WHITE SLAVES, AFRICAN MASTERS

WHITE SLAVES,

Edited and with an Introduction by

PAUL BAEPLER

AFRICAN MASTERS

An Anthology of

American Barbary Captivity

Narratives

THE UNIVERSITY OF CHICAGO PRESS

Chicago and London

Paul Baepler is a lecturer at University College at the University of Minnesota.

The University of Chicago Press, Chicago 60637
The University of Chicago Press, Ltd., London
© 1999 by The University of Chicago
All rights reserved. Published 1999

08 07 06 05 04 03 02 01 00 99   1 2 3 4 5
ISBN: 0-226-03403-8 (cloth)
ISBN: 0-226-03404-6 (paper)

Library of Congress Cataloging-in-Publication Data

White slaves, African masters : an anthology of American Barbary captivity
    narratives / edited and with an introduction by Paul Baepler.
        p.   cm.
    Includes bibliographical references and index.
    ISBN 0-226-03403-8 (cloth : alk. paper).—ISBN 0-226-03404-6
(pbk. : alk. paper)
        1. Slaves—Africa, North—Biography.   2. Americans—Africa, North—
Biography.   3. Prisoners of war (Islamic law)—Africa, North—
Biography.   4. Slavery—Africa, North—History—19th century—
Sources.   5. Americans—Africa, North—History—19th century—
Sources.   6. Pirates—Africa, North—History—19th century—
Sources.   7. American prose literature—19th century.   I. Baepler,
Paul Michel.
HT1345.W47   1999
305.5' 67' 092261—ddc21
    [B]   98-40368
                                                                   CIP

For

RICHARD AND SIMONE BAEPLER

MARIE-DANIELLE AND ROGER BURRUS

In Memory of

LEONA AND NORMAN WIDIGER

Contents

Illustrations

Preface

In 1994, four "Muslim extremists," as they were termed by the Western press, hijacked an Air France jetliner on Christmas Eve in what was called a "Christmas hostage drama." Armed with Kalashnikov rifles, they had dressed as Algerian airport workers and commandeered the Airbus A300. After killing three of the 170 passengers, they ordered the pilot to fly to Marseille. Once the jet landed, French officials refused to allow the plane to leave, and during the next two days, the hijackers released 65 passengers, though the freed hostages made it clear that the Algerians were preparing to execute more passengers. Eventually, about 30 commandos from the gendarmerie's elite antiterrorist unit stormed the plane and killed all four of what the French called "air pirates." The term "air pirate" is a fairly common French term used to denote what might be described in the United States as "skyjackers." Though these events describe a fundamentally different postcolonial situation in Algeria than that which obtained at the time of the Barbary pirates, this episode in which armed "Muslim extremists" engaged in piratical acts against a Western country on a Christian holiday accurately codes a long legacy of mutual hostility between North Africa and the West variously portrayed in Barbary captivity narratives.

The accounts gathered in this collection represent a small fraction of the experiences of thousands of captives held as slaves in North Africa over the past few centuries and are limited to the North American colonists and citizens of the United States who ventured across the Atlantic. It is a largely neglected history despite its continuing importance and a lost story that is still being recovered. The nine complete and excerpted narratives in this anthology can only begin to delineate this formerly well known abduction tale of primarily white slaves in Africa. The majority of the captives likely never recorded their experiences, or, if they did, they wrote about them in journals, letters, newspaper articles, or perhaps unpublished manuscripts. (James Cathcart's narrative, for example, was not published until decades after his death, and Joshua Gee's account, which we have only as fragments and therefore is not included here, existed for centuries before it made it into print.) Still other captives were illiterate and perhaps only made their accounts known orally; many died in captivity, and perhaps others chose to stay in Africa. But the story was well known in Britain, Europe, and North America, and was reimagined in novels by Royall Tyler, Peter Markoe, and Daniel Defoe; in plays by Cervantes, Sussana Rowson, and Moliere; in opera and in film. While the full story of African captivity remains incomplete, this book begins the recovery of that story by presenting the most popular published versions of this once familiar tale.

Literary historians have long recognized the importance of the American slave narrative and the Indian captivity narrative, and I would argue that the Barbary captivity narrative deserves our attention as well. Indeed, I would venture that the study of these three genres should be intertwined, that accounts of white captives enslaved in Africa have everything to do with accounts of white captives in America and African or African American slaves in the United States. Abolitionists and slavery apologists openly referred to captives in Barbary both to protest and justify slaveholding practices. Barbary captivity narratives provided Europe and America with some of their first impressions and reinventions of Africa long before Richard Burton or David Livingstone or Mary Kingsley set out to "explore" the African continent. These lasting impressions not only abetted the colonization of Africa, but aided in constructing the boundaries of "barbarity" and "civility" as they came to define "blackness" and "whiteness" in the United States.

I am indebted to many friends and colleagues who have read and commented upon this book, and their advice is interlaced throughout the text. Edward M. Griffin, Marcia Pankake, and Jean M. O'Brien encouraged this project since its germination, and they provided insightful reading and encouragement along the way. Peter Reed, Kent Bales, John Wright, Wayne Carver, and Mark Schwehn also offered their kind support at various stages in the development of this collection. Carol Urness, Brad Oftelie, Susan Hoffman, Charles Spetland, Karen Beavers, Dennis Lien, and Mary Pat Winters all helped me track down rare texts and images as well as answers to odd bibliographical queries. Alan Thomas and Randolph Petilos at the University of Chicago Press have been generous with their enthusiasm and care for the project from the beginning, and Michael Koplow has carefully copyedited along the way. The anonymous reviewers for the press made many helpful suggestions, and I thank them. Mark Olson, Risa Hazel, and Martina Anderson paid their ransom with close attention and sharp commentary. Chris Parker, Susy Gilbert, Caroline Scully, Tom Powers, Melissa Blum, and Stephanie Dumaine suffered excruciating close-reading agonies that can never be forgotten. Richard Carr, Samia Hollinger, Jean Buckley, Joyce Sutphen, Lois Vossen, Pat and John Wong, Bosco and Thea Petchler, Bruce Blacher, Betsy Wheeler,

Janet Johnson, Lisa Bergin, Karin Matchett, Corinth Matera, Kerry Brooks, Peter Scott, Steve and Meg Robertson, Hugh McTavish, Clinton Cowan, David Groos, Mel Stanforth, Luna Hazel, and Calamity, Grace, and Al Bosch were all held captive by this project and offered me profound relief and extreme kindnesses for which I am deeply grateful.

Introduction

Upon returning from her captivity among King Philip's "barbarians" and being reunited with the surviving members of her family, Mary Rowlandson declared, "Thus hath the Lord brought me and mine out of that horrible pit, and hath set us in the midst of tender-hearted and compassionate Christians."[1] These "tender-hearted" neighbors resided in Boston, where the Rowlandsons remained for three-quarters of a year until they moved to Wethersfield, Connecticut, in 1677. Among these Bostonians was an industrious man by the name of Joshua Gee, a shipwright by trade. Three years after Rowlandson's return, on January 25, 1680, Joshua Gee set sail from Boston harbor. Taking on a cargo of tobacco in Roanoke, Gee crossed the Atlantic on a trading voyage. Near the end of that journey, Algerian privateers boarded Gee's vessel and carried him into captivity. During his time in Africa, Gee served aboard one of the notorious Algerian slave galleys and went on numerous corsair raids, attempting to escape on at least one occasion. The famous judge and diarist Samuel Sewall helped to arrange his redemption, and Gee returned to a prosperous life; his son, also named Joshua Gee, eventually shared the pulpit of Boston's North Church with Cotton Mather. The elder Gee's story of seven years of slavery in Algiers—a captivity far longer than that of the more renowned Rowlandson—gives us the first Barbary captivity narrative from America.[2]

Cotton Mather, who is more commonly associated with Indian captivity, called Barbary servitude "the most horrible *Captivity* in the world" and described the "Hellish *Moors*" who held Americans in bondage as "worse than *Egyptian Task masters*."[3] Mather was well informed of African thralldom, and though Joshua Gee's narrative didn't see print until 1943—reason enough for Gee's obscurity—it is likely that many heard Gee's oral account of life in captivity as well as earlier tales of colonists lost in a far-off wilderness an ocean away. Although Barbary privateers began to take North American colonists as early as 1625, the written genre of the Barbary captivity narrative didn't flour-

1. Rowlandson, *The Sovereignty and Goodness of God,* 110.
2. See Gee, *Narrative.*
3. Mather, *The Glory of Goodness,* 31. See also Mather, *A Pastoral Letter.*

ish in the United States until the early nineteenth century. During these years, several survivors of Barbary captivity published immensely popular accounts of their suffering in North Africa, and the story of Barbary captivity became a common tale that involved hundreds of men and women, invoked public subscriptions for ransom funds, forced the government to pay humiliating tributes in cash and military arms to African rulers, stimulated the drive to create the U.S. navy, and brought about the first postrevolutionary war. Among other things, these narratives reveal some of the earliest impressions Americans had of Africa at a time when the issue of chattel slavery in the United States increasingly divided the country. The account by Captain James Riley, for example, sold nearly a million copies, and Abraham Lincoln's biographers credit Riley's narrative for helping to change the future president's stance on slavery.[4]

The word *Barbary*, which Europeans consistently used to mark the Maghreb or North Africa, evolved out of a place that Mary Louise Pratt has called a "contact zone," "a social space where disparate cultures meet, clash, and grapple with each other, often in highly asymmetrical relations of domination and subordination"; and consequently the word has a particularly revealing etymology.[5] While its derivation is uncertain, there are several likely theories. Most scholars agree that *Barbary* originated from the Greek *barbaros* or the Latin *barbarus* to signify non-Greeks or non-Romans, and thus uncivilized populations. Lotfi Ben Rejeb remarks that "the Arabs in the seventh century are reported to have used . . . *berbera* (to mumble) in reference to the natives' unintelligible language."[6] Similarly, Paulo Fernando de Moraes Farias suggests that *Barbara* was a categorical label used to denote African tribes who opposed communication and trade and thus "whose nature was like the nature of animals. . . . Behind such classifications is the notion of trade as a metaphor for language or vice versa, i.e., the symbolic equivalence of the exchange of messages and the exchange of goods."[7] So it is not strange that Saint Augustine, himself a native of North Africa, used the term *barbarus* to refer to his fellow natives who resisted Roman rule and Christianity. If we accept this derivation, then from virtually the beginning of its use in Africa, *Barbary* had not only pejorative connotations but a sense of commercial and cultural resistance; Africans were called "barbarians" because they refused to communicate

4. See McMurtry, "The Influence of Riley's *Narrative* upon Abraham Lincoln." For a longer discussion of Riley, see Alig, *Ohio's Last Frontiersman.*

5. Pratt, *Imperial Eyes,* 4.

6. Ben Rejeb, "To the Shores of Tripoli," 2.

7. Fernando de Moraes Farias, "Models of the World and Categorical Models," 39.

and were reluctant to cooperate. The Barbary corsairs themselves originated in part from the need to defend North Africa from European aggression.[8]

Beginning in the Mediterranean, the history of Barbary captivity coevolved with, if not predated, that of Indian captivity and reached to the sixteenth century, when the Barbarossa brothers swept into North Africa and solicited the help of the Ottoman Empire to fend off Spanish attackers.[9] For the ensuing three centuries, Europe clashed with Morocco and the new Barbary regencies—Algiers, Tunis, and Tripoli—on the Atlantic and in the Mediterranean. In addition to plundering trading vessels, each side captured slaves in what was cloaked as a Christian holy war or an Islamic jihad. Although both took slaves, and we know that Muslim survivors have written or spoken their own stories—Job Ben Solomon and Abd ar-Rahman, for instance, were both prominent African-born Muslim slaves in America—the "Barbary captive" has nevertheless come to refer to those thousands who were captured and held by North Africans.[10] Estimates vary greatly, but one source suggests Algiers alone held 20,000 Christian captives in 1621, and another puts the figures at 25,000 male and 2,000 female slaves around the 1630s.[11]

8. The term *barbarian* is often used by Indian captives to describe Native Americans; more interestingly, however, the entire Christian/Muslim conflict seems to have been superimposed onto the conflict between South American natives and European settlers in order to deny their humanity and label them "infidels." See Haberly, "Captives and Infidels"; and Frederick, "Fatal Journeys, Fatal Legends."

9. For an examination of early Barbary captivity narratives in English at the time when Indian captivity narratives were developing, see my "The Barbary Captivity Narrative in Early America."

10. Indeed, we have many records of African-born Muslims who were held as slaves in the United States, but until recently the story of Muslim slaves in this country has been largely overlooked. Their written legacy has been compromised in part by language differences and the prohibition slavemasters enforced on the propagation of "secret" scripts they themselves couldn't decipher. In addition, colonial and antebellum witnesses were largely ignorant of Islam and didn't bother to observe or record the wide variety of differences among slaves. Advertisements for runaway slaves sometimes described missing chattel as originating from "the Moorish country," though this could still refer more to a slave's Muslim identity than her residency in North Africa. Most Muslim slaves came from Islamized areas in the sub-Sahara, but Abd ar-Rahman, for instance, lived for a time in Timbuktu, where Robert Adams landed for a while when in captivity himself. One can certainly imagine the existence of narratives by North Africans taken captive by Europeans, particularly since many Muslims had an Islamic education and were literate—a fact many North Americans commented upon. These Muslim slaves in the United States were brought via the middle passage. Thomas Jefferson also argued for the political expediency of capturing North Africans. In a letter to James Monroe dated August 11, 1786, Jefferson hoped to exchange North African hostages for the enslaved Americans. See Austin's *African Muslims in Antebellum America: A Sourcebook* and his revised, albeit shorter, *African Muslims in Antebellum America: Transatlantic Stories and Spiritual Struggles*. See also Turkistani, "Muslim Slaves and Their Narratives"; Gomez, "Muslims in Early America"; and Judy, *(Dis)Forming the American Canon*. On capturing North Africans to use as hostages, see Sofka, "The Jeffersonian Idea of National Security," 535n, and Jefferson, *Papers,* 18:406.

11. See Braudel, *The Mediterranean and the Mediterranean World in the Age of Philip II,* 887. See also Wolf, *The Barbary Coast,* 151.

Fig. 1. Trinitarian monks redeeming
Christian captives. (Courtesy James Ford Bell
Library, University of Minnesota)

Fig. 2. Crucifying a Christian slave in a Muslim courtyard. (Courtesy James Ford Bell Library, University of Minnesota)

Fig. 3. Christian slaves attempting to escape Algiers in a homemade boat. (Courtesy James Ford Bell Library, University of Minnesota)

Captivity accounts in English begin to appear at least as early as 1563, if we include John Fox's captivity in Alexandria.[12] The British barber-surgeon William Davis suffered almost nine years of captivity beginning in 1597, but he wasn't a slave to the North Africans; alongside Muslim captives, he served aboard papal galleys carrying Turkish goods from Tunis.[13] By 1621, when Nicholas Roberts and John Rawlins wrote of their bloody encounters with Algerian privateers, the Barbary captivity narrative had begun to establish itself as a recognizable genre.[14] A decade later, Francis Knight, who endured seven years of slavery in Algiers before escaping, would write an account that seems fully formed, praising God's hand in his deliverance and lamenting the tribulations of a galley slave: "there is no calamity can befall a man in this life which hath the least parallel to this of captivity, neither are the endurances of captives equal, although the least without the divine assistance were insupportable; yet are they all easy in comparison to that of the galleys, which is most inhuman and diabolical."[15] By 1675, William Okeley had framed his experiences as a slave in Algiers into an account that stylistically and cosmologically parallels what Mary Rowlandson would write seven years later. Like a Puritan captive in America, Okeley interprets his suffering in Africa as God's trial, and he explicates his ordeal with extensive reference to the Bible.[16]

Although Joshua Gee's "pocket book" presents us with the first American Barbary captivity account, many North Americans had already been captured by 1680.[17] As early as 1625, just five years after William Bradford landed in Plymouth, rovers had claimed two American ships and escorted them into the Moroccan harbor at Sallee.[18] Fifteen years later, there is record of a colonist named "Austin," who, in his voyage from New Haven to England, was captured with his family by "Turks"—the generic name for North African pirates—and carried into slavery in Algiers.[19] What resistance these New England vessels marshaled remains a mystery, but according to James Feni-

12. Munday, "The worthie enterprise of John Fox," 150–56.

13. Davis, *A True Relation of the Travels,* 475–88.

14. Roberts, "A Letter contayning the admirable escape and glorious Victorie," 311–23; Rawlins, "The wonderful recovery of the Exchange of Bristow," 151–71.

15. Knight, *A Relation of Seven Years Slavery,* 478.

16. Okeley, *Eben-Ezer or a Small Monument of Great Mercy.*

17. While not properly a Barbary captive, Captain John Smith, before he was captured by Powhatan, was earlier captured by Tartars and with others sold "like beasts in a market-place" as a slave. He eventually "beat out the Tymors [Bashaw of Nalbrits in Cambia's] braines with his threshing bat," escaped, and toured Barbary before making his way to Virginia. His coat of arms displays the disembodied heads of three Turks he had slain, and it's conceivable that Smith's earlier Turkish captivity influenced his depiction of his capture by Powhatan and rescue by Pocahontas. See Smith, *The True Travels,* esp. 3:184–210.

18. Tucker, *Dawn Like Thunder,* 60.

19. Sumner, *White Slavery in the Barbary States,* 67–68.

more Cooper, the very first regular naval action in which an American vessel is known to have engaged did involve a Barbary rover. In 1645, a fourteen-gun ship built in Cambridge, Massachusetts, sailed for the Canary Isles with a crew of thirty: "This vessel fell in with a rover, of twenty guns, and seventy men, supposed to belong to Barbary, when an action took place that continued the entire day. The rover receiving some serious injury in her rudder, the New England ship was enabled to escape."[20]

Thus, from the beginning of European colonization in America, settlers and North African corsairs clashed. By 1661, Massachusetts merchants regularly encountered Barbary privateers on their way to Europe and sought to protect themselves: "One Captain Cakebread or Breadcake had two guns to cruise in search of Turkish pirates."[21] Colonists, however, could hardly defend their vessels when even well-armed British ships fell prey to the corsairs, and so we have many reports of captures. In 1671, Captain William Foster and his son from Roxbury, Massachusetts, were held captive for three years.[22] Less fortunate than the Fosters, Dr. Daniel Mason was imprisoned by Algerian privateers after sailing from Charlestown, Massachusetts, in 1678, and was never heard from again.[23] The following year, Captain William Condy, sailing in the *Unity* from Boston to England, was also driven into Algiers. Traveling with Condy was "a person of consequence" named William Harris, an associate of Roger Williams in Providence. That same year, Seth Southell, the king's appointed governor of Carolina, was abducted on his way to the colonies and held for several months in Algiers while he petitioned Charles II to ransom him. On July 2, 1679, the king signed a decree ordering "the peticoner to be redeemed in exchange for Hodge Omar ['late Commander of the Tiger of Argier'] and Buffalo Ball two Turkish Prisoners aboard Vice Admiral Herbert in the Mediterranean or either of them."[24] Southell was eventually released and assumed his post in Carolina, though complaints of some unsavory financial transactions in Algiers dogged him in America. Unfortunately, if any of these captives indeed wrote of their capture, none of the accounts has surfaced, except Joshua Gee's fragmented narrative and the accounts given in Cotton Mather's 1703 sermon, *The Glory of Goodness*.

Beginning at the close of the American Revolution, however, citizens of the new nation had greater cause for worry. The British treaties that had once protected colonial shipping no longer sheltered independent America, and pub-

20. Cooper, *The History of the Navy of The United States of America*, 18.
21. Paine, *The Ships and Sailors of Old Salem*, 22.
22. Sumner, *White Slavery in the Barbary States*, 67–68.
23. Sibley, *Biographical Sketches of Harvard University*, 213–14; Tucker, *Dawn like Thunder*, 60.
24. Quoted in Sha'ban, *Islam and Arabs in Early American Thought*, 65–66.

lic alarm grew as Morocco seized James Erving's vessel, the *Betsey,* in May 1784. Although the Moroccans quickly freed the crew, public fear grew as exaggerated press accounts—spurred on by shipping insurance underwriters in London—claimed that as many as a dozen ships had been seized by both Morocco and Algiers. Almost as soon as these fears were laid to rest, Algerian privateers seized two American vessels, the *Maria* and the *Dauphin,* with a total of twenty-one prisoners, in the summer of 1785. Once again news accounts stirred up public fears, and a rumor circulated that the illustrious Benjamin Franklin himself, who had set sail from Paris on July 12, had been seized by the corsairs. The rumor of Franklin's abduction eventually proved to be unfounded, but in one of his final editorials in 1790, Franklin, writing under the name "Historicus," used the Christian slave trade in Algiers to critique slavery at home. Reacting to a proslavery speech in Congress, Franklin posed as a high Algerian official who rejected a proposition for the manumission of Christian slaves in Africa. Building on the rhetoric of southern legislators, Franklin qua Algerian noted, "If we cease our Cruises against the Christians, how shall we be furnished with the Commodities their Countries produce, and which are so necessary for us? If we forbear to make Slaves of their People, who in this hot Climate are to cultivate our Lands? . . . Must we not then be our own Slaves?"[25]

The crisis of 1785 worsened when Britain, attempting to menace the United States, made great efforts to contract a peace agreement between Algiers and Portugal. Portugal patrolled the Straits of Gibraltar and had been refusing Algerian ships crucial access to the open waters of the Atlantic, where unprotected U.S. ships sailed. In 1793, Britain succeeded in temporarily opening the straits, and within a few weeks Algiers had increased the number of U.S. sailors in its slave bagnios to 119. At least two of these prisoners—John Foss and James Leander Cathcart—would eventually write captivity accounts and inaugurate the decades when Barbary captivity narratives reached the height of their popularity.

Because the fledgling United States had few monetary and diplomatic resources with which to negotiate these captives' release, the Americans remained hostage until the summer of 1796, when Joel Barlow, the famous poet and Connecticut Wit, helped to free the eighty-eight remaining sailors during a particularly virulent outbreak of the plague in Algiers. The price for freedom was around a million dollars or roughly one-sixth of the federal budget. As a favor to his new American friends, the enriched Algerian bashaw pressured Tunis and Tripoli into signing treaties with the United States for the comparatively paltry sums of $107,000 and $56,486. The peace bargains,

25. Franklin, *Writings,* 1158.

however, backfired, and the United States soon faced a new North African problem.

On May 14, 1801, the bashaw of Tripoli, demanding a greater price for peace than what the 1796 treaty had promised, cut down the American flagstaff in Tripoli and declared war on the United States. As early as 1784, Jefferson had strongly pushed for the creation of a navy to secure American trade routes and to assert the country's commercial rights in full view of the great European powers. With Adams, who had followed a more conciliatory path, out of office, Jefferson was determined not to pay "one penny in tribute" and sent the new navy to establish a blockade against the Tripolitans.[26] In 1803, however, catastrophe struck as the U.S. frigate *Philadelphia,* commanded by Captain William Bainbridge, ran aground on an uncharted reef just a few miles outside Tripoli harbor. Unable to free the warship, Bainbridge struck the flag without a fight and the Tripolitans soon captured the frigate with its full complement of 307 U.S. sailors. For the prisoners' release, the bashaw demanded $1.69 million, and the event, by far the single largest Barbary imprisonment of U.S. citizens, propelled the country into another national crisis that would last for the next fifteen months. The United States responded with even greater military force. After Commodore Edward Preble launched ceaseless cannonades against Tripoli, Stephen Decatur set aflame the captured *Philadelphia,* and William Eaton invaded Derna, the bashaw eventually relented and settled for a token tribute of $60,000. Several of the U.S. hostages—Doctor Jonathan Cowdery, William Ray, and Elijah Shaw—wrote narratives of their imprisonment and forced labor for a public eager to hear about the country's first post–Revolutionary War victory.

In the years immediately following the Tripolitan crisis, the Barbary regencies captured only a few U.S. ships, and even these abductions virtually ended when Stephen Decatur revisited the area in 1815. Although the threat of high-seas kidnapping had passed after Decatur's show of force, the public interest in Barbary abduction had not. When the U.S. sailor Robert Adams told of his shipwreck off the treacherous Moroccan coast and how he was carried into the African interior all the way to the fabled city of Timbuktu, where no Westerner had traveled, authorities in London eagerly transcribed and published

---

26. Although Tripoli did declare war on the United States, some of the blame must rest with John Adams's dilatory response to Tripoli's diplomatic overtures. Michael Kitzen argues that the lives of over a hundred men and nearly four million dollars might have been saved had Adams treated with Tripoli as he had with Algeria, Tunis, and Morocco. Jefferson, James Sofka suggests, had been spoiling for a war with the Barbary powers from at least 1784 despite his liberal Enlightenment rhetoric and his public denouncement of Europe's Machiavellian proclivities. See Kitzen, "Money Bags or Cannon Balls"; Sofka, "The Jeffersonian Idea of National Security."

his story. Soon after Adams's release, Captain James Riley also ran aground, and his narrative of how he was captured by "wandering Arabs" and forced to march through the cruel Sahara desert entranced his readers and became a best-seller. The various shipwrecked captives—Robert Adams, James Riley, Archibald Robbins, and Judah Paddock—suffered tremendous hardships at the hands of their captors but also owed their lives to these desert people who saved them from certain death in the Sahara. Unlike previous captives, however, these sailors were not held hostage by a nation seeking tribute but by individual desert dwellers who happened, upon the castaways and took possession of them as human salvage. Thus while these were certainly the most lengthy and popular Barbary captivity narratives, the captives' plights were not followed in the press as they happened, nor did they cause a national crisis.

Nearly a century after these events transpired and the figure of the Barbary pirate had faded into historical myth, a new national crisis emerged. In 1904, Ion Perdicaris, an aging American millionaire living in Tangier, was abducted from his home along with his British stepson by Muali Ahmed er Raisuli (which Perdicaris spelled "Raissuli"), a rebel Riffian chieftain, who wanted to embarrass the Moroccan sultan. Theodore Roosevelt, facing reelection, immediately sent seven warships to Tangiers demanding the American's release. Headlines in the American papers promised an imminent invasion, and the sultan was finally forced to acquiesce to all of Raisuli's extravagant demands. Perdicaris returned to Tangier after six weeks in the hinterlands, and he eventually traveled back to the United States, where he gave lectures on his captivity and wrote at least three accounts of the ordeal. When the dust settled, it became clear that the United States had no intention of ever invading Morocco, particularly when the secretary of state learned that Perdicaris had long ago renounced his U.S. citizenship—and was in fact a *Greek* national. However, the international affair captured the media's attention during a flagging Republican national convention, and Roosevelt's dramatic posturing helped catapult him to victory at the polls.[27]

Unlike the record of Indian captivity in North America, which was, in large part, epitomized by female writers such as Mary Rowlandson, Hannah Dustan, and Mary Jemison, no "authentic" Barbary accounts written by U.S. women have so far surfaced. Nevertheless, several of the early best-sellers were written by reputed female captives who underwent tremendous deprivations, though none of these accounts appears to be historically verifiable.[28]

27. For a detailed discussion of the Perdicaris episode see my "Rewriting the Barbary Captivity Narrative."

28. At this time, there seems to be no way to authenticate the female narratives, but we might be wise to recall the controversy surrounding the veracity of Harriet Jacobs's now-famous slave narrative and the

For instance, the title of Mary Velnet's 1800 narrative advertises the Gothic horror a reader could expect to find inside: *The Captivity and Sufferings of Mrs. Mary Velnet, Who was Seven Years a Slave in Tripoli, three of which she was confined in a dungeon, loaded with irons, and four times put to the most cruel tortures ever invented by man.* The existence of these ersatz accounts suggests that the demand for "true" African captivity tales, particularly accounts of women in peril, outstripped their availability. The two accounts in this collection reputed to have female authors—Maria Martin and Eliza Bradley—are almost certainly fictions.[29]

Why no verifiable female accounts have come to light we can only conjecture. Certainly there were far fewer women available to be captured on vessels traveling near the Mediterranean than there were homesteading on the North American frontier.[30] Of those who were captured, most were likely sequestered from the male captives, who rarely mention the presence of white women. In his 1797 account of Algerian captives, James Wilson Stevens suggests that the female slaves were "sent to the dey's seraglio, where they are made concubines, or subjected to domestic services, unless a considerable ransom is expected for them; or if young they are sold to such as want them for these purposes."[31] If female captives became part of an Algerian seraglio, then the survivor would be forced to recount her rape—something we rarely read in Indian captivity narratives—or her willful violation of the racial/sexual boundary or of her vigorous defense against imminent sexual violation. Instead, in the Martin and Bradley accounts, we find women who were forced into domestic service, tortured, and finally rescued.

That we label some narratives, like Martin's and Bradley's, fiction and others, such as Cathcart's and Cowdery's, nonfiction redraws a distinction that

---

struggle to verify Jacobs as the true author. Perhaps new evidence will emerge and provide a similar corrective for these accounts.

29. In addition to the Velnet, Martin, and Bradley narratives, there are unverifiable accounts reputedly by women, and all of them produced in multiple editions. See, for example, Laranda, *Neapolitan Captive: Interesting Narrative of the Captivity and Sufferings of Miss Viletta Laranda, A Native of Naples, Who, with a Brother, was a passenger on board a Neapolitan vessel wrecked near Oran, on the Barbary coast, September 1829, and who soon after was unfortunately made a Captive of by a wandering clan of Bedowen Arabs, on their return from Algiers to the Deserts—and eleven months after providentially rescued from Barbarian Bondage by the commander of a detached Regiment of the victorious French Army.* There is also at least one counterfeit male account: Nicholson, *An Affecting Narrative of the Captivity and Sufferings of Thomas Nicholson [A Native of New Jersey] Who has been Six years a Prisoner among the Algerines, And from whom he fortunately made his escape a few months previous to Commodore Decatur's late Expedition.*

30. Wives often accompanied their husbands on long trading or whaling voyages. Many performed critical work aboard ship: tending the sick, teaching navigation skills to the crew, and even taking the helm when the captain died. Nevertheless, women were likely to be extremely isolated during the voyage and considered a hindrance to the crew. For more on captains' wives and the "ambivalently gendered" way they recorded their experiences, see Springer, "The Captain's Wife at Sea."

31. Stevens, *An Historical and Geographical Account of Algiers,* 242.

A NEW AND INTERESTING PUBLICATION.

PUNISHMENT INFLICTED BY THE ARABS ON A FEMALE CHRISTIAN CAPTIVE.

Fig. 4. From the narrative of Miss Viletta Laranda, a native of Naples (published in New York, 1830). (Courtesy Boston Athenaeum)

has grown less apparent and meaningful. Many accounts we designate nonfiction draw on events that most likely did not occur or were influenced by previous travel accounts and histories. Did Robert Adams really see exotic animals that no one before or since would ever see? Did Doctor Cowdery witness a wild melee among the Arabs when William Ray, witness to the same event, directly stated that no such mutilation occurred? Fictional narratives, on the other hand, often borrowed directly from authentic accounts; Eliza Bradley's narrative, for instance, directly lifts entire paragraphs from James Riley's popular narrative. The distinction between fiction and nonfiction is further complicated by the intertextuality of tropes and style. For instance, John Foss breaks from his straightforward reportorial prose style to mourn his loss of liberty in a purple passage that draws directly from the sentimental tradition, while Maria Martin's fictional narrative always appeared in conjunction with a historical and geographical account of Algiers that lent it an air of accuracy and authenticity. If the fictional was sometimes read as true, then fiction helped to shape history, and we need to view these narratives side by side.

ALTHOUGH ON THE SURFACE the genre of Barbary captivity may appear fixed, the narratives themselves refuse easy categorization. They differ dramatically from one another, which is part of why they originally sold well and why today they are intellectually compelling. Christopher Castiglia has argued that Indian captivity narratives "refuse to be static texts," and that "they persistently explore generic and cultural changes, divisions, and differences occasioned by the captives' cultural crossings."[32] Similarly, the presence of white captives in a distant, exotic, and primarily black wilderness allowed for narratives that challenged as well as reinforced established identities and social hierarchies. When Ion Perdicaris, a twentieth-century captive, prepared to return home, he described his sentiments as "topsy-turvy," and indeed beyond its "insupportable calamities," the temporary world of the captive was reorienting and carnivalesque. What emerges from these narratives is a highly variegated and fluid mosaic of the captivity experience and the cultural divisions it describes.

While not properly a captivity account, Cotton Mather's sermon, *The Glory of Goodness,* contains first-person descriptive narratives of life in the thrall of "Black-a-moors" and "Negro-Boyes." Like the fragments of Joshua Gee's seventeenth-century account, Mather's sermon situates the captive within a Calvinist, Puritan theological paradigm in which the chosen undergo trials and are saved. Although he describes the "astonishing Hardships" the redeemed captives have undergone—the temptation of suicide, the diet of bread and water, the "torrid" climate, the backbreaking labor and the "African Monster" that captured them—he focuses on the fact that none of the Christians have become apostates, for Barbary captives were threatened not only by being cast into the Barbarians' strange wilderness replete with spectacular physical dangers but by being dragged into the heretical Islamic world where a person's soul might be lost forever. Commenting on Mather's Indian captivity writings, Gary Ebersole has noted, "Mather draws a connection between the moral 'wilderness' resulting from a disrupted or disordered family and the ever-present danger on the New England frontier of reverting to savagery. Only by making that connection can we appreciate the extent to which the external events of history unfolding over the physical topography of New England were held to mirror the interior movements of the hearts of the people over a spiritual landscape."[33] To preserve themselves during their long stay among the "infidels," Mather claims, the English captives re-created the social topography of New England by remaking their world in Africa, forming themselves into a society with a "Master" and "Assistents" and its own body of

32. Castiglia, *Bound and Determined,* 4.
33. Ebersole, *Captured by Texts,* 71.

laws to settle disputes and conduct communal worship services. Redemption for the captives, however, didn't begin until their brethren in New England made a "Cry of PRAYER" on their behalf. For Mather, the two orderly societies were interrelated: New England saved the captives through the spiritual "noise" of prayer and the captives presented a living example of faith and civilization at the "Hands of a Bitter and Hasty Nation."

Written almost a hundred years later, John Foss's captivity narrative reads much more like an ethnography than does Mather's sermon. Just as the Indian captivity narrative during this time departs from a theological framework toward the emerging adventure tale and sentimental novel, Foss scarcely mentions God let alone relies upon elaborate biblical reference as Gee, Rowlandson, and Mather had. Foss declares his text "a simple statement of facts," yet he is unable to write a detached report of his time in Africa, and indeed he hopes his readers' "tears of sympathy will flow."[34] Joanne Dobson has argued that we should think of the sentimental not as a genre but as an "imaginative orientation" with a focus on "affectional ties" in a turbulent and violent world: "Violation, actual or threatened, of the affectional bond generates the primary tension in the sentimental text and leads to bleak, dispirited, anguished, sometimes outraged, representations of human loss, as well as to idealized portrayals of human connection or divine consolation."[35] Although Foss intends his narrative primarily to inform, to be considered as fact, he nonetheless wishes to instruct his reader morally through the affect produced by his personal tale of loss and separation but not especially to demonstrate God's providential workings. Cautious of losing his readers' attention with an overly long tale, Foss moves between his generalized account of slave life and Algeria, which he writes in the third person, and his sentimentalized reflections, which he reports in the first person.

These registers overlap, however, as when Foss tells of the slaves' "common labor," which involves dragging twenty-ton stones over several miles to build a breakwater—a story that might have had Mather recalling Egyptian slavery of the Old Testament. Initially, Foss simply reports on the engineering process of excavating and moving boulders, but when he begins to explain how the guardians beat "the slaves," he cannot sustain the same illusion of objectivity, of relaying "a simple statement of facts." Foss switches back to the first person and begins to recount an anecdote of how one of the cruelest taskmasters tumbled off a wall to his death after taking a vicious swipe at a Christian.[36] Much

34. Foss, *A Journal of the Captivity and Sufferings*, 1.
35. Dobson, "Reclaiming Sentimental Literature," 267.
36. Foss, *A Journal of Captivity and Sufferings*, 20–21.

later in the narrative, upon learning of yet another postponement of his ransom, a delay that will continue to disrupt the union between him and his familial world, Foss's rhetoric grows much more arch and florid, and he uses the occasion to link the shameful plight of the captives with national disgrace: "How long, said we, may our country neglect us! . . . How long may our chains and torments be continued!"[37]

When James Leander Cathcart's vessel, the *Maria,* was commandeered in 1785, the Algerian captain, who himself had twice been a captive in Spain and Genoa, promised his American prisoners a more humane captivity than his own. "This world is full of vicissitudes," he said referring to his own startling transformation from a slave to an Algerian corsair.[38] This short opening anecdote prefigures Cathcart's own curious rags-to-riches captivity, a story in which he rises from a common slave to the highest position a slave could attain. Posthumously cobbled together from his journals, Cathcart's account records much of the ethnographic detail Foss's narrative had begun to record, but in a much more vivid and interior fashion. His description of the notorious slave prison as a "perfect pandemonium" where lions and tigers are treated better than slaves, and where Cathcart could own three profitable slave taverns, only magnifies the trope of a world turned topsy-turvy. Captivity, as described by Cathcart, is not only a state where Muslims and Jews dominate Christians, and where blacks hold sway over whites, but where captives, in rare instances, can grow rich while still enslaved.

Like Foss before him, Cathcart represents his own enslavement as a national humiliation. "I was convinced," writes Cathcart, "that the honor of our country was connected with our redemption."[39] At the time of Cathcart's abduction, the new nation had no direct diplomatic means for dealing with such a foreign crisis, and though several backdoor attempts to free the mariners were made, they failed. It was not simply that he felt the United States was being held hostage, but that his own country, which had just emerged from the tutelage of the British monarchy, had done very little to secure his freedom. He writes of feeling abandoned, "Why are we left the victims of arbitrary power and barbarous despotism, in a strange land far distant from all our connections, miserable exiles from the country for which we have fought, forgotten by our co[n]temporaries who formerly used to animate us in all our expedition with tales of liberty?"[40] His point that revolutionary rhetoric—"tales of lib-

37. Ibid., 61.
38. Cathcart, *The Captives,* 6.
39. Ibid., 41.
40. Ibid., 144.

erty"—didn't extend to his situation, gestures toward another way in which the captive's world was turned upside down: "freedom" was qualified—a critique that might just as easily have been applied to African-American slaves and disenfranchised women. In a later passage, Cathcart, not having heard otherwise while in Algeria, believes that "[t]he negroes have even had a share in your deliberations, and have reaped the benefits arising from your wise and wholesome laws and regulations," while he, who had fought during the Revolutionary War, suffers the ignominy of enslavement. "[W]e are doomed," he says, "to be the only victims of American Independence."[41]

The account attributed to Maria Martin explores quite a different form of victimization from Cathcart's. Contemporaneous with the Gothic and sentimental novels, the Martin narrative borrows heavily from both forms. Entombed in the tower of an "old decayed castle," Martin inhabits a starkly isolated world in contrast to her male counterparts, who share a communal space, as squalid as it may be, and labor together in work gangs. As did Mary Rowlandson before her, Martin must sew clothing for her board, but even Rowlandson was free to intermingle with her captors and other English captives. Besides her faceless guards, Martin's sole link to the world beyond prison is the chivalrous mate from her vessel, who promises to provide for Martin and in whose presence Martin is free to swoon and faint. In the final two years of her confinement, Martin's leash grows even shorter when blacksmiths manacle her in irons as punishment for her escape attempt, irons so heavy that she has to support them around her neck even in sleep for fear of choking. The space of her prison now virtually coterminous with her body, Martin revels in her own fortitude: "I glowed with the desire of convincing the world I was capable of suffering what man had never suffered before."[42]

In this sense, the Martin narrative parallels concurrent developments in sentimental fiction in which heroines everywhere gauged their moral strength by facing extreme adversity and bearing physical pain, often sacrificing their mortal bodies in order to preserve their sacred souls. Suffering, when made public in writing, becomes instructive, capable of reaching the reader's imagination and evoking a sympathetic understanding; the captive's body becomes an interpretable site where the reader gains from pain. "In giving expression to [the female captive's] pain and suffering," Gary Ebersole argues, "she provides the opportunity for her listeners' sympathy to find expression as well. Innumerable examples from history demonstrate that intense pain can be borne

---

41. Ibid., 145.
42. Martin, *History of the captivity and sufferings*, 37–38.

and can even be a source of ecstatic-pleasure for the sufferer when it is located within a meaningful structure."[43] Writing on Mary Rowlandson's captivity, Teresa Toulouse has noted that "self-sacrifice and affliction" become signs that, in addition to denoting the "true sainthood" of the Puritan captive, also denote "true womanliness," and "thus the height to which Rowlandson will rise, as woman and as Puritan, will be contingent on the lowliness, passivity, and utter dependence of her body."[44] Although Martin's narrative hardly resembles a Puritan captivity narrative, it is primarily concerned with reporting physical isolation, emotional trauma, and bodily degradation.

Before her removal to her tower prison, Martin is confined to a "small hut, adjoining the bashaw's habitation." The convenient proximity of Martin to the bashaw, along with the text's preoccupation with preserving Martin's body against all injury, would seem to prepare the reader for a seduction tale. June Namias has pointed to the lure of sexual fantasy and crossing tabooed sexual boundaries in Indian captivity narratives: "To cross these boundaries was to enter into a world of forbidden intimacies whether in fact or in the imagination of the reader or viewer."[45] Other Barbary captivity narratives, for instance, mention the abduction of handsome boys for the bashaw's pleasure, and many outline the penalties for illicit sex between a Christian slave and a Muslim woman. In spite of such penalties, Robert Adams's narrative strongly implies that he seduced his master's wife. The 1790s also saw the first publication of "Arabian Nights" with its tales of the harem.[46]

In spite of the traditional seduction markers, curiously, nothing disturbs the sexual order in the Martin narrative. The same can be said of Eliza Bradley's account from about the same period, but Bradley's text, like Rowlandson's, concerns itself far more with the role of God's will in her preservation. Indeed, Bradley's narrative was used in many Sunday schools as a teaching text, and the

---

43. Ebersole, *Captured by Texts*, 164.

44. Toulouse, "'My Own Credit,'" 661.

45. Namias, *White Captives*, 109.

46. Also known as "The Thousand and One Nights," the main story of "Arabian Nights" was taken from a no longer extant volume of Persian fairy tales called *Hazar Afsanah* (A thousand tales). It was likely translated into Arabic in A.D. 850, and subsequent editors added stories of Indian and Arabian origin until an Egyptian editor codified a standard version in the late eighteenth century. Antoine Galland produced the first English translation, which began to appear in 1704. For more on the explicitly sexual content in "Arabian Nights," see Robert Irwin's *The Arabian Nights*, esp. 159–77. Robert Allison has observed that the 1790s also saw a special edition of the story of Sinbad the sailor and two editions of a biography of the prophet Muhammad published in the United States (Washington Irving would write another biography of Muhammad thirty years later.) See Allison's *The Crescent Obscured*, xvii. *The Crescent Obscured* also serves as an insightful introduction to the tumultuous first contact between North Africa and the newly formed United States.

hint of seduction, it might be argued, would be out of place. The narrative upon which Martin's is based, that reputedly by Mary Velnet, "an Italian Lady," includes a woodcut of a bare-breasted enchained captive (fig 12) and points to a clear sexual fascination with enslaved women.[47] That Maria Martin avoids this complication altogether suggests that her narrative may not be as completely representative of the female Barbary captive, though we can't be certain without a greater number and wider variety of narratives by or about female captives.

The problem of viewing any single Barbary captivity narrative as representative of the genre becomes clear when two narratives contest the same set of events, and this is what we find in the accounts by Jonathan Cowdery and William Ray. While the Martin narrative is certainly a fiction based on a historical situation, one must allow that Cowdery's and Ray's clashing narratives engage in their own confabulations. Both men became prisoners when their frigate, the *Philadelphia,* was captured in November of 1803 during the Tripolitan War, but almost immediately the similarities of their imprisonment end. Jonathan Cowdery served as one of the *Philadelphia*'s doctors and, as a U.S. naval officer, was accorded preferential treatment by his captors.[48] Within two months of his arrival, he was called upon to minister to the bashaw's sick infant, and with the boy's return to good health came the bashaw's gratitude and Cowdery's virtual liberty. If Martin's narrative fetishizes her isolation, Cowdery's reads more like the journal of an inconvenienced gentleman on holiday. He lives in the home of the former American consul, dines with the bashaw, visits ancient ruins, picnics in the orchards, and is told he can have anything he wants, free of expense. William Ray and the majority of the U.S. prisoners, in contrast, live together in cramped quarters on a meager diet and without freedom to leave their prison.

Publishing his narrative two years after Cowdery, Ray presents his account as a much-needed corrective to the doctor's distorted version of events. In addition to impugning the doctor's courage, Ray contends that Cowdery covered up the fact that the Tripolitans had been able to refloat the stranded *Philadelphia* off the shoals almost immediately after the Americans surrendered. Ray knew that his readers would be shocked by this news because the *Philadelphia* was the well-publicized object of postrevolutionary heroism. Commodore Preble, realizing the dangerous potential of the *Philadelphia* in the hands of Tripoli, had sent Lieutenant Stephen Decatur with the ketch *Intrepid* on a daring nighttime raid to burn and destroy the *Philadelphia*. To sug-

---

47. See Lewis, "Images of Captive Rape in the Nineteenth Century."

48. Second Lieutenant Jacob Jones served alongside Cowdery and received the same preferential treatment. For more on Ray's colleague and naval medicine, see Estes, "Commodore Jacob Jones."

gest, as Ray did, that the officers too quickly surrendered the *Philadelphia* to Tripoli was to imply that Decatur and his men had risked their own lives to remedy the actions of men who had refused to save their own. This claim is part of a larger grievance in which Ray pits the hard-working patriotic sailor against the tyrannous rule of the officers, and he dedicates much of his account to complaints against the treatment he found in the brutish U.S. navy. Officers, he claims, routinely beat the sailors indiscriminately for the slightest offenses and worked the crew to a frazzle. Although a strident admirer of the heroes of the Tripolitan War—Decatur and Preble—Ray compares the naval officers under whom he served to the tyrants they were fighting: "Petty despotism is not confined alone to Barbary's execrated and piratical shores; but that base and oppressive treatment may be experienced from officers of the American, as well as the British and other navies."[49] In this instance, Barbary captivity served as a mirror with which to critique the integrity of democracy in the new republic, just as it was used to question the practice of slave holding in a newly freed nation.

Yet a third narrative about the captivity, published in 1843, by Elijah Shaw, a carpenter aboard the *Philadelphia,* generally confirms Ray's version of events, though Shaw, a veteran of four wars, refrains from criticizing the U.S. navy. Upon his capture, Shaw took his place alongside a team of men who were forced to transport four-ton stones to reinforce the ramparts that had been damaged by U.S. cannonades: "We worked bare-headed and bare-footed; and the climate being very warm, our necks and feet were burnt to a perfect blister. Add to this the soreness of our backs from the frequent application of the whips, and the famished condition of our bodies, and the reader can form some idea of our sufferings."[50] Shaw suffered further when he protested his treatment and received the bastinado—eighty-two lashes on the bottom of his feet. These were agonies Ray never experienced because shortly after he arrived, he grew ill. Instead of working on the earthenworks under the broiling sun, he oversaw the captives' meals and was in charge of rationing food among the prisoners. This explains how Ray found the luxury to write his journal in Tripoli, even finding time to scribble doggerel. Unlike Shaw, Ray claims to have been "pressed into the Maritime service of the United States," but he later admits that he was desperately poor and entered the navy as a last resort. That a prosperous country like the United States could allow the unfortunate to slip into penury galled Ray and informs his complaint with the officers along class lines, though clearly he was treated far better than Shaw, who himself never

49. Ray, *Horrors of Slavery,* 18.
50. Shaw, *A short sketch,* 23.

complained about the treatment he received under the same officers. Ray's competing narrative about the events surrounding the *Philadelphia*'s capture points to the extreme variation of the captivity experience for all the U.S. prisoners as well as the flexibility of the genre.

By the end of the Tripolitan War (1801–5), the United States had signed treaties with each of the Barbary states, and predation on American shipping virtually ended. Unfortunate sailors plying the waters off the Moroccan coast, however, sometimes foundered on the rocks and were cast upon the desert only to be reclaimed by "wandering Arabs." This was the case with James Riley, Judah Paddock, and Archibald Robbins, whose narratives of incredible struggle through the hot Saharan sands sold remarkably well; however, the most curious shipwreck account is that of Robert Adams. Adams's narrative, the only Barbary captivity narrative by an African-American, resembles a U.S. slave narrative in that the account was generated by a white amanuensis who, along with several dozen inquisitors, grilled the former captive with questions and later cobbled together a third-person narrative. The motive behind the quizzing stemmed from Adams's claims of having traveled to the fabled city of "Tombuctoo," a place shrouded in the myth that it held considerable riches. It was a town where no white man had traveled and that many well-outfitted explorers had died trying to find. That the black, illiterate Adams did not set out to discover Timbuktu but had simply been dragged there against his will as part of a slave caravan, and that he also refused to confirm the glittering majesty of the town—popular speculation that would not be disproved until a few years later by a white explorer—only added fuel to criticism of Adams's account, particularly in the United States. The publication of the original narrative was sponsored by the African Association, a group of middle-class British professionals who sought to explore and exploit the interior of Africa. Adams's account was carefully sandwiched between the editor's justificatory preface and an overwhelming sheaf of endnotes contributed by a second authority, the British vice-consul in Morocco. As John Sekora notes in writing about the American slave narrative, for many abolitionist editors, white authentication was more important than black storytelling, so that the "black message [was] sealed within a white envelope."[51] This appears to be the pattern for Adams's narrative as well. The final version of Adams's account, which of course might never have been transcribed without a careful amanuensis— and his editor clearly seemed to have believed Adams—is nevertheless highly mediated. Like the antebellum slave narrative's concern for information about slavery itself, the message of this Barbary captivity story is subsumed by the

51. Sekora, "Black Message/White Envelope," 502.

recorder's devotion not to Adams's personal experience as a captive but to the recorder's concern for accurate information about Timbuktu.

If the production of Adams's text is confused by the collision of an African-American author and a white editor, the narrative itself poses questions about constructions of race. For instance, upon his shipwreck, Adams is abducted by a group of Arabs who want to employ him in their hunt for "negro slaves." Upon capturing a few frightened slaves, Adams and the Arabs are set upon by a larger group of black villagers who transport them to Timbuktu. When Adams reaches the town, he is immediately singled out as a curiosity because he appears to be white to the villagers. After six months of relative freedom in Timbuktu, perhaps when the curiosity wore off, Adams was sold to another group of Arabs and traveled in the desert for several more years until he was ransomed by the British vice-consul, who described him as "perfectly resembling [an] Arab" and having an Arabic accent that "resembled that of a Negro." Adams's journey along the color line is almost as astounding as his trip to the interior of Africa. What is to be made of this chameleon, this man who can variously appear as "white," "Arab," and "negro"? The Barbary captivity narrative to this point had been about white slaves in Africa, but Adams's narrative confounds this defining trope as it also lays open a highly charged imperial project, the quest for wealth in Africa.

Adams's captivity barely resembles that of Foss or Ray or Martin, for his captors are also his saviors, and his struggle is not in the bagnios but across the open desert. Because Adams's editor writes the account in the third person, more as a cold debriefing than a personal narrative, his story lacks a sense of interiority—his thoughts and feelings are absent—as well as the typical plea for an empathetic readerly response. Unlike Maria Martin's, Adams's narrative doesn't dwell on extreme suffering, though clearly his situation was desperate, particularly in the final months of his servitude. To re-create part of Adams's missing experience, we must turn to the stories of the other desert captives such as Eliza Bradley, whose shorter narrative borrowed heavily from Captain James Riley's lengthy account of his shipwreck and captivity.[52]

As a result of her shipwreck, Bradley, like James Riley, landed on the hostile desert with no food or water and had to surrender herself to the care of her new master, whom she described as a "monster in human shape." She and her party,

---

52. In addition to noting how the Bradley narrative borrowed almost verbatim from Riley's 1816 account, Keith Huntress has suggested several other reasons to consider Bradley's account a spurious one. These include the facts that no insurance records on the *Sally* exist nor is there mention of ransom payments by Consul Willshire in the Public Record Office or a registry of the *Sally* in Liverpool. In addition, neither the first nor second original British edition with its publisher's guarantee of personal knowledge of the Bradleys seems ever to have existed. See Huntress, introduction.

including her husband, dragged themselves through the Sahara, subsisting on giant locusts, camels' urine, and very little else. Like Maria Martin, Bradley claimed to have conjured a superior strength: "my fortitude, by the blessings of Heaven, was much more, probably, than what would have been exhibited by many females in my situation—the extremity of the misfortune, with the certainty of its being inevitable, served to supply me with a sort of seeming firmness."[53] Her "firmness," however, is not the same as that of Martin, whose strength seems to grow spontaneously from her torture. Bradley draws courage from at least three sources: her husband, the Bible, and her master.

In her study on the Gothic novel and the American slave narrative, Kari Winter has noted how antebellum women linked their own plight to that of slavery: "During the nineteenth century, the comparison of women to slaves became pervasive in British and American women's writing and in the writings of progressive men like John Stuart Mill and Frederick Douglass. In particular, female Gothic novelists in Britain and feminist-abolitionists in the United States represented imprisonment and slavery as the central paradigms of woman's condition in patriarchal society."[54] The image of a female captive escorted by her husband would appear to magnify the gendered roles of the couple—Captain Bradley struggles to provide for Eliza's comfort and security and Mrs. Bradley offers spiritual succor to her flagging husband. Christopher Castiglia, however, has warned against reading female captivity narratives as "'straightforward' documents upholding religious and social hegemony" since there is frequently "a gap between what the narratives purport to say and what the anecdotes relate."[55] In the end, because the captain is carried away from her and leaves her to survive on her own and also because she narrates the story, Eliza's endurance and command of the situation appear to be independent of her husband's.

In part, Bradley draws her courage and authority, she claims, from the Bible that she is allowed to carry with her despite the fact that her captors are strict Muslims. The first U.S. edition of the narrative even includes an etching of Bradley tucked in a tent and reading her Bible, which she describes with eager salesmanship: "What book is there but the Bible, that contains so much to inform, impress, and delight reflecting minds, laid together in a manner extensively adapted to their various turns of understanding, taste and temper; which people of different and distant countries, through a long succession of ages, have held in so much reverence, and read with so much advantage."[56]

53. Bradley, *An Authentic Narrative*, 6.
54. Winter, *Subjects of Slavery*, 2.
55. Castiglia, *Bound and Determined*, 27.
56. Bradley, *An Authentic Narrative*, 40.

These sentiments are not the echo of Rowlandson or Mather, who carefully apply biblical passages to the captive's plight, but resound as more of a superficial nod to a former convention.[57] That Bradley was allowed to keep and read the book instructs us more than her biblical raptures and points to the evolution of her opinions of her captor. She admits that her master, whom she formerly called a monster, afforded her preferential care, allowing her to ride a camel while the others in her party stumbled through the sand. On several occasions her master physically defends her from attack, even taking a beating for her, and Bradley doesn't represent these episodes merely as a man protecting his property (though clearly the owner had a financial stake in his captive), nor as a noble barbarian with romance in his heart, but as stories of a monster growing more humane. She even recognizes her captors' devout, albeit "deluded" spirituality. As is true of many captives, Bradley grows to recognize the humanity of her captors. Other captives, such as Riley and Adams, go even further, learning the language, adopting the dress, and gaining a taste for the food of their captors.

In many regards, the captivity of Ion Perdicaris stands out not only because it took place in the twentieth century, well after the earlier captivities, but because Perdicaris had already made Morocco his home and possibly conspired with his captor in his own abduction. If ever there was a cozy relationship between captor and captive it was this one, for Perdicaris went far beyond extending his public sympathy for Raisuli and considered him "in the light of a patriot." When Raisuli promised to protect him, Perdicaris wondered if he "was living in the days of Robin Hood and Friar Tuck." Teddy Roosevelt, who sent seven warships to Morocco to demand Perdicaris's release, would hardly have called Raisuli a patriot, nor would the millions of Americans who followed the story as it unfolded in the press. While many captives rewrote their journals with their readers' concerns in mind (even John Foss wrote a letter to his mother which she later had printed in the *Salem Gazette*), Perdicaris was the first to be commissioned *during* his captivity—editors from *Leslie's Magazine* actually contacted him while he was a prisoner deep in the interior—to narrate his story for an eager audience. Because his time in captivity was largely unremarkable, Perdicaris emphasized the drama of his late-night kidnapping, the romantic bearing of his captor—who first appears on the scene raising his hand to declare "I am the Raissuli"—and his own feeble condition.

If Cathcart's narrative describes his accumulation of wealth in captivity, Perdicaris's account reflects the influence of an already wealthy man taken captive. Whether Roosevelt would have just as easily committed two U.S. naval

57. See Ebersole, *Captured by Texts*, 145.

squadrons for the safety of a common sailor, as he did for a millionaire, is moot; his bellicose posturing at the time of the Republican convention served its own political end. No other Barbary captive, however, took with him his own servant or was treated with such great care that upon the moment of his ransom he could write, "Yes! I was actually sorry to leave one of the most interesting and attractive personalities [Raisuli] I have ever encountered."[58] If one begins to read the narrative as an apology for the bandit Raisuli, who treated his invalid captive with civility and kindness, it becomes quite plausible that the two acted in collusion to embarrass the sultan of Morocco, who was an enemy to both the politically ambitious Raisuli and the landholding millionaire. Because Perdicaris was wealthy, Raisuli could use his captive's high visibility not to exact payment from the United States but to seek reparations from his own government.

ALTHOUGH THE BARBARY CAPTIVITY NARRATIVE in English existed for more than three centuries, it caught the attention of United States readers primarily during the first half of the nineteenth century. Between John Foss's 1798 narrative and the numerous printings of James Riley's 1817 account, which continued to be offered into the second half of the century, American publishers issued over a hundred American Barbary captivity editions. The rise in popularity of the Barbary captivity narrative coincides not only with the growing number of U.S. sailors held in North African bondage during these years, but also with the resurgent demand for Indian captivity tales during the revolutionary period.[59] At the time of the War for Independence, colonists increasingly viewed themselves as captives to a tyrannical king rather than as protected royal subjects, and Indian captivity narratives, like those of John Williams and Mary Rowlandson, enjoyed a renewed readership after having been out of print for decades. In 1779, The *Narrative of Colonel Ethan Allen's Captivity,* the first American prisoner-of-war account, modeled after tales of Indian captivities, sold nearly twenty thousand copies in its first year of publication and then appeared in nineteen editions between 1779 and 1854. The fact that in 1776, Jefferson, Franklin, and Adams proposed a captivity motif for the Great Seal of the United States in which Israelites are depicted safely crossing the Red Sea as their Egyptian captors drown illustrates the pervasiveness and propagandistic power of the collective captivity metaphor.[60]

58. Perdicaris, "In Raissuli's Hands," 522.

59. In some instances, publishers issued both Indian captivity narratives and Barbary captivity narratives. Matthew Carey in Boston, for example, published several of each, as well as a number of travel accounts about North Africa and Susanna Rowson's drama "Slaves of Algiers."

60. The great seal was rejected not because of the captivity image but because it was thought the image

After the Revolution, Indian captivity narratives still proved immensely popular, though the frontier where abductions took place gradually receded to the West. By the 1830s, the attitude in New England toward American Indians had slowly shifted from overt hatred to a sentimental interest as the threat of local Indian wars faded with the decline in population and presence of Indian nations in the East. Those who once represented a menacing savage presence now symbolized America's national heritage, or at least an antiquarian relic from the bloody past.[61] The new Barbary captives, on the other hand, were almost exclusively mariners from the East, and while North Africans posed no personal threat to the safety of the average citizen, they greatly disrupted shipping. The Revolutionary War had put the new nation at odds with its former trading partners—Britain (including the British West Indies), France, and Spain—and while the Baltic states and the Orient seemed like promising new markets for American merchants, the increasingly important trade was based in the Mediterranean. At a time when overseas trade was becoming more important for the United States, the North African corsairs promised to become a greater problem and, at the same time, a test of the country's diplomatic and military independence. While the removal of Indian nations from the East seemed exemplary of American vitality and domestic strength, Barbary captivity represented public humiliation and signaled the new nation's vulnerability in international affairs. The Tripolitan War, which resulted in the forced release of over three hundred U.S. captives, however, would change this perception, and North Africa would eventually become a world theater where Jefferson's navy could flex its new muscle.

The development of the Barbary captivity narrative also coincides with the dramatic increase in the number of black slaves held in the United States. The one million Africans and African-Americans owned by whites in 1807 doubled in just thirty years. At the same time, the country witnessed the emergence of an organized antislavery response as the abolitionist movement matured and promoted the cause of free blacks through the American slave narrative. More than one hundred former slaves wrote of their flight to freedom before the end of the Civil War, speaking for the tens of thousands who made that same perilous journey. Many of these accounts, like the 1845 *Narrative of the Life of Frederick Douglass, an African Slave,* quickly became best-sellers and endured as testaments to the cruelty of slavery, testaments that continue to inform American culture.

While the question of black slavery increasingly divided the country, white

was too busy. See Sieminski, "The Puritan Captivity Narrative and the Politics of the American Revolution."

61. See Derounian-Stodola and Levernier, *The Indian Captivity Narrative, 1550–1900,* 36.

intellectuals also battled over the concept of "race" as a significant category. Racial theorizing had been spurred on by advances in the study of heredity as well as by the rise of the study of physiology and physiognomy, what was then known as the science of ethnology. (Ethnology, a "new" science, rose, in part, from the epistemological rupture that Michel Foucault has traced to the seventeenth century, wherein discrimination or difference took precedence over similitude and resemblance in modes of scientific inquiry.)[62] No immediate consensus emerged on the question of whether race was a biological determinant or whether it was a rhetorical ordering principle imposed on people to make sense of economic and political hierarchies. Dana Phillips has suggested that the central paradox concerning the nineteenth century's notion of race was that "everything seemed to be racial, or 'racy'; but (especially in polyglot America) no one thing by itself seemed to be 'race.'"[63] It is within this unstable context—a time in which the question of black slavery increasingly divided the country and contesting theories of race competed for dominance—that the Barbary captivity narrative grew in prominence.

As a form of exploration and adventure literature, the narrative of captivity in Africa translated local issues of race and slavery onto a removed setting that had been made exotic by European lore about the "Dark Continent." Typically, the account is structured as a journey that through some ill fortune—kidnapping, war, shipwreck—leads the narrator off her original course and into Africa and consequently into slavery. The narrator recounts her discoveries, once she has been captured, much as an explorer does, noting the lay of the land, the climate, the natural resources, and particularly the manner and appearance of her barbarous captors as well as the other Africans she encounters. While eventually presented as the ostensible memoir of an American in Africa, the narrative actually stages a larger drama about racial struggle.

---

62. In *The Order of Things,* Foucault suggests that the seventeenth century marks the close of the "age of resemblance" and is replaced by an analysis of "identity and difference." Following Descartes's line of thought in his *Regulae,* Foucault writes:

> Comparison, then, can attain to perfect certainty: the old system of similitudes, never complete and always open to fresh possibilities, could, it is true, through successive confirmations, achieve steadily increasing probability; but it was never certain. Complete enumeration, and the possibility of assigning at each point the necessary connection with the next, permits an absolutely certain knowledge of identities and differences: . . . The activity of the mind . . . will therefore no longer consist in *drawing things together,* in setting out on a quest for everything that might reveal some sort of kinship, attraction, or secretly shared nature within them, but, on the contrary, in *discriminating,* that is, in establishing their identities, then the inevitability of the connections with all the successive degrees of a series. (55)

63. Phillips, "Nineteenth-Century Racial Thought and Whitman's 'Democratic Ethnology of the Future,'" 299.

For nineteenth-century readers in the United States, the plight of the captive in Africa appeared to transpose the traditional roles of black and white bodies. Karen Sanchez-Eppler has argued that in general the black body was marked as subservient. For instance, Dr. Samuel Cartwright, a southern physician writing in midcentury, suggested that the slave's body was particularly suited for genuflection: "in the anatomical conformation of [the black slave's] knees, we see '*genu flexit*' written in his physical structure, being more flexed or bent than any other kind of man."[64] In this case, the white doctor inscribed ancient Latin upon the "physical structure" of the black slave to illustrate white superiority. In the captivity narrative, however, such a formula does not obtain. White bodies no longer possess full authority; indeed, they become the property of their captors and subservient to black desire.[65] These texts thus create a site in which once-privileged white flesh can suddenly be whipped, maimed, coerced into labor, traded for other slaves, exchanged for money, and even killed. At the same time, the captive-narrator never loses control over the range of narrative strategies he can deploy to tell his story. He engages in what James Clifford has called a kind of "cultural *poesis*" or "the constant reconstitution of selves and others through specific exclusions, conventions, and discursive practices."[66] Thus while the status of black and white

64. Sanchez-Eppler, "Bodily Bounds," 30. Cartwright originally published his theory in "Diseases and Peculiarities of the Negro Race," *De Bow's Review* 11 (1851), which is excerpted in Breeden, *Advice among Masters,* 173. Sanchez-Eppler comments on this passage, suggesting that "God writes 'subservience' upon the body of the black" just as the bodies of women were read against them ("Bodily Bounds," 30). Breeden notes that Cartwright was a prominent spokesman for southern nationalism. How he used racial theory to political ends is apparent in an article he first published in the *New Orleans Medical and Surgical Journal* in May 1851 which was reprinted widely in the South. Stephen Jay Gould cites theories concerning black inferiority, which Cartwright traced to inadequate decarbonization of blood in the lungs, a condition he termed "dysesthesia." The disease was characterized by carelessness and insensitivity, and, not surprisingly, part of the cure included a form of whipping with a broad leather strap and hard work to stimulate blood flow. For more on Cartwright, see Breeden, "States-Rights Medicine in the Old South."

65. In several instances black Americans were captured and treated as slaves in Africa. In each case, they were highly prized as workers because they were black and never were allowed, so far as I know, to return to the United States. For instance, Richard Delisle, the black cook aboard the *Commerce,* was never returned despite Riley's pleas to be permitted to ransom him. Similarly, the Bedouins who captured the crew of the *Oswego* refused to ransom Jack and Sam, two black seamen who served with Judah Paddock. Paddock attempted to intercede on their behalf: "I assured Ahamed [his new master] . . . that if these men were of any more value to their masters than the rest of us, the surplus of their value our consul would pay for them," but Ahamed refused to believe Paddock, whom he accused of conducting a slaving voyage. Paddock, *Narrative of the shipwreck of the ship Oswego,* 68. In these cases, the strength and endurance of black bodies are highly prized attributes compared to the weak and withering white bodies. It is highly likely that a great number of African-American sailors were taken captive in North Africa, for seafaring was one of the few employments where northern black men could thrive, and their numbers aboard ship were large in comparison to their population in the northern states. For more on African-American men in the maritime trade, see Bolster.

66. Clifford, "Partial Truths," 24.

Fig. 5. Christian slave being bastinadoed. (Courtesy James Ford Bell Library, University of Minnesota)

bodies actually changes, the capacity to "decode and recode" the situation re-mains under the control of the white narrator.[67]

White slaves actually suffered greatly in captivity and were forced to live un-der humiliating conditions, eat rancid food, sleep with droves of vermin, bake under the desert sun, strain at the galley oars, cart massive boulders, and face inhuman punishments. The captive life, for some slaves, could be infernal; yet it would be wrong to equate it with institutionalized chattel slavery in the United States. Barbary slaves were not born into captivity or stolen from their homeland; they ventured into danger as travelers engaged in mercantile or military enterprises. Furthermore, many white captives were eventually ran-somed and liberated from their slavery. They could return to the intact family

67. Most of the Barbary captivity narratives can be read as African ethnographies. For instance, the en-tire second half of James Riley's narrative is given over to the description of the manners and customs of the Moroccans that he has observed. While they appear under the guise of scientific observation, these accounts are more closely related to imaginative writings, as James Clifford has observed: "Ethnographic writings can properly be called fictions in the sense of 'something made or fashioned,' the principal burden of the word's Latin root, *fingere*. But it is important to preserve the meaning not merely of making, but also of making up, of inventing things not actually real" ("Partial Truths," 6).

and social structures into which they were born.[68] Freedom for a slave in America, however, most often disrupted family ties, relocating the slave far from her natal home and never liberating her from the material and psychological effects of hegemonic racism. Thus while the Barbary captivity narrative might seem to mirror a slave narrative, the situations of white and black slaves differed, just as the ability of the narrators varied.

The image of the white captive in Africa nevertheless evoked comparison to the black slave in America. Most often, the captive used the situation to indirectly justify slavery in the United States or altogether denounce Africans as "barbarous." Archibald Robbins, for instance, who was shipwrecked off the coast of Morocco in 1815, felt fully justified in withholding his sympathy for U.S. slaves given his protracted captivity in the desert: "These Africans, of every name and feature and complexion, take delight in enslaving each other; . . . it can hardly be expected that an American, who has for months and years been enslaved by them, can feel so much compassion towards a slave *here* as those do who have always enjoyed the blessings of humanity and liberty."[69] Even James Riley, who captained the ship upon which Robbins served, and who in his immensely popular narrative eventually vowed to fight for the freedom of American slaves when he returned home, initially portrayed his African captor as a subhuman cannibal:

He appeared to be about five feet seven or eight inches high, and of a complexion between that of an American Indian and negro. He had about him, to cover his nakedness, a piece of coarse woollen cloth, that reached from below his breast nearly to his knees; his hair was long and bushy, resembling a *pitch mop*, sticking out every way six or eight inches from his head; his face resembled that of an ourang-outang more than a human being; his eyes were red and fiery; his mouth, which stretched nearly from ear to ear, was well lined with sound teeth; and a long

68. James Wilson Stevens, in his *An Historical and Geographical Account of Algiers,* comments on the varied conditions of Barbary slaves as well as the hyperbolized reports of their treatment that circulated in the United States:

The condition of those who are slaves to private individuals, depends very much upon the disposition of their master, and the slaves' own conduct. Some of them fare better in Algiers, than ever they did in their own countries, and if they are good for any thing, are entertained rather as companions than servants; though by far the greater number are barbarous masters, who treat their slaves with great cruelty. . . . While the Americans were enslaved in Algiers, the most exaggerated accounts were circulated respecting the severity of their afflictions. It was reported that the tongues of some were cut out, that others were emasculated; and captain Lawrence of the Hull Packet, who is said to have obtained his information at Cadiz, informs us that the Americans had their heads shaved close, and were not permitted to wear any kind of covering on their heads. Their calamities were indeed without a parallel, but the above accounts were entirely unfounded. (242–43)

69. Robbins, *A Journal,* 91.

curling beard, which depended from his upper lip and chin down upon his breast, gave him altogether a most horrid appearance, and I could not but imagine that those well set teeth were sharpened for the purpose of devouring human flesh!!⁷⁰

Less frequently, captives, or those who wrote about white slavery, attempted to reveal the hypocrisy of the American slave system. In *The Selling of Joseph,* the first antislavery tract written and printed in New England in 1700, the famous judge and diarist Samuel Sewall commented upon the duplicitous nature of complaints made against Barbary in the light of American slavery: "Methinks, when we are bemoaning the barbarous Usage of our Friends and Kinsfolk in *Africa:* it might not be unreasonable to enquire whether we are not culpable in forcing the *Africans* to become Slaves amongst our selves."⁷¹ In 1786, at the time of the first postrevolutionary captivity crisis, John Jay, the secretary of foreign affairs, issued a complaint against English authorities for "carrying away" from New York several African-Americans. In questioning the denominating of Africans as "goods and chattels," he invoked the example of Algerian captives: "Is there any difference between the two cases than this, that the American slaves at Algiers were WHITE people, whereas the African slaves at New York were BLACK people?"⁷² In 1797, James Wilson Stevens echoed this sentiment in *An Historical and Geographical Account of Algiers:* "With what countenance then can we reproach a set of barbarians, who have only retorted our own acts upon ourselves in making reprisals upon our citizens? For it is manifest to the world, that we are equally culpable, and in whatever terms of opprobrium we may execrate the piratic disposition of the Africans, yet all our recriminations will recoil upon ourselves."⁷³ Much later, in 1853, the ardent abolitionist Charles Sumner wrote a short history entitled *White Slavery in the Barbary States* in order to detail the antislavery battle in Africa and to illustrate the injustice of such practices in the United States: "The interest awakened for the slave in Algiers embraced also the slave at home. Sometimes they were said to be alike in condition; sometimes, indeed, it was openly declared that the horrors of our American slavery surpassed that of Algiers."⁷⁴ That the

70. Riley, *An Authentic Narrative,* 18. James Riley's son William published a sequel to his father's narrative that included journal entries and letters. Although James Riley was eventually elected to the House of Representatives, he appears never to have fought for emancipation. It seems, however, that Riley supported the recolonization movement and was willing to undertake an exploratory expedition along the African coast to find a suitable harbor to land former American slaves. See Riley, *Sequel to Riley's Narrative,* 55–56.

71. Sewall, *The Selling of Joseph,* 11. As early as 1688, Germantown settlers had signed a petition denouncing slavery in America, comparing it to slavery of Christians in North Africa. See "Germantown Friends' Protest against Slavery, 1688."

72. Quoted in Sumner, *White Slavery in the Barbary States,* 88.

73. Stevens, *An Historical and Geographical Account of Algiers,* 235.

74. Sumner, *White Slavery in the Barbary States,* 83.

Fig. 6. James Riley's initial escape from his Arab captors. (Courtesy Special Collections and Rare Books Department, University of Minnesota Libraries)

Barbary captivity narrative is used to portray African "barbarity" (just as accounts of Indian captives conjure portraits of Indian "savagery") as well as critique slavery in America (work more often associated with the traditional American slave narrative) suggests the semiotic plasticity of the Barbary narrative and the interconnections among all three genres.

WHEN TRIPOLI DECLARED WAR on the United States in 1801, John Adams authorized William Eaton's dramatic march across the desert to help install a friendlier bashaw—an event memorialized in "The Marine's Hymn": "From the halls of Montezuma to the shores of Tripoli." Fewer than a dozen U.S. marines, however, actually invaded Tripoli, a minor incursion compared to that of the French occupation of Algeria, which began in 1830. By the turn of the century, most of the region would be European colonial territories.[75] Though the United States never had a grand design to invade North Africa, this did not preclude many captives from musing about the eventual conquest of the Barbary coast. James Cathcart, for one, dreamed that France would

75. The events of the Tripolitan War helped to foster nationalist pride and homespun prestige. If we have long ago forgotten this war, the fact that the United States now has more than twenty-five towns named either Eaton or Decatur testifies to the former popularity of these men and the pervasiveness of their stories. Despite the pride the country took in its military action against Tripoli, the United States sought and accepted financial and tactical aid from the British. That the nation with its brand-new navy saw itself as acting in the interest of international commerce suggests the degree to which the war might be viewed as both a nationalistic and internationalistic affair.

march into Africa and overpower his own Algerian captors, whom he saw as unjust and capricious: "What a pity such a character as Napoleon Bonaparte, with one hundred thousand men under his command, had not a footing in Barbary; with that force he would subdue the whole of the Barbary States from Salu to Derna in less than twelve months."[76] Archibald Robbins, writing after the Tripolitan War, lamented the difficulty of invading Africa while recalling how the U.S. Navy used Tripoli as a proving ground to demonstrate its imperial muscle: "Destroy [Tripoli's] naval armaments, and batter down their capitals," Robbins complained, and "they still have a safe retreat in their mountains and in their deserts, where a civilized army cannot subsist. The mention of *Tripoli* calls up the proud recollection of the infancy of the *American Navy.* It was upon the coast of that country, that Americans began to learn how to conquer upon the ocean."[77] The fictional narrative attributed to Thomas Nicholson, which also reflects a strong desire to subdue Africa, suggests that military force would have to be combined with diplomatic guile in order to succeed: "An absolute conquest of the Algerine territory cannot be effected but by invasion from the interior, through the co-operation of the Grand Seignior or the assistance of the other Barbary states."[78]

The reason for bringing up these "conquest" reveries is not to suggest that the United States would have invaded North Africa if it had had the military wherewithal to do so, but to illustrate that the nation participated in the eventual subjugation of North Africa through narrative. Insofar as imperialism is a theory and practice of domination, it must also be understood as a cultural project expressed in myriad ways and by assorted nations, institutions, and individuals. As Edward Said points out, the imperialist struggle is not exclusively about territorial boundaries:

> The main battle in imperialism is over land, of course; but when it came to who owned the land, who had the right to settle and work on it, who kept it going, who won it back, and who now plans its future—these issues were reflected, contested, and even for a time decided in narrative. . . . The power to narrate, or to block other narratives from forming and emerging, is very important to culture and imperialism, and constitutes one of the main connections between them.[79]

The Barbary captivity narrative engages in this textual battle through a variety of rhetorical strategies that reinforce the image of the dominated captive as culturally superior. In this sense, these accounts both created and drama-

76. Cathcart, *The Captives,* 1.
77. Robbins, *A Journal,* 147.
78. Nicholson, *An Affecting Narrative,* 19.
79. Said, *Culture and Imperialism,* xii–xiii.

tized the conflict between Western "civilization" and African "barbarity." What we must keep in mind is that every captive who wrote a narrative survived the ordeal. We name these accounts "captivity" narratives, but they might just as easily be called "survival" narratives, a special form of the adventure story, because a survivor has, in most cases, returned home or to a place of refuge to write about her past experience as a captive. Her success—measured by her native ability to stay alive until such time as her compatriots can arrange for her redemption—illustrates her ability to overcome great hardship at the hands of barbarous captors and bring honor to her home. The text begins with the supposition that the captive's superior culture, and sometimes her superior devotion to God, has provided her with the fortitude to overcome the ordeal. That the writer has returned to a place where she is free to record and represent her experience is evidence of her success and the greatness of her society—as well as her God—in the face of barbarous circumstances.

The unbalanced relationship between captive and master plays a key role in establishing a defining boundary between the captive's own identity and that of her African captor. From the moment of first contact, the writer can clearly establish a moral and cultural difference based on the "unmoral," "unlawful," "inhuman" act of abduction itself, which begins to define a widening gulf between the civilized and the barbaric. The aggrieved captive can then easily insist upon other differences between herself and her new masters, differences that are usually framed in terms of something lacking and something a civilized country could eventually supply: rationality, progress, history, self-control, etc. To tell her story, the author relies not only upon the adventure tale but on the elements of travel narrative and ethnography that give her license to present "Africa" to her readers from the standpoint not only of a person of strong character in dismal conditions, but of a careful, even scientific, observer. Frequently, these observations offered a negative portrait of Africans while proposing the need for further study, assessment, and exploration.

A case in point comes from the opening pages to Judah Paddock's narrative about his 1800 captivity, which includes a letter of support from one Thomas Eddy, urging the former captive to write his narrative. Eddy suggests that Paddock's experience would be welcomed by the public because of a growing curiosity about Africa: "The civilized world is now looking towards that country with increasing interest, and any genuine information can hardly fail to be favourably received."[80] The "civilized" world's burgeoning fascination with Africa took several forms.

Western contact with Africa had largely been restricted to the coastal trad-

---

80. Paddock, *Narrative of the shipwreck of the ship Oswego,* vii.

Introduction

Fig. 7. Burning Christian captives. (Courtesy James Ford Bell Library, University of Minnesota)

Fig. 8. Disfiguring, impaling, burning, and burying alive Christian prisoners. (Courtesy James Ford Bell Library, University of Minnesota)

ing areas—the slave coast, the gold coast, the ivory coast, the pepper coast, etc. As a result of the Enlightenment and the scientific revolution, a growing curiosity arose about the African interior, a space filled by confused fiction on most maps. Questions often centered around geographic problems such as the sources of the Zaire and Nile Rivers and the course of the Niger River. The same British African Association that quizzed Adams (later to be known as the Royal Geographical Society) sponsored scientific expeditions like that of Mungo Park's excursion up the Gambia River in 1795. Other explorers, such as the famous David Livingstone, sought not only to survey the continent but to convert and eventually to "civilize" its inhabitants. Several Protestant missions established themselves in Africa by the first decade of the nineteenth century, although the Moravian Brethren first arrived in what is now South Africa as early as the 1730s. These same religious forces helped to curtail the British slave trade, and the first act banning slavery in Great Britain came into effect in 1772. By 1807, Britain had forbidden its citizens to trade in slaves, and by 1833 it had outlawed slavery in all of its colonies except India. With the decline in the slave trade came a concomitant increase in the demand for industrial raw materials such as rubber, ivory, beeswax, gum, coffee, and palm oil. Abolitionists viewed the shift to commodity exchange and a wider, more profitable trade in resources as necessary to reduce the incentive to market slaves, but the demand had grown primarily out of an expanding middle class, particularly in Britain, and the evolution of modern industrial capitalism based on wage labor. It was largely the middle class that sponsored the African Association and helped to finance exploration while feeding public interest in the continent. The United States, eager to develop its overseas markets, found the possibilities presented by Africa no less interesting.

Many captives noted the continent's well-known natural potential and marveled over the land's great possibilities in the hands of an industrial society. John Foss, for one, observed that although Algiers had seven principal rivers, none was currently navigated: "It is however likely that they might be made use of for this purpose, were the inhabitants of a more intelligent and industrious character, for some of them are of a tolerable depth. Such is the gross ignorance of the natives in whatever concerns domestic improvements, that there is not a single bridge over any of those rivers."[81] In Tripoli, several years later, William Ray noted that under Roman rule the land had been called "the garden of the world" but could scarcely lay claim to such fecundity any longer. He declared the town of Tripoli inferior to both Algiers and Tunis, and this owing to no fault of the soil: "The fertility of the soil cannot be controverted; for were it not extremely prolific, the exanimate inhabitants, oppressed by tyranny, and abandoned to indolence, could not possibly subsist."[82] A decade later, in Morocco, Archibald Robbins put it more succinctly:

> Although Africa holds the third rank in point of size among the four great continents that constitute our globe, in a moral, political, and commercial point of view, it is decidedly inferior to them all. While the continents of Europe and America have been making rapid progress in civilization, the arts and sciences, Asia may be said to have been, for the most part, stationary, and Africa retrograding.[83]

81. Foss, *A Journal of the Captivity and Sufferings*, 41.
82. Ray, *Horrors of Slavery*, 173.
83. Robbins, *A Journal*, 38.

For Foss, Ray, and Robbins, African land presented wondrous possibilities, while African people posed daunting impediments.

Before they wrote their narratives, several of the captives had researched what had already been written about Africa. Many wrote brief histories of Africa, never failing to measure the apogee of African civilization in terms of the rise of the Roman empire. Writers usually interpreted the years after the Roman decline as a period of stagnation or regression, certainly not one of great development or innovation. Thus North Africa was usually viewed as a decayed world built upon the ruins of Western civilization. Two examples must stand in for many. James Riley claims to have been keenly observant of his surroundings; his experience as a seagoing captain, he mentions, made him extremely conscious of geography and gave him a natural curiosity about foreign places. Near the end of Riley's captivity, when his strength was at its nadir, he claims that he could not help but speculate on the desert's lustrous past: "Notwithstanding my frame was literally exhausted, yet my imagination transported me back to a time when this region might have been inhabited by men in a higher state of civilization, and when it was probably one of the fairest portions of the African continent."[84] Riley's nostalgia for a more civilized past appears almost benign in contrast to William Ray's depiction of the heavily armed Tripoli harbor. To Ray's sensibility, what had followed the Roman legacy wrought only Gothic horror:

> For here [on the Tripoli beachhead] bribery, treachery, rapine, murder, and all the hedious [*sic*] offspring of accursed tyranny, have often drenched the streets in blood, and dealt, to the enslaved inhabitants, famine, dungeons, ruin and destruction. On yonder noddling tower, once waved the banners of the all-conquering Rome, when these fruitful regions were styled the Eden of that empire, now Gothic ruins, and barbarous inhabitants curse the half-tilled soil.[85]

Both Riley's and Ray's descriptions refuse any idea of progress, a notion particularly important to Enlightenment philosophers.[86] They recall Roman

84. Riley, *An Authentic Narrative*, 223.
85. Ray, *Horrors of Slavery*, 164,
86. Peter Hulme has remarked that the Enlightenment notion of history "was the idea of 'progress,' initially from 'savagery' to 'civilization,' but then through the stages of a more complex developmental model based on distinctions between hunting, pastoralism, and agriculture" (8). For John Locke, the mere existence of food mattered little. Locke made a key distinction between people who simply gathered and those who cultivated the land. Those who failed to improve the land or their material conditions and refused to learn what reason readily taught could be viewed as irrational or animalistic. To neglect reason was an indictment of moral lassitude and further evidence that a society had not progressed out of its savage past or had lapsed into a state of barbarity. This was also the argument used to discount American Indian agricultural practices as irrational. See Hulme and Jordanova, *The Enlightenment and Its Shadows*. See also Matar, "John Locke and the 'Turbanned Nations.'"

greatness and the potential for future wealth, but to them the present suggests only ruins and desert wastes. Their descriptions conjure a static picture of a society headed nowhere. Is it any wonder that Riley wrote of his captors as "wandering" Arabs?[87] The rhetorical gesture of erasing local history serves as a way to deny a sense of "movement toward a destiny." David Spurr has argued that Western travelers engage in an imperial rhetoric when they describe a country as having no legacy or worthy past: "This way of defining the African, as without history and without progress, makes way for the moral necessity of cultural transformation. The colonizing powers will create a history where there was none."[88]

Much of colonial discourse creates the imperative for "cultural transformation" in the manner Spurr describes and thus reproduces a notion of the African other as outside humanity. Christopher Miller, for instance, has noted how "Africa has been made to bear a double burden, of monstrousness *and* nobility."[89] Nowhere is this polarized account of Africa more apparent than in James Riley's narrative. We have already seen how Riley depicted his captors as monstrous cannibals, but much later in the narrative Riley's impression of Africans expands. Nearing the border of Morocco, Riley meets with Rais bel Cossim, an emissary for the British consul. Riley confesses that he feels extremely weak and that he fears he will die before ever regaining his freedom. Rais bel Cossim listens patiently and then chastises the Christian for doubting a merciful God who had preserved Riley through such trials. Riley is astonished:

> To hear such sentiments from the mouth of a Moor, whose nation I had been taught to consider the worst of barbarians, I confess, filled my mind with awe and reverence, and I looked up to him as a kind of superior being, when he added, "We are all children of the same heavenly Father, who watches over all our actions, whether we be Moor, or Christian, or Pagan, or of any other religion; we must perform his will."[90]

In this passage, Riley describes Rais bel Cossim as a superior being who understands all humanity as equal under the eyes of God. Commenting on similar passages, Spurr argues that the ultimate aim of colonial discourse is not to maintain a radical difference between colonizer and subject but to foreground

---

87. John Foss also imagines the indigenous people to be aimless wanderers: "The people in the country, have no houses, but live in tents, and remove from one place to another, as they want pasture, or as any other accidental circumstance may happen" (34).

88. Spurr, *The Rhetoric of Empire*, 98–99.

89. Miller, *Blank Darkness*, 5.

90. Riley, *An Authentic Narrative*, 209.

their common humanity: "[imperial discourse] seeks to dominate by inclusion and domestication rather than by a confrontation which recognizes the independent identity of the Other."[91] This is the logic that allows the colonizer to see his subjects as sympathetic to imperial aims. The colonizer can rationalize his civilizing mission—often violently implemented—as one that brings humanity together.

Depictions of Africans as noble or exemplary are infrequent, indeed rare. "Monsters," "savages," "cannibals," and "torturers" typify the descriptions captives give of the Africans they encounter. Judah Paddock, for instance, confessed that his reading of travel literature had done little to prepare him for his first contact with Africans: "Their figure, and ferocious look, to say nothing of their behaviour, were as savage, and even exceeded in savageness, any thing that I ever have read in narratives of voyages. . . . Before I proceed further, I will describe, as well as I can, these monsters."[92] John Foss portrayed his Algerian captors as more hostile than the indigenous wild animals: "Indeed a considerable part of the back country is a savage desert, abounding with Lions, Tigers, Leopards, Jackalls, Buffaloes, wild Boars, Porcupines, &c. And it must be acknowledged, that these animals are not the least amiable inhabitants of this country."[93]

Soon after his capture, Riley describes an interesting scene in which two groups of Arabs clash over who properly owns the American captives. Eight Arabs jump off their camels with their scimitars "naked and ready for action." They lay hold of the Americans, pulling and hauling in every direction, claiming them as their own. Soon, the disagreement escalates to blows:

> They cut at each other over my head, and on every side of me with their bright weapons, which fairly whizzed through the air within an inch of my naked body, and on every side of me, now hacking each other's arms apparently to the bone, then laying their ribs bare with gashes, while their heads, hands, and thighs, received a full share of cuts and wounds. The blood streaming from every gash, ran down their bodies, colouring and heightening the natural hideousness of their appearance.[94]

This passage is of particular interest because Jonathan Cowdery describes almost an identical scene when the Tripoli navy boarded the U.S.S. *Philadelphia*. After the flag was lowered, "the Tripolitan chiefs collected their favourites, and, with drawn sabers, fell to cutting and slashing their own men,

91. Spurr, *The Rhetoric of Empire*, 32.
92. Paddock, *Narrative of the shipwreck of the ship Oswego*, 47–48.
93. Foss, *A Journal of the Captivity and Sufferings*, 41–42.
94. Riley, *An Authentic Narrative*, 55.

who were stripping the Americans and plundering the ship."[95] These scenes of mutual mutilation among captors are particularly important not only for how they define barbarity but for their larger implications for self-governance. They represent in miniature what has been implied about the political corpus; that is, individuals who exhibit a lack of self-discipline and a strong proclivity toward self-destruction are the products of a society that is unable to govern itself. Primitive passions that go unrestrained reflect the utter debasement of an entire culture as well as moral and intellectual degradation.

In addition to such wild melees, the Barbary captivity narrative writers create a pool of bizarre episodes and images: spectacularly gruesome punishments, meals of camel sores and human urine, "ourang-outang" men, etc. Barbary becomes a safe repository for the grotesque and bizarre.[96] James Riley, for instance, is convinced that many inhabitants of the desert live to be two hundred years old.[97] His claim imbues the desert with mysterious, life-granting properties, even though its harsh climate threatens to kill Riley at every moment. This description reinforces the notion that Barbary is a land of extremes, a country either lush or barren and rarely conventional. We see this again in James Cathcart's depictions of the notorious prison, the bagnio belique, as he conjures an image of utter bedlam. In this portrait of Algiers, the world is turned upside-down and the comfort of wild animals is prized over the health and safety of civilized men:

> The greatest inconvenience in this prison is in consequence of the lions and tigers being kept there which creates an insufferable stench, which joined to the common shore of the hospital which communicates with that of the prison corrodes the atmosphere that in the summer season it is nearly suffocating. I have known twenty-seven animals of this description to have been kept at once in this prison

95. William Ray, who was aboard the *Philadelphia* at the time, disputes Cowdery's account. He admits that there was "a sort of mutiny" among the Tripolitans but nothing to the extent Cowdery describes: "For my part I never saw any hands amputated, nor do I believe there were any lives lost, for myself and a hundred others were in the ship much longer than the Doctor, and none of us ever saw or heard of this carnage amongst themselves." Ray, *Horrors of Slavery*, 79. In this section of his account, Ray aims to discredit Cowdery and call attention to the doctor's cowardice; his correction may indeed be a much more accurate picture of what actually occurred.

96. David Spurr has suggested that

> [t]he Third World continually provides what writers call "material" of a special nature: the exotic, the grotesque, the bizarre, the elemental. . . . The atavism of the Third World becomes the object of interest and attraction, as if it offered an image of our own more primitive being. Madness, revolution, barbarism, natural disaster—all seem closer to the surface there, offering a constant source of pathos. But, like Proust at his breakfast table, one can experience this pathos safely by virtue of an aesthetic mediation whose transforming power increases with cultural distance.

Spurr, *The Rhetoric of Empire*, 46.

97. See Riley, *An Authentic Narrative*, 313–14.

which are maintained at the expense of the Christian tavern keepers. They frequently break loose and have killed several of the slaves as they dare not destroy them even in their own defense, and if very ferocious, an order must come from the Dey and some of his guards are then dispatched to shoot them before the evil can be removed. The offals from their dens serve to maintain an enormous number of rats, the largest I ever saw, which frequently serve to satisfy the craving appetite of some of the poor slaves. Cats are likewise eaten from mere necessity, and once in particular I asked a Frenchman what he was going to do with it after skinning, he laconically answered, "Ma foi it [*sic*] faut Manger." During the plague this prison, in consequence of its communication with the hospital, had the greatest number of its inhabitants destroyed with that contagion.[98]

For James Riley, the exotic took many forms, including the very desert terrain that caused him such sustained agony. When we recall that most captives wrote or rewrote their narratives as survivors, the fact that they could retrospectively take pleasure from the vistas they encountered as if they were on the Grand Tour should not come as a surprise. Their expression of a cultivated aesthetic reaffirms the captive's position as a civilized person. This ability to recognize "beauty" in the "wild" appears in several guises, most notably in the captive's aesthetic appreciation for the African landscape. While often the landscape appears horrid and inhospitable to the suffering captive, she frequently comes upon a view that astounds her. This is particularly the case for the shipwrecked captives who were forced to travel across great expanses of desert and mountains. Note how James Riley writes about the encroaching mountains as he approaches them from the south:

> We had seen these mountains for several days past, in the distant horizon, when we were on the high ridges, which we were obliged to pass; but we now beheld them from this wide-spreading plain in all their awful magnitude: their lofty summits, towering high above the clouds in sharp peaks, appeared to be covered with never-melting snows. This sight was calculated to fill the mind of the beholder with wonder and astonishment.[99]

Once again Riley expresses a particularly Romantic appreciation for the "lofty" and "towering" vista. His observation that the view was "calculated" to fill him with "wonder and astonishment" reminds us that the "calculation" was formulated as an invisible aesthetic imposed upon the scene and describes Riley's own cast of mind.

If what Riley saw filled him with visual rapture, then his ears delighted him

98. Cathcart, *The Captives*, 56–57.
99. Riley, *An Authentic Narrative*, 201.

Fig. 9. Public punishment of
Christian criminals.
(Courtesy James Ford Bell
Library, University of
Minnesota)

no less. All captives wrestled with communication problems and were forced
to make do with hand signals and gesticulations. Riley, however, claims to
have learned a form of Arabic tolerably well and thanks his creator that he "en-
dowed me with intelligence to comprehend a language I had never before
heard spoken."[100] To Riley, however, who aestheticizes the experience, com-
prehension is less important than the images that are called to his mind when
he listens only to the sound of his captors' speech: "Their language . . . thrills
on the ear like the breathings of soft wind-music, and excites in the soul the

100. Ibid., 256.

most soothing sensations; but when they speak in anger, it sounds as hoarse as the roarings of irritated lions, or the most furious beasts of prey."[101] Riley's shipmate, Archibald Robbins, was similarly awed by his captors' voice and claimed "there is a kind of peculiar mystery in their language."[102]

This mystification of language is particularly important when we recall the etymology of the term *barbary*, traced earlier, which refers to unintelligibility. According to this history, Africans were named *barbarians* because they refused to communicate. Riley and Robbins, who are not invaders per se but strangers in a foreign land, do not expect the burden of communication to be placed on their captors—it is they themselves who must learn the lingua franca. In essence, they are the "barbarians" who cannot speak the native tongue. Unintelligibility thus takes on a Romantic cast and is translated into melody and mystery. For Riley, rudimentary language acquisition becomes a source of intellectual pride and a new sphere of mastery.

A danger exists, however, as we see in Robert Adams's narrative. To Joseph Dupuis, who was one of the first to meet Adams upon his return from captivity, Adams's speech represented a form of contamination. Dupuis writes in a letter included in the introduction to the narratives:

> I had difficulty at first in believing him to be a Christian. When I spoke to him in English, he answered me in a mixture of Arabic and broken English, and sometimes in Arabic only. . . . Like most other Christians after a long captivity and severe treatment among the Arabs, he appeared upon his first arrival exceedingly stupid and insensible.[103]

Dupuis's remarks suggest a fear that the boundary of identity is closely linked to language and that language acquisition—particularly under the duress of captivity—comes perilously close to cultural assimilation.

Perhaps it was a real source of fear since as many as two-thirds of the Algerian corsair *reis* or captains in the seventeenth century were Christian renegades who had served in the professional armies of France, England, or the United Netherlands. We also know that many Christian slaves never returned home and likely "took the Turban," but we know very little about them. Kathryn Zabelle Derounian-Stodola and James Levernier have noted that transculturated Indian captives often chose to remain silent because of their decision to disassociate themselves from their natal culture, and this may have been the case with returning renegades who chose not to write of their conversions. In addition, Western publishers were less likely to publish accounts of Barbary

101. Ibid., 316.
102. Robbins, *A Journal*, 72.
103. Adams, *The Narrative of Robert Adams*, xxiii–xxiv.

that went against the prevailing image of a sinister North Africa.[104] Nabil Matar has suggested that during the Renaissance at least, captive Christian apostates were the rule, not the exception. Many were forced under penalty of death to convert. Others who lived among Muslims slowly grew accustomed to the habits and rituals of Islamic life and gradually chose to accept the dominant culture as their own. Certainly many chose to renounce their faith to receive better treatment and avail themselves of Islamic privileges: freedom from slavery and opportunities for marriage and employment. "Evidently," Matar notes, "Mohammad was more attractive than Christ because he paid higher wages to those who served him."[105]

Occasionally, a captive does document the presence of a renegade. Adams, for instance, describes the miserable condition of two of his fellow mariners, Williams and Davison, who regretfully renounced their religion, believing there was no other alternative. For their conversion, they were given a horse, a musket, a blanket, and the opportunity to marry a Muslim woman. It is likely that they were eventually ransomed and partly responsible for contesting the veracity of Adams's account because of their own embarrassment. Other captives may have "turned Turk" and lived quite a good, long life. That their stories are not reported is a sign of the troubling picture a "white barbarian," like a "white Indian," posed. What "civilized" person would voluntarily join an "inferior" culture? What white American would allow his whiteness to be symbolically erased?[106] For theologians, the figure of the Christian apostate might suggest the possible superiority of Islam and the legitimacy of the prophet Muhammad.[107] While ostensibly about African barbarity, these accounts delimit the boundary of the civilized United States as they discuss matters of history, rationality, aesthetic development, cultural degradation, theological hegemony, and transculturation.

In many ways, the captive writer participates in and is encircled by a culture grounded in imperial pursuits. I do not mean to suggest that Foss, Riley, and the other captives should have been expected to write differently. On the contrary, they wrote within a climate that limited their vision, and that, as Mary Louise Pratt has suggested of the European travel writer, invested the captive with "imperial eyes [that] passively look out and possess."[108] Basil Davidson

---

104. See Derounian-Stodola and Levernier, *The Indian Captivity Narrative*, 73–74.

105. Matar, "'Turning Turk,'" 38.

106. See Axtell, "The White Indians of Colonial America."

107. Many Christians resisted apostasy. One extreme form of resistance involved tattooing newborn children on the face with the sign of the cross so that the child's body was indelibly marked as Christian flesh. See Matar, "'Turning Turk,'" 38–39.

108. Pratt, *Imperial Eyes*, 7.

characterized the general myopia of early travelers in Africa when he wrote, "If they tried to understand the minds and actions of Africans they knew, it was by the way, and it was rare. Nearly all of them were convinced they were faced by 'primeval man,' by humanity as it had been before history began, by societies which lingered in the dawn of time."[109] These narratives, then, must be read with an awareness of the writers' immersion in imperialist culture if both their confining limits and how they expressed a dominating attitude are to be understood.

WESTERN WRITERS HAVE LONG USED the trope of Barbary captivity. Miguel de Cervantes, for example, along with his brother Rodrigo, was captured by Algerian corsairs on September 26, 1575, and was held for sixty-one months. Twice he attempted to escape, sufficient cause to have him put to death, but the bashaw spared Cervantes and substituted a "less expensive Christian," whom he repeatedly dashed on the head until the man drowned in his own blood. Cervantes wrote two plays about his experience, *Life in Algiers* and *Dungeons of Algiers,* and the figure of the Barbary captive also appeared in several of his poems as well as in *Don Quixote* (1605).

In "The Old Woman's Story" in *Candide,* Voltaire creates a farcical Barbary captivity episode in order to poke fun at Christians as well as Muslims: "We embarked on a papal galley gilded like the altar of St. Peter's in Rome. Suddenly a corsair from Salé swept down and boarded us. Our soldiers defended themselves as papal troops usually do; falling on their knees and throwing down their arms, they begged of the corsairs absolution *in articulo mortis.*"[110] Later, Voltaire rewrites the stock scene of barbarians wildly slicing each other with scimitars as they fought for possession of the captive booty. The Old Woman remarks:

> A Moor snatched my mother by the right arm, the first mate held her by the left; a Moorish soldier grabbed one leg, one of our pirates the other. In a moment's time almost all our girls were being dragged four different ways. . . . My captive companions, their captors, soldiers, sailors, blacks, browns, whites, mulattoes, and at last my captain, all were killed, and I remained half dead on a mountain of corpses. Similar scenes were occurring, as is well known, for more than three hundred leagues around, without anyone skimping on the five prayers a day decreed by Mohammed.[111]

Most readers of Daniel Defoe's adventure novel understandably forget that Robinson Crusoe's first misadventure landed him in Morocco for a

109. Quoted in Said, *Culture and Imperialism,* 99.
110. Voltaire, *Candide,* 20.
111. Ibid., 21.

short time. After Crusoe set himself up as a "Guiney" trader, a slave dealer, and his luck fails, he is taken by a "Turkish" rover and is held for two years: "At this surprising Change of my Circumstances from a Merchant to a miserable Slave, I was perfectly overwhelmed."[112] Given the wealth of well-known imaginative works that have recounted, satirized, moralized, and embellished captive life in North Africa, it is not surprising that several of the first American novels drew upon the tension between North Africa and the United States.[113]

Thomas Atwood Digges was an American who while in Britain wrote the picaresque *Adventures of Alonso* (1775), arguably the first "American" novel.[114] In his travels, Alonso falls prey to the Moroccan corsairs and the lusty whims of Aldalid, a rich slave owner:

> As soon as they were alone, [Aldalid] proceeded to caresses; but Alonso, disgusted with his familiarities, treated him with contempt and disdain. Aldalid, however, was not to be so easily repulsed.—"Come, (said he) lay aside these airs, and comply with my desires.—If I did not love you, I would not be trifled with. I chuse rather to gratify my passions with good-will, than by force; but if that is necessary, you muste be sensible it is in vain to resist."—This he delivered with a kind of emphasis; but immediately changing his tone, he resumed his fondness, and was proceeding to the most disgusting indecencies, when Alonso, pushing him aside with violence, desired him, with a peremptory voice, to desist; that he would sooner part with his life, than be subservient to his lust.[115]

To prevent his rape, Alonso kills one of Aldalid's slaves, who was about to tie him up. Soon Alonso meets a Christian renegade who conveniently recognizes him from a previous adventure and helps him escape from Morocco. The episode highlights the vulnerability of male captives to sexual violation, a real threat alluded to in several narratives. It also rewrites the formulation established in the narratives of female African-American slaves, who are frequently figured as victims of white sexual aggression.[116]

---

112. Defoe, *Robinson Crusoe*, 17.

113. Further novelistic examples include Penelope Aubin's *The Noble Slaves* (1722) and William Rufus Chetwood's *The Voyages and Adventures of Captain Robert Boyle* (1726), which appeared in twenty-three printings. For an insightful discussion of how these novels participated in Orientalist discourse and the formation of imperial subjectivity, see Snader.

114. See Elias, "The First American Novel"; and Elias and Finch, introduction to *Letters of Thomas Atwood Digges*, xxxi–xxxix.

115. Digges, *Adventures of Alonso*, 83–84.

116. Frances Smith Foster acknowledges the extreme vulnerability of African-American women slaves, but she suggests that this fact has been overworked in traditional U.S. slave narratives:

> Widely accepted as being, if not the slave's own true story of slavery, at least the versions of slave life most sympathetic to the slaves, most slave narratives stereotyped slave women as sexually exploited beings.

46

Introduction

Another early American novel, written in 1787, at the time of the Constitutional Convention, is Peter Markoe's *The Algerine Spy in Pennsylvania*.[117] The spy Mehemet, who comes to hold quite a good opinion of the United States, nevertheless schemes to meet with the leaders of Shays's Rebellion and secure Rhode Island as an Algerian port. While the plot might seem laughingly farfetched, Algerian corsairs had ventured as far as Iceland in 1633, capturing eight hundred slaves, and Moroccan privateers had hijacked forty ships off the coast of Newfoundland in 1625. For tribute, Mehemet suggests that his new American allies can pay the sultan not in gold or military supplies as is usually the case, but curiously "in a certain number of virgins."[118] At the close of the novel, the spy is betrayed and must live permanently in Pennsylvania, where he buys a farm and sings the praises of freedom. His sudden conversion to Christianity reverses the typical threat of "taking the turban" and easily transforms even a scheming barbarian into a beneficiary of revolutionary democracy. Yet another American novel, *Humanity in Algiers: or, the Story of Azem,* published anonymously in 1801, tells the story of a virtuous slave, Azem, who upon his death leaves a legacy to free one honest slave every year. Written as a sentimental tragedy in North Africa, the novel criticizes slaveholding practices everywhere. It also denounces religious intolerance, blending Christian and Islamic precepts to create a universal God and thus denying both Christian and Islamic exceptionalism.

Of the Barbary novels, Royall Tyler's *The Algerine Captive* (1797) is the best known and the one that most closely parallels the captivity genre, particularly in the second of the two volumes. Like Robinson Crusoe, Updike Underhill falls prey to corsairs while serving aboard a slaving vessel. At first, his captors force him to perform brute labor, but like Jonathan Cowdery, Underhill receives special treatment when the Algerians learn that he was a ship's doctor. Perhaps copying authentic captivity narratives, Tyler writes in the ethnographic mode with chapters on language, government, marriage, religion, and more, so that the novel, which began by describing the sufferings of the innocent captive, ends with a detailed portrait of Algiers and an exploration of Islam. As Cathy Davidson has noted, *The Algerine Captive* was roundly criticized by early reviewers for seeming "singularly ambivalent about its own

---

Most slave narratives, however, were related by men. Narratives by slave women present a significantly different perception of slave women. It is this discrepancy which has not been duly noted, and it is this neglect of slave women's versions of their lives that is a basic reason for the perpetuation of the current and inadequate image of women slaves.

Foster, *Witnessing Slavery,* xxx.

117. For forerunners to Markoe's novel, see Giovanni Marana's *Turkish Spy,* which plants an Islamic mole in Paris, or Montesquieu's spy in *Persian Letters.*

118. Markoe, *The Algerine Spy in Pennsylvania,* 105.

Christian principles," and angling more for open-minded religious toleration than dogmatic allegiance to Christianity.[119] As Tyler critiqued Algerian slavery, he also allowed that slavery in the United States was likely far worse. "Algiers thus becomes a distorted mirror version of America," Davidson argues. "Or, more accurately, it become the mirror version that especially shows up American distortions."[120] In these early novels that espouse religious tolerance and civil freedoms, David Reynolds has argued that the authors have "capitalized on similarities between Islam and liberalism to make disguised attacks on orthodoxy and to call for a benevolent religion of works."[121] He further argues that the larger genre of the "oriental tale," which included a vast collection of stories and novels that explored the collision of Christianity and many Eastern religions, "was a crude incubator for nearly every variety of American religious fiction."[122]

African captivity also found its place on the American stage. In 1794, Susanna Rowson wrote *Slaves in Algiers,* a romance set among captives and court figures, complete with song.[123] The "slaves" are not only American captives but include several Algerian women who somehow have become chattel and who must devote their lives to serving the dey. These Algerian slaves "learn" about liberty from the American captives and plot their own revolt. Witnessing the Americans' willingness to die for their freedom, however, the dey has a change of heart, liberates his slaves, and abolishes slavery in Algiers. The play refrains from making an explicit connection between African-American slaves in the United States and white slaves in Africa as Tyler's novel would, but this analogy was likely well understood already by 1794, the year Congress passed the Navy Act in defiance of the Algerian dey's demands for ransom. Another play, James Ellison's *The American Captive, or Siege of Tripoli* (1812), is a highly charged patriotic romance that reenacts the Tripolitan War.[124] In Ellison's

119. Davidson, *Revolution and the Word*, 208.

120. Ibid., 209.

121. Reynolds, *Faith in Fiction*, 19.

122. Ibid., 37. In the later twentieth century, the mass marketing of Barbary captivity narratives shifted from the male-identified dime novel to the female-oriented romance novel in such pulp fiction as Victoria Holt's *The Captive* and Sergeanne Golon's *Angelique in Barbary.* The advertising for *Angelique* reads, in part, "The Prey of Lust. Angelique begins a perilous search for her lost love in the lawless, savage world of the Mediterranean, where her beauty is plunder for pirates, treasure for the slave traders, a helpless plaything for the lust-crazed Sultan."

123. In some subsequent performances, the play was retitled *Americans in Algiers* and *Slaves Released from Algiers.*

124. This play was adapted by Joseph Stevens Jones into his 1835 play, *The Usurper; or, Americans in Tripoli,* which was produced at the National in 1840–41. Jones also likely wrote *The Adventure; or, The Yankee in Tripoli.* Another play, entitled *Siege of Tripoli,* has been attributed to Mordecai Noah and was produced in New York in 1820 and again in 1822 in Philadelphia.

drama, the ruling despot, Abdel Mahdi, is not affected by the freedom-loving Americans, and instead of renouncing slavery, the bashaw is killed by his principal American slave. Benilde Montgomery has commented upon the subversiveness of this murder: "Written after the slave revolts in Santo Domingo in 1798 and perhaps in frustration with those who continued to resist abolition, *The American Captive* contains a rather chilling warning and perhaps a presage of the [Civil War] that lay ahead."[125]

Slaves in Barbary (1817), by David Everett, takes Ellison's "chilling warning" even further by using the captivity scenario to bring a former white slave owner to justice. "Kidnap," a white sea captain and slave owner who talks in his sleep of whipping his slaves for singing a liberty song, finds himself on the auction block in Tunis. His former slave, "Sharp," identifies the cruel slave master to the bashaw: "He get drunk! he whip me! he knock a me down! he stamp on a me! he will kill a me dead! No! no! let a poor negur live wid a you, masser planter; live wid a masser officer; wid a dat a man; or any udder man, fore I go back America again; fore I live wid a masser Kidnap again."[126] Eventually, a Tunisian buys Kidnap and insinuates that the former slave owner will suffer a reverse of fortune and feel the other end of the lash when he becomes Sharp's slave.[127]

In contrast to the abolitionist undercurrent of these three plays, southerner Maria Pinckney's *The Young Carolinians, or Americans in Algiers*,[128] "explodes the very analogy from which the northern plays derived their power," according to Montgomery.[129] In scenes that cut between the Carolinas and Algeria, the story of the slave-owning Woodburys unfolds, and we see white Carolinians abused in Africa and a subservient African-American slave, Cudjoe, under the paternalistic care of the white slave owners. The point of Pinckney's comparison is not the similarity of the two situations, but the contrast, as well as the suggestion that comparing African-American slaves to white slaves in Africa is merely dubious northern rhetoric.

125. Montgomery, "White Captives, African Slaves," 624.

126. Everett, *Slaves in Barbary*, 111.

127. Richard Penn Smith wrote another Barbary play in 1829, *The Bombardment of Algiers,* but it was neither printed in its day nor produced. It was based on a play by Frederic du Petit-Mere, *Le Bombardement d'Alger; ou, Le Corsaire reconnaissant* (1815). See also William C. Reynolds's *An American Pasha, an Original Comedy in 3 Acts* (1883). A British opera, *The Fall of Algiers,* was scored by H. R. Bishop and first performed at the Theatre Royal, Drury Lane, on January 19, 1825. It may have been authored by John Howard Payne, who had been American consul at Tunis, and also author of "Home Sweet Home." In 1813, when he was only twenty-one, Gioacchino Rossini scored the comic opera *The Italian Girl in Algiers,* and it was well received.

128. The play was likely never produced.

129. Montgomery, "White Captives, African Slaves," 628.

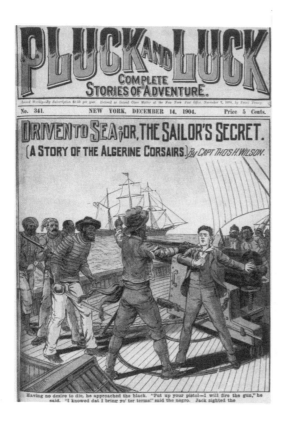

Fig. 10. Former U.S. slave turned Barbary pirate forcing a New York boy to fire upon a friendly ship. Originally appeared in *Golden Weekly* nos. 90–97 (July 30–September 17, 1891). (Courtesy Hess Collection, University of Minnesota)

James Riley's popular narrative returned to print in 1854 when Samuel Goodrich turned it into an illustrated children's book.[130] In the last quarter of the nineteenth century, captivity narratives filled the juvenile pulp fiction market with titles like *The Algerine, The Corsair Prince, The Boy Bedouins, We Three* (subtitled *or, The White Boy Slaves of the Soudan*), and *Seven Boy Slaves* (subtitled *or, Wrecked on the Desert of Sahara*). Many of these dime novels saw numerous incarnations as they were reissued under different imprints, and they remained popular well into the twentieth century. Alexander Armstrong's *Driven to the Sea; or, the Sailor's Secret, A Story of the Algerine Corsairs,* typifies the wild plot turns of *Pluck and Luck* and the other Tousey dime novel series.[131] In Armstrong's novel, a former Kentucky slave flees to Algeria, where

130. Goodrich, *The Story of Captain Riley and his Adventure in Africa.*

131. Alexander Armstrong used the name Capt. Tho's H. Wilson as a pseudonym. See Armstrong, *Driven to Sea.* It is difficult to trace dime novel authors and reissues, and I have relied upon the personal work of Edward T. LeBlanc and J. Randolph Cox as well as the knowledgeable curators of the Hess Collection at the University of Minnesota.

he is enslaved once more but rises to become the Algerian dey's right-hand man. When the treasure map to the dey's fortune is stolen by a New York sailor, the slave returns to New York, kidnaps the white boy who now has possession of the parchment, and brings him back to Algeria as his own slave . . . and from there, as one may imagine, the plot only thickens.

In the twentieth century, the Barbary captive arrived on the big screen, and at least eight films were produced. With John Milius's 1975 film, *The Wind and the Lion,* Hollywood dramatized the historical events surrounding the 1904 Perdicaris kidnapping. MGM recruited Sean Connery to play the Riffian sharif, Raisuli, and Milius cast the youthful Candace Bergen in the role of Eden Pedicaris [*sic*] as a substitute for the elderly, real-life Ion Perdicaris. When Raisuli's bandits capture her, it becomes clear that the noble sharif must now protect her from sexual threats. Though they never physically consummate their bond, Raisuli becomes Eden's surrogate lover as well as her protector. In one pivotal scene in this oddly edited film, Raisuli rescues Eden from certain defilement by a clan of "hideous men." Riding his Arabian steed, Raisuli literally sweeps Eden off her feet. A version of John Milius's screenplay reads:

> Eden gasped in awe and found her feet frozen, unable to flee, a weakness in her legs. At the last minute Raisuli leaned down with his sword hand and swept her off the ground and up onto his saddle. Her face was close to his and she could feel him breathe. The sword was between them and hot blood ran down its blade over his hand and onto her breast.[132]

132. Milius, *The Wind and the Lion,* 60. There are at least seven other films that dramatize the Barbary captivity scenario. Based on Rafael Sabatini's 1915 novel by the same name, Associated First National Pictures' *The Sea Hawk* (1924) is a love saga in which the sixteenth-century Moors and Spaniards capture and recapture each other, delaying the union of Rosamund and Oliver. (*Variety* declared it "[a] work of art that will go down in screen history as a really great picture"; Warner Brothers remade it in 1940, excising the North African conflict.) Two years later, in 1926, Paramount filmed a historical treatment of the Tripolitan War, *Old Ironsides,* at the bank-busting cost of $2.4 million, which included a new wide-screen process, Magnascope, to highlight the patriotic battle scenes. *Variety* enthused, "What a thrill and what a kick!" In 1947, Columbia Pictures produced *Slave Girl,* a send-up of swashbucklers that depicts a U.S. diplomat's attempt to ransom ten U.S. captives. The film includes a talking camel that comments, with a Brooklyn accent, upon the action in the film. Columbia also produced *Barbary Pirate* (1949), a film that posits a conspiracy theory that involves a Washington mole who delivers secret intelligence to Tripolitan corsairs. Maureen O'Hara stars in *Tripoli* (Paramount, 1950), which attempts to re-create scenes from the Tripolitan War, but to less effect than the earlier *Old Ironsides.* O'Hara, a French diplomat's daughter, joins Eaton on his march across the desert to capture Derna. In 1953, United Artists produced *Raiders of the Seven Seas,* a far-fetched swashbuckler starring Donna Reed as the love interest of Barbarossa (John Payne) set, oddly, in the West Indies. *Yankee Pasha* (Universal, 1954), based on Edison Marshall's novel of the adventures of Jason Starbuck, transports a Yankee frontiersman to Morocco, where he teaches the bey's son Yankee rifleman techniques. To create the harem scene, director Joseph Pevney paraded Miss Universe and her cohort, Misses United States, Japan, Panama, Norway, Uruguay, South Africa, and Australia. Also of interest is *Pirates of Tripoli* (Columbia, 1955). Although it doesn't present a captivity scenario, it delivers plenty of clashing sabers and swagger in sixteenth-century Tripoli.

This safe sexual fantasy, which crosses racial borders without explicit sex, is nested within a larger imperialist fantasy. The film rewrites the historical record by marching a garrison of U.S. soldiers into Morocco to forcibly rescue the brash American woman and her children. None of this, of course, ever occurred in 1904. The United States never invaded Morocco, but instead was forced to negotiate for Perdicaris. Although Raisuli rose to his most powerful position as a direct result of the Perdicaris kidnapping, the film has him riding off into the endless desert landscape pursuing an unknown fate. Throughout the film, Raisuli is portrayed as a noble and endangered figure, much like the *bon sauvage* or noble savage icon that was used to portray the vanishing and vanquished American Indian.[133] This figure might be termed "The Last Barbary Pirate," a romanticized image that can safely recede into the timeless desert as it helps to enact imperialist reveries.

Surviving for over three centuries in America, the Barbary captivity narrative has filtered through religious and popular literature, reaching millions of readers in various forms of nonfiction, fiction, drama, and film. The figure of the white slave in Africa not only produced a mirror image of the black slave in America, it both rationalized and critiqued slavery in the United States and produced some of the first and longest-lasting images of Africans for an American audience.

133. See Carr, *Inventing the American Primitive.*

BIBLIOGRAPHY

Adams, Robert. *The Narrative of Robert Adams, A Sailor, who was wrecked on the Western Coast of Africa, in the Year 1810, was detained three years in slavery by the Arabs of the Great Desert, and resided several months in the city of Tombuctoo.* Ed. S. Cook. London: William Bulmer and Co., 1816.

Alig, Joyce L. *Ohio's Last Frontiersman, Connecticut Mariner: Captain James Riley.* Celina, OH: Messenger Press, 1996.

Allison, Robert J. *The Crescent Obscured, The United States and the Muslim World, 1776–1815.* New York: Oxford UP, 1995.

Armstrong, Alexander [Capt. Tho's H. Wilson, pseud.]. *Driven to Sea; or, the Sailor's Secret. A Story of the Algerine Corsairs. Golden Weekly,* nos. 90–97 (July 30-September 17, 1891); reprinted as *Pluck and Luck,* no. 341 (December 14, 1904) and *Pluck and Luck,* no. 1142 (April 21, 1920).

Austin, Allan D. *African Muslims in Antebellum America: A Sourcebook.* New York: Garland, 1984.

———. *African Muslims in Antebellum America: Transatlantic Stories and Spiritual Struggles.* New York: Routledge, 1997.

Axtell, James. "The White Indians of Colonial America." In *The European and the Indian: Essays in the Ethnohistory of Colonial North America*. New York: Oxford UP, 1981.

Baepler, Paul. "The Barbary Captivity Narrative in Early America." *Early American Literature* 30, no. 2 (fall 1995): 95–120.

———. "Rewriting the Barbary Captivity Narrative: The Perdicaris Affair and the Last Barbary Pirate." *Prospects* 23 (forthcoming).

Ben Rejeb, Lotfi. "'To the Shores of Tripoli': The Impact of Barbary on Early American Nationalism." Diss., Indiana U, 1981.

Bolster, W. Jeffrey. *Black Jacks: African American Seamen in the Age of Sail*. Cambridge: Harvard UP, 1997.

Bradley, Eliza. *An Authentic Narrative of the Shipwreck and Sufferings of Mrs. Eliza Bradley, the Wife of Capt. James Bradley of Liverpool, Commander of the Ship Sally, which was wrecked on the coast of Barbary, in June 1818*. Boston: James Walden, 1820.

Braudel, Fernand. *The Mediterranean and the Mediterranean World in the Age of Philip II*. Trans. Sian Reynolds. New York: Harper & Row, 1972.

Breeden, James O., ed. *Advice among Masters: The Ideal in Slave Management in the Old South*. Westport, CT: 1980.

———. "States-Rights Medicine in the Old South." *Bulletin of the New York Academy of Medicine* 53 (March–April 1976): 348–72.

Carr, Helen. *Inventing the American Primitive: Politics, Gender and the Representation of Native American Literary Traditions*. New York: New York UP, 1996.

Castiglia, Christopher. *Bound and Determined: Captivity, Culture-Crossing, and White Womanhood from Mary Rowlandson to Patty Hearst*. Chicago: U of Chicago P, 1996.

Cathcart, James Leander. *The Captives, Eleven Years a Prisoner in Algiers*. Compiled by J. B. Newkirk. La Porte, IN: Herald Print, 1899.

Clifford, James. "Partial Truths." In *Writing Culture: The Poetics and Politics of Ethnography*. Eds. James Clifford and George E. Marcus. Berkeley: U of California P, 1986.

Cooper, James Fenimore. *The History of the Navy of The United States of America*. Ed. R. D. Madison. Del Mar, NY: Scholar's Facsimiles & Reprints, 1988.

Cowdery, Jonathan. *American Captives in Tripoli; or, Dr. Cowdery's Journal in Miniature. Kept during his late captivity in Tripoli*. 2d ed. Boston: Belcher and Armstrong, 1806.

Davidson, Cathy. *Revolution and the Word: The Rise of the Novel in America*. New York: Oxford UP, 1986.

Davis, William. *A True Relation of the Travels And most miserable Captivity of WILLIAM DAVIS, Barber-Surgeon of London, under the Duke of Florence*. In *A Collection of Voyages and Travels*. Ed. Awnsham Churchill. London, 1704.

Defoe, Daniel. *Robinson Crusoe*. Ed. Michael Shinagel. New York: Norton, 1975.

Derounian-Stodola, Kathryn Zabelle, and James Arthur Levernier. *The Indian Captivity Narrative, 1550–1900*. New York: Twayne, 1993.

Digges, Thomas Atwood. *Adventures of Alonso*. New York: U.S. Catholic Historical Society, 1943.

Dobson, Joanne. "Reclaiming Sentimental Literature." *American Literature* 69, no. 2 (June 1997): 263–88.

Ebersole, Gary. *Captured by Texts: Puritan to Postmodern Images of Indian Captivity.* Charlottesville: U of Virginia P, 1995.

Elias, Robert H., and Eugene D. Finch. Introduction to *Letters of Thomas Atwood Digges.* Raleigh: U of South Carolina P, 1982.

Ellison, James. *The American Captive, or Siege of Tripoli.* Boston: Joshua Belcher, 1812.

Estes, J. Worth. "Commodore Jacob Jones: A Doctor Goes to Sea." *Delaware History* 24, no. 2 (1990): 109–22.

Everett, David. *Slaves in Barbary.* Boston, 1817.

Fernando de Moraes Farias, Paulo. "Models of the World and Categorical Models: The 'Enslavable Barbarian' as a Mobile Classificatory Label." In *Slaves and Slavery in Muslim Africa.* Vol. 1, *Islam and the Ideology of Enslavement.* Ed. John Ralph Willis. London: Frank Cass, 1985.

Foss, John D. *A JOURNAL,* of the Captivity and Sufferings of *JOHN FOSS;* several years a prisoner in ALGIERS: *Together with some account of the treatment of Christian slaves when sick:—and observations on the manners and customs of the Algerines.* Newburyport, MA: A. March, 1798.

Foster, Frances Smith. *Witnessing Slavery: The Development of Ante-Bellum Slave Narratives.* Madison: U of Wisconsin P, 1979.

Foucault, Michel. *The Order of Things: An Archaeology of the Human Sciences.* New York: Random House, 1970.

Franklin, Benjamin. *Benjamin Franklin, Writings.* New York: Library of America, 1987.

Frederick, Bonnie. "Fatal Journeys, Fatal Legends: The Journey of the Captive Woman in Argentina and Uruguay." In *Women and the Journey: The Female Travel Experience.* Ed. Bonnie Frederick and Susan H, Mcleod. Pullman, WA: Washington State UP, 1993.

Gee, Joshua. *Narrative of Joshua Gee of Boston, Mass., While he was captive in Algeria of the Barbary pirates 1680–1687.* Intro. Albert Carlos Bates. Hartford: Wadsworth Atheneum, 1943.

"Germantown Friends' Protest against Slavery, 1688." In *Am I Not a Man and a Brother?: The Antislavery Crusade of Revolutionary America 1688–1788.* Ed. Roger Bruns. New York: Chelsea House, 1977.

Gomez, Michael A. "Muslims in Early America." *Journal of Southern History* 60 (November 1994): 671–709.

Goodrich, Samuel G. *The Story of Captain Riley and his Adventure in Africa.* Philadelphia: Lippincott, Grambo & Co., 1854.

Gould, Stephen Jay. *The Mismeasure of Man.* New York: Norton, 1981.

Haberly, David T. "Captives and Infidels: The Figure of the *Cautiva* in Argentine Literature." *American Hispanist* 4 (October 1978): 7–16.

Hulme, Peter, and Ludmilla Jordanova. *The Enlightenment and Its Shadows.* New York: Routledge, 1990.

Humanity in Algiers: or, the Story of Azem. Troy, NY: R. Moffitt & Co, 1801.

Huntress, Keith. Introduction to *An authentic narrative of the shipwreck and sufferings of Mrs. Eliza Bradley, the wife of Capt. James Bradley of Liverpool, commander of the ship* Sally *which was wrecked on the coast of Barbary, in June 1818 . . . Written by herself.* Fairfield: Ye Galleon Press, 1985.

Irwin, Robert. *The Arabian Nights: A Companion.* New York: Penguin, 1994.

Jefferson, Thomas. *The Papers of Thomas Jefferson.* Eds. Julian Bond et al. 25 vols. Princeton UP, 1950.

Judy, Ronald T. *(Dis)Forming the American Canon: African-Arabic Slave Narratives in the Vernacular.* Minneapolis: U of Minnesota P, 1993.

Kitzen, Michael. "Money Bags or Cannon Balls: The Origins of the Tripolitan War, 1795–1801." *Journal of the Early Republic* 16, no. 4 (winter 1996): 601–24.

Knight, Francis. *A Relation of Seven Years Slavery under the Turks of Algier, Suffered by an English Captive Merchant.* In *A Collection of Voyages and Travels.* Ed. Awnsham Churchill. London, 1704. 465–489.

Laranda, Viletta. *Neapolitan Captive: Interesting Narrative of the Captivity and Sufferings of Miss Viletta Laranda, A Native of Naples, Who, with a Brother, was a passenger on board a Neapolitan vessel wrecked near Oran, on the Barbary coast, September 1829, and who soon after was unfortunately made a Captive of by a wandering clan of Bedowen Arabs, on their return from Algiers to the Deserts—and eleven months after providentially rescued from Barbarian Bondage by the commander of a detached Regiment of the victorious French Army.* New York: Charles C. Henderson, 1830.

Lewis, James R. "Images of Captive Rape in the Nineteenth Century." *Journal of American Culture* 15, no. 2 (summer 1992): 69–77.

Markoe, Peter. *The Algerine Spy in Pennsylvania: or, Letters Written by a Native of Algiers on the Affairs of the United States in America, from the Close of the year 1783 to the Meeting of the Convention.* Philadelphia: Prichard & Hall, 1787.

Martin, Lucinda [Maria Martin]. *HISTORY OF THE* Captivity and Sufferings *of Mrs. MARIA MARTIN, who was six years a slave in ALGIERS: two of which she was confined in a dark and dismal dungeon, loaded with irons.* Boston: W. Crary, 1807.

Matar, Nabil I. "John Locke and the 'Turbanned Nations,'" in *Journal of Islamic Studies* 2 (1991): 67–78.

———. "'Turning Turk': Conversion to Islam in English Renaissance Thought." *Durham University Journal* 86, no. 1 (January 1994): 33–41.

Mather, Cotton. *The Glory of Goodness. The Goodness of God, Celebrated; in Remarkable* Instances *and* Improvements *thereof. And more particularly in the REDEMPTION Remarkably obtained for the English Captives, Which have been Languishing under the Tragical, and the Terrible, and the most* Barbarous *Cruelties of BARBARY. The History of what the Goodness of God, has done for the Captives, lately delivered out of Barbary.* Boston: T. Green, 1703.

————. *A Pastoral Letter to the English Captives in Africa.* Boston: B. Green and J. Allen, 1698.

McMurtry, Gerald R. "The Influence of Riley's *Narrative* upon Abraham Lincoln." *Indiana Magazine of History* 30 (1934): 133–38.

Milius, John. *The Wind and the Lion.* MGM, 1975.

Miller, Christopher L. *Blank Darkness: Africanist Discourse in French.* Chicago: U of Chicago P, 1985

Montgomery, Benilde. "White Captives, African Slaves: A Drama of Abolition." *Eighteenth-Century Studies* 27, no. 4 (1994): 615–30.

Munday, Anthony. "The worthie enterprise of John Fox an Englishman in delivering 266 Christians out of the captivitie of the Turkes at Alexandria, the 3 of Januarie 1577." In *The Principal Navigations Voiages and Discoveries of the English Nation.* Ed. Richard Hakluyt. Cambridge: Cambridge UP, 1965.

Namias, June. *White Captives: Gender and Ethnicity on the American Frontier.* Chapel Hill: U of North Carolina P, 1993.

Nicholson, Thomas. *An Affecting Narrative of the Captivity and Sufferings of Thomas Nicholson [A Native of New Jersey] Who has been Six years a Prisoner among the Algerines, And from whom he fortunately made his escape a few months previous to Commodore Decatur's late Expedition. To which is added, a Concise Description of Algiers of the Customs, Manners, etc of the Natives— and some particulars of Commodore Decatur's Late Expedition, Against the Barbary Powers.* Boston: Printed for G. Walker, 1816.

Okeley, William. *Eben-Ezer or a Small Monument of Great Mercy Appearing in the Miraculous Deliverance of John Anthony, William Okeley, William Adams, John Jephs and John Carpenter.* London, 1675.

Paddock, Judah. *Narrative of the shipwreck of the ship Oswego, on the coast of south barbary, and of the sufferings of the master and the crew while in bondage among the arabs; interspersed with numerous remarks upon the country and its inhabitants, and concerning the peculiar perils of that coast.* In *An Authentic Narrative of the loss of the American Brig Commerce, Wrecked on the Western Coast of Africa, in the Month of August, 1815. With An Account of the Sufferings of her Surviving Officers and Crew, who were enslaved by the wandering arabs on the Great African Desert, or Zahahrah; and Observations historical, geographical, &c. Made during the travels of the author, while a slave to the arabs, and in the empire of Morocco.* By James Riley. 3d ed. New York: Collins & Co. 1818.

Paine, Ralph D. *The Ships and Sailors of Old Salem: The Record of a Brilliant Era of American Achievement.* New York: Outing Publishing, 1908.

Perdicaris, Ion H. "In Raissuli's Hands: The Story of My Captivity and Deliverance May 18 to June 26, 1904." *Leslie's Magazine* 58 (September 1904): 510–22.

Phillips, Dana. "Nineteenth-Century Racial Thought and Whitman's 'Democratic Ethnology of the Future.'" *Nineteenth Century Literature* 49, no. 3 (1994): 289–320.

Pinckney, Maria. *The Young Carolinians, or Americans in Algiers.* In *Essays Religious and Moral.* Charleston: 1818.

Introduction

Pratt, Mary Louise. *Imperial Eyes: Travel Writing and Transculturation*. New York: Routledge, 1992.

Rawlins, John. "The wonderful recovery of the Exchange of Bristow, from the Turkish Pirats of Argier, published by John Rawlins, heere abbreviated." In *Hakluytus Posthumus or Purchas His Pilgrimes*. Ed. Samuel Purchas. Glasgow: James MacLehose and Sons, 1905.

Ray, William. *Horrors of Slavery, or the American Tars in Tripoli.* Troy, NY: Oliver Lyon, 1808.

Reynolds, David S. *Faith in Fiction: The Emergence of Religious Literature in America.* Cambridge: Harvard UP, 1981.

Riley, James. *An Authentic Narrative of the loss of the American Brig* Commerce, *wrecked on the western coast of Africa, in the month of August, 1815, with an account of the sufferings of her surviving officers and crew, who were enslaved by the wandering Arabs on the great African desert, or Zahahrah; and observations historical, geographical, &c. made during the travels of the author, while a slave to the Arabs, and in the empire of Morocco.* Hartford: Published by the author, 1817.

Riley, William Wilshire. *Sequel to Riley's Narrative; being a sketch of interesting incidents in the life, voyages and travels of Capt. James Riley, from the period of his return to his native land, after his shipwreck, captivity and sufferings among the Arabs of the desert, as related in his narrative, until his death.* Columbus: G. Brewster, 1851.

Robbins, Archibald. *A Journal, Comprising an Account of the Loss of the Brig Commerce, of Hartford, (Con.) James Riley, Master, Upon the Western Coast of Africa, August 28th, 1815; Also of the Slavery and Sufferings of the Author and the Rest of the Crew Upon the Desert of Zahara, In the Years 1815, 1816, 1817; with Accounts of the Manners, Customs, and Habits of the Wandering Arabs; also, A brief Historical and Geographical view of the Continent of Africa.* 20th ed. Hartford: Silas Andrus, 1831.

Roberts, Nicholas. "A Letter contayning the admirable escape and glorious Victorie of Nicholas Roberts Master, Tristram Stevens his Mate, and Robert Sucksbich Boatson of a Ship of Dover, taken by Algier Pyrates." In *Hakluytus Posthumus or Purchas His Pilgrimes*. Ed. Samuel Purchas. Glasgow: James MacLehose and Sons, 1905.

Rowlandson, Mary. *The Sovereignty and Goodness of God.* Ed. Neal Salisbury. New York: Bedford Books, 1997.

Rowson, Susanna. *Slaves in Algiers; or, a Struggle for Freedom: A Play, interspersed with songs, in three acts.* Philadelphia: Wrigley and Berriman, 1794.

Said, Edward. *Culture and Imperialism.* New York: Vintage Books, 1993.

Sanchez-Eppler, Karen. "Bodily Bounds: The Intersecting Rhetorics of Feminism and Abolition." *Representations* 24 (1988): 28–59.

———. *Touching Liberty: Abolition, Feminism, and the Politics of the Body.* Berkeley: U of California P, 1993.

Sekora, John. "Black Message/White Envelope: Genre, Authenticity, and Authority in the Antebellum Slave Narrative." *Callaloo* 10, no. 3 (fall 1987): 482–515.

Sewall, Samuel. *The Selling of Joseph: A Memorial.* Ed. Sidney Kaplan. Amherst: U of Massachusetts P, 1969

Sha'ban, Fuad. *Islam and Arabs in Early American Thought: The Root of Orientalism in America.* Durham: Acorn Press, 1991.

Shaw, Elijah. *A short sketch of the life of Elijah Shaw, who served for twenty-two years in the Navy of the United States, taking an active part in four different wars between the United States & foreign powers; namely, first—with France, in 1798; second—with Tripoli, from 1802 to 1805; third—with England from 1812 to 1815; fourth—with Algiers, from 1815 to 1816: and assisted in subduing the pirates from 1822 to 1826.* Rochester: Strong & Dawson, 1843.

Sibley, John Langdon. *Biographical Sketches of Harvard University, In Cambridge, Massachusetts.* Vol. 2. Cambridge: Charles William Sever, 1881.

Sieminski, Greg. "The Puritan Captivity Narrative and the Politics of the American Revolution." *American Literature* 42, no. 1 (March 1990): 35–56.

Smith, John. *The True Travels, Adventures, and Observations of Captaine John Smith.* In *The Complete Works of Captain John Smith (1580–1631): in Three Volumes,* vol 3. Ed. Philip L. Barbour. Chapel Hill: U of North Carolina P, 1986.

Snader, Joe. "The Oriental Captivity Narrative and Early English Fiction." *Eighteenth-Century Fiction* 9, no. 3 (April 1997): 267–98.

Sofka, James. "The Jeffersonian Idea of National Security: Commerce, the Atlantic Balance of Power, and the Barbary War, 1786–1805." *Diplomatic History* 21, no. 4 (fall 1997): 519–44.

Springer, Haskell. "The Captain's Wife at Sea." In *Iron Men, Wooden Women: Gender and Seafaring in the Atlantic World, 1700–1920.* Eds. Margaret S. Creighton and Lisa Norling. Baltimore: Johns Hopkins UP, 1996.

Spurr, David. *The Rhetoric of Empire: Colonial Discourse in Journalism, Travel Writing, and Imperial Administration.* Durham: Duke UP, 1993

Stevens, James Wilson. *An Historical and Geographical Account of Algiers; comprehending a novel and interesting detail of events relative to the American Captives.* Philadelphia: Hogan & M'Elroy: 1797.

Sumner, Charles. *White Slavery in the Barbary States.* Boston: John P. Jewett, 1853

Toulouse, Teresa A. "'My Own Credit'": Strategies of (E)Valuation in Mary Rowlandson's Captivity Narrative. *American Literature* 30, no. 4 (December 1992): 656–76.

Tucker, Glen. *Dawn like Thunder: The Barbary Wars and the Birth of the U.S. Navy.* Indianapolis: Bobbs-Merrill, 1963.

Turkistani, Abdulhafeez Q. "Muslim Slaves and Their Narratives: Religious Faith and Cultural Acommodation." Diss., Kent State U, 1996.

Tyler, Royall. *The Algerine Captive.* Ed. Don L. Cook. New Haven: College and UP, 1970.

Velnet, Mary. *The Captivity and Sufferings of Mrs. Mary Velnet, Who was Seven Years a Slave in Tripoli, three of which she was confined in a dungeon, loaded with irons, and four times put to the*

most cruel tortures ever invented by man. To which is added, The Lunatic Governor, and Adelaide, or the Triumph of Constancy, a Tale.* Boston: T. Abbot, 1828.

Voltaire. *Candide.* Ed. and trans. Robert M. Adams. New York: W. W. Norton, 1966.

Winter, Kari. *Subjects of Slavery, Agents of Change: Women and Power in Gothic Novels and Slave
Narratives, 1790–1865.* Athens: U of Georgia P, 1992.

Wolf, John B. *The Barbary Coast: Algiers under the Turks 1500–1830.* New York: Norton, 1979.

∾ COTTON MATHER

The Glory of Goodness

In March 1703, Cotton Mather recorded in his diary: "Our Captives in Barbary, have been the Subjects of many Prayers, among the People of God: and poor I have had a special Share in these Prayers: wherein also I received and uttered my Assurances many Years ago, that I should also have a Share in offering Praises to our glorious Redeemer; for the Answers of those Prayers. The Prayers are now answered; gloriously answered. The Captives have been returned." Five years earlier, Mather had codified his prayers for the captives in his "Pastoral Letter to the English Captives in Africa." In that meditation, Mather reminded his countrymen that every "Sinful Child of Adam" was born into slavery to the "Powers of Darkness." Christ's blood, Mather continued, constituted the captive's ransom and his agent of deliverance. Thus despite the present agonies of their current bondage in Africa, Mather argued, their true danger was the challenge posed to their faith. In the margin of his diary, Mather noted that the captives had received his letter and that it had "proved the Preparation and the Introduction unto their Deliverance."

His sermon excerpted here, *The Glory of Goodness,* claims that the redemption of the captives from the "Filthy Disciples of Mahomet" is a testament to God's mercy. That other Christians succumbed to the temptations of apostasy and the relief from servitude it promised was a demonstration of the power of prayer in New England. Mather thus contrasts the order and devotion of the Christian churches and political body in the colonies to both the laxity of other Christians and the infernal chaos of Morocco. To emphasize this comparison, Mather relies upon the captives' anecdotes and first-person narrative, and these accounts magnify the gruesome conditions in Barbary. Unlike Mary Rowlandson's narrative, which Mather's father likely brought to the print house, *The Glory of Goodness* tells the story not of an individual but of an entire community of captives and weaves it into the fabric of Mather's covenant theology.

The Glory of Goodness. The Goodness of God, Celebrated; in Remarkable *Instances* and *Improvements* thereof: And more particularly in the REDEMPTION remarkably obtained for the English Captives, Which have been languishing under the Tragical, and the Terrible, and the most *Barbarous* Cruelties of BARBARY. The History of what the Goodness of God, has done for the Captives, lately delivered out of Barbary. Boston: T. Green, 1703.

H AVING BEEN thus far carried along with a stream of more *General Reflections* upon the *goodness* of God, we are now arrived unto the *Falls* of our Discourse, and are easily and pleasantly carried over, into a more particular Contemplation of the Divine *Goodness* towards our Friends, with whom we are now Uniting our THANKSGIVINGS unto our *Lord-Redeemer.*

We have been so called upon, Psal. 107. 1, 2. *O give Thanks unto the Lord, for He is Good; for His Mercy endureth forever. Let the Redeemed of the Lord say so, whom He hath Redeemed from the Hand of the Enemy.* Behold, some that have been remarkably the *Redeemed of the Lord,* are at this Day to *Say so;* and we are invited now to joyn with them when they *Say so.*

These our Brethren, are delivered through the *Goodness* of God, from the most horrible *Captivity* in the world; and, we may observe several Remarkables in their Deliverance: 'Twill be an agreeable and an acceptable Revenue of Glory unto our *Lord-Redeemer,* for us to observe such Remarkables.

I. It is a Remarkable *Goodness* of God That the *Lives* of these our Friend [*sic*], have been prolonged and preserved under a *bitter Servitude,* that was enough to have made them, even *weary of their lives.*

Their *Way* of *Living,* (or, shall I not rather say, their way of *Dying*) 'twas full of astonishing Hardships. Many, many *Dyed* under the Hardships: But these are this Day declaring, *Having obtained Help from God, we continue to this Day.*

Their Condition cannot perhaps, be more livelily in a few words painted out, than in the words, of the Brief, which their late Majesties, K. WILLIAM and Q. MARY, granted on their behalf.

"A Great Number of Our Good Subjects peaceably following their Employments at Sea, have been taken by the Turkish Pirates of *Algiers, Salley, Barbary,* and other places on the Coast of *Africa,* and now remain Slaves, in Cruel and Inhumane Bondage, without any *Dayes of Rest,* either on the *Turkish Sab-*

bath or Ours, except Four Dayes in a Year; being kept to Extream *Labour;* from which, some endeavouring a little Rest, several of them were barbarously Murdered. Neither is their *Diet* any more tolerable than their *Labour;* Great Numbers being allow'd no other Food, than decay'd *Barley,* which stinketh so, that the Beasts refuse to eat it. And often they are not permitted to go from their Labour, to fetch Water, which is their only Drink; and sometimes driven about by *Black-a-moors,* who are set over them as Task-masters; and some of them have been so severely Whipp'd, that they have dropp'd down Dead.

ONE THAT WAS A SUFFERER, has given us this further Account, of the *Barbarian Cruelty* undergone by his Fellow-sufferers.

"The poor Christian Captives, that are taken by any of those Hellish Pyrates, belonging to the Emperour of *Morocco,* are brought up to *Macqueness;* being kept at Hard work, from Day-light in the Morning till Night: carrying Earth on their Heads in great Baskets, driven to and fro, with barbarous Negroes by the Emperours Order; and when they are drove home by the Negroes at Night, to their Lodging, which is on the cold Ground, in a Vault or hollow place in the Earth, laid over with great Beams athwart, and Iron Bars over them; they are told in there, like Sheep, and out in the Morning; and if any be wanting, he quickly secures the Negroes, and sends out a parcel of his Guard, to look for them. Their Food is Bread, made of old rotten Barley; and their Drink, Water, when they can get it: Many times, when they are hurried unto their work in a Morning, not knowing, whether they shall be able to undergo their Afflictions till Night and when they are drove Home, expecting Rest, the Tyrant sends some of his Negroes, to hurry them again to work, either to hale down Walls, cut Gates, or the like; keeping them both Day and Night, many times without either Bread or Water, which is all their Sustenance. When they have done That, the Negroes dare not drive them home, before he gives Order, lest they be kill'd for their so doing. When they have his Order, they drive them home, tell them over, and so lock them up until Day-light in the Morning. There are Three Hundred and Forty Englishmen (*sayes he*) in this sore Captivity.

This is the Captivity, that has been *On-lived,* and now *Escap'd,* by these our Brethren.

It is much, that their horrid *Labour* did not *Kill* them, in a Climate, so hot at some Times, and so wet at others. One would have said, *Their Strength must have been the Strength of Stones, & ther Flesh of Brass,* Or their Life could not have been prolonged under such prodigious Fatigues.

It is much, that their forlorn *Diet* should not rather *Kill* them, than *Feed* them. So finall, and so vile their Allowance of *Bread,* that it is plain, *They lived not by Bread alone, but by the Word of God.*

It is much, that they have *Out-Lived* the Sorrows, the *Deadly Sorrows,* that must sieze upon their Spirits, when the fierce Robbers had siez'd upon them. By the *Sorrows of their Hearts,* why were not their *Spirits broken,* and Killed, when they saw themselves dragg'd away from all the Comforts of Life, and felt themselves fearfully *broken in the place of Dragons,* and were Hopeless of ever being recovered out of their doleful Circumstances? Methinks, I see them *Crying from the Belly of Hell, Lord, The Waters compass me about, even to the Soul, the Depth closes me round about; the Weeds are enrapt about my Head; the Earth, with her stars, is about me forever.* Oh! My Children, How did you do Live, in the midst of these Agonies? Truly, *The Lord* has at last *Loosed the Prisoners:* 'twas He, who *raised up,* those that were thus *bowed down:* Some of them for a whole prentice-Ship of Years, and One here even for Nineteen Years together. This preservation of our Friends, has been yet more signalized, where any of them, endeavoured a *Fight* out of the Hands of their Enemies, but were unhappily Retaken by those bloody Hands. For it was the manner of the *Tygre,* whom they call the *Emperour,* when such Retaken Prisoners were brought before him immediately to run a *Lance* through the Hearts of them. We have some with us at this Hour, who once expected the stroke of the *Lance,* and can ascribe it unto nothing, but this, *That the Heart of the King was in the Hand of the Lord.*

Oh! That men would Praise the Lord, for His Goodness, and for these His wonderful Works unto the Children of men.

II. It is Remarkable *Goodness* of God, That these our Friends enjoyed so many *Supports,* which Heaven and Earth afforded unto them, under their Insupportable Calamities.

How, One would wonder *How,* were their minds kept from Fainting under the Grievous Things that continually befel them, while, for many Years together, their *Lives hung in doubt before them, and they were in fear day and night, and had no Assurance of their Life; In the Morning they said, Would God it were Evening, and at Evening they said, Would God it were Morning!* Doubtless, the Good Spirit of God often irradiated their minds, with such Considerations, as were their Consolations.

Behold, A Support from the *Goodness* of God!

If they cannot say, *The Barbarous people show'd us no little Kindness,* yet some happy Things fell out now & then, to shelter them from some *Unkindnesses* as would else have been offered.

Behold, A Support from the *Goodness* of God!

It was a mighty Relief unto them that the English Captives there formed themselves into a SOCIETY, and in their *Slavery* enjoyed the *Liberty* to meet on the Lords Day Evening, every Week & annually chuse a *Master* and *Assistents,* and form a *Body of Laws,* to prevent and suppress Disorders among themselves. The *Good Orders* of their Society, were a great *Repastation,* and *Preservation* unto them. And it afforded them no small *Comforts to delight them, in the multitude of the Griefs upon them,* that at their Meetings they still had one or other, who by his *Prayers,* and other Exercises of Religion among them, greately Edified them.

Behold, A Support from the *Goodness* of God!

And God Supported them, with Raising up such as were concerned more ways than one, to supply them in their deplorable Necessities. There were some (as a *Carver*) among themselves, that were able to advise & assist the rest, and others (as a *Balam*) at home, were full of Charitable endeavours to send them Comfortable Assistences. And, a, *Pastoral Letter* or two, Published, and Scattered among them, was blessed of God, for their unspeakable Advantage, and perhaps, had no little Influence, to prepare them for the *Salvations* which they have now received.

Oh, That men would Praise the Lord, for His Goodness, and for His wonderful Works unto the Children of men!

III. It is a Remarkable *Goodness* of God, That none of these our Friends proved *Apostates,* from our Holy Religion, when they were under so many *Temptations* to Apostasy.

There was now and then a wretched Christian, who Renounced *Christianity* & Embraced *Mahometism.* If These our Friends had been left unto themselves, under their amazing Trials, *They,* They would have done so too! Sirs, I hope you readily own, That you did not keep your selves from Falling! Wherefore unto Him that kept you from *Falling, be Glory and Majesty, Dominion and Power, both now and forever.* Oh: Let us admire Sovereign *Grace,* and shout, *Grace! Grace!* upon it, that though these our Friends, were *covered with the shadow of Death,* yet they did not *Forget the Name of our God,* into which they had been Baptised, nor *deal falsely in their* Baptismal *Covenant;* nor stretch out their Hands unto the Impostor *Mahomet,* and his accursed *Alcoran!*

Our Glorious Lord JESUS CHRIST has now and then had a *Martyr,* of late, in the *Torrid zone of Africa.*

One Story (related by *Brooks,*) may not unprofitably be now repeated.

"An *English-man* and a *French-man* were taken, endeavouring an Escape: The next Day, the *English-man* and the *French-man* were carred [*sic*] up to *Macqueness* in Irons, before the Emperour, who by the Moors was informed, what was done. The Emperour, upon Examination, told them, if they did not immediately turn *Moors,* he would kill them. The *French-man* yielded; the

Emperour then threatened the *English-man,* if he did not turn, he would quickly kill him. He mad Answer, Gods Power was greater than the Devils, & let him do what he would, he should not make him turn *Moor.* The emperour called for his Sword, and immediately fell to cutting him, threatening him still, to turn. He said, *He was brought up in the Faith of Jesus Christ, & he would not forsake it.* Then this inhumane Wretch in great spleen, Cut him till he fell down, and hack'd & hew'd him, as if had been butchering an Oxe, and caused the Negro-boyes to run his Body full of Holes, with Knives, till his Body was as full of Holes as possible it could be. When he had so done, *Bring,* said he in his own Language, *Four English Dogs to fetch that Dog away.* And as they carried his Body away, the Negro-boyes stoned them, saying, That should be the end of them, if they did not turn *Moors:* But they were glad to go quietly without answering again; if they had made any Reply, they had certainly been fallen upon by the *Negro-boyes.* So their greatest satisfaction was, his Dying in the Christian Faith, and his counting that more precious than his own Life, holding the same stedfast before that Cruel Tyrant, while he had Breath in his Body. Then they carried him to the place, where they lodged under ground; so took off his Irons, and kept there all Night; and the next Morning carried him where he was to be buried, the Negroes still stoning of them as they went along. As soon as they had laid his Body in the ground, they were hurried by the Negroes to work again after their usual manner.

These our Friends, have not thus *Resisted unto Blood.* But yet they have not been without Bloody *Temptations.* And, O my Hearers, Will you not now Glorify the *Faithfulness* of our Lord Jesus Christ, who would not suffer these our Friends to be *Tempted above what they were able,* but made even their *Temptations* to be their *Preservations!* One would have thought, that if any thing should have made them turn *Infidels,* it would have been their *Adversity,* and the Hope of getting thereby some Relaxation of their *Adversity.* No; It was remark'd, That the *Renegade's* for the most part, were those who suffered the least share of *Adversity.* The Fellows who enjoy'd more *Prosperity,* & lived in Gentlemens Houses with much of Idleness, and Luxury, and Liberty, THESE for the most part were they that fell into *the Snare of the Wicked;* when those who were toiling about *Castles* or *Brickilns,* continued stedfast in the Faith of our Lord JESUS CHRIST. It was also a notable thing; That few did ever come to cast off the Faith of our Lord JESUS CHRIST, until they were first grown very Vicious in their Morals, and fallen into Vices and Scandals, which made 'em asham'd of appearing before their better disposed Countrey-men; THEN 'twas that they grew desperate, and they departed from the Lord with such a total and final Backsliding, that the *Soul of God had no pleasure in them.* How Forlorn, how Undone, how Damned for both Worlds had you been, if you had been given over to become such vile *Deserters?* You saw the strange Hand of God, upon *Them:* You saw them Hated, Loathed, Scorned, both by the *Baptised* and the *Circumcised:* You saw they got nothing, but were *Temporally* more abject than they were before, & *Eternally* siezed by *Chains of Darkness* impossible ever to be taken off. You are Glad, that you have been saved from your *Apostasy.* Did you save your-selves? No; We hear you humbly saying this Day before the Lord and His People: *Not unto us, Not unto us, O Lord, but unto thy Name give Glory!* And, *Lord, Thou art He who has delivered my Soul from Death, my Eyes from Tears, and my Feet from Falling.*

Wherefore yet once again; *Oh! That men would Praise the Lord for His Goodness, and for His wonderful Works to the Children of Men.*

IV. It is a Remarkable *Goodness* of God, That now the Deliverance of these our Friends is accomplished, and in a signal *Answer to Prayer* accomplished, and this not without great Obstructions to the *Accomplishment.*

Such was the known Treachery and Perfidy of the False Tyrant, who held these our Friends in Bondage, that every one despaired of their Deliverance.

For instance;

In the year, 1680, the English Captives, which were under this fierce Tyrant, sent over a Petition to the King of *England,* that something might be done for them. An English Captain being sent over, came to an Agreement with him, for their Deliverance, and the Captives were actually put into his Hands. The *Shack* of the Jews, who had order to build a Town for this Faithless Monarch, came to him, telling him that if he would let him have the *Christians,* to build the *Jews-Town,* he would give him as much Money as the English Captain had agreed with him for. The next Morning, this *African Monster* sent out his Negroes, to drive back the Christians, which were hurried again to their old Slavery, in the Cruellest manner imaginable: And there was an end of the matter! Though the Vengeance of God quickly pursued that Jew, who not without the Connivance of the Emperour, had his Brains horribly trod out, by one who purposely Rode over him.

The Time, the Test Time for Favour, was not *then* come. Now 'tis; and this with a Touch from Heaven upon the Heart of a *Devil Incarnate* compelling him to deal more truly than he use to do.

The Difficulty of Gathering the *Ramsome* was at last got over; every other Impediment was removed: And, *who art thou, O Mountain, that shall stand in the way,* when Gods Time is come? Who is the *Persherd* [Shepherd?] *of the Earth,* that shall propose to *Command the Lord concerning His Children?*

To what a sweet *Change* of their Condition, are these our *Friends* now arrived! Instead of Hellish *Moors* at their pleasure Kicking and Scourging and Plaguing of them, they are in the Arms of their most agreeable Relatives, and others whom they daily behold with mutual Delight. Instead of being driven to Servile, Tedious, Vexing *Employments,* they are now Employ'd Easily, and as they would be. Instead of the *Sabbaths* which they saw without any *Rest* in them, they have now as many Opportunities for the Service of God and their Souls, as they wish for.

What has brought all this about? Oh! 'Tis PRAYER, 'Tis PRAYER, that has done it all. Give me leave to speak it with all due Humility; This Deliverance never began thoroughly to operate, until God began to awaken a *Spirit of Prayer* in the Churches of poor NEW-ENGLAND for it. When the Sons of *New-England,* and of some very Praying people here, fell into so dire a Captivity, presently a Cry of PRAYER made a Noise that reach'd up to Heaven. We did not *Sin by ceasing to Pray for them.* Thus was the *Arm of the Lord awakened* for the Deliverance of these our Sons; and, thou, O *Mully Ishmael,* with all the Diabolical Fury, art no longer able to with-hold from us, the Friends, about whom God gave thee an Efficacious Order, *To let them go.*

But, For what, O my Sons, For what are you thus *let go* from your Servitude but that *being Delivered out of the Hands of your Enemies, you may serve the Lord without Fear, in Holiness and Righteousness before Him, all the dayes of your Lives.* Your Friends, are with Raptures of Love and Joy, beholding your Deliverance from your Captivity. When we see your *Captivity-turned,* we are *like them who dream;* and with astonished Souls, we make that Acclamation, *The Lord hath done Great Things for them!* Now, as a most proper Expression of the Affection, wherewith we bid you *Welcome* unto us, we cannot but set before you, the Desire of our Souls after the *Improvement* and *Perfection* of your *Deliverance.* If nothing else, yet the *Prayers* that we have Day and Night been putting up to Heaven for you, in your *Troubles,* may bespeak for us the Freedome of tendring you the *Counsels,* which you may do well to take, now you have received the Answer, and the Harvest of those *Prayers* in the Period of your *Troubles.* Indeed our *Prayers* are not answered, until our Counsels be followed; and the greatest service now to be done for you, is freely & plainly to tell you, What those Points are, for which our *Prayers* are therefore continued.

WE DO IN THE FIRST PLACE, *Pray* to the God of all *Grace,* that you may have the *Grace* to be very sensible of the matchless Favours that God hath bestowed upon you. Look, Oh! Look back, upon your doleful and woful Circumstances in the Hands of a Bitter and Hasty Nation. Read the Book of *Lamentations,* as one of the Ancients tells us, he did use to do, when he felt *Vanity* growing upon his mind; and from thence Revive to your own mind, the Remembrance of your own *Lamentable* Miseries. But herewithal Remember, how much you would once have given, to be brought out of those miserable Confusions. And acknowledge that you have Deserved all your Sufferings, from the Hands of a Righteous God, before whom you must indeed say, *Lord, Thou hast punished us far less than our Iniquities have deserved.* It is a *Surprizing* Mercy of God, that has rescued you from the *Horrible Pit,* into which you were fallen; But that which makes it the more *Surprizing,* is, that it is a *Singular* Mercy. In former Years, the *Lions Den,* in that part of *Barbary* where you have been cast, had this unhappy Character upon it, *Few or none Returned.* That we now see a Return of so many, who have been a *Pray to those Terrible ones,* truly, 'tis a New, a Strange, & a Great Sight. We may say upon it, *This is the Lords Doing, and it is marvellous in our Eyes!*

WHAT WILL YOU NOW DO, but Sing the *High Praises* of your Almighty Redeemer? Don't so regard *Second Causes,* as to neglect the *First* and *Chief* Cause of all or account Him any other than the *First* and *Chief* of all. Methinks, the *Hundred and Sixteenth Psalm,* the *Hundred and Forty Sixth* Psalm, the Second Paragraph of the *Hundred and Seventh* Psalm, the Beginning of the *Hundred and Third* Psalm, the Conclusion of the *Fifty Sixth,* and *Fifty Seventh,* and *Sixty Sixth* Psalms, will afford some good strokes of *Thanksgiving* for you, when you come to *Sing* the *Praises* of God. On all fit occasions also, why should you not make a *Thankful mention* of what you have received! Yea, *Mention* it not only in *Speaking,* but also in *Writing* thereof, & keep a *Record,* of *How Great Things the Lord hath done for you.*

BUT WHAT SIGNIFIES a *Thanksgiving,* without *Thanksgiving?* Sirs, You are under infinite Obligations, to *keep the Commandments* of that Good God, who hath *brought you out of the Land of* Barbary, *Out of the House of Bondage.* It is the most Reasonable, and the most Adviseable thing imaginable, That you should seriously *Consider* with your selves, and ask Divines and other Christians, to Assist you in Considering, *What Lessons you should learn, by the Changes that have passed over you?* And apply your Cares, to learn those *Lessons,* and *Live* as you have been *Lesson'd.* But in a very particular manner, it becomes you, to get from under your *Slavery* unto *Satan,* and unto *Sin,* which is worse than *Satan:* for that is a *Slavery,* a Million times worse, than what you have seen at *Maquiness.* Every Unrenewed man, is a *Slave* to those Destroyers; and *You* will be so, till you have heartily Resigned up your selves unto the Conduct of the Lord JE-SUS CHRIST with a lively *Faith* in Him, to be made *Righteous* and *Holy:* But, *When He shall make you Free, you will be Free indeed.* Be perswaded now to enter into *Covenant* with God, and become the Bound *Servants* of the Lord JESUS CHRIST, who hath brought you out of your dismal Servitude. Hereupon often think with your selves; *What shall I render to the Lord for all His Benefits? And,*

What special thing shall I do for the Honour of Him, to whom I owe my All? God hath Returned you to the Blessings of His *Day*, and of His *House*, whereof you were deprived, when the Filthy Disciples of *Mahomet* were Lording it over you: You should now make a better use of *Them* than ever you did, and bring forth more of that *Fruit*, by which your Blessed Redeemer may be *Glorified*. Oh, Let the *Goodness of God lead you to this Repentance*. Truly, There should now be seen in you, a Remarkable Difference from *other Men*, that never were so Remarkably Delivered as *You* have been and from what *you your selves* were before you were thus Remarkably Delivered. There is one awful Scripture, which 'tis pitty, but you should have your Eyes more than a Thousand Times upon: Even That; Ezr. 9.13, 14. *After all that is come upon us, for our Evil Deeds, and thou hast given us such Deliverance as This; if we should again break thy Commandments, wouldest thou not be Angry with us, till thou hast Consumed us?*

FINALLY, BRETHREN; You see by your own happy Experience, what *Prayer* can do: Oh! Let it make you in Love with *Prayer*. If this *One* Point may be gain'd, *All* will be gain'd; *Prayer*, Fervent *Prayer*, Constant *Prayer*, Daily *Prayer*: Oh, *Pray without ceasing*, and with every sort of *Prayer;* and very particularly, for a Good Effect of all the Divine Dispensations towards you. Resolve with him; Psal. 116.2. *Because the Lord hath inclined His Ear unto me, therefore will I call upon Him as long as I live.*

ADDITIONAL WRITING BY MATHER

A Pastoral Letter to the English Captives in Africa. Boston: Printed by B. Green and J. Allen, 1698.

A Journal, of the Captivity and Suffering of John Foss

On Tuesday, September 10, 1793, the brig *Polly* set sail from Baltimore. The American ship's original destination had been Tobago, but when Captain Samuel E. Bayley discovered that his freight had already been shipped to that port, he quickly picked up new cargo and made full sail for Cadiz. This change in destination would have dire consequences, for on October 25, just two days from Cadiz, the crew spotted "a strange sail" that they mistook for an English privateer. Bayley had no way of knowing that the British had negotiated a tentative truce between Algiers and Portugal just a month before. For a long time, Portuguese men-of-war had kept the Algerians out of the Atlantic, but on September 29, eight Algerian ships sailed through the Strait of Gibraltar under the newly signed (and short-lived) treaty. Within a few hours, the *Polly* was boarded by "Moors" and the crew securely stowed in the hold of the Algerian *Babasera*. Captain Bayley would eventually die of the black plague just days before his repatriation, and of the eight remaining crew aboard the *Polly*, only four are known to have survived. One of these was John Foss.

Official negotiations for U.S. captives had been ongoing with little success since 1785, when Algerian privateers first captured the new nation's shipping. In addition to the *Polly*, the Algerian privateers brought in ten more U.S. ships, which brought the total number of U.S. captives to 119. To make matters worse, the dey demanded an exorbitant ransom of $2.435 million. Back in Washington, Jefferson, who had originally opposed the creation of a federal navy, acted with the Congress to authorize the building of six warships. He also appointed Colonel David Humphries to negotiate a peace settlement with Algiers in the amount of $642,500 in cash and an annual tribute of

$21,600 in naval stores. Because the United States lacked credit in North Africa, delays in payment ensued, and Joel Barlow, the famous Connecticut Wit, appeased the dey by promising him a thirty-six-gun U.S.-built warship. Eventually, the price of the treaty, annual tribute, frigate, and "presents" ballooned to nearly a million dollars—about one-sixth of the annual $5.7 million federal budget.

Algeria released the U.S. captives on July 13, 1796, but because of seemingly endless delays, Foss didn't return to his home in Newburyport, Massachusetts, until August 23, 1797. He brought with him his journal, which he claimed to have written to divert his mind from his sufferings, having never imagined anyone would read it. The full account appeared in two editions in 1798 and marked the start of the most prolific period of Barbary captivity narratives written by Americans.

A JOURNAL, *of the Captivity and Sufferings* of JOHN FOSS; *several years a prisoner in ALGIERS:* Together with some account of the treatment of Christian slaves when sick:—and observations on the manners and customs of the Algerines. Newburyport, MA: A. March, 1798.

To the Public.

MAN SELDOM UNDERTAKES a more difficult, or at least a more disagreeable task, than that of relating incidents of his own life, especially where they are of a remarkable or singular nature. And he must be fortunate indeed, who does it without having his veracity called in question by the ignorant or censorious.

The following narrative (extracted from a Journal kept merely for the writer's satisfaction, and without the most distant idea of its ever being made public) contains a simple statement of facts, which can be attested to by many living evidences this day in America. It is now published at the repeated and urgent solicitations of some esteemed friends—confident that the candid reader will pardon the inadvertent inaccuracies of an illiterate mariner.

The tears of sympathy will flow from the humane and feeling, at the tale of the hardships and sufferings of their unfortunate fellow countrymen, who had the misfortune to fall into the hands of the Algerines—whose tenderest mercies towards Christian captives, are the most extreme cruelties; and who are taught by the Religion of Mahomet (if that can be called a Religion which leads men to the commission of such horrid and bloody deeds) to persecute all its opposers.

In this work I have not attempted a full description of the many hellish tortures and punishments those piratical sea-rovers invent and inflict on the unfortunate Christians who may by chance unhappily fall into their hands—my design being principally confined to narrate in as concise a view as possible, some important matters of fact that occurred, during our long, tedious and cruel captivity.

As some may inquire what opportunities could be obtained for writing a journal under such severe captivity; I would here observe, that I wrote in the night, while in the Bagnio or prison, after our daily labour was over, the principal events of the day, merely to amuse and relieve my mind from the dismal reflections which naturally occurred—that I could have no inducement to ex-

aggerate our sufferings, not supposing my narrative would ever be seen here—
these circumstances being known, I flatter myself the facts herein stated will
not often be called in question.

Sincerely wishing that none of my fellow-citizens may ever be so unhappy
as to experience the miseries of Algerine slavery, I commend the following to
their candor and patronage.

J. Foss.

A JOURNAL, &c.

On Saturday the 27th of July, 1793, I sailed from Newburyport in the State of
Massachusetts, in the capacity of a Mariner, on board the Brig Polly, belonging
to the above mentioned place, Samuel E. Bayley, Master, bound to Baltimore,
expecting to take a freight from thence for the Island of Tobago.

On Tuesday the 6th of August, were brought too [*sic*] by a French privateer,
and permitted immediately to proceed on our voyage. Being then in sight of
the Capes of Virginia, we took on board a pilot, and stood in for the Chesa-
peak.

Wednesday the 7th of August, we entered the Capes, and were until Saturday the 10th, before we arrived at Baltimore, and found on our arrival, that the
freight, which Capt. Bayley expected, was embarked and sailed on board another vessel.—Nothing particular happened, until Monday 19th when we
were ordered by the Capt. to discharge the ballast, and were informed by him,
that he agreed for a freight for Cadiz.

Thursday 29th, Paul Noyes, one of our mariners, was attacked with a severe
fever, and continued on board, until Monday the 9th September, when he was
carried on shore, and put under the care of a woman, who was well qualified
for attending sick people: And I understand he died in a few days after our departure. Tuesday the 10th, we sailed from Baltimore, bound to Cadiz; and on
Friday the 13th we left sight of the Capes of Virginia. Nothing of any moment
happened, until Thursday 24th of October, when we fell in with, and spoke
[to] two brigs from Elsmore, bound to Barcelona. On Friday 25th early in the
morning we saw the same brigs about two miles to windward standing on their
larboard tack, with the wind, about E.N.E.

We got our breakfast and eat it in the greatest jollity, not apprehending any
danger nigh, and expecting to reach the port of our destination within 48
hours; As we judged ourselves to be about 35 leagues westward of Cape St. Vincent. At nine A.M. we saw a strange sail bearing about E.N.E. and standing directly for the two Danish brigs: We then discovered (with a prospect glass) that

she had boarded them; that she had the English Flag displayed at her peak. We supposed her to be an English Privateer; she soon dismissed them, and then bore down upon us. By this time we could see that she was a Brig; and discerned by the cut of her sails, that she was not an English vessel, although had still the English flag flying; we then supposed her to be a French Privateer, hoisting the English flag to deceive their enemy. We immediately clued down top gallant sails, and hove too [*sic*] in order to wait 'till she came along side.—— When she came near enough to make us hear, she hailed us in English, asked from whence we came, and were bound; which was immediately answered by Capt. Bayley. The man who hailed us, was dressed in the Christian habit, and he was the only person we could yet see on her deck. By this time the Brig was under our stern, we then saw several men jump upon her poop, to hall aft the main sheet, and saw by their dress, and their long beard, that they were Moors, or Algerines. Our feelings at this unwelcome sight, are more easily imagined than described: She then hove too [*sic*] under our lee, when we heard a most terrible shouting, clapping of hands, huzzaing, &c. And saw a great number of men rise up with their heads above the gunnel, drest in the Turkish habit, like them we saw on the poop.——They immediately hoisted out a large launch, and about one hundred of the Pirates, jumped on board, all armed; some, with Scimitres and Pistols, others with pikes, spears, lances, knives, &c. They maned about 20 oars and rowed along side. As soon as they came on board our vessel, they made signs for us all to go forward, assuring us in several languages, that if we did not obey their commands, they would immediately massacre us all. They then went below into the cabin, steerage, and every place where they could get below deck, and broke open all the Trunks and Chests, there were on board, and plundered all our bedding, cloathing, books, Charts, Quadrants, and every moveable article, that did not consist of the Cargo, or furniture. They then came on deck, and stripped the cloathes off our backs, all except a shirt and pair of drawers, (myself being left with no shirt at all.) The next day an old Turk, with an air of kindness, gave me an old shirt without sleeves, blaming those who had taken mine from me. It was soothing to find a spark of humanity in my barbarous masters.——Having chosen a sufficient number of the Algerines to take command of the prize, they ordered us all into the launch: and, when they were all embarked, they rowed along side their own vessel, and ordered us on board. We embarked accordingly, and were conducted by some of the sea-rovers to the door of the poop, at which place we were received by a negro man, who conducted us into the cabin[:] when we entered the cabin, we saw the commander of the Pirates, sitting upon a mat, on the cabin floor; who, (with the help of an interpreter,) asked us many questions, concerning the vessel, and cargo, the places of our nativity, & many others, as void of sense as he was that asked them. He then informed us that he was an Algerine, and his vessel belonged to Algiers, that her name was Babasera, & his name was Rais Hudga Mahomet, Salamia, and we were his prisoners, and must immediately experience the most abject slavery, on our arrival at Algiers, which we soon found to be true. Our embarrassments were still greater, when we found that they were Algerines (for before we supposed them to be moors;) knowing, that the Algerines used the most severity (toward Christian captives) of any state in all Barbary. He then informed that Charles Logie, Esq. British Consul at Algiers, had negotiated with the Dey, for a truce with Portuguese, for the term of twelve months, and before that time was expired, they would have a firm peace, and the Algerines could cruise in the atlantic when they thought proper. He then told us we must do our duty as seamen on board his vessel; We told him we had no cloathes, for his people had taken every thing from us except what he saw on our backs, which was not sufficient for us to stand the deck with. He answered in very abusive words, that we might think ourselves well used that they did not take them.—And he would teach us to work naked. And ordered us immediately to our duty.

When we came out of the cabin, we saw the Polly, just making sail, and standing after us, and that night we lost sight of her, and saw her no more until our arrival at Algiers. About sunset they brought us a dish of Oil, Olives, and Vinegar, and some bread, and told us, to eat heartily, while we were on board, for after our arrival at Algiers, we should not be allowed such dainties. Although we were very hungry, we could eat but very little, considering the situation we were in, and not being used to such diet. When we set down to eat, we were accompanied by three Dutchmen, whom we had not seen before. And on asking them the particulars of their being on board, they informed us, that they sailed from Amsterdam, bound to Malaga three weeks, before, on board the Ship Hope, belonging to New-York, commanded by John Burnham, and had been captured by an Algerine frigate, within ten leagues of Gibraltar. And the frigate having taken several vessels; had a great number of Christian captives on board, and the Capt. of the frigate, being fearful lest they should make an attempt to rise upon the vessel, had distributed them on board the other corsairs, which had not taken any prizes. After we had finished our supper they divided us (twelve in number) into two watches, and ordered us to stand the deck, in our respective watches. It fell to my lot to have the first watch below, and as we went down they ordered us into the sail room to sleep, and shewed us the door. We were obliged to creep in, on our hands and knees, and stow ourselves upon the sails, in the best manner we could. We endeavoured to get a little sleep, but could not as our minds were filled with horror, and dreadful apprehensions of the fate we might experience, and expecting additional severity on our arrival at Algiers. We lay in this unhappy condition, bemoaning our hapless fate, until we supposed it to be past midnight, and could not conceive the reason that the watch was not relieved, as it is customary among Americans, and English.—And being strangers to their manner of relieving the watch, we supposed we had (innocently) neglected our duty, which made us very uneasy, fearing the watch had been relieved, and we not knowing it, they would inflict some corporal punishment.—I then proposed to my fellow sufferers, that I would go on deck, in order to know, whether they had called the watch or not; but they advised me not to go, adding, that if the watch was not called they might treat me very ill, for appearing on deck in the night, when my duty did not call me there, we then resolved to wait 'till we were called, and to bear patiently, our punishment if they inflicted any: We waited in this suspence for near an hour longer, when I resolved to go on deck, by myself, and know the issue, with this resolution, I crept upon my hands knees, to the sail room door; on my appearance at the door, a Turk came to me, armed with a Scimitre, and a pair of pistols, and made me to understand by signs, that he wanted to know where I was going. I answered him in the same manner, made him understand that necessity called me on deck. He then conducted me to the hatchway, and spoke to some person on the deck, in his own language, which I could not understand; and, pointing with his finger, I found I had permission to go up. I accordingly went on deck, and was received by another Turk, armed in the same manner he asked me in French, if I wished to go in the head, which I answered in the affirmative. As I understood some French, and could hold a tolerable discourse with him, I asked him if the watch was not called, which he answered in the negative, and on asking him if it was not past twelve o'clock he told me it was past two. And on enquiring the manner of their standing a watch, he informed me, that they kept ten hours for one watch; that it commenced at 8 o'clock in the evening and continued until 6 in the morning; then relieved, and kept 'till 4 in the afternoon, and their dog watch was from 4 in the afternoon, 'till 8, having only three watches in 24 hours. I then, went below and informed my fellow sufferers of what had passed, which gave them great satisfaction to think we had not committed an innocent offence, as before we feared we had done. We were happy in being freed from the terrors of punishment.—We then made ourselves as easy and comfortable as we could, considering the deplorable situation we were in. But could not sleep any the remainder of the night, for by this time, the vermin, such as lice, bugs, and fleas, had found their way to our apartment, and in such quantity that it seemed as if we were entirely covered with those unwelcome guests.

However we passed the remainder of the night, in condoling our miserable condition, and rubbing those vermin from our bodies, in the best manner we could. At 6 A.M. we were surprised by three heavy knocks, we heard on the deck, and with such force, that it seemed as if they endeavoured to knock the deck to pieces, and not hearing any thing said, we could not imagine the meaning; we lay a few minutes, and were then called by a Turk, and ordered on deck, and were informed, that that was their fashion of calling the watch, which office is generally performed by the Boatswain, or one of his mates, in the following manner. A large block is laid on the deck, near the hatchway, and struck upon with a very large beetle, which makes such a horrid noise, as nearly sufficient to stun the brain of a strong headed person, and which was the cause of our surprise before mentioned. This being Saturday, the 26th October.—We passed the rock of Gibraltar on Monday the 28th and nothing of any consequence, happened on our passage to Algiers, spoke [to] several vessels, but none proved to be their enemies. We having a very fresh breeze from the W. we arrived at Algiers, on Friday the 1st. of November.

After they had brought their vessel to an anchor in the roads, they hoisted out their boats and ordered us to embark, and to lay ourselves down in the bottom of the boat: And having obeyed their commands, we were rowed on shore, and landed, amidst the shouts and huzzas, of thousands of malicious barbarians. We were conducted to the Dey's palace, by a guard, and as we passed through the streets, our ears were stunned with the shouts, clapping of hands, and other acclamations of joy from the inhabitants, thanking God for their great success, and victories over so many Christian dogs, and unbelievers, which is the appellation they generally give to all christians. On our arrival at the gates of the Palace, we were received by another guard, and conducted before the Dey, who after taking a view of us, told us he had sent several times to our Government, entreating them, to negociate with him for a peace, and had never received any satisfactory answer from them. And that he was determined, never to make a peace with the United States, (in his reign) as they had so often neglected his requests, and treated him with disdain, adding "now I have got you, you Christian dogs, you shall eat stones." He then picked out four boys to wait upon himself, in the palace, as follows, Benjamin Church, Benjamin Ober, Charles Smith, and John Ramsey, and then ordered the rest of us to be conducted to the prison Bilic. When we arrived there, we found several other Americans, who landed a little before us, and they informed us that the Corsairs had captured ten sail of American vessels, and that their Captains and crews were chiefly in the same prison.

After condoling our hapless fate, for a considerable time; a French priest came to us and enquired, if any among us understood the French language, and was answered in the affirmative. After conversing sometime with the person who spoke French, he left us, and told us he should return in a few minutes. About half an hour afterwards he returned, and two moors with him, who brought two baskets full of white bread, and he gave each man, a loaf weighing nearly a pound, which was a very delicious meal for us, we having eaten nothing during the day, it now being about 4 o'clock in the afternoon. He likewise informed us that it was a custom among those sons of rapine and plunder, not to allow the slaves any kind of food on the first day of their landing, except one small loaf of bread at night. And what we then received, he gave us, out of his own pocket, and said if he was able, his charity would further extend. We thanked our kind benefactor, and he took his leave of us, and left us. We then walked from one part of the Bagnio to another, not knowing in what part we might be allowed to remain. We wandered in this manner, bemoaning our deplorable situation, 'till about 5 o'clock, when we saw (according to the best of our judgment) about 600 men enter the Bagnio,—all appearing to be in a more miserable condition than ourselves, with wretched habits, dejected countenances, and chains on their legs, every part of them bespeaking unutterable distress. I enquired of the prison keeper, who those people were, and of what crimes they had been guilty, that they were loaded with such heavy chains. I was answered, that they were christian slaves, had been captured in the same manner as myself, seeking an honest livelihood: A few minutes afterwards, we heard a man shouting out in a most terrible manner, and not understanding his language, made it sound more terrible.—We were immediately informed by a man, who understood the English language, that all of us (Americans) must appear in the third gallery.—We made all haste up, we possibly could, and as we entered the gallery, we passed one at a time, through a narrow door, on one side of which stood a task-master, and on the other side a christian slave. The former had a large stick in his hand, and the latter a book, in which was written the names of all the Christian captives in that prison. The christian asked each man his name, and then wrote it in the book, and as we passed, the Turk gave each man a small bundle. On examining it, we found it contained a blanket, a capoot, (which is a sort of jacket with a head,) a waistcoat, made something like a frock, to draw on over the head, it not being open at the belly, a shirt, with neither collar or wrist-bands, a pair of Trowsers, made somewhat like a womans petticoat, (with this difference,) the bottom being sewed up, and two holes to put the legs through, and a pair of slippers. There was neither button, or button-hole in the whole suit. Such a suit excepting the blanket, of which they never get but one, is given to each captive once a year. The day they receive this suit is on Friday ensuing Christmas: And the first friday in January all the captives are obliged to go about seven miles into the country, and gather reeds, and carry them to the Dey's garden for Beans, Peas,

&c. to run upon, and which is a very tedious days work.—At this season of the year the rains fall in abundance in that country and renders the walking very disagreeable, as we do not follow the road, but are obliged to cross fields, and meadows.—The distance those reeds must be carried is about eight miles. We go out at the easternmost gate (called Babazoone,) and it is near 7 miles from said gate to the place where they are gathered, and from thence they must be carried to the Dey's garden, which is near a mile westward of the gate called Babel-wed which is the west gate of the city.

I shall omit the particulars of the usage of the slaves at present and give an account of our first nights lodging in this doleful mansion. Soon after we received the above mentioned bundle, we were again called into the third gallery, and passed in the same manner as before, and having our names called by the clerk we passed the task master, and received each man a small loaf of very black, sourbread weighing about three ounces and a half, which we ate, although it was not so delicious as the bread we received from the french priest. Having finished our supper, we lay down upon the stone floor, and went to sleep, and made ourselves as comfortable, as we could, having neither bed, nor beding, except the blanket before mentioned but being very much fatigued, we slept tolerably well until about three o'clock, when we were alarmed with a terrible shouting, as before, and were all ordered to go down into the lower part of the prison. When we arrived there, they put a chain on each man's leg, reaching up to the shoulder, and weighing about 25 or 40 lb. This done, it now being day break—Saturday the 2d. Nov. we were all driven out of the Bagnio, and from thence to the marine, where I experienced the hardest days work, I ever underwent before. The dreadful clanking of the chains, was the most terrible noise I ever heard.—And never during my whole captivity did I feel such horrors of mind, as on this dreadful morning. As it is not in my power to write the particulars of each day of my captivity, (which would be too tedious to my readers,) I only intend to give you a short narrative of some of the most particular occurrences, which happened while I was in this abject slavery, and the common labor, and usage of the slaves, which is as follows.

At day break in the morning, the Prison-keeper calls all the slaves out to go to work, and at the door of the Bagnio they are met by the *Guardians* or taskmasters (who have their orders from the *Guardian Bachi,* who is the master of all the slaves that belong to the Regency) and we are conducted to whatever place he has directed.

The greatest part of their work, is blowing rocks in the Mountains. While some are drilling the holes, others are diging the earth off those rocks, which are under it, and others carrying away the dirt in baskets. When the rocks are blowed, they take such as will answer their purpose: (Rocks less than twenty

Tons weight, will not serve.) Many are hauled by the slaves, two miles distance, which weigh forty tons. They roll them to the bottom of the mountain, where is a convenient place to put them on a sled, from thence they are hauled to a quay, about two miles distant, and left. Those rolled down the mountain are left at the bottom, until Friday, (which is their Mahometan Sabbath,) on which day all the christian slaves belonging to the Regency, are driven out haul them to the Quay. At day light in the morning they pass through the gates of the city, and arrive at the bottom of the mountain, sometime before sunrise. On their arrival, they are divided by the task-masters, into different gangs, and each gang has one sled. They must haul as many in a day as the task-masters think proper, and are treated with additional rigor and severity on this day. For the drivers being anxious to have as many hauled as possible, (because the number they haul must be reported to the Dey.)—they are continually beating the slaves with their sticks, and goading them with its end, in which is a small spear, not unlike an ox goad, among our farmers. If anyone chance to faint, and fall down with fatigue, they generally beat them until they are able to rise again. The most Tyrannical guardian, or taskmaster, we had, during my captivity, was known by the name of Sherief. This cruel villain never appeared to be in his element, except when he was cruelly punishing some Christian captive. In the month of April 1795. He and another task-master being sent with 20 slaves, to remove a pile of boards, which was in a magazine, upon the walls of the city, and having beat several unmercifuly without any provocation; an American exclaimed (in the English language, which the Turk did not understand) "God, grant you may die, the first time you offer to abuse another man." A few minutes afterwards, as a slave was going upon some plank, which were laid from the first wall to the second, having his load upon his back. Sherief thinking he did not proceed as fast, as he might, ran, and endeavouring to strike him missed his stroke, his stick gave him such a sudden jirk, that he fell from the planks, between the walls, and was dashed to pieces.

Thus ended the days of a Godless wretch, apparently in a moment, swept away by the devout breath of a suffering Christian.

When a slave is found to be so sick that he is incapable of doing any kind of work, they then permit him to go to a hospital, until they think he can work again.

This Hospital was erected by the Spaniards for the benefit of christian slaves, in the year ———, and is still maintained by them, when a slave goes in, he is used very well by the doctors and priests. They generally allow three or four doctors, and eight or ten priests to attend this hospital. The Doctors order what is to be given to the patient, and the Priests prepare it. While a slave is sick, he is no manner of expence to the Regency, for he is maintained with victuals[,] drink, medicine and attendance by the Spaniards; every morning one of the task-masters goes into the hospital to view the slaves, and if he finds any one whom he thinks able to perform any kind of work, he drives him out, not even asking the Doctors whether they think he is able or not. And often times they are driven out in this manner, to work, and are obliged to return within two or three hours to the hospital again, and often expire within a few hours after their return.

A circumstance of this kind, happened on the 30th of January 1796. When one Scipio Jackson, (a black man) had been for some time very sick, and was recovering (to all appearance,) very fast; he had been able to walk the room, but the day before, and was walking on the said morning when the task-master came in, who on perceiving him walk, declared he was well, and ordered him to the marine to work. He told the task-master he was not able, at which he gave him several strokes with his stick saying if you are not able, I will make you able, and drove him to the marine. The Doctors used their utmost endeavours to dissuade him from it; all was to no purpose, he would not hearken to any thing they said, but drove the poor man before him, to work. He did the best he could for about half an hour, and then fell down insensible. Upon this he was again sent to the hospital, expired at two o'clock in the afternoon, & was in his grave before sunset.

At night when they have done hauling, all hands are called together, and have their names called by the Clerk, and every one must pass the Guardian Bachi, as his name is called. After they have done calling, and find that none are missing they are driven by the task-masters, into the city, and then left to go to the Bagnio, by themselves, and must appear there within half an hour after they must enter gates of the city. The roll is called every night in the prison, a few minutes before the gates are locked. If any one neglects his call, he is immediately put into irons hands and feet, and then chained to a pillar, where he must remain until morning. Then the irons are taken from his feet, and he is driven before a task-master, to the marine, and the Vigilhadge, (who is the Minister of the marine) orders what punishment he thinks proper, which is immediately inflicted, by the task-masters. He commonly orders 150, or 200 Bastinadoes. The manner of inflicting this punishment is as follows, the person is laid upon his face, with his hands in irons behind him and his legs lashed together with a rope.—One task-master holds down his head and another his legs, while two others inflict the punishment upon his breech, with sticks, some what larger than an ox goad. After he has received one half in this manner, they lash his ancles to a pole, and two Turks lift the pole up, and hold it in such a manner, as brings the soles of his feet upward, and the remainder of his punishment, he receives upon the soles of his feet. Then he is released from his bands, and obliged to go directly to work, among the rest of his fellow slaves. There is several other punishments, for the christian captives, for capital offences. Sometimes they are burned, or rather roasted alive. At other times they are impaled. This is done by placing the criminal upon a sharp iron stake, and thrusting it up his posteriors, by his back bone 'till it appears at the back of his neck. For being found with a Mahometan woman he is beheaded, and the woman, is put into a sack and carried about a mile at sea, and thrown overboard with a sufficient quantity of rocks, (or a bomb) to sink her. For suspicion of being with them the slave is castrated, and the woman bastinadoed.

A slave for murder of another slave, is immediately beheaded. But for murder of a Mahometan he is cast off from the walls of the city, upon iron hooks, which are fastened into the wall about half way down.—these catch by any part of the body, that strikes them, and some times they hang in this manner in the most exquisite agonies for several days before they expire. But should the part that catches, not be strong enough to hold them (for sometimes the flesh will tear out,) they fall to the bottom of the wall and are dashed in pieces.

Another punishment they have for slaves endeavouring to make their escape is, they are nailed to the gallows, by one hand and opposite foot, and in this manner they expire, in the most undescribable torture. But this is not always practiced for desertion, for sometimes they are only bastinadoed, at other times they are beheaded.—I never knew an instance of the former, during my captivity. Though I have been an eye witness to the latter several times.

In the month of October 1793, fourteen slaves of different nations, made an attempt to run away, with a boat, but were overtaken and brought back to Algiers. When they were landed, the Dey ordered the steersman, and bowman, to be beheaded, and the rest to receive 500 bastinadoes each, and to have a chain of 50 lb weight fastened to their leg for life, and a block of about 70 lb. to the end of that, which they were obliged to carry upon their shoulder when they walked about to do their work. And those of them that were alive when I left Algiers, (which was the 13th of July, 1796,) were still in this miserable situation. When they are at work they lay the block down & can only work within the length of their chain. When they have occasion to go further, they must carry the block, to the place where the work calls them.

When a slave commits any crime, except murder, or speaking ill of their religion or striking a Turk, if he can get into one of their Marabout Mosques, they will not inflict any kind of punishment, except an additional chain upon his leg, with a large block at its end.

A Turk is strangled for offences capital, in the following manner. The criminal is confined, with his back against a wall, in which is two holes, right opposite the back of his neck, through which holes is reaved a rope with the two ends on the opposite side, and the bite, or double of the rope comes about the criminal's neck and when the two ends are knotted together, the executioner puts a stick in and twists the rope, which brings it tight about the criminal's neck, and he is soon dispatched. So the executioner does not see the criminal while performing his office. This is counted the most honorable death, for persons who are executed. And beheading the most ignominious. A moor or arab convicted of theft, hath sometimes his right hand cut off and hung about his neck; Then he is led through the city upon an ass, with his face toward the tail; but at other times they are hanged upon a tree, or bastinadoed.

A Turk is pardoned, let his crime be ever so capital, if he can get into one of them before he is taken into custody. And those Marabout Mosques are an asylum for persons of any religion whatever, having committed a small offence, except the Jews, who would be burned if they were to offer to enter one of them. Those Marabout Mosques, are particular Mosques, in which has been buried a Marabout or Hermit, whom they account Saints. And their religion teaches them to pardon a Mahometan, having committed any crime whatever, if he flees to those Saints for protection. When a Mahometan, who has committed a crime, and has taken to the marabout, it is immediately reported to the Mufti, and he reports it to the Dey, who sends a string of beads by the Mufti, to the keeper of the Mosque, and the criminal then comes out. Tho' he might come out before if he pleases, but should he leave the Mosque before the Mufti comes with the beads, he would be liable to the same punishment he was before he had taken the Marabout. The Mufti then returns with the beads, to the Dey, and they are laid by, until some other similar occasion.

At the gates of the Deys Palace, there is a chain which is fastened at the top o the gate, and at night the lower end is locked down, and any one that has committed an offence, and can get hold of this chain before he is taken, it serves the same purpose as the Marabout Mosque.

If a slave has been cheated by any Turk, Cologlie, Moor, Arab, Renegado, or Jew, and he takes hold of this chain, and says he wants justice, one of the principal officers of the Deys corps of guards, goes to him & asks the particulars of his being wronged; and who the person is that has wronged him and justice is immediately done him.—But should he give a wrong account, and it be proved that he has not told the truth, he is immediately bastinadoed. If it is a Jew that is complained of, and he is found guilty, he must make the slave reparation and is bastinadoed.

I mentioned before, that on Friday, all the slaves work in the mountains, but on other days only a part of them work there. They have commonly a part of the captives at work in the marine. When they work in the marine, they have different kinds of employ. Sometimes they are cleaning the corsairs, and fitting them for sea. At other times they are striping them, and hauling them up, discharging the prizes, cleaning the harbor, bringing those large rocks before mentioned, from the quay, on board a large flat bottomed kind of vessel which, they call a Puntoon, discharging them at back of the mole, with the help of wheels. These rocks are laid there in order to break off the sea, that the mole may not wash away, which must have a continual supply, for every gale of wind that comes, washes them into the deep water. After a gale they have as much need of them as they had the first hour after the mole was built. So we may conclude this is a work that will never be finished. And every article that is transported from one part of the Marine to another, or from the Marine to the city or from the city to the marine, or elsewhere must be carried by the slaves with poles upon their shoulders. For the streets are so narrow that no kind of carriage is used here, not even a wheelbarrow. In many streets it is difficult for one man to pass another.

When their prizes are discharged, their cargo must be all carried into the city, and stowed in Magazines, so that some part of the slaves are constantly carrying, hogsheads of sugar, pipes of wine, casks of nails, cannon, &c. They work from day break, in the morning, until a certain hour in the afternoon, (which they call Laza) which is just half an hour before sunset, summer and winter. At which time they hoist a white flag upon the mosques, to denote that it is the hour of prayer, it being contrary to their religion to have a bell sound among them.

All the slaves at this hour, are ordered to leave work and go up to the gate, called Babazia, which is the marine gate, and before they can pass, they are searched by the task-masters, to prevent their stealing any thing from the Regency, and if they are found with any thing, (except a few chips,) they do not escape punishment.

I have known a slave to receive 100 bastinadoes for being found with three board nails.

Having related the common labors and punishment of the slaves, I now proceed to give you an account of the provisions they are allowed to subsist on, to enable them to perform this laborious slavery. About eight o'clock in the morning they are called by one of the task-masters from their work to take their breakfast. The order of receiving it, is as follows. When they are called they all leave their work, and go near some sacks of bread. As they pass by, they are counted by one of the drivers, while another gives each man a loaf of bread. And to every eighth man he gives a wooden bowl with about a pint of vinegar, in this manner they pass until all have received their allowance. They then sit down upon the ground to eat, and are commonly called to work in about ten minutes, and are seldom allowed more than twelve minutes. The same ceremony is passed at twelve o'clock, and at night when the roll is called they receive another loaf of bread, but no vinegar. This is all they have allowed from the Regency. But oftentimes when they are at work on board the corsairs, the steward will give them a little sweet oil, and sometimes some olives, and this they count a feast. These loaves of bread weigh about three ounces and an half. I have weighed several and never found one to exceed three ounces and eleven drachms. So what bread they have allowed them for a day, will not exceed eleven ounces, and it is so sour that a person must be almost starving before he can eat it. The reason of its being so sour is, they mix the dough three days before it is baked. To make this bread they sift the bran of wheat, after the flour and midlings are taken out.

Perhaps you may think what I have already told you would not be augmented with additional severity, but alas, this is not all. The Bagnio in which they sleep, is built with several Galleries, one above another, in each gallery is several small rooms, where the slaves sleep. And they must pay a certain sum, every moon to the Guardian Bachi, or sleep in the open Bagnio, where they have nothing but the firmament to cover them. On the evening after the moon changes, the keeper of the Bagnio calls out for all hands to pay for their rooms. And if any one that has slept in a room during the moon, has not procured the money, and cannot pay it down, his hands are put into irons behind him, and his legs chained to a pillar every night, until the money is paid. And those miserable objects are commonly relieved by the rest of their fellow sufferers. Some of the slaves are allowed a small pittance from their country, which enables them to pay this demand. Others are mechanics and work at their trade in the night, to procure this sum, and others get it by theft, tho' they often hazzared their lives by so doing; and many are obliged to sleep every night upon the cold stones with nothing but the heavens to cover them, for want of money to pay this tribute. In the Bagnio, where the slaves sleep, is kept a great number of animals of prey, they are confined with chains in different apartments from where the slaves sleep. And are maintained by them; with Bullock's and Sheep's heads; this money must be paid every moon when they pay for the rooms they sleep in. There is still another demand as unreasonable as the former.

After their Ramadan, a fast which they keep a whole moon, and during which they cannot eat, drink, smoak, or even wet their lips while the sun is in the horizon, (what they do eat, is in the night) they have a great feast, which continues two days, on the evening previous to the feast, every slave must carry as a present to the task-master, two fowls; and a certain number of sheep is given to them, for which each slave must pay his proportionable part. During those two days the slaves are locked in the bagnio, and are allowed no kind of subsistence from the Regency except one small loaf of the bread which I mentioned before, and this they receive each night when the roll is called. The drivers, on the first morning of the feast, give each slave a loaf of good white bread, weighing about half a pound, for which they had received two fowls from each slave the evening before.

In this deplorable situation, were upwards of 1,200 Christian captives, (dragging out a miserable existence) when I left Algiers.

The present inhabitants of the territory of Algiers are composed of many different nations. The Turks, are the first people among them, and have all the government and power in their own hands, and no man can hold any post of great distinction among them except he is a Turk. The Cologlies, are next the Turks, in power. These are those persons born of a Morish mother the father being a Turk. The Arabs, who trace their descent from the disciples of Mahomet, who formerly subdued Algiers. Moors or Morescoes, who were driven out of Spain, about the end of the 16th century. Renagadoes, Levantines, Jews, and Christian slaves, with a croud formed of the posterity of all these different people, make the rest of the population. The people in the country, have no houses, but live in tents, and remove from one place to another, as they want pasture, or as any other accidental circumstance may happen. The Dey demands a tribute from them, which is procured by the Beys, and carried to Algiers.

The manner of gathering the tribute is as follows: The Dey informs the Bey what sum he must pay him the ensuing year, and then the Bey goes with a large number of Cavalry, and if they do not pay his demand immediately, he takes from them what he pleases, and if they make the least resistance, or even intimate that they are dissatisfied with his proceedings, he cuts off their heads and sends them in triumph to the Dey. And after they have carried it twice from the Dey's palace to the gate Babazoon, and exposed it to public view, they then bury it. The Beys seldom are in office more than two or three years, before they are so rich that the Dey finds something against them, and haves them executed, and all their property is brought to the city and deposited into the treasury.

The dress of the men, (who live in the country) is only a coarse woolen cloth wrapped round the shoulders, which falls down as far as their ancles, with a cap of the same cloth, with a twisted turban of woolen over that.

The women pay some more attention to ornament themselves with dress. They are dressed with a long piece of coarse woolen cloth, not unlike that of the men's, with a great number of pewter, and brass, broaches, fixed upon it, about the shoulders, arms and breast.

They adorn their heads, with several of these broaches fixed in their hair, and a braided woolen string passed several times round their heads, and filled with several kinds of flowers. The children are suffered to go naked, 'till eight or nine years of age. The Sheik or chief of a tribe is known by a linen garment instead of a woolen, and a linen turban, he also wears a pair of shoes, made of dressed leather.

The common sort of people, seldom wear any shoes, and when they do, they are made of undressed leather with hair on the out side.

When a young man would marry, he drives a number cattle to the tent where the parents of his mistress reside. The bride is then set on horse back and led to the tent where the young man resides, amidst the shouts and huzzas of a multitude of young people, who have been invited to the nuptial feast. When she arrives at the tent of her lover, a mixture of milk and honey is given her to drink, and a song is sung suitable to the occasion. She then alights, and receives a stick from her husband, which she thrusts into the ground, and holding her right hand upon its end, she repeats some words to the following effect: "As this stick is fastened in the ground so am I bound in duty to my husband, as nothing can remove it, but violence so nought but death, shall force me from his love." She then drives his flock to water and back again, to shew her willingness to perform any duty that he may assign her. These previous ceremonies being settled, all the company set down by the tent, and the evening concludes with the greatest jollity. They feast upon Dates, Almonds, Raisins, Olives, and Oil, and drink sherbot, which is water, having run through Raisins, somewhat like making lye of ashes. Subsequent to the marriage, the wife is vailed and never stirs from the tent, for the space of a whole moon, and no one can see her, except her parents, during this time. These are the ceremonies, which (I have been Informed by the Algerines) are customary, in celebrating a marriage, among those savage barbarians, but I never had an opportunity of viewing one of them.

The people of Algiers in general speak a compound of Arabic, Moresco, and the remains of the ancient Phenician languages. The inhabitants of all denominations, for the most part, understand the Lingua Franca. This is a kind of dialect, which without being the proper language of any country whatever, has a kind of universal currency all over the Mediter[r]anean, as the channel of information for people, who cannot understand each other through any medium but this. The public business of the nation, and the records are transacted in the Turkish tongue.

In Algiers, the men wear large turbans, having their heads close shaved, and for the most part they wear their beards—some only wear their whiskers. Their longest jackets, which have sleeves, they wear next to their shirt, and then a vest over that, always taking care to have the shortest garment outside. Their shirts are made with neither collar nor wristbands, their breeches, something like a woman's petticoat, reaching down to their knees. Stockings are entirely unknown among them. Their shoes have square toes, with no heels. People of any denomination whatever, (except the Jews) are allowed to dress in this habit. No person is allowed to dress in green, except a Sherief, whom they say descended from Mahomet, they are known by a green turban. The Jews are obliged to dress entirely in black, and wear shoes without any quarters.

I have known 50 in one day, to be punished with five hundred bastinadoes, for being found with a small red sash about their waist.

The women dress, with a sort of cap upon their heads, of either Gold, Silver, Brass, Pewter, or Tin, according as their fortune will afford; and wear short jackets, and long trowsers. After they are married, they are obliged to have white trowsers, but before their trowsers are a sort of Callico; they are obliged to wear a veil when they go out of their houses, though very few are allowed to go out at all. They mark the forehead, nose and chin, with india ink, and stripe the backs of their hands, and fingers black, and colour their finger nails red.

The husband never sees his wife before marriage but accepts her upon the description of her father. When the match is agreed upon, and the man has paid the father for the daughter, (for in this country every man is obliged to buy his wife, from her parents,) the bridegroom sends a present of fruits and sweetmeats, and entertains her relations with a feast, and musical entertainments. He is then conducted into the presence of his wife, by four women, who are veiled. He then retires and goes to his own house, and the bride is set on horseback and led to his house. After she is safe delivered to her husband, the females who were invited to the nuptial feast, assemble themselves, and walk through the street, and at several corners they pronounce the bans by shouting out all together, as loud as they can, with such strong shrill voices, that they may be heard two miles.

Algiers is a country which derives its name from its metropolis, and extends four hundred and eighty miles in length from east to west, along the northern coast of Africa. And is in breadth three hundred and twenty miles from the sea-coast, it becomes a barren desert, almost uninhabited by either man or beast. Algiers is situated between thirty-two and thirty-seven degrees of north latt. which coresponds to that of the United States, from Virginia to Carolina, inclusive. It is bounded on the north, by the Mediterranean sea; on the south, by Mount Atlas; on the east, by the country of Tunis; and on the west by the River Mulvia, which separates it from the empire of Morocco.

The principal rivers which water the territory of Algiers, rise in Mount Atlas, and run by a northerly direction into the Mediterranean sea. They are seven in number. None of them has a long course, or is navigable: at least none of them are made use of in navigation. It is however likely that they might be made use of for this purpose, were the inhabitants of a more intelligent and industrious character, for some of them are of a tolerable depth. Such is the gross ignorance of the natives in whatever concerns domestic improvements, that there is not a single bridge over any of those rivers. And ferry boats are entirely unknown.—When they are to be crossed, the traveller hath sometimes to wander several miles in search of a ford.

The climate in this country is remarkably delightful. The air is pure and serene. The soil is covered with almost a perpetual verdure. Extreme heat is not common.—In the winter it is seldom cold enough to freeze. I have been informed, that it has been known to freeze at the depth of two or 3 inches. I once saw frost during my residence there, but I never saw any ice.—This description applies to the land on the sea-coast; for as you advance into the country, the soil becomes more barren.—Indeed a considerable part of the back country is a savage desert, abounding with Lions, Tigers, Leopards, Jackalls, Buffaloes, wild Boars, Porcupines, &c. And it must be acknowledged, that these animals are not the least amiable inhabitants of this country.

The City of Algiers lies in latt. 36, 50 North, and in long. 3, 47 East, over against the Island of Minorca, 380 miles from Tunis, it lies upon the side of a very high hill, with such an ascent, that when you are at sea, you may see almost every house in it. At a great distance it appears like a snow bank; which is occasioned by the houses being white-washed on the outside. The city is of a quadrangular form, and is near three miles in circumference, compassed with two walls, about 25 feet distant, and in some places 100 feet in height. The outward wall is defended by upward of 300 brass cannon, and outside the wall is a deep entrenchment 40 feet wide, over which are built bridges at the gates of the city. In the intermediate space between the walls are magazines, for public stores.

The Mole of the harbour is about 500 paces in length, extending from the continent to a ledge of rocks, where there are three castles, with large batteries of guns.

The houses are all built with stone and lime. The principal buildings are the Dey's palace, and several large Mosques; The former stands near the center of the city; is very large but not magnificent. The Mosques are fine buildings, though they make no great appearance at a distance.—There is a great number of hot baths in this city, people of any denomination whatever are allowed to go into them and bathe, on paying double the sum which a Turk pays. If a stranger happens to go in, they generally extort eight or ten fold. The men spend a great part of their time in bathing, smoking, and drinking coffee.— Their religion obliges them to bathe four times a day, but many of them do much oftener, for their own pleasure. There are also several baths for the use of women, who are not allowed to bathe, only in the afternoon. Those among them who are able, have these conveniences in their own houses, that their women may not go out. Few white women walk the streets, except prostitutes, and those far advanced in years, and when these do they are obliged to be veiled. The principal street extends from the east gate of the City, to the west, is tolerable wide and some what magnificent.—The rest are all very narrow, which renders it very difficult for passengers. The men by their Laws, and religion, are allowed to have four wives (if they are able to purchase them) but they generally content themselves with two or three.

The present Dey of Algiers, is between sixty and seventy years of age—is a thick well built man, with his white beard covering his breast. He is of a very light complection. Does not appear to be much decayed by the weight of years, which have rolled over his head. He is of a very malicious disposition, and often when he is in a rage, commands deeds of inhumanity to be committed, of which he repents afterwards.

His family consists of himself, wife and one daughter. His wife and daughter have a separate palace, at a little distance from that of the Dey's, and have a great number of female christian slaves to serve them. The Dey visits them every Thursday evening, abides with his wife the night, and returns to his own palace on Friday morning. The Dey has also a number of Christian captives to wait upon him. One cooks his victuals, another sets his table, waits upon him while eating, makes his bed, and sees that all things in his apartment are kept clean. The others do any kind of work that is necessary. He keeps no Seraglio as is generally reported—has but one wife, and sleeps with her but once a week.

When the Dey eats, he has a table about four inches high, on which is set several different dishes, with neither plates, knives or forks, they eat only with spoons, their victuals being cut small before it is set on the table and can touch their victuals only with their right hand. They sit always on the floor, as chairs are entirely unknown among them. The common people only differ from the Dey, by having no table whatever, their dishes being set upon the floor.

The Dey is an absolute Monarch, and the Haznagi, is the next man to him in dignity and power—the Aga is next the Haznagi—the Hoodge de Cabellos, is next to him—and the Petit Mell next to him—The Aga de Baston, is next to him, who enjoys his post but two moons, and then retires with a pension. The other officers of importance are, a Secretary of State, twenty-four Chiah Baffas, or Colonels subordinate to the Aga, about two hundred seinor [*sic*] Raifes, or Captains, and about four hundred Lieutenants. The Mufti, the Cadi, and the grand Marabout, are known by the largeness of their turbans. The two former are the High Priest and Supreme Judge in ecclesiastical causes. The latter is the chief of an order of Saints or Hermits. The inhabitants of Algiers live very meanly, altho' their country plentifully produces the conveniences and luxuries of life. The chief of their diet is bread, oil, olives, vinegar and sallad. They very seldom eat any meat. When they do, one pound is sufficient for six or eight people, and this they count extravagant. They profess not to drink any kind of spiritous liquor, and if any one is seen intoxicated, he is no more counted a true Mahometan. Many of them will however, drink to excess when they are out of sight of any others of their religion. Many instances of this kind I have seen, particularly one Mustafa, an Algerine, would often go into the Bagnio and purchase wine from the slaves (at double price) which they had bought for their own use, and sit down and drink among them. One evening as I went in, after returning from my labour, I saw Mustafa, drinking wine, and eating pork sausages. I asked him if he knew what he was eating, he answered in great rage, uz coot fanza fida, un ta main schelim, un a main arsshi, which is, "Hold your tongue you unbeliever, if you do not tell me, I shall not know."

The Cologlies, Moors and Arabs, are the most numerous in Algiers. They compose the great body of the inhabitants; but it may be supposed, that amidst such a variety of different races, immense numbers cannot be said to belong to any particular tribe or nation whatever.

The Turks are a well built robust people, their complexion not unlike Americans, tho' somewhat larger, but their dress, and long beards, make them appear more like monsters, than human beings.

The Cologlies are somewhat less in stature than the Turks, and are of a more tawney complexion.

The Moors, or Morescoes, are generally a tall thin, spare set of people, not much inclining to fat, and of a very dark complexion, much like the Indians of North America.

The Arabs, or Arabians, are of a much darker complexion than the Moors, being darker than Mulattoes. They are much less in stature than the Moors, being the smallest people I ever saw, very few arrive at the height of five feet, tho' they are in general nearly of a size. These people compose the greater part of the Piscaras, or porters in the city. As they are not allowed to trade in any mercantile line, nor even to learn any mechanic art, they are obliged to be drudges to their superiors, to gain the hard earned morsel on which they subsist.

They bury their dead in the following manner. The corps is washed, then sewed in a winding sheet, put upon a bier, and carried to the grave, where they are buried in a sitting posture. No females are allowed to follow any corps whatever. Any Mahometan who dies with the plague is carried to the grave as fast as the bearers can run. All the followers sing while they are going. They imagine all Mahometans who die with this disorder, are called by the Supreme

Being, and are happy to eternity. But people of any other religion, who die with it, they suppose are damned. At each end of the grave they place a small earthern [*sic*] pot, containing about half a pint, which they keep filled with water, presuming that their friends, if not happy, will be relieved or comforted with this drink. They also plant Pease and Beans on the graves of their friends, and lay fragrant bushes on them, for the comfort and support of their departed relatives.

The old women also every Friday morning repair to the mansion of the dead, to carry such provisions as bread, beans, pease and plumbs. These they expect their friends if unhappy, will receive; if they be happy, they are willing the cats should partake the repast. These animals croud their grave yards in hundreds.

The greatest part of their commerce, is with the Swedes, Danes, Dutch, French, Spaniards, Raguscans and English. The commodities they trade in, are Wheat, Barley, Oil, Olives, Figs, Raisins, Wax, Honey, Silks, Almonds, Dates, Wool, Leather of different colours, which is commonly called Morocco Leather, Horses, Mules, &c.

Their manufactures are chiefly Silks and Woolen Carpets.

In Algiers are about five hundred christian slaves, of different nations, who deserted from Oran, while it was in possession of the Spaniards. They have no hopes of relief till death. The Spaniards will not ransom them because they are deserters. In November '95, one of them having grown desperate, was drinking wine one evening in the Bagnio, and making some noise; the Guard[1] beat him without mercy. The slave drew a knife and stabbed him to the heart, and he fell instantly dead. The rest of the Guards commanded the slaves to endeavour to secure him. In attempting this, he killed one slave, and wounded three more. He was then taken, secured while morning and then beheaded.

Another circumstance of this kind happened in March '96. One of those Oran slaves having been informed, that the money for the redemption of the Spaniards, (who deserted from that place) was lodged in the hands of a Spanish priest, resident at Algiers; that he had neglected their liberation. The slave went to the priest, asked if he had money for the redemption for the Spaniards. Being answered in the negative, he drew a knife, and stabbed him in fourteen different places, and left him to all appearance dead. However, the Priest recovered. The slave then went to the house of the Spanish consul, intending to kill him, and finding he was at his garden, he went to the Bagnio, where he killed a Christian slave, with whom he had had some dispute before. He then

---

1. These Guards or Corvos, are slaves who are ordered by the Guardian Bachi to keep peace among the rest of the slaves in the night, and have power to put any one in irons who misbehaves, and keep him till morning when he is punished. [Foss's note]

threw down his knife and delivered himself up, and was beheaded the same evening.

Perhaps some of my readers may wish to know something more particular, concerning Oran, I therefore give the following description.

Oran is situated about eighty leagues west of Algiers; is a mile and an half in circumference. It lies partly on a plain and partly on the ascent of a hill, and is well fortified. As the Spanish coasts and merchant ships had suffered much from the corsairs of this port, Ferdinand, King of Spain, determined to attempt its reduction. Accordingly he transported into Africa, an army under the command of his prime minister, Cardinal Ximenes. The wonted good fortune of this officer did not, at this juncture desert him. He had maintained a correspondence with some of the people of Oran; and when the Moors sallied out to attack the Spaniards, their perfidious countrymen shut the gates against them. Ximenes killed four thousand of the barbarians, and set at liberty sixteen thousand Christian slaves. The Algerines, during near two hundred years, made frequent but unsuccessful attempts to recover it. In 1708, they retook it. In June, 1732, a Spanish army was landed not far from Oran. The Turkish troops and the inhabitants were seized with a panic, and abandoned their fortifications without any resistance. The Moors not long after attacked it with great fury, but were finally repulsed, with much slaughter. In '91, the Algerines went with a strong force against it, under the command of Alli Bey of Mascara. After a siege of several days, they withdrew their troops, having received much damage. In '92, the Dey of Algiers and the King of Spain having agreed upon terms, very advantageous to the former, Oran was given up to the Algerines, and is still in their possession.

Having given a short account of the common labor of the slaves, their provisions, cloathing, punishments, &c. and a short sketch of the manners and customs of the inhabitants, in the city and country of Algiers. I now proceed to give an account of the most particular circumstances which happened to myself and fellow sufferers during my captivity, and some other circumstances equally entertaining. Nothing of any great moment happened after our arrival, which was on the first of Nov. 1793, until the eleventh, when a courier arrived from Alicant, (sent by Colonel Humphreys, the Ambassador from the United States, for Algiers,) to obtain the Dey's permission for him to come to Algiers, and make a peace. The Dey answered, that "he would not receive him, either to make peace or redeem the American slaves—that he had been soliciting the American government to send an ambassador to make a peace with the Regency for three years before, and they had treated his propositions with neglect—that as he had a truce with the Dutch and Portuguese, and had captured ten sail of American vessels, and had a fair prospect of capturing many more, he would not make a peace with them—that he made the truce with Portugal for the purpose of having the straits open for his vessels to cruize in the Atlantic, for capturing American vessels—that he could not be at peace with all nations at once."

At this dreadful news we despaired of ever tasting the sweets of Liberty again; here we expected to end our days in the most laborious slavery, pregnant with unutterable distress, in whose presence reigns eternal horrors, and meagre famine leads its doleful train; where subjugation adds to the weight of each curst load, and the pain of the vassal is doubled; It spreads a gloom over the sprightly face of nature, and dooms every pleasure to the grave.

On the 29th, a prize arrived, and she proved to be the Minerva of New-York, loaded with Wine, Oil, Fruit, and Marble, Commanded by Joseph Ingraham, from Leghorn, bound to America. She was captured by the Algerines, on the 25th within 7 or 8 miles of Cape St. Sebastian. When the captors arrived they brought the crew of the said brig. Seven more were now added to our number to participate in our distress & partake with us the horrors of unspeakable slavery, & bemoan the loss of the blessing of Liberty, draging out the unwelcome existence of a slave, on Barbary's hostile coast, persecuted by the hands of merciless Mahometans.

On the 23rd of Dec. we were informed by Mr. Skjolderbrand, the Swedish Consul, that we were allowed a valuable supply from the United States. And he had that day received orders, and money, to pay each Capt. belonging to the United States, 8 Spanish Dollars per month, and each mate, 6, and the rest three dollars each.

Our country also furnished us with a sufficient quantity of cloathing, decent and comfortable. This was happy news for us, for from the time of our being captured, to this day, we had been draging out a miserable existence, scarce worth possessing with no kind of subsistence except bread and vinegar, and water to drink.

This generosity of the United States to us their enslaved countrymen was of inestimable value. It was more precious from being unexpected. No nation of christendom had ever done the like for their subjects in our situation.

The Republican government of the United States have set an example of humanity to all the governments of the world.—Our relief was matter of admiration to merciless barbarians. They viewed the caracter of Americans from this time in the most exalted light. They exclaimed, that "Though we were slaves, we were gentlemen;" that "the American people must be the best in the world to be so humane and generous to their countrymen in slavery." The goodness of my country I shall never forget.

Our money would now enable us to purchase some kind of provision, that we might have something to eat at night, when we went to the Bagnio, that gloomy mansion of horror and despair. But these avaricious sons of plunder and rapine, would endeavour to extort this little relief out of our hands, and as they were not allowed to take it by force, they would endeavour to get it by art. For when we were in the Bagnio, and wished to buy any kind of provision, we must pay them for going to buy it, and they would tell us they gave double what they really did give. In this manner they cheated us out of one half our money. This supply was allowed us until the day of our liberation, with the addition of three quarters of a dollar a month, for the seamen, the officers being allowed the same they were at first, with no addition.

About the first of February, 1794, several Americans were attacked with the smallpox. Of this epidemical disease four Americans died in the course of the month, as follows, Samuel Milborne, Richard Wood, John Mott, and Thomas Furnace. A short time after, the city was alarmed with the plague, which carried off many Americans, whom I shall name hereafter.

On the 16th of April, as all hands were at work in the mountain, Joseph Keith, and Peter Barry being very much fatigued, they went to a spring of water about 50 yards distant, and after having drank some water they felt faint, and sat down upon the grass. The Guardian Bachi observing them, sent two task-masters and brought them to him and ordered them 100 bastinadoes each.—This punishment was inflicted for being about 5 minutes absent from their work.—And many instances of this kind I have witnessed. Particularly on the 14th August 1794, when a slave received 300 bastinadoes for no greater offence, than pulling 6 hairs out of a horses tail, which belonged to one of the great men of the Regency.

About the last of April, a Dutch Admiral arrived in the bay, with four sail of the line, and two frigates, and in a few days effected a peace with the Regency. He ransomed all the Dutch captives, which the Algerines had in their possession. It being an old custom among the Algerines, when they make a peace with any christian nation to oblige that nation, to ransom the Dey's Chief servant, and sweeper of the palace, should they be of a different nation from the one ransomed. Accordingly when the Dutch ransomed their captives, they also ransomed one Philip Sloan, an American, who was captured in the year 1785, on board the Ship Dolphin of Philadelphia, Commanded by Richard O'Brien, he being at this time sweeper of the palace.

In the Month of Sept. they captured 201 Corsicans. The manner of capturing them was somewhat singular. The corsicans, when they were under the government of France had licence from the Algerines, to fish for Coral on the coast of Africa, from the bay of Bona, to the Island Galette. And having surrendered the Island of Corsica, to the English, they supposed they still enjoyed the same privelege. Accordingly they equiped about thirty boats for this purpose. They sailed under the convoy of an armed brig. Having been a few days upon the coast, a french frigate captured their convoy and several of the boats. The rest took refuge in the harbour of Bona. The Aleaid or Mayor on their arrival, not knowing their flag, (which is a white field with a Moors head in the centre) confined them all in the Mortimore, or dungeon, secured their boats & sent and informed the Dey of Algiers what he had done, asking his orders concerning them. The Dey commanded them all to be brought to Algiers, and made slaves.

They remained in captivity until the month of March '96. And were then ransomed by the English, at the rate of 1,200 dollars each.

We heard many encouraging stories during our captivity, but none proved to be fact, until the month of July '95, when we were informed that *David Humphreys Esq.* and *Joseph Donaldson jun. Esq.* had arrived at Gibraltar, and that *Mr. Donaldson* was ordered for Algiers, to make a peace, for the United States. This news was confirmed about the 10th of August, when a Spanish courier arrived from Alicant, with a letter from Mr. Donaldson, to the Dey of Algiers for permission to come and effect a peace with the Regency. At this time the Dey being very anxious to have an American Ambassador come, and negociate with him for a peace, and the redemption of the captives, he chartered a Raguscean polacre, and sent her to Alicant, to bring Mr. Donaldson to Algiers.

On Thursday the 3d Sept. '95, the wind being W. b, S. at 9 A.M. saw a sail from the marine, bearing N. b W. standing direct for the harbour. At 11 A.M. could discern that she had a white flag, at her foretop gallant mast head, the American flag at the main top gallant mast head, and the Ragusa flag over her stern.—This being a flag of truce, and denoting the American Ambassador was on board.

Our transports are more easily imagined than described. At 3 P.M. she being within one mile of the mole, the harbour-master went on board with permission from the Dey, for Mr. Donaldson to land when he thought proper. At 4 he landed and was conducted by some of the chief men of the place, to a very elegant house, which the Dey had provided for him, previous to his arrival.

Friday, 4th, being the Mahometan sabbath, he could not do any kind of business with the Dey. The suspence, the hope, fear, and agitation we suffered this day may be conceived but not described. An Ambassador to redeem us had arrived. What would be his success we knew not—a whole day was passing away and nothing done. Never was there a longer, more tedious day in the annals of slavery—Again we must repair to our mansion of misery and in suspense wear out a night of sleepless anxiety.

Saturday, the 5th, about 11 A.M. Mr. Donaldson, was invited to the Dey's presence. Accordingly he went, and about 12 o'clock the American flag was hoisted on board the Ragusean polacre. And the banner of the United States was saluted from the castles of Fenelle and Cordalares, with the thunders of 21 Cannon.

Sounds more ravishing never vibrated in the air; our hearts were joy. We imagined ourselves already freemen. In idea, our chains were falling off and our task-masters no longer at liberty to torture us. In imagination we were already traversing the ocean—hailing our native shore—embracing our parents, our children and our wives. This delirium of joy was of short duration; like a dazzling meteor in a dark night, which blazes for a moment, making succeeding darkness more dreadful; our enchanting hopes left us to despondency, horrible beyond description. In about five hours we were informed that the cup of our sufferings was not drained—that we could not be released till our ransom was paid.

Never was there a more sudden or affecting change in the countenances and conversations of men. Instead of sprightly looks, cheerful congratulations and sanguine anticipations of finished bliss; there was nothing but faces of sadness and the most gloomy silence, interrupted only with sounds of complaint, or sighs of despair. "Not released till our ransom is paid?" How long, said we, may our country neglect us! How many fatalities befall our redemption on its passage! How many disappointments may yet occur! How long may our chains and torments be continued!

After we had done work that evening and come to the Bagnio; myself, Abel Willis and Thomas Billings were sent to the Ambassador's house; he informed us the Dey had granted him three captives as servants to him, and that he was responsible for our good behaviour. We tarried with him and Mr. Barlow, until the day of our liberation.

On Friday the 11th, Captain O'Brien was sent from Algiers, on board a Spanish vessel, with dispatches for Mr. Humphreys at Lisbon. About the middle of March '96, we understood that the Dey had got impatient with the delay of the money, and had ordered Mr. Donaldson to leave the place, and declared that he would send out the corsairs and bring in every American vessel they met with; that he would never make a peace with the United States in his reign. At this we again despaired of ever seeing a christian shore again.

On the 21st of March, a brig appeared in the bay, with the American colours over her stern, and she proved to be the Sally of Philadelphia, commanded by ———— March. She brought as a passenger, Joel Barlow, Esq. Consul General of the United States, for the city and kingdom of Algiers. This worthy gentleman, whose compassionate services for his distressed countrymen, can never be estimated too highly, nor praised too much, gave us all the encouragement he could; assuring us he would never quit Algiers and leave us in slavery, altho' at this time he was not permitted to enter the Dey's palace. While we were in this suspense, we received the following letter from Col. David Humphreys, Esq. who likewise faithfullly did for us all that could be done.

Lisbon, Feb. 16, 1796.

MY DEAR FELLOW CITIZENS.

THE object of this letter is to assure you, that you are neither forgotten or neglected by your country. I have written to his Excellency the Dey, by this conveyance, stating truly the inevitable obstacles which have retarded the completion of our arrangements with the Regency until this period; and which may perhaps still protract the delay for a considerable time to come. I have also written explanatory letters, in a copious manner, on the subject, to Messrs. Barlow (who I hope will soon be in Algiers) Donaldson, Cathcart, &c.

Impossibilities cannot be effected: But whatever is in its nature practicable, will be done in your behalf.

Let me therefore my dear Countrymen, once more (and God grant it may be the last time I may have occasion to do it;) exhort you to be of good courage, to exert all your fortitude, to have a little more patience, to hope always for the best, and to be persuaded that every thing is doing and shall be done, which the nature of the circumstances will admit, for your relief.

In all events, be assured of my persevering efforts in your favour, and of the sincere attachment and regard, with which I shall ever remain,

My dear Countrymen,

Yours, &c.

D. Humphreys.

A few days afterwards, Mr. Barlow got permission to see the Dey, with whom he made new arrangements, and our hopes were again revived.

About the first of April Mr. Donaldson sailed from Algiers destined for Leghorn (as we were informed) to procure the money for our Redemption.

At the time of his departure, the Plague that fatal epidemical disorder, had spread its alarm, in the country adjacent. And which soon made its appearance in the city, and carried off many of my fellow countrymen, when they were expecting every day to be called free men.

On the 9th of July we were informed by a letter from Mr. Barlow that we might expect to be at Liberty within three or four days.

This filled our hearts with joy, and we imagined ourselves the happiest people in world. For a long period we had been suffering the most inhuman slavery; loaded with almost an insupportable weight of chains, and now expecting to enjoy Liberty; the greatest blessing human beings ever possessed. And our expectations at this time were not visionary nor unfounded, as had often been the case with us before. For that worthy gentleman, Mr. Barlow had procured money for our redemption from Mr. Machio Baccri, a Jew belonging to Algiers, which should be paid as soon as it could be counted.

What a joyful night, was this, we passed it with praises to our kind deliverer. And anticipations of ensuing freedom.

On the 10th at day break in the morning the Bagnio-keeper, informed us that all taken under the American flag must stay in the Bagnio, and hold ourselves in readiness to go to the Dey's palace, and receive our (tiscaras) or passports from the Dey, and that we should be embarked the next morning.

On the 11th after the slaves of other nations had gone out to work, we were all called out of the Bagnio, and conducted by the Dey's chief clerk to the palace where we received our pass-ports from the Dey, and at 9 A.M. we all embarked on board a ship which had been captured by the French (formerly English) and condemned at Algiers, and she now being the property of Mr. Baccri, a Jew belonging to that place.

On board of this ship were also forty eight Neapolitans, who had been ransomed three days before us.

On the 12th we received the provisions on board, and got ready for sea.

On the 13th, at 5, A.M. we got under way and stood to sea, at 7, A.M. we found a Neapolitan below, sick with the Plague, we then tack'd and stood into the bay again, and made signals for the harbour master to come on board. He boarded us at 9, and took the sick man on shore, we then tack'd and stood to sea again with a fresh breeze from the eastward, bound to Leghorn.

On the 14th, another Neapolitan was attacked with the plague, and died on the 16th.

On the 15th Captain Samuel E. Bayley was attacked with the plague, and we finding the plague beginning to rage on board the ship, made all possible haste for Marseilles. On the 17th capt. Bayley died, and on the 20th we arrived at Marseilles, and on the 22d, all hands, except twelve who were left on board to take care of the ship, went on shore to the Lazaretto, where we performed a quarantine of Eighty Days, and nothing particular happened, during our residence here.

On the 7th October, we were visited by several Doctors, who finding us all in good health, gave us Praddick, at 10, A.M. we were conducted by a company of the city guards to the house of Stephen Catherlan, jun. esq. Vice Consul of the United States, for the city of Marseilles; he provided lodgings and provisions for us all.

On the 8th, I shipped myself in the capacity of first mate, on board the ship Fortune of Philadelphia, commanded by Michael Smith.

On the 17th November we sailed from Marseilles, bound to Bona, (in the state of Algiers) where we arrived after a passage of twenty days, which brought it to the 7th of December.

On the 21st we began to take on board our cargo, and finished loading on the 15th of January '97, and sailed for Marseilles on the 17th.

On the 24th, being in latt. 37, 26, N. and long. 6, 56, E. was boarded by his Britannic Majesty's ship Pallas, treated politely and permitted to proceed on our voyage.

Feb. 5th, at 6, A.M. Marseilles light house bore N.N.E. about nine leagues distance, wind N.N.W. at 11, A.M. was captured by his Britannic Majesty's ships, Inconstant and Blanche, and ordered to Porto Ferrajo, in the island of Elba, where we arrived on the 15th and were all sent on shore on the 16th, and not allowed to stay on board the prize or frigate, except we would enter in his Britannic Majesty's service, and none being willing to enter; George Tilley was impressed on board the Inconstant; Richard Hales, Matthew Johnson and William Lackey entered on board the Union, a British transport. The rest of us determined not to enter, we procured a passage for Leghorn. Having been robbed of the greatest part of our cloathes, and all our money, by the captors, we found it very difficult to subsist until the vessel was ready to sail.

We sailed for Leghorn on the 23d, and arrived on the 24th, and were kept in quarantine until the 5th of March, on which day capt. Smith arrived from Porto Ferrajo, and sailed for Marseilles on the 10th, with all the rest of the ships crew, but myself and Moses Brown, Brown being sick in the hospital.

On the 20th I sailed from Leghorn in an open boat for Piombino, in the dominions of the king of Naples, to which place Mr. Donaldson went by land. I arrived at Piombino on the 21st, and Mr. Donaldson arrived the 22d; on the 23d we sailed for Porto Ferrajo, and arrived the same evening.

On the 24th, we sailed for Leghorn, and arrived on the 26th.

On the 2d of April I embarked on board the Madona del rafario e fan vincenzo faeraro, of Ragusa, in the capacity of a passenger, bound to Philadelphia, and sailed on the 4th, and on the 11th was captured by a Spanish privateer and carried into Barcelona; was cleared on the 12th and sailed again, and on the 20th was captured by a French privateer and carried into Almeria, treated politely and cleared on the 22d and sailed. On the 29th, the wind having been contrary for several days, we run into Malaga, where we waited for a fair wind until the 21st of May. We then sailed, and on the 22d was boarded by his Britannic Majesty's ship Petterel, treated very well and permitted to proceed on our voyage.

On the 23d at 6 A.M. was boarded by two Spanish privateers, (Gibraltar then bearing W.N.W. 3 leagues distant) and carried into Ceuta, and I having struck one of the privateers men with a sword, and wounded him on the arm; was put into a dungeon, ironed hands and feet. Where I was kept about an hour and a half, and then let out. The vessel was cleared the same evening, and we sailed for Philadelphia.

On the 28th lat. 31, 54 N. long. 17, 25 W, was boarded by a Spanish privateer, and robbed of a quantity of provisions, and the greatest part of our cloathes, and then permitted to proceed. On the 1st July was boarded by his Britannic Majesty's ship Woolwich, treated politely, and permitted to proceed on our voyage. We being very short of provisions, endeavoured to get some from on board the Woolwich, but could not be supplied, she being as short as ourselves.

On the 24th, lat. 38, 20. N. lon. 74, 10, W. spoke [to] the brig Jefferson from St. Croix bound to Philadelphia, from whom we got a supply of provisions, having been about 40 days upon less than one biscuit per day, and nothing else except oil, and wine.

On the 25th at 4 A.M. saw Cape May bearing W. b. N. about 6 leagues distant, at 11 took on board a pilot and stood in for the land, wind N.W. on the 28th arrived at Philadelphia, where I remained (being in an indisposition) until the 11th August.

I then sailed in the quality of a passenger on board the Schooner Jay, belonging to Edgartown, commanded by David Smith, for Boston where we arrived on the 17th.—On the 23d I took passage for Newburyport where I arrived the same evening.

Thus out of 9 persons who left Baltimore on board the Brig Polly, 4 only returned, as follows: Michael Smith, first mate, Benjamin Edwards second Mate, Moses Brown mariner, and myself, the rest all died with the plague.

ADDITIONAL WRITINGS BY FOSS

"The Algerine Slaves; a poem." Newburyport: Angier March, 1798.

"Letter From Algiers." *Salem Gazette,* August 11, 1795.

"A Solemn Call to the Citizens of the United States." Newburyport: Angier March, 1797 [published under the byline "A Citizen of Newburyport"].

The Captives, Eleven Years a Prisoner in Algiers

Eight years before John Foss became a captive, another ship set sail from Boston to Cadiz. On July 25, 1785, after six weeks on the Atlantic, the American schooner *Maria* cruised along the Portuguese coast, three miles southeast of Cape Saint Vincent when a fourteen-gun Algerian xebec captured the American vessel and its crew of six, stowing them in the dank sail locker below deck. Among the miserable captives sat James Leander Cathcart, the future U.S. consul general to the Barbary States. Throughout his eleven years as a captive, Cathcart curried favor with anybody who could help him, and he eventually rose to the highest position a Christian slave could hold—chief Christian secretary to the Algerian dey. Whether by luck, industry, bribery, or willingness to inform on his fellow sufferers, Cathcart knew how to take advantage of his situation, and the story of his financial success as a captive is remarkable.

Official negotiations for all the American prisoners began right away, but without great success. John Lamb, who had been sent by the U.S. and authorized to spend only $200 per captive, promised the dey a price of $50,000, which Lamb knew he could not raise. In fact, when he returned to Europe, he refused to report to Congress and resigned his commission. Time passed slowly for Cathcart although his fortunes rose dramatically. Over the years he progressed from palace gardner to "coffeegie" (coffee brewer), clerk of the marine, clerk of the bagnio galera, and finally to "Chief Clerk of the Dey & Regency of Algiers." Because of his status, Cathcart took an active role in the final treaty that eventually led to his own emancipation. Although Joseph Donaldson, Jr., had successfully concluded his treaty negotiations already in September 1795, the dey had not received his money by the follow-

Fig. 11. James Leander Cathcart, U.S. captive in
Algiers. (Courtesy Minneapolis Public Library)

ing May and finally sent Cathcart back to Philadelphia to deliver the articles
of peace and to urge prompt payment. Because of his financial acumen,
Cathcart was able to return to the United States in a ship he had purchased
with the profits he made while in Algiers.

Cathcart's narrative didn't appear until long after his death. His daughter,
J. B. Newkirk, compiled the original journals in 1899. Like Gee's narrative,
Cathcart's had little if any effect on his contemporaries, although throughout
the U.S.-Barbary wars, he frequently exchanged correspondence with the
highest government officials, including the president. Much of this correspondence was collected by Ms. Newkirk in a second volume entitled *Tripoli.*

The Captives, Eleven Years a Prisoner in Algiers. Compiled by J. B. Newkirk. La Porte, IN: Herald Print, 1899.

Chapter I

POLITICAL STATE OF ALGIERS IN 1785

THE PIRATICAL STATES OF BARBARY, especially Algiers, having for a succession of years withstood the attacks of Spain and several of the smaller Christian powers, bordering on the north side of the Mediterranean, coadjuted by a small squadron from Portugal, and, having compelled a number of their armaments to retire from the object of this enterprise, and their chiefs to abandon their hopes of possessing themselves of that city, among which, since the grand expedition by the Emperor Charles the V, in 1541, those under the command of Don Pedro Castigon and Gen. O'Riley in 1775 and Don Antonio Barcelo in 1784 were the most formidable, now resolved to accept a valuable consideration from that Monarchy as the price of peace, and thereby liberate themselves from the annual apprehension of bombardment as well as to obtain a larger field for committing depredations on the commerce of other nations. The preliminaries, or, rather, the foundations, upon which a peace between those nations might be established, were adjusted in 1777 and 1778 by Ciddi Hassan Vikilharche, of the marine of Algiers, during his detention at Carthagena, and would have been carried into effect long ere this, had not the war in which Spain was afterward involved with Great Britain rendered the measure unnecessary, and the Dey of Algiers partiality for that nation, even after peace took place in 1783, rendered it improvident for Spain to solicit a peace on his own terms. Accordingly a small armament was sent to bombard Algiers in 1784 in order to prove that Spain had sufficient force to impede the depredations of the Cruisers of Algiers, which had no other effect than to render the wished for accommodation more popular among the soldiery and inhabitants of that city, and to give the Dey and Divan of Algiers an opportunity to persuade them that it was entirely on their account, that he wished for peace with a nation that had for so many years been their implacable enemy.

There was one small obstacle remaining to be removed on the part of his Catholic Majesty, this was a clause in the Coronation oath which prohibits that Monarch from concluding peace with the Infidels; but, as a truce only implies a cessation of arms for a certain time, that impediment was easily gotten over by concluding a truce for a century, for which was paid to the treasury, one million dollars, and about as much to the Dey and grandees of the Regency among whom Ciddi Hassan was most liberally rewarded for his friendly interposition and ever afterwards made it a pretext for extorting valuable presents from the Court of Spain.

At this period Algiers was at peace with Great Britain, France, Spain, Holland, Denmark, Sweden, Venice, and the little Republic of Ragusa. With the Empires of Russia and Germany the Dey was upon indifferent terms and waited for information from the Sublime Porte before he took his position with those powers and consequently had not captured any of their vessels. With Portugal, Prussia, Naples, the Italian States, the Hanstowns and all the rest of the world that did not pay him tribute he was at war. Great Britain, by her superiority at sea and in consequence of her garrisons in the Mediterranean, during the war which concluded in acknowled[g]ing the independence of the United States, was both feared and respected by the Divan of Algiers, exclusive of the Dey's partiality to that nation, but from the death of Mr. Benton, late British Consul who had died at Algiers, none had been appointed until the arrival of Charles Logie, Esq., a very short time before peace was concluded between Algiers and Spain, consequently the Dey was ignorant of the differences which had existed between her and her ci-devant colonies; as it was by no means incumbent on the Agents of France or Holland to give him information either of those differences or the result of the war before they received instructions from their respective Courts, which, had circumstances permitted, would have prevented, in a great measure, the many disagreeable events which have since happened. It would be as impolitic as disagreeable to revive the remembrance of transactions dictated by the exigencies of the times, and which the interests of both nations would induce us to consign to oblivion; but a faithful narrator ought to write things as they really were, or not at all. I therefore will not interrupt the thread of my narration by any evasion of truth, but am sincerely inclined to believe, that many of the facts which will be herein mentioned, were owing more to individual inveteracy than national animosity.

Consul Logie, who arrived at Algiers too late to impede the progress of the negotiations between that Regency and Spain, whether to ingratiate himself with his own government or that of Algiers, is immaterial and hard to determine, immediately gave the Executive of Algiers a circumstantial detail of the motives of the late war and the results, declaring that the United States were no longer under the protection of his Master, and, that wherever the Cruisers of Algiers should fall in with the vessels of the United States of America, they were good prizes and wished them success in their attempts to capture those who refused allegiance to his Master. The Cruisers of Algiers were fitted out with all expedition and sailed on the 30th of June, bound direct to the Atlantic ocean, where they had not cruised for a number of years before. Their aim was the capture of some rich Portuguese-Brazil ships which were expected at Lisbon about this time and did not suppose they would meet with any Americans, whom Consul Logie had represented to be a set of beings without strength or resources, and so contemptible, that his Master did not think us worth the trouble or expense of subduing.

The Cruisers proceeded to cruise on the coast of Portugal but were disappointed in their expectations of capturing the ships from Brazil but took several others, Portuguese, Genoese and two Americans. The Maria of Boston on which I had embarked was captured three miles southeast of Cape St. Vincent (southeast point of Portugal) on the 25th of July, 1785, and arrived at Algiers on the 4th of August following, and the Dauphin of Philadelphia was captured 70 leagues to the westward of the Rock of Lisbon on the 30th of said month, and arrived at Algiers on the 12th of August, being captured by the Admiral's ship, and the Maria by a Xebec of fourteen guns. On being boarded the Mahometans asked us for our flag and papers. Of the first they had no knowledge and the papers they could not read and Mediterranean pass we had none; consequently, they conceived us to be a good prize but my feelings were very different from the rest of my fellow sufferers. I understood the Spanish language which they all spoke and was the only person on board who had any knowledge of the Barbary States. I knew that a few months before Spain was at war with the eastern states and prevented their Cruisers from coming into the western ocean and, not having spoken [to] any vessel at sea to inform us of that event, I conjectured that this boat must belong to some pirate from that part of Morocco, which was then at war with the Emperor, and that they concluded that the "Kingdom of Heaven" was at hand. They were twenty-one in number and we were only six, which precluded the possibility of overpowering them had we been so imprudent as to have made an attempt. In this state of mind I remained more than two hours before we joined the Xebec, there being very little wind, and the first salutation we received was a shout from the whole crew of the Cruiser indicative of our being a good prize. We were then driven into the boat without being permitted to go into the cabin and taken on board the Cruiser and conducted to the quarter deck, every person having a pull at us as we went along, in order to benefit by our capture. Our hats, handkerchiefs and shoes were the first articles that were taken from us and which we most wanted as we could not endure the scorching heat of the sun on our heads nor were our feet calculated to bear the heat of the deck. We were welcomed on board by the Rais or Captain, a venerable old Arab, who had been a captive for several years, both in Spain and Genoa, and who was really a good man. "Christians," said he, "be consoled, this world is full of vicissitudes. You shall be well used, I have been a slave myself, and will treat you much better than I was treated; take some bread and honey and a dish of coffee and God will redeem you from captivity as he has done me twice, and, when you make your peace with your father, the King of England, the Dey of Algiers will liberate you immediately." He informed me that they were a Cruiser of Algiers, that they had come through the Straits in consequence of their having concluded a peace with Spain and of the arrival of a British Consul, (Charles Logie), who informed them that they might take all such vessels that had not passports of a particular cut. They had taken several Portuguese fishermen, and two pretty large vessels, the crews of the whole amounting to thirty-six men, and one woman, a Spaniard by birth, a facetious creature, who seemed perfectly reconciled to her situation, and endeavored to reconcile every one to theirs. I had entered into a conversation with her and began to thank God that our situation was no worse, when a sail was descried from the mast head and we were all ordered down to the sail room, except the woman. It is impossible to describe the horror of our situation while we remained there. Let imagination conceive what must have been the sufferings of forty-two men, shut up in a dark room in the hold of a Barbary Cruiser full of men and filthy in extreme, destitute of every nourishment, and nearly suffocated with heat, yet here we were obliged to remain every night until our arrival at Algiers and wherever we were either chased or in chase. The vessel proved to be a friend and was liberated immediately, the prize master and crew taking the Captain's quadrant perspective glass, charts and some wearing apparel, to indemnify themselves for the trouble of examining their papers and we were permitted to come upon deck and were regaled with some very bad black olives, mixed with a small quantity of rank oil, and some vinegar to which was added some very coarse bread and water, which was corrupted, and which we were, literally, obliged to strain through our teeth, and, while we drink, to stop our noses. This was all our allowance except twice they served us burgul, which we could not eat, notwithstanding the calls of nature were very great, and we must [i]nevitably have perished, had it not been for some Turks, who were more charitable than the rest who gave us some onions, oranges, raisins and figs from their own private stores. I likewise received relief several times for standing at the helm for the sailors, and actually learned to smoke, by the kindness of the ship's steward, who gave me a pipe and tobacco, and whom I lived to repay, at Algiers more than two years after. Whether the Algerian Cruisers were apprehensive that Portugal would fit out a squadron to cruise against them or were content with the booty they already had made, I know not, but fortunately for us they made but a short cruise and returned into the Mediterranean the first westerly wind after our capture. Had they remained thirty days longer in the western ocean they would undoubtedly have captured as many American vessels as they could have manned and, probably, several rich Portuguese.

We arrived at Algiers on the eve of the feast that follows Ramadan and being private property were conducted to the owner of the Cruiser's house, having been first entirely stripped of the remnant of our clothes which remained, and I was furnished in lieu thereof with the remains of an old dirty shirt, and brown cloth trousers which formerly belonged to a Portuguese fisherman, and were swarming with myriads of vermin, which, with the crown of an old hat, composed the whole of my wardrobe. The rest of my brother sufferers were in no better condition. We were first carried to the Kieuchk or Admiralty office and were permitted to regale ourselves with as much good water as we pleased, which flowed from a neat marble fountain and was as clear as crystal. My desire was so great to partake of this refreshment, that I really believe that I should have expired had I been refused this gratification. Those who have been on long voyages know how to appreciate this greatest of luxuries, and how grateful it must have been to people in our situation. It has made so permanent an impression on my mind that I shall remember the Fountain of the Kiosk of the Marine of Algiers, to the latest hour of my existence.

We were marched from the Kieuchk through the principal streets and market place of Algiers and to several of the Grandee's [*sic*] houses followed by the mob who had gathered to view Americans, we being the first they had ever beheld, and, at last, arrived at our owner's house, having received no refreshment but water since the evening before. Here we remained but a few minutes, when we were visited by Christian slaves of all denominations, they not being at work in consequence of the festival, and those, who could afford it brought us the fruits of the season, wine, bread, and everything that was cooked, or could be eaten without cooking. At our owner's house we were all put into an empty room, on the ground floor, where we all sat or laid on the bare bricks. In the centre of the area was placed a large cauldron in which clothes had lately been boiled, filled with water, and a quantity of coarse flesh, which we supposed to be ordinary beef, but afterwards was informed was camel's flesh, which prevented us from tasting it. This enraged our Master considerably and he declared he never would put himself to so much expense again to accommodate Christian slaves. To this again was added a quantity of burgul and some grease which was extremely rank and then served up in wooden platters, which with a quantity of black bread composed the whole of our nourishment until that time the next day; as the Mahometans, of his rank, seldom eat themselves or feed their slaves above once a day and that is after sunset.

Thus forlorn, without food or raiment, anticipating the horrors of a miserable captivity, we stretched ourselves on the bare bricks where we remained all night, tormented with vermin and mosquitos, and at daylight, were driven down to the marine to unbend the sails and do other necessary work on the Cruisers that had captured us. Here we received some biscuit and olives such as was given us at sea, and plenty of good water, and in the evening we were marched back to our Master's house and passed the night in the same manner we had done the one before, with the exception that we got, in lieu of camel's flesh, some boiled mumsa, vegetables and fruits with which, with some wine and provisions given by Christian slaves, we made out tolerably well, but still our fate was not decided and we did not know whether we would be placed at the oar in the galleys or sold to the Arabs in the interior of the Regency. Although our fears proved groundless, they prevented us from enjoying the least repose for, when we slumbered, our imagination painted the horrors of our situation in such lively colors, that we started from the arms of Morpheus very little refreshed.

The next day we were taken, in a kind of procession, to several of the Grandee's [*sic*] houses whom we had not visited on our arrival and who were curious to see Americans, having supposed us to be the aborigines of the country, of which, some of them had an imperfect idea from viewing figures which ornament charts of that continent, and were much surprised to see us so fair or, as they expressed themselves, so much like Englishmen. Ultimately we were taken to the British Consul's house who had ordered us some refreshments and passed his word to our Master that he would be answerable for our conduct while in his house, but advised him to leave a person to prevent us from strolling about the streets. But even here we were made sensible of our situation and exposed to new species of indignities which we did not expect and therefore felt in a superlative degree.

We remained here two days and on the third, in the morning, were marched to the Bedistan or Slave Market where we remained from daylight till half past three o'clock without any refreshments, and were treated thus for three days successively, the first and second nights being lodged in our Master's house, and having no better accommodations than we had the first day of our arrival. On the afternoon of the third we were taken into the Dey's palace and paraded before his Excellency when, of our crew, he took five, only leaving Capt. Stephens, and, of the Portuguese, eight, for the service of the palace, and the others sent to the Slave prison as the Regency purchased them all except four or five old men, who had been sold at vendue, and the woman, who, immediately on her arrival, had been sent to the Spanish hospital, there to remain until ransomed, was likewise purchased by the Regency. We were now taken to the hot bath by the other Christian slaves and cleansed from the filth of the Cruiser, our old rags were changed for a large shirt with open sleeves and a large pair of cotton trousers, a pair of shoes and red cap, all made in Turkish fashion, in which no doubt, we made a curious appearance. We were allowed to remain together that night and fared sumpt[u]ously in comparison to what we had some time before, and, being clean, slept for several hours as sound as any people could do in our situation. In the morning we awakened much refreshed, and were stationed at our respective duties; two were retained as upper servants, one was sent to the kitchen and myself and another were doomed to labor in the palace garden, where we had not a great deal to do, there being fourteen of us, and, the taking care of two lions, two tigers and two antelopes excepted, the work might have very well been done by four.

Here I had sufficient time to bewail my unfortunate situation, but was ignorant of its full extent. Had I known the different vicissitudes I was to experience, and the length of my captivity, I should have sunk beneath the weight of such accumulated woe. But hope, that sweet soother of all earthly cares, represented that our situation was really not so bad as we had expected, and that we had not been used worse than many of our fellow citizens had been during the Revolutionary war in the different British prisons; and, being confident that our country would immediately redeem us, I resolved to bear my captivity with as good a grace as possible and not give the Mahometans the satisfaction of seeing me dejected, but alas! I had seen the best part only, I had as yet experienced but few of the bitters of slavery in comparison to what I afterwards suffered.

As I have promised to give a detail of the treatment that Christian slaves receive in Barbary, and as I have experienced a great variety of scenes myself, I will give the particulars as they occur and will likewise take the liberty of making as many digressions as I deem necessary to facilitate my plan for which I most humbly beg the rigid critic's indulgence.

Chapter II

Economy of the Dey's palace will describe the situation of slaves in all the Grandees and rich peoples' [*sic*] houses in the Regency of Algiers, making allowance for the caprices of Masters, some being better and some worse, as in other countries. The Dey's palace is governed by two Hasnadars or Chamberlains and two chief cooks, the latter always eat with the Dey, no other person having any interference with the internal regulations of the Dey's household. The two chief cooks on my arrival at Algiers had thirty-three Christians of different denominations, under their command, besides a number of Moors for doing the out door work, the Christians only being permitted to go out twice a year, on the second day of their two chief festivals. Those Christians are employed in the different offices of the kitchen and magazines of provisions in the palace. The chief cooks only superintend the whole. The two Chamberlains, of which the celebrated Ciddi Aly, afterwards Bashaw of Tripoli, was the chief, had the same number of Christian slaves under their jurisdiction. They were divided as follows:

In the Dey's apartments, which are higher than the rest, the Capo di Golfa, (who is the head slave in the Regency, the Dey's chief Christian clerk excepted), and four others. These are the Dey's body guards and do nothing else whatever. In the first gallery, or Chamberlain's apartment, fourteen, whose duty it is to keep that part of the house clean, take the dishes of meat for the Dey's and Chamberlain's tables from the kitchen, and in general whatever they were ordered to do, either by the Dey or Chamberlain, no other person interfering with them. Of this class the two coffee servers, whose duty it is to serve the Day and Grandees with coffee of which mention will be made hereafter. As those are maintained from the Dey's table, they live in general much better than they would in their own country, the use of wine excepted, as no inebriating liquor is permitted to be used in the palace on pain of a severe bastonading and being turned to hard labor in chains, nor is tobacco to be used, when the Dey does not use it himself, which was the case while I remained there. Not so in the garden. Here we had nothing allowed us but a small plate of meat and another of rice mumsa or burgul, and a basin of sour milk twice a day, which was hardly sufficient for four of us, with some oil and vinegar now and then and black bread, such as is given to the slaves at the Marine, and in the fruit season some musk and watermelons. The fruit of the garden was prohibited and kept for the Dey's own use and I have actually known several of my brother sufferers bastonaded for having been detected eating an orange or a small bunch of grapes. Those, who had friends in the kitchen or upper apartments, sometimes would get small supplies, but notwithstanding we were often seduced to making a kind of salad from the vine leaves to stay our craving appetites, and not unfrequently have committed depredations on the Dey's pigeon house, at the risk of breaking our necks, exclusive of a severe bastonading if detected. We were under the jurisdiction of the Chamberlains and were often used by them in the most petulant, humiliating and cruel manner, of which more in the sequel. There were likewise two Christians called "captains a proa" whose duty it was to keep the lower part of the palace clean, to light the Dey down stairs in the morning, as he always takes his seat at the break of day, to remove the soldiers' beds who sleep at the doors of the treasury and whatever the Prime Minister and store-keepers of the palace should order them, under whose jurisdiction they are all day, but at night they are classed with the cooks, as neither the Prime Minister or store-keepers sleep in the palace. Besides the Christians already mentioned there are a number of blacksmiths who work in the palace but sleep at the prison, and several mulateers to take away the filth of the palace which is considerable, as all the meat that is killed for the use of the palace is kept and slaughtered within the gates, and often have I seen the butcher cut a sheep's throat already dead and set it apart for the Christians in the garden and the blacksmiths; besides the Dey's horses are also kept in the palace with a number of mules and asses for labor, which creates a great deal of dirt which is carried out of the gates of town and heaped up for manure which is sold by the head scavenger as one of his perquisites. Thus are employed sixty-eight Christians, and the numbers that are employed in the great men's houses are treated nearly in the same manner, and those in the gardens not near so well.

On the 12th of August arrived the Cruiser that captured the Dauphin with her crew on board, being fifteen in number they had been used nearly in the same manner that we had, but being public property were brought from the Cruiser direct to the palace where they remained all night. It was a consolation to find us here as we informed them of many particulars very pleasing to people in their situation, especially, that there were no galleys in Algiers and that they would not be made to wear chains any longer than the ships of war of England and France were in the bay unless they committed crimes to deserve them; that the officers would be sent to work in the sail loft and the seamen in the Marine, this was so much better treatment than they expected that they began to reconcile themselves to their situation, and, as the clothes which they had on were not taken from them in consequence of their having an old English Mediterranean passport; when washed and cleaned they made a much better figure than we did. When paraded before the Dey the next morning his Excellency chose several of them for the palace and the rest were sent to the Slave prison, which I shall describe when I become an inhabitant of it myself. Captain O'Brien, Stephens and Coffin, the latter was a passenger on board the Dauphin, were immediately taken to the British Consul's house to serve as domestics where they remained suffering every indignity that inhumanity could devise to render their situation humiliating in the extreme, until the arrival of the Count de Expilly who by the orders of Mr. Carmichael, Charge des Affairs at Madrid, took them under his protection, and hired a small house where they lived very comfortably for sometime upon the supplies furnished them by Mr.

Carmichael and their friends in the palace. The Mates were likewise taken out of the Marine and placed with the Captains, but the Marines were left at hard labor and were only allowed three masoons a day to clothe and maintain them which is equal to 7½ cents.

I shall now return to the palace. The slaves in the upper apartments received two suits of elegant clothes trimmed with gold, those in the palace garden had the same quality of clothing with less gold, and the cooks were supplied with clothing somewhat inferior, trimmed with silk, those that are sent to the Marine to hard labor receive one suit of clothes which is seldom worth more than one dollar and a half, and each slave receives two coarse blankets which is supposed to last them the whole of their captivity; the slaves in the palace never receive anything else from the Dey, but those who work at hard labor are allowed a suit of clothes every year of the same value as is given them on their arrival, but no blankets. From what has been said of the slaves in the palace, the reader will be apt to believe that their situation is at least supportable, but humiliations he undergoes verily make a person of any sensibility even more miserable than he would be at hard labor, as he has more time to reflect on the rigor of his fate. I shall enumerate a few of the acts of injustice which I either suffered myself or saw others suffer, while I remained in the palace and which every slave is subject to in so great a degree, that a Genoese on his redemption, kissing the hand of Mahomed Bashaw, Dey of Algiers, inadvertently said, "thank God I have been your servant ten years and never received the bastinado once." "Did you not," said the Dey? "Take this Christian and give him one hundred blows on the soles of his feet, that he may not have so great a miracle to tell his countrymen when he returns to his home." The poor man, thunder struck, exclaimed "I am free! surely your Excellency will not punish me for not having committed a fault in ten years' captivity?" "Give him two hundred blows," replied the Dey, "and if the Infidel says a word more, send him to the works again and inform the person, that has redeemed him, that he may have anyone of the same nation in his room. I will keep him till he dies, for his insolence." The poor man received the punishment, immediately went to the hospital to be cured, and embarked as soon as possible with no very favorable opinion of the Dey's justice and clemency, notwithstanding, he was supposed to be the least of a tyrant of any Dey that ever reigned in Algiers. It is written of Hassan Bashaw that he was always in dread of assassination. I will here mention that Hassan Bashaw succeeded the present Dey, Mahomed Bashaw at his death, in 1791. Once, when one of his attendants was assisting Hassan Bashaw to change his linen, the shirt which he put over his head had not been altered since it came from the Levant, consequently had no place open to put his head through. The Dey's head was in a sack and he, supposing they were going to assassinate him, caught his attagan (sword) and flew at the youth, who being more nimble than the Dey, got out of his reach and his attendants did the same until he grew calm and put up his sword in its place, being convinced that he was in no danger of losing his life and that he was thus encased by the ignorance of the American. Another time, one of his attendants, who frequently walked in his sleep, one night, in his perambulations, frightened the Dey exceedingly. He called aloud for his servants, who awakened the youth, and the blame was thrown on the cats, of which the palace was full. A few nights after the same person dreading the consequence of being met by the Dey in his night walks, agreed with one of his comrades to tie their legs together. At a dead hour of the night the Dey was alarmed by something and called his attendants with great vociferation, the youths, forgetting that they were tied, sprang forward to receive the Dey's orders and overturned one of their comrades against the door of the Dey's apartment, which flew open with a great noise. The Dey thought he was surprised and drew his sword and would certainly have put them to death, had not the darkness of the room prevented his seeing them. This gave an opportunity for them to escape the first impulse of the Dey's wrath and, having tumbled headlong down stairs to loosen themselves, while another was procuring a light, the cause of the disturbance was explained, which pacified him for the present, but the next day they were both punished with bastinado. Thus was the lives of those unfortunate youths rendered extremely miserable. Every moment they were menaced with bastinadoes, hard labor, chains and death, and, when we consider that the Dey has the power of putting his menaces into execution with as much ease as he has to do any act, no matter how frivolous, we will readily conceive that their situation was by no means enviable, their fine clothes, money and good living not excepted. The Christian slaves in the upper galleries are subject to the same indignities from the Hasnadars, (ie) Chamberlains that those above suffer from the Dey and are often bastinadoed for mere trifles, such as speaking loud, procrastinating any part of the service assigned them, being found out of their rooms after a certain hour, or speaking to any of the cooks or the Christians in the garden, and on a thousand other pretenses. I have heard those illiberal minded Renegades commence an absurd argument with some of the slaves and on being confuted beat their opponents most unmercifully, and tell them they would teach them better manners than to dare to contradict them when they condescended to converse with them. The cooks have harder labor and less money than the other slaves, but have more liberty and, when the chief cook is a good man, which was the case while I remained in the palace, their situations were by far the most tolerable.

The first two months I was stationed in the palace garden nothing very particular happened. We watched the wild beasts in rotation and performed the other duties assigned us without murmuring and were generally or individually abused by the Chamberlains once or twice a day when they came to wash in order to purify themselves before they said their prayers, and very often some were bastinadoed from mere caprice. As I understood the French and Spanish languages sufficiently to read their authors, I employed myself in reading such books as I could borrow from the other slaves and writing, or teaching some of my companions practical navigation; this procured me the title of the false priest, the moshabbe, and many other names of a similar nature from the Chamberlains, and as the lower class, to ingratiate themselves with their superiors, generally imitate them, these appellations proved a great source of disquiet and involved me in continual disputes both with the Chamberlains and Christians, and as I always refuted their arguments, it ultimately procured me many enemies among whom was Ciddi Aly the Chief Chamberlain, who uniformally persecuted me through the rest of my captivity until he was ultimately expelled from the Regency by Hassan Bashaw. A little more than two months after my admission into the Dey's garden, the slaves were permitted to go out into the town in consequence of the great festival of which the first and last day is celebrated in the palace with feasting, music, wrestling, and fireworks of very poor construction, before the palace gate. In the morning on the first day the banner of Mahomet is hoisted on the palace and the national flag on the fortifications, the cannon of the fortifications are fired, those next the sea with ball. When the wrestling is ended, the officers of the Regency and inhabitants kiss the Dey's hand while seated on his throne, having the Hasnagi Agas at Hodga Beitelmel and Vikilharche of the Marine standing on his left hand, and the Chauxes and other inferior officers behind them. After the Mussulmen have all performed this act of humiliation and respect, not even excepting the hangman and scavengers, the Consuls have that *honor* conferred on them, next to them the head clerk and then the chief of the Jew brokers of the palace and their dependents. The Dey then invited the five Grandees to dine with him in his apartments, they are joined chief cook, and after dinner they retire to their respective houses and the Dey generally goes to visit his lady if he is married, if not he retires to sleep.

The second day is a day of recreation for the slaves, and third is celebrated in the same manner as the first except the firing of the cannon and visits from the Consuls. The British and French Consuls sensible of the indignity they would suffer by waiting on the Dey the first day of the festival always wait on him the day before, neither do they kiss his hand. On the second day of the festival the slaves are permitted to visit their friends and to absent themselves from six or seven in the morning until one in the afternoon, but are generally excused if they return by three, some few in particular employment excepted. By special grace we were permitted to visit our countrymen at the British Consul's garden which was about three miles from the city, and there, to our surprise, we found Captain O'Brien with a hoe digging a hole to plant a tree in the Consul's garden; Stephens, with the capote given him by the Regency tied round his middle with a straw rope, driving a mule loaded with manure for the root of the tree, and Coffin, who was consumptive, feeding the hogs and poultry. We could not refrain from tears at viewing their humiliating situation which affected us the more as they suffered this indignity from a person, (the British Consul), who ranked among Christians and gentlemen, was of the same religion and spoke the same language, and from whom a more humane treatment might naturally have been expected. We stayed but a short time, shared the money that had been given to us in the palace among them and returned to town, visited the poor fellows in the prison, borrowed some money from our comrades to give them and returned to the palace with a heavy heart, in order to be immured for ten months, where I remained without once being permitted to go out and was then sent to the Marine in consequence of some young Hollanders being captured on board a Russian prize. I had not been long in this garden before the persecutions of the Chamberlain became intolerable. I was prevented from reading or writing except by stealth and likewise forbidden to speak to any of my countrymen, who were stationed in other parts of the palace. This was occasioned by my frequently retorting on them their insolence and barbarity, and in consequence of my observing in conversation that those, who were base enough to renegade the faith of their forefathers, generally became the most bitter enemies of those who continue faithful, in order to induce the secretaries [*sic*], whose tenets they embrace, to believe that they were really converted and had renounced their former opinions or convictions, that they were really erroneous and thus made up for their ignorance by hypocricy and a pretended zeal for what they did not understand. This was reported to Ciddi Aly and Ciddi Mahomed (who were both renegades from the Greek church) probably with additions and afterwards they continued my most inveterate enemies. These deprivations (being prevented from reading and writing) I felt most sensibly and have nothing now to divert my mental faculties[.] I really became a victim to melancholy reflections, my spirits were so much depressed that I fainted several times in a day and, ultimately, was obliged to keep my bed. This was construed by the Chamberlain as a pretense in order to be sent to the hospital to divert myself. The Spanish surgeon petitioned for me without effect; however, he rendered me assistance and with the help of a good constitution I soon recovered. During my illness the Portuguese and Spaniards were continually persuading me to change my religion, to confess immediately to restore myself to the bosom of the Holy Mother church. One old man, who had been nineteen years in the garden, and who had experienced better days, seemed particularly interested for my soul. He very charitably offered to take all my sins upon himself, and to guarantee my full absolution both in this world and the next and then laconically asserted that if I died in the state of heretical reprobation that I was now in, he would pawn his own salvation that I would be d——d to all eternity. So intent were these poor slaves on my conversion that I really believe, had I proposed to change my faith by subscription, that I would have raised a sum sufficient for my redemption. I had been about four months in captivity when one evening I heard a noise in another part of the garden. Induced by curiosity to know the cause, I went to where the sound proceeded from and found to my no small astonishment the two Chamberlains, diverting themselves, beating with two sticks on the soles of the feet of a Portuguese who roared most tremendously. I asked his crime but received no answer before I was seized by four stout Moors who threw me down, pinioned my legs and arms and the same game was played on the soles of my feet to the tune of twenty-eight hard blows, which produced the most excruciating pain and left me with four toe nails less than I had before this game commenced. All the fourteen were served in the same manner, none were pardoned for age or infirmity, but old men of sixty and children of ten years of age received the bastinado without ever knowing what it was for. After some days had elapsed, we found that we were indebted to the head gardener, a native of Malta, for this refreshment. It seems he had complained that he could not keep us in subjection, that we made use of the fruit which was intended for the Dey, and several frivolous charges, but, as he could not particularize the offenders, the Chamberlains concluded that by chastising the whole, they would undoubtedly find those who had offended. As for the innocent suffering unjustly that was a trifle of such little moment that it either entirely passed their notice or was deemed unworthy of attention. Twice more was I bastinadoed while I remained in the palace, once for writing and the last time for speaking to some of the Americans who belonged to the upper apartments. In the last were involved seven or eight. My comrade was included who was a simple, ignorant lad who was so much terrified that it had a sensible effect on his mind and I am sure it was the first step which caused him to lose his reason, of which more will be said hereafter. I could never have endured the anxiety and degradation under which I labored for any length of time had I not placed the greatest confidence in the generosity of my country. I thought it impossible that a nation just emerged from slavery herself would abandon the men who had fought for her independence to an ignominious captivity in Barbary, when they could be immediately redeemed for less than $50,000. I was not ignorant of the embarrassments that our government labored under before the adoption of the present Constitution, yet the sound policy of redeeming their citizens immediately appeared so evident that I was confirmed in my hopes, and, although I knew the treasury at that period was very poor, I was so sanguine as to believe that the sum would be loaned immediately to the government by individuals, or that our fellow citizens would have raised it by subscription, but I reckoned "without my host," as I lived more than ten years after this in captivity, experiencing every indignity that Barbarians could invent to render the life of a Christian miserable in the extreme, and I hesitate not to assert that no class of men suffered in any degree so much by the consequences attending the American Revolution as those who were captured by the Algerines in 1785.

The infirmities of age prevented Mahomed Bashaw from visiting the different apartments of the palace so often as formerly. He now only came to the bath in the garden once a month and always before daylight. The Chamberlains, being thus delivered from the apprehension of complaints being lodged against them by the slaves, gave loose to their tyranny and never came to the garden without a stick in their hands and never failed to use it on some of the unhappy captives, and, frequently, I became the victim of their rage. To divert themselves they had two small brass cannon with which they fired at marks, but if they missed they never failed to vent their spleen on the bystanders. To complete my sufferings Ciddi Mahomed had a great propensity to study alchemy and pitched upon me for his assistant, he asked me my opinion of the science. I treated it with ridicule. Sometimes I told him the Emperor Caligula was the first who prepared natural arsenic in order to make gold of it, and left it off in time, as many others would be obliged to do, if they did not wish to ruin themselves as they found the expenses exceeded the profits considerably, and many stories of a similar tendency, but these observations had no effect upon this infatuated man. He still persevered and every crucible of metal procured me the most opprobrious language; at length he took it into his head that I knew something of the art, and relaxed the rigor of his treatment, and descended to mean adulation in order to induce me to divulge all the secrets of the art with which he supposed I was acquainted. With a little address I might have converted this alchymist from being my inveterate enemy to be my temporary friend at the small price of my conscience, but the truth is I dispised him and my vanity would not permit me to temporize with a person of his character who daily had taken advantage of my situation, and treated me so inhumanely merely because he could do it with impunity. Ciddi Aly likewise ridiculed the idea of making the philosopher's stone, and one day came into the garden and being in a good humor exclaimed, "What the devil is the false priest likewise a gold maker? If the Bashaw knows this he will not let him be redeemed until he turns every cassarole in the palace into pure gold." I said nothing is farther from me my lord, than to have any pretention to the knowledge of so sublime an art. I have read that it has been said in times of ignorance, that the Arabians were supposed to have invented this mysterious art, wherein they were followed by Raymond, Lullius, Paracelsus and others of different nations who never found anything but ashes in their furnaces and repentance in their hearts. So many have been ruined by this infatuating science that it is now entirely neglected and the authors who treated on that subject ridiculed as it is well known that the quadrature of the circle, perpetual motion, inextinguishable lamp and philosopher's stone have engaged the attention of philosophers and mathematicians from time immemorial without any effect, and with all just deference to Ciddi Mahomed's superior judgment is it reasonable for him to expect to succeed with the small assistance he receives from a few leaves of an old Arabic author, two or three crucibles and a small portable furnace, when so many who have made this art their study for their whole lives and had every convenience that a large fortune could provide, have ultimately failed and ended their pursuits in ruin? "Yes," answered Ciddi Aly laughing, "But they did not possess the charms that Ciddi Mahomed knows." That is possible my lord, but permit me to observe that it would be as easy to charm me into a good Mussulman as to convert that metal in the crucible to pure gold. "Ah! thou false priest, though hardened Infidel! I know that to be impossible, you are destined to take up your eternal residence in the mansions of the d——d." With this he gave a kick to the crucible and walked away with Ciddi Aly who laughed very heartily and Ciddi Mahomed muttered something in the Turkish language which I did not understand. During the time I remained in the palace no mention was made of the philosopher's stone, nor was I used any worse than my fellow prisoners, but in all reason that was bad enough to satisfy the malevolence of a disappointed Greek alchemist, or even the persecuting spirit of the inquisition.

The period now approached that was to put an end to my sufferings in the palace, and to give birth to a new species of indignity. Two large vessels, the one a Russian and the other a Leghornese, were captured by the Cruisers of Algiers, on board of which were several handsome youths who were taken into the palace, and eight of the oldest and ugliest were sent into the Slave prison called the Bagnio Belique in order to be sent to hard labor the next day, among whom was myself and my American comrade before mentioned, but as we had not committed any crime we had none of our clothes taken from us but were permitted to depart with all our wardrobe. As this closes the first year of my captivity, and the next opens with fresh scenes of horror I shall conclude this chapter and in my next give a circumstantial detail of Mr. Lamb's negotiation with the regency of Algiers which proved extremely detrimental to the captives as it fed them with false hopes of obtaining their liberty soon, and prevented their friends from exerting themselves to procure their ransom, and by deceiving the Dey with unwarranted expectations he committed the honor and dignity of his country and led the Dey and Grandees to believe that the government of the United States was trifling with them and in the event of a negotiation for peace prevented that explicit confidence being placed in the promises of the negotiators on the part of the United States, a sacred adherence to, and compliance with, ought forever to characterize the public operations of contracting powers, especially those divided by so great a distance as the United States and the Regency of Barbary.

Chapter IV

Three months had elapsed since the departure of Mr. Lamb, when the Christians arrived which caused our expulsion from the palace garden. We were in lively expectation of a speedy redemption, but I must candidly confess that I was not so sanguine as a number of my fellow sufferers; we had heard nothing from Mr. Lamb since his departure, and I conceived that in three months (had he a credit in Europe) he would have given the Regency some account of his proceedings, and considering that he had likewise requested to negotiate a peace, I naturally concluded that he would be obliged to communicate his proceedings to congress before any step would be taken towards our redemption, and consequently, did not expect to be redeemed in less than nine or ten months from his departure from Algiers; nevertheless I was rejoiced to leave the palace garden, as at that period I could not conceive that a more humiliating situation than mine was in existence. I was convinced that the honor of our country was connected with our redemption; that it could not possibly be protracted for more than a year at the utmost, and I finally resolved to bear the hardest labor accompanied with hunger, nakedness and all their concomitant miseries in preference to the sentimental afflictions I then suffered. I was likewise actuated by so strong a desire to change my situation in hopes of procuring information which would enable me to ameliorate it, and be the means of alleviating the sufferings of my unfortunate fellow citizens, that I really viewed my expulsion from the palace garden as the greatest blessing that could befall me under the existing circumstances. On the evening of the 29th of July, 1786, the Christian chief clerk of the Dey and Regency informed the captives in the palace garden that he had orders to conduct eight of them to the Bagnio Belique, as the Dey had thought proper to replace them with the captives newly arrived. Accordingly two Portuguese, two Americans, and four Spaniards, among whom was myself and unfortunate companion, were selected and ordered to prepare ourselves immediately. My wardrobe was contained in a small basket, which with two blankets, a few books and papers, a four-dollar gold coin and two sequins in gold, constituted the whole of my worldly possessions. We left the palace without regret as we were ignorant of the situation we were destined for, but we were soon undeceived, and for myself I candidly own that I found a great deal of difference between the Bagnio Belique and hard labor at the public works, and the palace garden with all its evils, but the nature of mankind is such that they are never sensible of the blessings they enjoy until they are deprived of them, when they learn to appreciate their value by comparison. We rejoiced that we had escaped the humiliation of taking care of wild beasts and keeping the garden in order, and the tyranny of the two Hasnadars, but did not consider that seeking to avoid Scylla we had fallen upon Charibdis and were now exposed to the more ferocious Ibram Rais Guardian Bashaw, and his numerous minions, a more motley crew than whom never breathed the ambient air. I observed that the Regency only allows the slaves in the palace their living on their first arrival, they are ever afterwards obliged to furnish themselves with every article of apparel from the perquisites they receive, which are collected from the coffeegies in the following manner. When the Beys, Caliphs, Alcaides, Sheiks and in general every stranger who is permitted the honor of drinking coffee with the Dey, including Christian Ambassadors and sometimes Consuls, are presented with coffee, when they return the cup they put a quantity of gold according to their rank into it and give it to the coffeegie, who deposits it in a box in the Dey's apartment. His Excellency generally makes a small addition to it himself and divides it twice a year among the captives according to his own pleasure. It sometimes amounts to $3,000 annually and is seldom less than $2,000, which is sufficient to supply all their wants as well as to enable them to assist their brother sufferers at hard labor in the nauseous prisons called the Bagnios, of which there are three, which shall be described in due season. The coffeegies, in addition to their share of the money extorted in a manner from the Dey's visitors, are allowed to pester the Beys and Caliphs when they visit the Hasnagi and chief cooks, and seldom fail to benefit by their impudence. Several of the other slaves are likewise permitted to waylay those great men on the palace stairs and under the pretense of paying their devoirs by kissing their hands, likewise levy their contributions while they show their respect in proportion to the sums they receive, which, if not equal to their expectations, which seldom is the case, never fail to curse the supposed parsimony of the donor. Once when Salah Bey of Constantine, who was very liberal, was retreating from the Dey's palace with as much expedition as possible, his patience and cash being nearly exhausted, he was saluted by an inferior Moor of his province, who was employed by the Dey. Here, says Salah Bey, take your revenge, giving him some money, your countrymen shall reimburse me on my return to Constantine. I am at Algiers what your Sheiks are there, they complain of the exactions which it is my duty to make upon them in order to pay the tribute due to the Dey and Regency; but if they had once made a tri-ennial visit to Algiers they would marvel at my moderation and be no way ambitious of the apparent respect which is shown me by the different classes of the inhabitants, which has cost me so many thousands; but so long as Bobba Mahomed (meaning the Dey) is content, then I am perfectly satisfied. May the immortal Allah prolong his reign in happiness and internal peace, beloved by his subjects, and feared by his enemies. There are other Christians who have likewise a right, founded on custom, to pay their respects to the Beys and Caliphs among whom are the Dey's chief attendant in the palace (who carries them the Caftan or role of honor from the Dey, who is rewarded by the Beys with about two hundred dollars and by the Caliph with about half that sum) the Dey's chief Christian clerk, his clerk and several others, besides those unhappy men are made to disgorge their ill acquired wealth in all the Grandee's houses where they visit, and, generally, return to their government completely fleeced, and commence their impositions on the Moors, the different tribes of Arabs, the Jews, and every other class of beings whom Almighty Providence has subjected to their yoke, with surprising alacrity and without the least shadow of remorse, being stimulated thereto by the treatment they themselves have received at Algiers, and the fear of being deficient in the sum to satisfy the avarice of the Dey and Grandees and inhabitants of that city, when the period arrives for their return with the tri-ennial tribute.

On our arrival at Bagnio Belique we were introduced to Ibram Rais, who acted as the Guardian Bashaw, in consequence of his age and sickness he was soon afterwards confirmed in the post, the superior guardians having died of the plague. I shall only take notice of him in that station where he remained during the rest of my captivity and several years afterwards. He was at this period guardian of the large pontoon for cleaning out the harbor and was generally supposed to be the most cruel, unrelenting guardian that had ever been in Algiers. He had lately returned from Malta, where he had remained in captivity for fourteen years, and having been cruelly treated himself on board the Maltese Galleys, he was determined to retaliate on the slaves whom he had under his command, and revenge the insults he had received at Malta, upon the innocent men who were not even of the same nation, for at this period he had not even one Maltese under his command and there were but two of that nation in the Regency, who were captured under the Portuguese flag by the same cruise that I was. The reception that we received from this petty tyrant will both characterize the man and deliniate the horrors of our situation. He was sitting under the gallows at the outer gate. In the porch were a double row of guardians Sbirro all armed with sticks, thick rope, and other offensive weapons, the guardians who were soldiers being also armed with attagans (swords) and pistols, and the walls of the porch were decorated with clubs, halters, chains, shackles and handcuffs, the whole forming the most dejecting "Coup de Oeil" that imagination can possibly conceive. "Well, gentlemen," commenced Ibram Rais, "so you were not content with your situation in the palace and have preferred my acquaintance to the Hasnadars. You are all young and healthy and too well clothed for slaves, you shall have something to divert you tomorrow at Bebel Wey'd, I will show you there how I was treated at Malta. Here, Sbirro, put stout rings on these gentlemen's legs and let them be awakened and brought to me before daylight at the Marine gate."

The head clerk now interfered and informed him that we had committed no fault and that the Hasnadar had ordered him to have them sent to the Marine. "They shall go to the Marine," answered the surly Guardian, "but from thence I will send them where I please, they don't know what slavery is yet; it is time they should learn; I have not forgot the treatment I received from Christians when I was a slave." I observed that I was an American and that it would be extremely hard for me to suffer for the injuries he had received from the Maltese, who were situated at the distance of 6,000 miles from my country and were likewise of a different religion, which taught them from time immemorial to view the Mahometans with emnity [*sic*]; but that in America there probably had never been a Mussulman and that we never had been at war with any nation of that religion. "True," answered he, (curling his whiskers), "but you are Christians and if you have not injured Mussulmen it was not for the want of will, but for want of power, if you should chance to take any of our Cruisers how would you treat our people?" "That will entirely depend on how you treat those of my nation whom you have captured," I answered, "and you may be assured sir that my nation will retaliate upon those who treat their unfortunate citizens with undeserved cruelty." "Slave!" answered he, "I am not accustomed to listen to the arguments of Infidels; you are too loquacious for a young man; retire immediately and for the future be silent and obey." "I shall obey sir, but never be silent while there remains a higher tribunal to appeal to." My fellows by this time had all kissed this tyrant's hand, and we were ushered into the prison yard and there left to shift for ourselves, having first had a large iron shackle bolted and riveted above our ancles, which weighed about 20 ounces. The Sbirro informed us that we might have it changed for a small iron ring, by paying a sequin each to the Guardian Bashaw and 12 masoons to him for his trouble for the ring. I felt too indignant to give him any answer, and my

American companion did not understand him. No sooner had this ceremony ended than we were obliged to give in our names to the clerk of the prison, and were ordered to hold ourselves in readiness to march to the Marine gate at daylight the next morning; at the same moment the Sbirro called out in a most tremendous tone thrice distinctly Capi Capar (ei) which in the Turkish language means we are closing the gate, when immediately emerged from the taverns a motley crew of Turks, Moors, Arabs, and even some Jews, all intoxicated, some half naked, having sold or pawned their clothes to the Christian tavern keepers for liquor, others singing or shouting, some with drawn swords swearing they would kill the first person that offended them and some few reeling peacefully to their habitations or, if soldiers, to the public barracks. The gates of the prison were then shut for the night and a heavy chain was drawn across the inside of the outer gate and the inner one was bolted and locked; the prison was now under the control of the Christian Corporals who were all deserters from the Spanish garrison of Oran, where they had been banished from their country, either for murder or theft, and before their appointment here, had in general signalized themselves as the most hardened villains in the Regency. As these Corporals have a tavern allowed them free of excise they generally mark such Christians as they suppose to have money or are in the way of earning any, and if they do not frequent their tavern, are continually persecuted by them, as the prisoners at night are entirely under their command and an unfavorable report in the morning from one of those miscreants will not fail to procure the person complained of a severe bastinadoing and several weeks in chains besides. They have power to keep any person that displeases them the whole night chained by the leg or the neck to a stone pillar, of which there are several in each prison, and in the day time they can persecute any of the slaves with impunity while at their labor and place them at the hardest and most disagreeable work. It is therefore at least prudent to keep on as good terms as possible with these petty despots and to occasionally bribe them, which will not fail to procure rest and frequently exemption from labor for several weeks successively. They are likewise receivers of stolen goods and share with the Guardians the product of this kind of commerce, and not unfrequently the blame is thrown on innocent persons to whom they own some private pique, while the culprit is allowed to go unpunished and revel with them on the plunder they have taken from some poor Jew or Christian, and frequently Turks and Moors share a similar fate; nevertheless a number of those robbers are detected and severely punished when they have not made their peace with the Guardians through the agency of the Corporals. It is necessary to observe that these robberies are in general committed by deserters from Oran (which are here called Carneros (i.e.) sheep) as they come into slavery like sheep to the slaughter and are not captives but voluntary slaves. Between such classes great distinctions are made, as none of the former were ever employed in the palace or Grandee's [*sic*] houses, or were made clerks of by the Regency until very lately that the latter became so scarce that they could not find enough to do their domestic work. They are now more mixed than formerly and it is worthy of observation that few crimes are committed by people taken at sea, and when a crime is committed the mistrust falls on those people as their iniquities have made it a proverbial saying among the Mahometans that any bad person has acted like a "Carnero from Oran" as they believe them with great reason to be capable of anything. In this prison are kept all the criminals, and sometimes forty or fifty are here chained two and two together for months, nay, some for years, for different crimes. The jingling of chains adds horror to this dismal dungeon beyond conception, which with the stench and unnatural imprecations and blasphemy of some of its miserable inhabitan[t]s, makes it really a perfect pandemonium. I will now proceed to describe this receptacle of human misery.

The Bagnio de Belique is an oblong hollow square, 140 feet in length and 60 in breadth, is three stories high and may be about 50 feet high to the top of the terrace. The whole of the apartments are built upon arches and have no windows except a small iron grating in each of the upper apartments, and receive the light and air from the doors. The lower story has no grating and is converted into taverns which are kept by the Christian slaves who pay their rent and very high duties for permission to sell liquors and provisions in them. They are perfectly dark and in the day are illuminated with lamps, and when full of drunken Turks, Moors, Arabs, Christians, and now and then a Jew or two, especially on Fridays, the day the Christians are sometimes permitted to rest in the prison from their labor, forms the most disgusting "Coup de Oeil" that can be imagined, especially when you add to the noise an instrument called a triboocca, a tabor or quinterra, and a guitar and sometimes a fiddle and Turkish guitar, and not unfrequently an Italian mandolin and Spanish guitar, each singing or rather shouting in different languages, without the least connection, the place filled with the smoke of tobacco which renders objects nearly impervious to the view, some wrangling with the tavern keepers for more liquor and refusing to pay for it, that upon the whole it must resemble the infernal regions more than any other place in the known world, especially, when they frequently quarrel among themselves and proceed to blows and even murder often takes place in those receptacles of vice and immortality, which generally occasions the tavern keeper to lose all his property as the tavern is in the most instances seized by the Regency and the tavern keeper sent to hard labor unless he bribes the Guardian to make a favorable report of the case. It is impossible for any person to conceive or even to believe when related what innumerable ways and with what avidity the Corporals and Guardians search for occasions to plunder those poor wretches and in general all those that receive money during their captivity from friends or having ingenuity or industry to earn it. In all the prisons in the evening may be seen different tradesmen at work, among which shoemakers, tailors, carpenters, coopers, sawyers, and some hucksters are those who meet with the most constant employment and make the most money. Before slaves became so scarce in the Regency a number of slaves of this description were permitted to remain in the prisons to work by paying the Regency one dollar per month and bribing the Guardians and spending their evenings at the Corporal's tavern, but latterly few can gain this permission and none except some Christian Consul or merchant becomes responsible for their conduct. Formerly this favor was obtained through the influence of the slaves in the palace or Grandees' houses, but so many misbehaved that at present the free Christians will not be responsible for any only those whom they employ in their own houses, even if permission could be procured from the Regency. The second and third story of this dungeon is surrounded by a small corridor or gallery from whence are entrances into long, narrow rooms where the slaves sleep. They are hung in square frames one over another, four tier deep, and they repose as well as miserable wretches can be supposed to do who are swarming with myriads of vermin of all sorts, many nearly naked and few with anything more than an old tattered blanket to cover them with in the depth of winter; for those who have the means of subsistence either live in the tavern or little boxes called rooms, built of boards hanging round the galleries for which they pay the Regency from twelve to fifty-four masoons per month, notwithstanding, before the Spanish and Neapolitan redemptions in 1787, and the mortality by the plague, numbers of those forlorn outcasts were obliged to lie in the galleries or wherever they could find shelter from the inclemency of the weather. In the center of the prison or very near is the well from which water is drawn from the cistern, which is nearly as large as the whole prison and was formerly supplied from the terrace of the prison with rain water, but is now partially supplied when necessity requires it from the waterworks of the city which shall be described hereafter. The whole of the building is covered with a terrace which has only two communications with the prison. It would be a great recreation to the slaves, especially in the summer, were they permitted to walk or sleep there, but that is strictly prohibited; one communication is through the Dey's chief clerk's apartment and the keys of the other are kept by the head Corporal, consequently none are permitted to go on the terrace but whom they please, and as they are generally such different characters the Corporals seldom make use of the privilege to the great satisfaction of the chief clerks who are by no means ambitious for the society of this class of men. The chief clerk's apartments are comprised of two handsome rooms and a kitchen, which with convenience of the terrace renders them both pleasant and commodious, and as they have four large windows which serves to ventilate them they are exempt from the stench which is insufferable in other parts of the prison. As there are two other prisons I will proceed here to describe them in order that the whole miserable scene may be comprehended by the reader at one view and a comparison drawn between them. They all have their inconveniences but the Bagnio Belique is the most miserable.

The Bagnio de Gallera of the prison of the galley slaves was so called because those who formerly used to row in the Algerine galleys were here confined and after it was rebuilt the name was continued because the Neapolitans who ran away with two galleys of that nation about the year 1750 were the first inhabitants of it when completed. It is built on the same plan as the former but is only two stories high and not so long, the taverns are the same and so are the long rooms, but on the terrace are two tiers of small rooms, one above the other, inhabited by those who are able to pay for them, which is one great reason why the better sort of slaves prefer this prison to any of the others. The greatest inconvenience in this prison is in consequence of the lions and tigers being kept there which creates an insufferable stench, which joined to the common shore of the hospital which communicates with that of the prison corrodes the atmosphere that in the summer season it is nearly suffocating. I have known twenty-seven animals of this description to have been kept at once in this prison which are maintained at the expense of the Christian tavern keepers. They frequently break loose and have killed several of the slaves as they dare not destroy them even in their own defense, and if very ferocious an order must come from the Dey and some of his guard are then dispatched to shoot them before the evil can be removed. The offals from their dens serve to maintain an enormous number of rats, the largest I ever saw, which frequently serve to satisfy the craving appetite of some of the poor slaves. Cats are likewise eaten from mere necessity, and once in particular I asked a Frenchman what he was going to do with it after skinning, he laconically answered, "Ma foi it [*sic*] faut Manger." During the plague this prison, in consequence of its communication with the hospital, had the greatest number of its inhabitants destroyed with the contagion.

The Bagnio Siddi Hamouda. This is the smallest Bagnio of the three and has every misery common with the other two, but is not regularly built, being composed of three or four old houses with communications made from one to the other. It takes its name from its former owner. Thus have I described the three prisons in which from two to three thousand miserable wretches have been confined, in consequence of the policy of those commercial nations which make a point not only to suffer their incorrigible insolence and arrogance, but likewise to feed their avarice and forge pretexts for them to commit depredations upon every nation which endeavors to share the commerce of the Mediterranean with them; when by stopping the dishonorable tributes paid by them to those Pirates, redeeming their slaves and stationing two Frigates each in that sea for four or five years, the Barbary States would become as contemptible as the little Republic of Lucca, and if we add to this the influence such a coalition would have at the Ottoman Porte their total annihilation would eventually take place. The dissensions which such a measure would produce among an idle soldiery would open a prospect of success, should the inhabitants of the city or Arabs of the country revolt, and could the Divan of the Sublime Porte be prevailed on to prohibit recruits from enlisting themselves under their banners, Algiers would be the first to feel the effects and with her would fall Tunis and Tripoli, which would inevitably tend to a change of government, which in the event would produce a change of measures, and the nations of the world would be liberated from the excursions of those Pirates who have, from time immemorial, committed depredations on their property and enslaved their citizens and subjects. But this union of sentiment is rather to be wished for than expected, for it is an incontrovertible fact that no war has been declared by those marauders for the last century that has not been instigated by some of the commercial powers in opposition to their rivals in trade, and the failure of all the Armadas sent against them by Spain may be justly attributed to the advice and assistance they constantly received from France, and especially through the medium of the Chamber of Commerce at Marseilles, which had in a great measure monopolized all the most valuable branches of commerce in all the Barbary States.

I now return to my initiation into the dungeons of Algiers. While ruminating on the horrors of my situation I received an invitation from the Dey's chief clerk to stay in his apartments until I had time to provide for myself which I thankfully accepted, but could not enjoy his civilities, my imagination was wound up to such a degree that I was nearly insane. I retired to rest on his sofa but slept but little and awaited the approach of day in anxious expectation of knowing my fate. About 3 o'clock in the morning the awful summons was given from the tremendously cadaverous lungs of the Sbirro, "Arise! all those who sleep, the day approaches!" and a short time afterwards, "Depart, sleepers!

each one to his daily labor." We all marched out at this warning and proceeded through a narrow street toward the gates of the Marine just at the time that the gates of the city were opened, and the influx of camels, mules, asses and laborers was so great that we could hardly pass. The animals were loaded with provisions for the market, palace and Grandees' houses, and the slaves, instigated by hunger, were endeavoring to steal as much as they could which produced such a scene as I have not words to describe. The Moors uttering curses and threats of "Which Christian dog, Infidel dog without faith, I will have you bastinadoed to death" were the most distinguishable among this motley crew. We proceeded until relieved by the turn of the street towards the mole, and then marched at my ease to the gate where we were all paraded in rows, the Guardians being in front, seated on a brick seat made for the purpose. Here we waited about a quarter of an hour when the Vikilharche, Belique, Bashaw, Captain of the Post and other officers made their appearance and marched through the gate followed by the Guardians and slaves who on the Vikilharche's first appearances must stand uncovered until he passes them some distance. The Dey's chief clerk took us to the Guardian Bashaw who presented us to the Vikilharche, who after asking a number of questions and receiving a favorable account of us from the clerk, we were ordered to our respective destinations. My comrade and myself were sent to the carpenter's shop. I was immediately apprenticed to a genteel looking Spaniard, a native of Barcelona, who had been a cadet in the Spanish service, but for some irregularity was sent to serve in the garrison at Oran from whence he deserted in hopes of regaining his liberty, but was taken into custody by the Arabs of the western province and sold to the Bey of Mascara, who brought him with a number of others as a part of his tri-ennial present to the Regency of Algiers, of which a proper mention will be made when we come to treat of the Bey's public entry, of which I was several times a witness during my captivity. This man despairing of ever being redeemed by Spain, abandoned by his relatives, had applied himself to learn the trade he was put to on his first arrival at Algiers so effectually that at present he was really the best house carpenter in the Regency, and consequently was employed on the out-door business, such as working in the Grandees' houses, and was very much in favor. The eight months I was with him I constantly accompanied him and as I understood French, Spanish and Portuguese tolerably well I had an opportunity to get much information and to study the manners and customs of the people to whom Divine Providence had made me subject. During the period that I worked in the city or for the Marine I was well provided with one good meal a day, which the Regency paid for exclusive of the allowance which we had in common with the rest of the slaves, and had our duties been confined to the duties of the carpenter's shop alone there would have been no reason to complain of hard usage, but that was not the case, for whenever any hard loads were to be carried, the ships of friendly powers that brought presents to be discharged, the ballast, guns, and ammunition to be taken out of the Cruisers or put on board again, which was done every cruise be it ever so short, then the apprentices in all the shops in the Marine were taken out and employed on that duty as well as in clearing out the magazines, fortifications, and other occasional jobs, and not unfrequently they were sent on board the Pontoons to clear the harbor of mud and stones and likewise to bring heavy stones from the Ponto Piscado to throw at the back of the mole to prevent the sea from breaking over in stormy weather; and at this period a large magazine war building adjoining the Vikilharche garden at Bebel Wed, about one mile from the city, large enough to contain all the gunboats belonging to the Regency. This magazine was built upon arches, and the earth that was dug out to lay the foundation was afterwards used to form the terrace. During this work frequent drafts of men were sent from the Marine and on Friday, the Mahometan Sabbath, all the slaves that worked at the Marine, with the exception of a few favored workmen, were sent to this employment which was much worse than the labor of the whole week. Figure to yourself above a thousand poor wretches, many of them half naked without hat or shoes, at work in the heat of the sun all day till four and sometimes till five or six o'clock on a summer day, carrying earth in a basket to the top of a high building, exposed to the heat and often blistered with the sun, chafed and scalded with the weight of their load, the perspiration flowing from them; add to this that they only received two small loaves of black bread of seven ounces each in all the day and a very small portion of horse beans, probably without any oil, as their small allowance is given out the day before and is generally either stolen or made away with in some way or another by the people to whose care it was intrusted, and on their arrival at the prison at night they then receive a loaf of the same sort of bread, but weighing twelve ounces which is all they ever receive on Friday, but on working days there is a mess of burgul boiled in the Marine, mixed with a quantity of butter worse than tallow, and as it is taken out of the jars by the slaves without any caution in order to get as much as it is possible to sell to the Moors; it frequently happens that they find rats, mice and other animals boiled in the burgul, which is by no means a pleasant addition to their mess; nevertheless I have seen many hundred during my captivity sit down to some buckets of this stuff, substitute a chip for a spoon and eat as voraciously as some of our epicures would turtle soup, terrapin or venison pastry. The grease that is used in this mess is what remains in the stores after the soldiers are occasionally served from the annual tribute which Tunis pays to this Regency, and of course is the worst part of it, and some of it has been laying several years with the mouth of the jars uncovered; formerly a certain amount of this stuff was served out, but as no Christian ever eats it that can get anything else the officers find it advantageous to let the Christian cooks take what they please, of which a quantity is always left which the cooks daily distribute to the dogs and cats of the Marine, and certain poor Arabs who attend for that purpose always giving preference to the former, so that a person whose stomach could bear such nause[o]us food need not starve, but if that was the case with all the slaves or were the provisions of such a quality that they could partake of it the abundance would cease and burgul would be as scarce as any other provision. This magazine before it was finished fell in two or three times with the weight of earth that was placed on the top; in every instance all the people who could be spared from the other works were sent to clear this earth away and to assist in repairing the work. No rest was allowed on Friday and even those slaves who paid by the month were called for on those occasions with the exception of two or three from each Consul's house. This place was built under the inspection of one Demetrius, a Greek master mason, and when finished was found not to answer the purpose it was intended for near as well as a common shed would have done, for, exclusive of the distance those heavy gunboats had to be hauled before they were housed, the arches interfered with each other in such a manner and took up so much room that the boats were obliged to be turned several times and stand one on the top of the other, and as this was done by main force, strength of the slaves, the boats when put by frequently were in a worse condition than before they were repaired, and in case of a sudden armament appearing could be of no service whatever. Since that period the Algerine have placed their gunboats close under the walls of the city in a dry ditch where they can launch them in a very short time and I am informed are kept in readiness for actual service. It would however take them three or four days to mount the artillery and make preparations in sufficient force to annoy an enemy that might make his appearance on their coast or bay, and as those boats have no sails and are quite open like Spanish launches. In a sea, nay, or even in a fresh breeze, they could easily be destroyed, provided they came from under the fortifications which in number of guns are really formidable so that the gunboats of Algiers may be considered rather as a defensive armament than calculated to act on the offensives, but in a calm would annoy an enemy exceedingly unless they were furnished with small vessels with oars to counteract their operations. As I have commenced with a description of the Marine force of Algiers I will conclude this chapter with an account of their actual Marine force in 1786 and a description of the Marine or mole of Algiers with all its fortifications, moorings, magazines, workshops and conveniences, which shall in some measure include a description of the site of Algiers.

Chapter VII

CONTINUATION OF MY SITUATION

I have already stated that when I was sent from the palace garden, my whole wardrobe was contained in a small basket, and in cash my funds did not amount to quite eight dollars, two of which I was obliged to pay to the Corporals to make interest to procure me leave to go to the Bagnio Gallera, where the rest of the American prisoners were, and as many as it could hold, of the most respectable prisoners. I therefore, and my companions in adversity, took leave of Bagnio Belique for the present. A large ring of iron, which was put on my leg there, I got changed for a small one, and my next occupation was to look out for quarters. Some of the Americans were fortunate enough to have a small room to themselves, but this was so crowded that it was impossible to hold any more inhabitants, and most of them slept on tables in the taverns. We arrived so late that all the births [*sic*] in the tavern where we put up were taken, and I was obliged to spread my blanket on the interstice of the bilge of a large wine cask and the wall, with my basket containing all my worldly possessions under my head, to serve for a pillow and prevent the contents from being stolen. The weather being very sultry, the stench of the prison, the quantity of rats which were continually running over us, joined to myriads of fleas which attacked on all sides, did not render the night's lodging very agreeable, and I was glad when I was summoned to work in the morning.

From this to the month of March 1787, I continued in nearly the same situation, working in the carpenter shop in the day time, occasionally sent to carry heavy loads to disarm the Cruisers, load vessels with wheat, carry ballast on board the Cruisers, and on Friday, either be sent to Bebal Wed to work at the Magazine, or to the Ponto Piscado to load the Pontoon with heavy stone to throw at the back of the mole, to prevent the sea from breaking over it. In short every other sort of labor, which the most common slave in the Regency was obliged to do; but this was not all, the Guardians or slave drivers supposing we had money, would send us to the worst work, abuse us in the worst manner, using the most opprobrious language, and often giving us cuts with their twisted rattans, "en passant," in order to oblige us to purchase our peace with them, which generally could be done for thirty or forty cents; but for those who had it not to give, it might as well have been a million. It might well be supposed that my treasury was soon exhausted, and that the clothes which I got in the palace, were disposed of to supply my most urgent wants. It is true, we were allowed seven and one-half cents a day for some time from our own country, but that allowance was soon withdrawn from us, and for years no more notice was taken of us than if no such unfortunate men were in existence. It may therefore well be imagined that our situation could not well be worse, especially as the plague, which had been introduced from the Levant, began to make its appearance in the slave prisons. This, however, produced no mitigation of our labor—as long as we live we must work.

I continued in this miserable situation until the 17th of March, 1787, when the King of Naples redeemed all his subjects who were taken at sea, except those who were taken in the Galleys which fled from Naples. A Neapolitan Frigate arrived with the cash on board, and they were permitted to embark under a flag of truce. They were about three hundred in number, and many of them being employed in the most eligible situations, many vacancies remained to be filled by those unfortunate men who remained; among whom, my fellow prisoner and myself were taken from carpenter's shop and ordered to attend on the Intendant or Vikilharche of the Marine. There are generally from six to nine Christians in this department, whose duty it is to attend to the Vikilharche at meals, to take care of the stores, carry the keys for the Belique Bashaw, serve the oil and bread out to the slaves, and in general, whatever the Intendant and Belique Bashaw order them to do; but they are not subject to the Guardians nor to the orders of any one else. They are well fed and receive some emolument from the Intendant's visitors, especially the Beys, Caliphs, Alcaides, Ambassadors, and Christian Consuls, who are expected to put some money into the cup every time they take coffee with him; and this money is divided among these Christians every Thursday night—and they always have Friday to themselves. This was no small alleviation from our sufferings, especially as we were nearly naked; and now we received two pieces of cotton sufficient to make two jackets and two pair of trousers, and money to pay for making them. Although you are subject to hard labor, sometimes, in clearing out the stores, it is nevertheless considered one of the best situations, and a great deal of interest is made to get there.

Although peace with Spain took place in June, 1785, still the Spaniards remained in captivity. The plague had commenced, and in January there died sixteen Christian slaves, and in February forty one, and in March the number was increasing, when the Neapolitans were redeemed. The Spanish priests now thought seriously of their captives, as they became very refractory and blamed the priests for their being detained so long in captivity after peace had taken place, and even threatened their lives. They, therefore, with the assistance of the Spanish Ambassador, became security to the Dey for the ransom of all the Spaniards who were taken at sea, to the number of about four hundred, and on the 19th of March they were embarked on board a large Russian prize vessel, which was purchased for that purpose, and soon sailed for Minorca to perform quarantine. The slaves who had deserted from Oran, who were about one thousand of all nations, had always expected to have been included in the general redemption. Some of these unfortunate men had been in captivity for fifty years, and certainly had suffered sufficiently to have expiated any crimes which they might have committed in their youth, and finding this not so, all their hopes vanished and they gave themselves up to dispair, threatened the priests and Ambassadors and all the free subjects of Spain with death, as being the cause of their not being included in the redemption; and were with difficulty appeased by the priests promising, in the most solemn manner, to write to the King of Spain in their behalf, and to the heads of their order to use their influence in their favor. This quieted them for the present; nevertheless their dissatisfaction frequently led them to acts of violence and riot, and often the priests were in danger of their lives; which, considering the class of people they had to do with, is not to be wondered at, especially as the priests did not fulfill their promises; for twelve years after I wrote this, in 1799, when I touched at Algiers, some of those poor creatures were still in captivity. The greatest number had died of the plague, some had been redeemed, and the remainder were ransomed sometime afterwards. When the Spaniards who had been redeemed embarked, the scene was truly affecting; they separated from their countrymen, who were left behind, with embraces and tears for their speedy liberation; they divided their clothes and money with them; some even gave away their all; and probably never was generosity more conspicuous or carried to a greater length. When the ship sailed she was followed by the eyes of those poor captives, and when she disappeared in the horizon, a universal groan was heard from those unfortunate men; and they sunk into despondency, declaring that now their last hope of ever being redeemed had vanished, and they cared not how soon they were struck with the plague and terminated their existence. The plague still increased, notwithstanding more than seven hundred captives were redeemed, which lessened the number considerably. Forty-three died this month and one hundred and five in April; nevertheless, the usual work was carried on and the labor being increased, no doubt exposed the poor slaves to the miasma of the infection more than otherwise they would have been, of which I will take particular notice when I come to treat of that dreadful disease.

By the redemption of the Spaniards, the places of the coffeegie and clerk of the Marine department became vacant. Giovanni de la Cruz, a native of Leghorn, who had been chief mate of a large Leghornese ship, which I had left at Boston, and who was captured last year, and with whom I was acquainted, was appointed to the latter situation and I was appointed to the former. His duty was to keep the books, and mine to make coffee and hand it to the Intendant and his visitors; I likewise had the superintendency of the other slaves and was accountable for their good behavior and was obliged to report them if they behaved improperly.

The clerk of the Marine is allowed a small room in the Bagnio Galera, gratis. I took up my quarters with him, and with the exception of people dying with the plague all around us, our situation was very tolerable. We were obliged to be in the prison at the same hours as the other slaves were, and to go to the Marine as soon as the gate was opened, in order to have the Intendant's seat made and coffee ready for him on his arrival. On Fridays, as we were confidential slaves, we could generally get leave to go out of town as far as the Consul's country seats. In May, one hundred and fourteen Christian slaves died, and in June, one hundred and fifty-five died, among whom was my friend Giovanni de la Cruz. He lingered a few days, and on the 11th of June departed this life, regretted by all who knew him. He was a most amiable young man. During his illness I rendered him all the service in my power but to no effect. When he was struck with the plague, I was ordered to take charge of the books of the Marine department until he died or recovered, and on the 12th I was appointed clerk of the Marine. Here I remained until all the people of the Magazine, the Vikilharche of the Marine excepted, had died and been replaced three different times. My former ship mate, of whom I will have occasion to mention hereafter, had been sent out of the Magazine soon after he was taken into it for incapacity, as he was a very simple ignorant lad, and could not learn the duty exacted from him. The Belique Bashaw died; another was appointed, he died also; and a Turk, a fisherman in the Turkish language (Baluckgee), was appointed in his stead. This man had never been in any office before, and was in rank only a common soldier. He was extremely ignorant, poor, and proud, and very morose in his manners, finding fault without reason and not over honest. Several things were missing from the stores, but no person dare accuse him of purloining them; besides they wanted proof. My situation was then rendered very unpleasant. I remained, however, at my post until April, 1788, when one Thursday, having made out a (Tischera) or account of the money to be delivered to the treasury that day by the Belique Bashaw, it amounted to a considerable sum more than he had in his possession. He first tried to pursuade [*sic*] me that I had made some mistake, and requested me to alter it without making any noise. This I positively refused to do and read to him all the items of the money he had received, and what he had paid away. He then endeavored to throw the blame on the Christian slaves, saying that they must have taken the money out of his drawer, although he had always kept the key himself. This produced altercation, when he complained to the Vikilharche, saying that I had accused him of embezzlement and that either he or I must leave the Marine. The Vikilharche endeavored to pacify him, but without effect; and the policy of these people being never to take part with a Christian against one of themselves, especially if he is a Turk or a soldier, [o]ccasioned him to order me to leave the Marine and remain in my tavern, declaring that he never would appoint another clerk in my place. This promise he kept, and the duties of my place were done by the Turkish clerk, until the Belique Bashaw was removed, which happened shortly after; and frequently I have met him with his cane and basket coming, after this time, from fishing. I remained in the tavern some time when, in consequence of the great mortality among the slaves, I was appointed clerk of the Bagnio Galera, three clerks having died in less than one month. The duty of this station was to muster the slaves in the prison every evening, to report when any died or were taken sick, to see their black bread served out to them, and to go to the Marine every morning, and on Friday, to the out works to muster the slaves, to call their names over, and to report them when any [were] missing; but as several of the clerks of the sheep skins and charcoal died with the plague, I was frequently obliged to do this duty, which kept me constantly employed, and probably was conducive to my health and may have been the means, under Divine Providence, of my being alive at the present moment.

Chapter IX

The clerk of the Bagnio Gallera is allowed to keep a tavern in the prison, and only pays half duty to the Regency. This, with my having purchased the Mad House tavern, will account for my having money at my command, and when my fellow sufferers had none, and I believe those who survive will do me the justice to acknowledge, that they never wanted a good meal while I had it in my power to give it to them; that they were attended in the hospital when sick, and that those who died were buried in a decent coffin at my expense. Nay, never was any American buried without my attending them to the grave, reading prayers over them, and remaining until they were decently covered. This was particularly taken notice of by the Consuls and Catholic priests. The plague raged all this year; nevertheless I never enjoyed better health, and I frequently stopped at the gates of the city to count the dead as they were carried out, not knowing nor indeed caring when my time should come. In 1789 the plague subsided, although it never was thoroughly exterminated, as no pains were taken to erradicate [*sic*] it. In this year only nineteen Christians died of all disorders, and the same number the next year. In 1791 only fifteen Christians died, and in 1792 seventeen, but in 1793 the plague broke out again and continued, with the intermission of the year 1795, when only thirty-one Christian slaves died, until 1796, but I am persuaded that the city and environs were never clear of the contagion, as it raged again and carried off several of our countrymen who were captives, of whom I will make mention when I come to treat of that terrible disorder. From 1788 to 1791, three years, I was employed as above stated, except about six months that I was in Dr. Werner's office to make out accounts. I ate at his table, but as I had money enough to serve all my wants, I was entirely independent of him until I closed all his accounts. He treated me tolerably well but having no further use for my services, he changed his mind and manner of treatment, making use of improper language, and pretending that I should not go out of his house without his leave, I therefore asked him to make out his account for my board, which he refused to do, and I retired to my room in the Bagnio Gallera, which I had rented to some of the captives during my absence. I was likewise one week at Mr. Logie's house, while he was out of town this was occasioned by Capt. O'Brien, who had lived there for considerable time, being sent to the Marine to make sails for the Cruisers, and the Consul requested me to take care of his house until he could get him back again. Capt. O'Brien had been through his whole captivity in one Counsul's [*sic*] house or another, except called occasionally to make or mend old sails for the Algerine Cruisers, and once that he was sent to hard labor and put on board the Panton Grand to cleanse the mold where he was kept some weeks during which time, however, I furnished him with a good dinner and a bottle of wine daily from my tavern, and as the guardian, Monto Negro, had no objection to a glass of wine himself, an extra one was sent to him by which Capt. O'Brien was treated very kindly, and only made to work under the eyes of the Vikilharche of the Marine, who was offended with him or rather was offended with the British Consul, and took this opportunity to revenge himself upon one of his dependents, as he could not upon the Consul himself. Little alteration took place in my situation until the arrival of the crews of the American vessels in October 1793. Sometimes I was employed as before mentioned and at other times I remained in my room at the Bagnio Gallera. I owned the Mad House tavern and half a tavern in the Bagnio Gallera, and another in Bagnio Liddi Hamuda, these were kept by Christian slaves, who paid me so much per pipe for wine and brandy. This gave me a profit sufficient for all my purposes, and an over-plus to serve the immediate wants of my unfortunate fellow sufferers taken in 1785, who had been a great part of the time without any assistance whatever from their country. Some of them had been at hard labor all the time, until their numbers were considerably reduced by the plague and hard usage, and at no time had they more than seven and a half cents allowed them per day to find them both food and raiment, and had it not pleased God to have placed me in a situation to have assisted them, they would certainly have been worse off. Those who were in Dey's palace, likewise gave them temporary assistance according to their means. People in our situation are generally liberal to each other. One probable reason, which might prevent them from hoarding, was the consideration that the plague was carrying off great numbers; that the Regency took possession of all the property belonging to the deceased, even their tattered garments and blankets, if they had any, and as we did not know when it would be our turn to die, we set no great value upon money, and made a merit of assisting our unfortunate brother sufferers, who were not in as good a situation as ourselves. Had we not been afraid of dying, I think it is likely enough that we would have been less liberal or at least more careful.

It must not, however, be supposed that notwithstanding I was much better off than many of my fellow prisoners, that I was not exposed to many sentimental afflictions. The Turkish Guardians frequently levied contributions on me on various false pretenses. The Paga Lunas were sometimes called to perform extra work on Fridays, and on any emergency such as fitting out Cruisers, covering in the waterworks at Bebazoon, clearing the Marine and fortifications, when any hostile armament was reported to be destined against Algiers, clearing away the rubbish of old houses, which were thrown down to augment the Dey's palace, discharging stores from the vessels of tributary nations, loading Christian vessels with wheat and barley, and in general everything that was an extra addition to the ordinary routine of duty from which the other slaves, whose numbers were greatly reduced by the redemption of the Neapolitan and Spanish slaves, and more by the dreadful plague, could not be spared, which occasioned frequently all the slaves, even those who were in the Consuls' houses, to be called to labor for a few days at a time. Many by bribing the guardians would get clear or not be forced to work hard; this would make the labor come harder on those who had nothing to give, and consequently create discontent, which was by no means to be wondered at; and would at times prevent the Guardians from showing lenity to any person whatever, for fear those who were not favored would complain to their superiors. In these several instances I suffered very much by accident. The first time I was standing by the Mad House tavern door, which belonged to me, when two Turks quarreled about a woman, one of the Turks was in the window of a house opposite, the other standing close by me, whose name was Hassan Chioux, said something which exasperated the one at the window to such a degree that he opened his door and shot Hassan through the thigh and with his attagan run him through the body without offering me the least injury. Hassan fell down dead into the tavern, and the pistol wounded another Turk in the foot, who was standing in the tavern. The murderer marched out of the gates and took refuge in the tent, which was pitched in the Rebat, as a sanctuary for all soldiers who had committed crimes, and would serve against the Arabs until pardoned. Hassan was carried to his barracks, washed and interred. The tavern was shut up and all the Christians who were present, among whom I was one, were sent to the Marine to work, by order of Ciddi Aly, who was Vikilharche of the Marine and by no means my friend. I remained at hard labor two days and then made application to the Hasnagi or Prime Minister and Treasurer, who gave orders that the tavern should be restored to me, and the Christians who were my servants permitted to go there as usual, but more than a week elapsed before my servants were returned, and not before I made a present of ten sequins to Ibraim Raiz, Guardian Bashaw. Not long afterwards a Kuluglo named Cara Burmuz of so infamous a character that he was deemed even unworthy to be a Turkish soldier, and his pay was taken from him—was insolent to a Greek Renegade called Mahommed Grittiti in the Mad House tavern, who beat him unmercifully. The next day Cara Burmuz complained to the Scheran Bashaw or head surgeon, whose duty it is to take cognizance of such acts and make the delinquent pay for drawing blood; but knowing that he could not expect more than two or three sequins from a soldier, induced Cara Burmuz to swear that it was I that had beaten him. I accordingly was summoned before this despot, who after a long discourse in which he wished to impress upon my mind the greatness of the crime of which I had been guilty, in beating so unmercifully a true believer, said he was willing to compromise the matter with me, provided I would pay him two hundred sequins as the price of blood, and if not I must go to prison. Mahommed Grittiti appeared and declared that I had not even seen Cara Burmuz when he had chastised him for his insolence. The Scheran Bashi, with a great deal of sang froid, said he supposed the Christian had paid him well for appearing in his favor, that it was a singular thing to see a Mussulman take the part of a Christian against one of his bretheren, and hinted that he formerly was a Christian himself, accounted for his partiality. Mahommed indignantly replied that he was a better Mussulman than he was, that Cara Burmuz was a vile character, and that although he had it in his power to extort money from a poor Christian captive with impugnity, that for every sequin he paid, Cara Burmuz should receive a drubbing, and he was as good as his word for every time he met him he broke his pipe over his head, until ultimately he was obliged to leave the city. Scheran Bashi then went to the Hasnagi and made out his own story—the Dey being at his country seat—this being Thursday evening he would not return until Friday, and no business would be done until Saturday, consequently had I went to prison I must have remained there until the Dey determined on the justice of the case which would have depended entirely upon the humor he might be in. I, therefore, concluded to make a virtue of necessity and agreed to pay this man one hundred and thirty manboobs, as the price of blood which I had not drawn, and returned home.

The third affair had liked to have been of a more serious nature. It happened on the anniversary of the eighth year of my captivity, and as it will show the temperature of my mind at this epoch of my captivity, I will copy my journal July 25, 1793:

Oh, Heavens! this is the anniversary of the eighth year of my captivity. Is it possible that so young as I was when I was captured, that I could have incensed the Divine Disposer of all human events so much as to merit perpetual captivity, an exile forever from my dear but cruel Patria, lost to my dearest connections and friends, never more to see those who in early life guided, protected and educated me in the paths of virtue, and who with unavailing tears regret my loss? For eight years have I been exposed to every indignity that a Mahomedan could invent, to render the life of a Christian captive truly and sentimentally miserable; destitute of friends to console me in time of affliction—at times without either meat, drink or raiment, but the small miserable pittance of black bread, olives and horse beans allowed us by the Regency of Algiers, even the small allowance of seven and a half cents a day, which was allowed us by our country, has been long discontinued—ever since September, 1789, and no notice whatever taken of us for years, except that now and then some person would ascertain the sum demanded for our ransom, which for a time would revive our hopes, but ultimately would sink us into the abyss of despondency and despair, when we found that the report of our redemption being near would die away "and like the baseless fabric of a vision leave not a wreck behind;" continually inclosed in those pandemoniums called Bagnios or Slave prisons, where every vice was not only tolerated but encouraged; exposed to the plague for several years, where hundreds of our fellow prisoners were dying around us, and thousands of the inhabitants, and not knowing but the present moment would be our last. O! America, could you see the miserable situation of your citizens in captivity, who have shed their blood to secure you the liberty you now possess and enjoy; and who now have their misery augmented by the consideration that the country for which they fought is now free and in a flourishing condition, you are the first that set the example to the world, to shake off the yoke of tyranny, to expel despotism and injustice from the face of the earth. The negroes have even had a share in your deliberations, and have reaped the benefits arising from your wise and wholesome laws and regulations, and we, the very men who have assisted in all your laudable enterprises, are now cast off because we have been unfortunate; are denied the rights of our common country. Have we sold our birth right? Are we excluded without a cause from the privileges enjoyed indiscriminately by the lowest class of our citizens? Was it not the calamities attending our country, that involved us in the misery we have so long experienced? Why then must we not be taken notice of? Why are we left the victims of arbitrary power and barbarous despotism, in a strange land far distant from all our connections, miserable exiles from the country for which we have fought, forgotten by our co[n]temporaries who formerly used to animate us in all our expedition with tales of liberty? O! Tempora! O! Mores! Thou art the people that now leave us neglected, buried in oblivion in the dungeons of Algiers, suffering the most ignominious captivity, when the paltry sum of $48,300 would have redeemed us years ago, and none of us would have been buried in the sand of "Bebal Wed" at the present when from twenty-one, who were captured in 1785, we are reduced by the plague and contingencies to only twelve, we might have been redeemed for a much smaller sum—nay, for less than $25,000; but it seems that we are doomed to be the only victims of American Independence. No means as yet have been pursued to extricate us from this terrest[r]ial purgatory, before the plague, which now rages in our prison, puts a final period to our existence.

O! America, if my sufferings could be of any benefit to you my beloved country, I would be happy in being the victim and glory in my chains; but as I am sure it cannot in the least degree, let me enjoy the melancholy privilege of bewailing my deplorable situation, which to a sentimental mind presents hor[r]ors easier to imagine than to describe.

I had remained in the room allotted me in the Bagnio Gallera all day without having eaten anything, and about 3 o'clock went to the Mad House tavern to get my dinner, and to give some to my unfortunate brother sufferers, when they came from hard labor as was generally my custom to do, but whether the thought of my situation or not having eaten anything since the morning or both, aided by a glass or two of wine impaired my reason or not, I am not aware, but I certainly acted very imprudently which had nearly ruined me forever. A sheriff—that is one who pretended to be a de[s]cendant of their Prophet Mahommed—desired me to rise and let him sit down, I told him that I was in my own house, and would finish my dinner before he, or any one else, would sit in my place. "What, dog without faith," answered this exasperated Moslem, "Will you presume to sit while one of the faithful and a sheriff stands?" You dare not call me a dog answered I; was I not a captive? You are an ungenerous cur for taking advantage of my situation; in any other I would cut your ears off; as far as being without faith I believe in the faith of my forefathers (la illah, ila Allah), there is no God but the true God. But as I was not born in the same country that you was, I have not been taught the symbol of your faith, but I know it. You say "la illah, ila Allah wa Mahomed Arasule Allah there is no God but the true God, and Mahomed is his prophet." I do not know Mahomed as a prophet, but I believe him to have been a very great law giver, who converted millions of Idolaters and induced them to worship the only true

God as I do; but I question if you know the tenets of your own religion as well as I do, or even know the history of your saints who succeeded your prophet and propagated the religion you profess. This harangue from a Christian drew the attention of all true believers in the tavern and prevented the sheriff from remembering that I threatened to cut off his ears; and an old sheik asked me where and how long was it since Mahomed was born, and who were his successors, as he said that he believed that I had assumed more knowledge than I possessed, building he supposed on the sheriff's ignorance, who was a soldier and not a learned man; that he was a Hadgi and had been twice to Mecca, and had the Koran by heart and consequently could not be deceived. I answered I had read the Koran and the life of Mahomed likewise in my own language, and as a proof that the translation was correct that I would answer his questions.

Mahomed the great law giver, I said, was born at Mecca in the month called Mary, in the year of Christ 571, and died at Medina on the 12th day of the 3rd month of Rabi-a-thani A.D., 632, and the 11th year of the Hegira, being 63 lunar years old at the time of his death. He was succeeded in the government by Ayesha's father, Abn Beckir, who was succeeded by Oman or Othman, who was succeeded by Ally Mahomed's son-in-law, who married Fatima, his daughter, by Cadigha, and had the best right to the succession, but was opposed three times successively by Ayesha and her party, and when ultimately he succeeded in obtaining the government, she and her party took up arms against him, and was the cause of the ruin of himself and his house. This was not a little facilitated by the death of his wife Fatima, which happened only sixty days after the death of her father, and considerably weakened his party. He, however, is adored to this day by the Persians, and some sects both in Asia and Africa. I was going to proceed when most of the Mahomedans exclaimed contemporaneously "Allah! Allah! Allah! this Christian is a Mahomedan, or the son of some renegade who pretended to turn Christian to serve his private purposes, he must become one of us. What did you say is the difference between your faith and ours?" I foolishly repeated as before la illah, illa Allah is mine, "and ours" they rejoined, "la illah, illa Allah wa Mahomed Arasule Allah!" This was a trap they had set for me; "he is ours" cried they; "he has pronounced the symbol of our faith." The Cadhi who lived but a few doors off was called upon, but fortunately was not at home. Another went to the Turkish barracks to get the Muden; he was at the Mosque, and as the Turks were obliged to be in their barracks before dark, some dispersed and only a few remaining I desired my tavern keeper to satisfy the sheriff by giving him some money and cordials, and likewise to treat all others who were most intent on what had happened, and the Hadgi, who was a sober man, I presented with ten sequins, requesting him if any questions were asked in the morning to say that what I had said I had rehearsed from the Koran, which I had in my possession in my own language without any intention whatever. I then returned to my prison, and thus escaped the greatest danger I had ever been in since my captivity commenced. The next day all was quiet except that some person had informed the Dey that a respectable Christian slave had wanted to become a Moslem the evening before. The Dey sent for the Hadgi who in consequence of the ten sequins reported favorably, and threw all the blame upon the sheriff, who in the first instance had exasperated me. "That young man has a hard head," said the Dey; "he has no more intention to turn Moslem than I have now to turn Christian; had he been so disposed he might have done it years ago much more to his advantage; for when I was Vikilharche of the Marine I offered him full pay if he would turn Turk, and the command of my largest cruiser, in which Salah Rais afterward lost his life in the engagement with the Russians in the Black Sea, a wife and a house and garden and likewise to take care of his fortunes in future; and probably, had he accepted my offer, he might at this instance be either Vikilharche himself or at least Post Admiral; but his answer was worthy of even a Turk, he said he thanked me for the good opinion I entertained of him, and that he would endeavor to retain it, but that he would deserve contempt if he should become an apostate from the religion of his forefathers merely to promote his worldly interests. "I should dispise [*sic*] a Moslem" said he, "Was he to renounce his faith merely to better his situation, and pray Effendi" said he, with a tear glistening in his eye, "what have you seen in my conduct to induce you to form so contemptible an opinion of me? Do you suppose that I can not bear slavery with all its concomitants and degradations sooner than renounce faith which I was taught to hold sacred by my mother, whom I hope yet to live to see and to thank more for her instructions than her nourishment."

"You see" says the Dey, "that this American has made fools of you all. In future you had better let him and his countrymen alone, and make converts elsewhere, for they are as hard headed as Arnahauds or as Englishmen themselves."

This conversation was recited to me in the first instance by the Hadgi on whom the ten sequins and some small presents afterwards had a most wonderful effect, and likewise in part by the Dey after I became chief secretary to him and the Regency in 1792. The escape which I have just recited prevented me from ever disputing with a Moslem upon points of religion again, and ought to serve as a warning to all who read this journal and travel in those countries; for in fact had the Cadhi been at home he was in duty bound to have demanded my admission among the true believers, the Dey himself dare not have opposed it; and had I refused after having recited the symbol of their faith

I would have been put to death as an apostate from it; so that I may conceive that I had a lucky escape.

From July 1791, I remained clerk to the Prime Minister, and to settle the accounts of the Dey's new house, which was not quite finished and which he sold to his Prime Minister when he became Dey himself.

Invocation

Oh! Omnipotent and Omnipresent Being, who beholdest the most hidden recesses of our hearts, influence that most august assembly of the United States of America, headed by the immortal Washington, in our favor, in order to extricate us with honor, from this state of incomprehensible misery in which we have remained seven years, without any one period of sentimental relief. This, O! most merciful God, is the anniversary of my departure from Boston, little imagining that I was to be buried from my country, my fellow citizens and all my dearest connections, to incur the displeasure of a just God; for surely nothing else could provide such a superlative degree of horror from one extreme of wretchedness to another, as I have experienced since my miserable captivity commenced. But sustained by the Almighty grace and that philosophy, which I have always taken pains to cultivate in extreme danger, I am preserved, myself to be a spectator of the small ray of hope we see reflected from our western world, through the channel of our present negotiation, magnified by the anxiety of our minds, longing to behold our beloved country. We are now in longing expectation of seeing our flag displayed in Africa, and we restored to our country, our liberty; and inspired by our long period of adversity with a spirit which, I hope, will make us worthy the patronage of the humane and benevolent Washington, the protector of his country and father of his people. The poor slaves in general never were in a more miserable situation than they are at present; wretchedness is painted on almost all their countenances, hard labor, scant provisions, injurious treatment, and blows from their cruel and most inhuman task masters. O! heavens, to insult distress in captivity and extreme wretchedness; what an unnatural deed, and is too much to bear to add to the load of misery that is borne by an afflicted slave, is unhuman beyond expression, and barbarous in a superlative degree. God forgive the perpetrators of such horrid deeds!

I became secretary to the Dey and Regency of Algiers, in March, 1792. This office became vacant by the redemption of my friend Mr. D'Andreis, with whom I was acquainted in Boston. The Dey remembered me and said that as I had fulfilled the duties of the different subordinate offices of clerk of the Marine, etc., that I ought to be preferred to the highest post a Christian can attain.

He, therefore, appointed me the same day. Notwithstanding that the Dey appointed me in consequence of my former services, he had it not in his power to exempt me from paying 1000 sequins to the Hasna or public treasury, and 383 sequins, the customary fee, to the officers of the government. This is paid in consequence of being entitled to redemption by any nation whatever, who either concludes a peace or ransoms their citizens, even should it take place the next day after his appointment, besides other perquisites. The Dey himself (strange as it may seem) loaned me 500 sequins, and my generous friend, the Messrs. Skjoldebrands (the Swedish consul and brother) loaned me 500 more, which I paid as the fee to the public treasury. I must not forget to mention my obligations upon this occasion, but upon a former one when I was by no means in so eligible a situation. These worthy and generous men loaned me $5000 to purchase a prize loaded with wine, on which I made a good speculation, without any interest or reward whatever, out of pure friendship. Although they knew the risk they run, for had I died or committed any fault, real or imaginary, before they were paid, the Regency would have seized all my property as their slave, and they would have lost every dollar of their money. Such unprecedented acts of generosity ought to be recorded on the tablet of our memory forever, never to be effaced. My gratitude to them is eternal and knows no bounds. The property I accumulated enabled me to purchase the vessel, of which I took the command, when I came to Philadelphia in 1796, to bring the articles to secure the peace.

ADDITIONAL WRITINGS BY CATHCART

Tripoli. Compiled by J. B. Newkirk. La Porte, IN: Herald Print, 1901.

❧ Maria Martin

History of the Captivity and Sufferings of Mrs. Maria Martin

Maria Martin's gruesome account of her long imprisonment in an Algerian dungeon enjoyed the greatest popularity of any of the spurious Barbary captivity narratives. From its first printing, likely in 1807, until its last in 1818, the narrative appeared in twelve editions by nine different publishers. The writer likely derived the Martin account from a fictionalized tale that appeared seven years earlier by the same publisher and under a very similar title, *The Captivity and Sufferings of Mrs. Mary Velnet, Who was Seven Years a Slave in Tripoli, three of which she was confined in a dungeon, loaded with irons, and four times put to the most cruel tortures ever invented by man.* While her narrative calls Mary Velnet "an Italian lady," Maria Martin's nationality remains a question. Two pieces of evidence within the narrative, however, suggest that readers might have understood her to be an American. First, she loathes the idea of "kingdom" and feels it is an epithet that should be struck from the land. Second, her voyage home took forty-five days, sufficient sailing time to return to America.

While the North African regencies captured many Western women, none of these captives appears to have written a narrative that has survived. Two other fabricated accounts, by Mary Gerard and Viletta Laranda, as well as several American plays with female captives suggest a public fascination with female captivity, perhaps derived from the Indian captivity tradition and accounts by Mary Rowlandson, Hannah Dustan, and Mary Jemeson among others. The female Barbary captive has also survived into the twentieth century through mass-marketed fiction in such romance titles as Victoria Holt's *The Captive* (1983) and Sergeanne Golon's *Angelique in Barbary* (1961).

Fig. 12. Bare breasted and
enchained, Mary Velnet
endures her torture. The
narrative by Maria Martin is
in part based on Velnet's
account. (Courtesy Rare
Book Room, Buffalo and Erie
County Public Library)

History of the *Captivity and Sufferings* of Mrs. Maria Martin, who was six years a slave in Algiers: *two of which she was confined in a dark and dismal dungeon, loaded with irons:* to which is annexed a history of Algiers, a description of the country, the manners and customs of the natives—their treatment to their slaves—their laws and religion—&c, &c. Boston: W. Crary, 1807.

H AVING IN THE FOREGOING PAGES given an account of the customs and manners of the Algerines, shall now proceed to relate some particulars of my Captivity and unparralleled [*sic*] sufferings while a slave among them. In the year 1800, I took passage at Madeira, in the sloop Triumph, for Cadiz—the object I had in view was to visit an aged uncle, with whom I had lived in the early part of my life. Nothing worthy of record took place from the time of my departure, until within sight of the rock of Gibraltar, when a man at mast head discovered a strange sail, steering directly for us. The sail in chase was soon within hail, and proved to be an Algerine corsair, armed and full of men. Our distracted feelings at this moment, can be better immagined [*sic*] than described—as we possessed but feeble means to defend ourselves, to surrender quietly our persons and property was the only alternative.—The corsair came along side, and in less than three minutes, more than half of her crew boarded us, sword in hand.—From this moment I must date the commencement of my sufferings.—The barbarians were no sooner on board, than they began their favorite work, cutting, maming [*sic*] and literally butchering, all that they found on deck. Having succeeded in clearing the deck of the sloop's people, they closed the hatches upon those who had sought shelter below, and took charge of our vessel, altering her course.

From the time of our capture they gave us nothing to subsist on but a few mouldy buiscuit, and a few quarts of stinking slimy water. On the eighth day they came to anchor in the harbour of Algiers—the hatches were now taken off and those below permitted once more to breath fresh air, and to witness the cheering rays of the sun. In a few moments after our arrival, we were successively boarded by more than one hundred boats from the shore, filled with men, women and children, who, apparently, strived to surpass each other in abusing us—the women (by whom I flattered myself I should be more humanely treated) would not unfrequently accost me with the epithet " *Chefti Oji*" (christian bitch!) These people were not only permitted, but encouraged to rob us of whatever they pleased—and to have resisted, would have been almost instant death—one took away my necklace, another my ring, and a third divested me of my shoes—the men were stripped of their cloathes, and in return, a few old duds were given them, hardly suffic[i]ent to cover them.

The commander of the corsair having now returned from the city, where he had been since our arrival, gave orders for the mooring of the sloop nearer the city. The orders of the commander were immediately executed, and in a few moments after, several boats were along side to take us on shore. The landing place was thronged with spectators, whose curiosity to view us, had brought them there, and by whom we were treated worse if possible than by those on board the sloop—he or she would think themselves fortunate indeed who could have an opportunity to level a blow at, or spit in the face of a Christian.

From the shore, we were conducted to the slave market, a place where all slaves are disposed of to the highest bidders. The bashaw, who had been sent for, and made acquainted with our capture, in a few moments arrived, to select from among us the usual number allowed him.—The bashaw is a short thick set man, of a tawny complexion and with whiskers which cover nearly the whole of his face—he wore neither shoes or stockings. On his arrival, he first enquired if there were any passengers among the captured, upon which, I was immediately conducted to him; he next demanded the captain, mate, second mate, carpenter, &c. Having obtained his number, we were led out of the market, and severally mounted upon mules, about twenty armed Turks, (the Bashaw's life guard) then conducted us to a house, where we were compelled to exchange our cloathing, for such as were worn by the slaves in general, which, for the men, is a large coarse pair of trousers, made so short, as to extend but a little way below the knees, a frock, and a thick coarse cloth cap—being thus garbed, each in a new suit, we were seperated [*sic*] and from that time, with the exception of the mate, I saw none of them afterward. I was conveyed to a small hut, adjoining the bashaw's habitation, it was dirty, mean and contracted. A few hours after my confinement, an old Turk (who was ever afterwards my attendant) brought me a jug containing about half a pint of inferior water, and a small piece of wormy beef—he likewise brought with him, a few yards of coarse cloth, a skein of thread, a jacknife [*sic*], and a rusty needle; with these he signified to me by his signs, I was to make up the cloth into garments for the slaves, and that in case of failure, severe punishment would be inflicted.

Gracious God! what were my feelings at this moment—no sooner had my attendant left me, than I, in a fit of dispair, seized the knife, and should had I not given myself time for a moment's reflection, certainly have put an end to my existence. I first viewed, and then cautiously tasted of the water which my jug contained, then of the rotten beef which accompanied it—but to taste, was all that I could do—"nought but extreme hunger (said I to myself) can compel me to partake of such nauseous food." After sometime contemplating upon the miseries which were likely long to attend me, I went to work with my jacknife [*sic*] (which I was to use as a substitute for scissors.) Being but a poor tayloress, the garment which I patched up, would I doubt not, have suffered considerably in a comparison with those made by the ingenious workmen of my own country.—However, as my orders were "work or be punished," I spared no pains in the performance of my work. At the sitting of the sun, the old Turk again visited my cell, and demanded my work, upon being presented with which, he left me, locking the doors after him. Hunger, I must now confess, compelled me to taste again of the beef, and to take a draught of the water, it was with much difficulty I succeeded in swallowing either. I next sought for something on which I might repose my wearied limbs during the night—I could find nothing but a few branches of the callabash tree, which probably were conveyed there for that purpose.

The succeeding morning, at sun-rise, my old attendant again visited me, bringing with him a like quantity of beef and water as before, and of no better quality. By signs he represented to me that my work on that day was to be the same as on the day preceding—in this way did he continue to visit me during my confinement in this desolate and dreary hovel, which, according to my calculation, was nearly twelve months.

Early one morning the old Turk entered, accompanied by the Mate of the unfortunate vessel in which I was captured, who accosted me with "well madam, I have had the good fortune to become the favorite of our master (the bashaw) and have perhaps been better treated than any other of our unfortunate ship's company—through my intercession, you are this day to be removed to a much more comfortable apartment than the one which you now occupy."—I thanked him for the great favor which he had rendered me, and promised him reward in case we should be so fortunate as to visit our native country once more.

The old Turk now made signs for me to follow him, which I gladly did, believing it not in his power to render my situation more deplorable than what it had been from the time of my capture. At the door of my apartment I found a guard of soldiers, who were sent to conduct me to my lodgings—the old Turk led the way, commanding us to follow—he took a circuitous rout round the city, and halted at the door of an old decayed castle, on entering of which, by the command of my attendants, I ascended two or three pair of stairs, and passed several narrow entries, in which lighted torches were burning, as they contained no windows. At the extremity of one of those dark winding entries, a large iron door presented itself to view—it was unlocked, and I commanded to enter—I found myself in a large spacious room, tolerably descent [*sic*] and comfortable, it however contained no furniture but an old matross [*sic*], a stool, and a small oak table—my attendants left me as soon as they had secured the doors.

The day being now far spent, and being much fatigued, I sought repose upon the matross [*sic*], and had the satisfaction soon to fall into a sound sleep, from which I did not awake until late the next morning, when I was suddenly aroused by the unbarring of the door of my apartment.—I arose hastily, and soon had the satisfaction to see my deliverer, the mate, enter, bringing with him a cup of coffee, a loaf of new baked bread, and a slice of ham.—"I have come madam (said he) this morning to present you with something, which to you, I presume, will prove a rich repast—and what is still more agreeable, to inform you that hereafter, I am to be your attendant—keep up good spirits, madam—I will spare no pains in my attempts to render your situation as comfortable as possible—you shall no longer suffer for food or cloathing while I can obtain either—I want to say a great deal more to you, but dare not at present, for fear of detection—through the goodness of God, madam, I hope I shall hereafter have an opportunity to discourse more freely with you,"—saying this, he hastily retired, as if fearful of being overheard. Alas! no tongue can tell what comfort his words afforded me.

What a strange thing is that called happiness! How shall I express my extreme joy, when after eleven months intolerable hunger, I was indulged with a sweet loaf of bread free from mould? The fond lover never rushed more eagerly to the arms of his bride; the famished tiger more ravenously on his prey than I upon this loaf; I eat, rested, surveyed the precious morsel, eat again, and absolutely shed tears of pleasure.

Oh Nature! what delight hast thou combined with the gratification of thy wants! remember this ye who rack invention to excite appetite, and which yet you cannot procure; remember how simple are the means that will give a crust of mouldy bread a flavour more exquisite than all the spices of the east, or all the profusion of land or sea: remember this, grow hungry, and indulge your sensuality.

A few moments after the sitting of the sun, my generous and noble benefactor again visited me, and brought with him my supper, he likewise presented me with some yams, which grow spontaniously [*sic*] Algiers. He informed that I should not be again compelled to do any kind of work, but in all probability, would be held a prisoner, until ransomed by my country—that, should not this soon take place, he would do all in his power to procure my liberation, but if unsuccessful in this, he would, at the hazard of his own life, leave no plans unpracticed to aid my escape, which he said he thought was practicable, since the whole care of me had been entrusted to him.—I thanked him for his kind offer, but begged of him not to endanger his life for my sake—that it was my sincere prayer that I should be one day enabled to repay him for the many favors he had already rendered me. He bid me good-night and retired. The succeeding morning he early again visited me—he informed me that he had the night previous been long in conversation with the bashaw, relative to my imprisonment, that he had represented to him that the imprisoning of female captives would be considered barborous [*sic*] in other countries, and was contrary to the law of nations, that if he (the bashaw) would grant me the liberty of the city, he would be answerable for my appearance at any moment that it should be requested—but that he could not prevail on the bashaw to allow me this indulgence, on no other condition than that I would renounce christianity and embrace the religion of Mahomet!—and since 'tis so (continues the mate) I am determined madam to convey and secret you on board of the first European vessel that arrives, let the consequence be what it may—this can be easily effected in the night time without creating suspicion—I am alone possessed of the keys of your apartment, and have orders to entrust them with no one—therefore, madam (said he) be prepared for a speedy departure, for what I now declare to you, shall be fulfilled the first opportunity that presents.

I could hardly believe my friend in earnest at first, but on recollection of the past services he had rendered me, I could not believe otherways.—I assured him that I would hold myself in readiness to depart at a moment's warning, and follow whatever directions he should be pleased to dictate.

Nothing from this time occurred worthy of note, until about six weeks after, when very early in the morning, my friend as usual entered with my breakfast—their [*sic*] was, I soon perceived, an unusual smile upon his countenance—"glad tidings, madam, glad tidings,"—exclaimed he, as entered,—"prepare yourself for a speedy departure—a ship from London has this moment arrived with presents to the bashaw, and will speedily return.—On board this ship it is my intention to take passage and return to my disconsolate family, and you, madam, must not fail to embrace this opportunity to return to your friends—already have I conversed with the captain upon the subject, and acquainted him with your deplorable situation, and have had the satisfaction to hear him declare his willingness to receive us on board, to protect us, and to do all in his power to aid our escape—tomorrow morning I may possibly be enabled to inform you of the precise time when the ship will depart—keep up good spirits, madam, and hope for the best—adieu for the present."—On saying this, the mate left me, his situation would not permit his continuing longer as it might have given rise to suspicion.

Through the whole of this day nought but mingled emotions of joy and grief invaded my mind—I could neither lie down, sit or stand still—the prospects before me, of a successful escape, would for a moment afford the most pleasing sensations—I would fancy myself half seas over and sometimes at the very door of my father's house, but, when I contemplated upon the possibility of detection and the nature of the punishment that would most assuredly be inflicted in such a case, my joy would be turned into grief. Night approached, but alas, I felt no inclination to slumber, my eyes I could not close, too impatient did I feel for the arrival of a moment, which, alas, proved the most disagreeable of my life.

Never did I witness the break of day with more pleasure than on the succeeding morning—the sun arose and shone with uncommon brilliancy—"Heaven quicken the footsteps of my friend,"—was my prayer—the doors of my apartment at length resounded—delightful sound!—The mate entered, and addressed me thus—"Madam, as usual, I have brought your breakfast, and through the goodness of God, may it be the last meal that you ever eat beneath the roof of a tyrant! This night, madam, will be either the most happy or the most wretched and unfortunate of our lives!—"Ere the rising of tomorrow's sun, we shall be either the most happy persons on earth, or the most wretched in existence."—"Heaven preserve me["] (cried I) and swooned!—When I recovered, I found myself supported by my friend, who continued thus—"fortitude, madam, is essentially necessary in this our important undertaking, if we have none of this, we cannot expect to succeed—were I not almost positive of success, never should I attempt any thing so hazardous, and which would inevitably prove destructive to our liberties forever, in case of detection.—This night, madam, the ship will sail, wind and weather permitting, every thing is prepared on board for our reception, about midnight I shall come for you, and as secretly as possible convey you on board—be not overcome by fear, offer up a prayer for our safe deliverance, and put your trust in Him whose creatures we are, and in whose power it is to protect and deliver us from our enemies."—My friend left me, he left me weeping!—two hours or more elapsed before I could muster sufficient fortitude to collect what little cloathing I had, together; after the elapse of a few hours, however, I became more composed, and by the time appointed by my friend, was in perfect readiness to depart.

About midnight my friend appeared, and in a low tone of voice, desired me to tread lightly and follow him—terror and darkness compelled me to take hold of the skirts of his coat, and was in this way re-conducted out of the dismal mansion, from whence we repaired with the utmost precipitancy on board the ship.

The Officers of the ship met us on deck and conducted us into the cabin, where we were solicited to partake of some refreshment.—"give yourself no uneasiness, madam, (said the captain) in three weeks, if the wind favours us, we will land you in a christian country,"—then turning to his mate "go (said he) and order the windless manned immediately, for it is time we were under way."

The orders of the commander were immediately executed, and in less than half an hour, I had the pleasure to discover the ship in motion. Fortune at this moment seemed to favour us—we were blessed with a good breeze and the wind favourable.

At day-break, land could but just be perceived, but to our sorrow we at this instant perceived the wind shifting and getting a-head—at sun-rise, it was completely so!—Alas! alas! I could at this moment read my fate in the countenances of all on board!—they gazed!—they pitied!—they wept.

In vain were the attempts of my friend to lull my fears—poor man! his countenance exhibited too much proof of the agitation of his own mind!—I now became like one distracted!—going on deck and finding the ship within plain sight of the city, and still losing ground, was about to throw myself overboard, when the mate perceiving my intentions, interfered.—Being strongly solicited by the captain, I again returned to the cabin, where I continued until I could distinctly hear the yells of the barbarians on shore, and in a few moments after, I heard the motion of oars along side!—Alas! O heavens! what were my feelings at this moment!—I fainted! . . . and recovered alas but to behold myself once more in the power of my unfeeling enemies!—they bound the mate and myself hand and foot, and carried us on shore—soon after, we were summoned to appear before the bashaw and his court to hear our sentences read, my friend being represented as having forfeited the confidence of his majesty, the court gave it as their opinion that for such a crime the criminal ought to suffer death. It now remaining for the bashaw to determine how and when he should suffer, he ordered him to be impanneled the succeeding day at sun-rise, and as is customary, in presence of all the slaves in the kingdom—my unfortunate friend heard the sentence read with a great deal of composure, it was interpreted by the French consul, in reply to which my friend observed, that "if I suffer thus inhumanly, it is a consolation that I suffer for no other crime than that of attempting to liberate from unjust and cruel slavery an innocent woman."

With regard to myself, the court gave it as their opinion that I ought to be kept in close confinement, fed on bread and water, and denied the priviledges allowed other slaves. The bashaw concurring, I was hurried off to my prison which had been built expressly for the purpose and of which the following is a description.

It was built of rough stone, and the walls were about 8 feet in breadth, it contained but one small window, with large iron gratings, and which afforded so little light that I could hardly discern an object four feet from me. My furniture consisted of a three legged stool and a gallon jug, which was filled once a fortnight with water.

God of heaven!—what were my feelings when I observed, on the 11th day of my confinement in this dismal cell, two smiths enter with their hammars, bringing along with them chains in abundance. They no sooner entered than they began the barbarous work of chaining me; an enormous collar was fixed round my neck, and another still larger round my waste [*sic*], to both of these was attached a large iron chain, the end of which, was fixed to a ring in the wall. This ring was five feet from the ground, and only allowed me to sit down on the stool above mentioned. They next rivited [*sic*] two iron rings around each of my wrists, to each of which a chain was fixed.

In this situation they left me, helpless and wretched, preyed on by all the torture of thought, that continually suggested the most gloomy, the most dreadful images. My fortitude after some time, began to revive; I glowed with the desire of convincing the world I was capable of suffering what man had never suffered before. Often did I reflect how much happier I was in innocence, than the malefactor doomed to suffer the pangs of death, the ignominy of men, and the horrors of internal guilt.

The enormous iron round my neck pained me, and prevented motion. The chains that descended from the neck collar were obliged to be supported first with one hand, and then with the other, for, if thrown behind, they would have strangled me, and, if hanging forwards, occasioned most excessive headachs. The little sleep I could have in such a situation may easily be supposed, and at length body and mind sunk under this accumulation of miserable sufferings, and I fell ill of a burning fever. Reason, fortitude, heroism, all the noble qualities of the mind, decay when the corporeal faculties are diseased, and the remembrance of my sufferings at this dreadful moment, still agitates, still enflames my blood, so as almost to prevent an attempt to describe what they were. Yet hope had not totally forsaken me. Deliverance seemed possible, especially should peace ensue.

I continued ill about two months, and was so reduced at last, that I had scarcely strength to lift the water jug to my mouth. What must the sufferings of a female be who is confined in a dungeon so damp, so dark, so horrible, without bed or straw, her limbs loaded as mine were, with no refreshment but dry mouldy bread, without so much as a drop of broth, without a consoling friend, and who under all these afflictions, trust for her recovery to the efforts of nature alone.

Sickness itself is sufficient to humble the mightest [*sic*] mind; what then is sickness with such addition of torment? The burning fever, the violent headachs, my neck swelled and inflamed with the irons, enraged me almost to madness. The fever and the fetters together flead my body so that it appeared like one continued wound.—The irons every where round my body, and their weight was insupportable; nor could I imagine it was possible I should habituate myself to them, or to endure them long enough to expect deliverance. A thousand reasons convinced me it was necessary to end my sufferings. I shall not enter into theological disputes: let those who blame me imagine themselves in my situation; or rather let them first actually endure my miseries, and then let the reason.

As I had passed nearly two years in this dismal cell I began to dispair of ever again enjoying my liberty. In one of my most serious hours, as I was sitting meditating upon the various scenes of my life, the doors of my dungeon I suddenly heard unbarring—the doors of my dungeon for the last time resounded!

A Turkish officer at this moment entered, and gave me to understand that my liberty had been purchased by my country.—Heavens! what joy did I feel on this occasion, it was a long time before I could be convinced of the truth of what was told me, nor would I believe it until a smith entered to take off my irons.

For some weeks after I first obtained my freedom, I was generally absent in mind, and deep in thought. This was a habit I acquired in prison, and the objects of sight appeared but as the visions of sleep. I often stopped in the streets, stared around me, doubted my own existence, and bit my finger, in order to convince myself that I was really awake and alive.

Three weeks after my liberation from the bitterest captivity ever experienced by man, I embarked once more to visit my native country, with a view of which, after a long and tedious passage of 45 days, my eyes were once more regaled. My friends had received the disagreeable news of my captivity, and dispaired of ever again seeing me. Before I conclude, it may be well to mention, that my friend the mate who was to suffer agreeable to the orders of the bashaw, the night preceding bribed his keepers and escaped to Morocco, where he took passage in an English vessel, and returned in safety to his friends.

FINIS.

American Captives in Tripoli

As part of the 1796 peace accord, the Algerian dey agreed not to disclose the huge price he had won from the Americans so that U.S. diplomats could negotiate comparatively inexpensive treaties with Tunis ($107,000) and Tripoli ($56,486). Eventually, however, this strategy backfired. The bashaw of Tripoli grew increasingly angry over the discrepancies and delays in tribute, and on May 14, 1801, he had the American flagstaff in Tripoli chopped down, officially declaring war on the United States (the Tripolitan War of 1801–05). After a two-year stalemate between the two powers, Jefferson sent Commodore Edward Preble to enforce an embargo on Tripoli harbor. When he finally approached Tripoli, however, he received devastating news—one of his two frigates, the *Philadelphia,* captained by William Bainbridge, had been piloted onto an uncharted reef just a few miles outside of Tripoli harbor and captured with its entire complement of 307 U.S. sailors. Tripoli, now holding more U.S. captives than Algeria ever had at one time, demanded $1.69 million for their release. The event, by far the single largest Barbary imprisonment of U.S. citizens, propelled the United States into another captive crisis.

Jonathan Cowdery served as one of several of the *Philadelphia's* surgeons and lived out his time in Tripoli among the officers, who were very well treated. The bashaw extended his courtesy to Bainbridge and his staff, and they enjoyed a great number of privileges denied to the ordinary seaman. The only work Cowdery was called upon to perform during his captivity was medical in nature. The bashaw asked the doctor to be his personal physician, and Cowdery readily agreed. Indeed, in most ways, Dr. Cowdery's captivity—replete with garden strolls and the fruits of the bashaw's personal

Jonathan Cowdery

gardens—hardly resembled the difficult experience of most of the Tripolitan prisoners.

Jonathan Cowdery's narrative, *American Captives in Tripoli; or, Dr. Cowdery's Journal in Miniature,* appeared in 1806, the first account to be published after the war. His editor assures the reader that Cowdery kept a "regular journal" throughout the war, and that this "journal in miniature" is Cowdery's selection of extracts from the original. Prior to his narrative, which came out in two 1806 editions, Cowdery had apparently published excerpts of the journal in several newspapers, and it was perhaps because of their favorable reception that he was encouraged to publish this condensed version.

Fig. 13. Chopping down the U.S. flagstaff and declaring the start of the Tripolitan War. (Courtesy University of Minnesota Libraries)

American Captives in Tripoli; or, Dr. Cowdery's Journal in Miniature. Kept during his late captivity in Tripoli. 2d ed. Boston: Belcher and Armstrong, 1806.

THE PARTICULARS of the unfortunate capture of the *Philadelphia* frigate, by the Tripolitans, have already been before the publick. She run on a bank abreast of the harbour of *Tripoli,* on the 31st of October, 1803, at 11, A.M. and kept up a brisk cannonade, with the gun boats of that regency, until 4, P.M.; when, failing in their efforts to get her off, they surrendered to superiour force. The *Philadelphia* mounted 44 guns, and had 350 men; she was afterwards got off by the Tripolitans, and moored in their harbour; but was destroyed by Capt. STEPHEN DECATUR, jun. in a schooner, with three boats, a part of our Mediterranean squadron, who boarded and burnt her upon the night of the 18th of Feb. 1804, four months after her capture. On the capture of the *Philadelphia,* the Tripolitans demanded *one million six hundred and ninety thousand dollars,* for the release of our captured brethren! they, however, have been very glad to take 60,000 dollars for their release, and to enter into new bonds for future good behaviour! This much premised, we now proceed to Dr. COWDERY's Journal; which he commences immediately after his capture.

AFTER THE FLAG of the *Philadelphia* was struck, (says the Doctor,) and the officers and crew were waiting the pleasure of their new masters, the Tripolitan chiefs collected their favourites, and, with drawn sabres, fell to cutting and slashing their own men, who were stripping the Americans and plundering the ship. They cut off the hands of some, and it is believed several were killed. After this battle amongst themselves was a little over, we were ordered in the boats to be carried on shore. One of their officers, whom I had taken by the hand, and who promised me his friendship, came to me, took me by the arm, and told me I must go. I asked him to let my boy go with me, which he refused. I then took hold of my small trunk, which contained my best clothes; he gave me to understand that I could not take it, but should have every thing taken care of and restored to me. He took hold of my hand and hurried me over the side of ship, while his other hand was employed in rifling my pockets, from which he took about ten dollars. I had concealed some gold in my clothes, which he did not find. I then went down into one of their boats, from whence

Jonathan Cowdery

I was to pass into the next, which was almost full of our officers and men. I made all haste to get into it, for I observed that the Turks in the boat where I then was, were stripping my messmate, Dr. Harwood, and the carpenter, Mr. Godby; but I was soon stopped by three of the ruffians, who stood over me with drawn sabres and cocked pistols, and wrested my surtout from under my arm. Whilst they were picking its pockets, and quarrelling with each other for the booty, I sprung for the next boat, which was waiting for me. In my way, I met a little fellow, who seized me, and attempted to take off my coat; but I hurled him into the bottom of the boat, and jumped into the one which was waiting, amongst my fellow officers, where I thought the Turks more civil. They then set off for the town, compelling our men to row the boat, and standing with drawn sabres over our heads. When we had got near the shore, they ordered our men to stop rowing. Two of them came to me and gave me a severe blow on the side of the head. They then searched me, and took a case of surgeon's instruments from my pocket. They took my pocket book, but finding it contained nothing but papers, they returned it. One took my silver pencil, and another the handkerchief from my neck. They then began upon Mr. Knight, sailing master, Mr. Osborne, lieutenant of marines, and all the officers in the boat, plundered their pockets and took the handkerchiefs from their necks. They then landed us at the foot of the Bashaw's palace, where we were received by a guard, who conducted us into the palace before the Bashaw. He viewed us with the utmost satisfaction, and had us conducted into an apartment where we found the captain and several officers, who arrived in another boat just before us. Here was a table set in the European style. The servants appeared to be Maltese and Neapolitan slaves. Here we supped, after which it was announced that another boat had arrived with our officers and men, who were before the Bashaw. Capt. Bainbridge requested me to go and look for Dr. Harwood, whom it was feared was killed. I found him with the carpenter before the Bashaw, stripped of every thing but their shirts and trowsers. They afterwards informed us, that they were stripped in the boat where I lost my surtout; and when they got within a few rods of the shore, they were thrown into the sea, and left either to drown or swim ashore. The Bashaw's servant gave them dry clothes, and we were all again conducted before the Bashaw, and formed into a half circle. He was seated on his little throne, which was decorated in the Turkish order, and made a handsome appearance. He is a good looking man, aged about 35. He counted us, viewed us with a smile, and appeared highly pleased with us.—We were then conducted by the minister of exteriour relations and a guard, to the house formerly occupied by the American consul—a very good house, with a large court, and roomy enough for our convenience. We were seated here about nine o'clock in the evening. Capt. Bainbridge got permission from the Bashaw to send for the Danish consul, who paid us a visit and offered every assistance in his power. We slept upon mats and blankets spread upon the floor, which was composed of tiles.

November 1.—This morning the Danish consul, Mr. Nissen, paid us another visit. Capt. Bainbridge engaged him to furnish us with provisions and such other necessaries as we might want. Our dwelling was furnished in a plain style and we were supplied with fresh provisions that were tolerably good. We were allowed to go to the front door, and to walk on the terrace or top of the house, which commanded a handsome prospect of the harbour, the sea, the town, the palace, and the adjoining country. Here we could see our ship on the rocks, full of Turks, and surrounded by their boats, and a constant stream of boats going to, and bringing off, the plunder of the ship. We could see these robbers running about town, with our uniform coats and other clothing on. The minister of exterior relations promised to be friendly, and collect as much of our clothing and effects as he could, and return them to us.

Nov. 3.—The Bashaw sent for the carpenter to go on board the ship; he went and found six feet water in the hold. The carpenter's crew and fifty men were ordered and carried on board to work at night. A gale of wind and heavy sea hove the ship off the rocks, and the carpenter returned.

Nov. 4.—In the morning lieutenants Hunt and Osborne, and myself, were at the Danish consul's observatory, on the top of his house, upon a plain with and adjoining ours, which together made a large and handsome walk. We were looking at the ship with Mr. Nissen's glass, when our drogerman came and informed us that the Bashaw had ordered us not to walk upon the terrace any more. We immediately returned to our house.

Nov. 5.—Our new masters came and closed up the passage which led to the top of the house; and a guard was set at the front door to prevent our going into the street. The minister sent his chief secretary with a parole of honour, written in French, which we all signed.

Nov. 6.—We found that we were not allowed to go out, notwithstanding our signing the parole of honour. The minister of exterior relations sent us word that he had got eight of our trunks, which we might have for twelve hundred dollars. We did not take them, nor thank him for his hospitality. We purchased new blankets, sent to us by the Danish consul. The English consul, Mr. M'Donald, paid us a visit and offered us every assistance in his power.

Nov. 8.—The Jews purchased some of our clothing and offered it to us at an enormous price; but we purchased but little of it. The Bashaw sent for captain Bainbridge and told him that John Wilson had informed that captain Bainbridge, before hauling down the colours, threw over nineteen boxes of dollars and a large bag of gold. Captain Bainbridge assured him it was false, and gave his word and honour, that there was no money thrown over to his knowledge; but that the money in question was left at Malta. In the evening, the Bashaw not being satisfied, sent for the captain's servant, and ordered him to be flogged if he did not tell the truth concerning the money. The boy denied having any knowledge of it. After repeating the threat several times, and the boy insisting that he knew nothing about the money, he was acquitted. Wilson had turned traitor, and given the enemy all the assistance in his power. He now acts as overseer over our men.

Nov. 9.—Our captain established a credit with the Danish consul, who supplied us with necessary provision, and with cloth for matrasses. A guard was posted at our door, to prevent our going into the street, or purchasing any books or clothing.

Nov. 10.—Several Turks came and informed captain Bainbridge that the Bashaw had been told that captain Rogers who commanded the U.S. frigate John Adams, treated the Tripolitan prisoners taken last summer, very bad; and that they feared we should suffer for it.

We have plenty of pomegranates, dates and oranges. The Danish consul visits us every day.

Nov. 13.—The minister of exteriour relations sent his drogerman to captain Bainbridge and informed him, that if he would send an immediate order to commodore Preble, to deliver up the Tripolitan prisoners captured by captain Rogers last summer, amounting to about eighty in number, we might remain where we were, but if he did not comply, we should fare worse. Captain Bainbridge replied, that he could not command commodore Preble, and therefore could not comply with his request. At 9, in the evening, a Tripolitan officer came armed with two pistols and a sabre, and said, *To night nothing; to-morrow the castle.* We accordingly prepared for the castle.

Nov. 14.—Breakfasted early, to be ready for our new habitation. At 9, A.M. a guard came and ordered us to the castle. We formed agreeable to rank, and marched to the castle. We were huddled into the most gloomy cell, among our men, where there was hardly room for us to stand. Here we spent the day without food, and were scoffed at by our foes until night, when, to our happy surprise, we were conducted back to our old place of abode. The minister of exteriour relations sent for captain Bainbridge, and affected great surprise at our going to the castle, saying that he knew nothing of the measure, which we all knew to be false. He told captain Bainbridge that we should remain where we were until he heard from his people, the prisoners, in the hands of the Americans.

Nov. 17.—Visited our sick, who were quartered in a small house without a floor, near the palace, and about half a mile from our lodgings. The Danish consul supplied the sick with fresh provisions, by the request of captain Bainbridge.

Nov. 20.—The minister permitted us to purchase our clothes. We got but a few, and at a high rate. One of our men, by the name of Thomas Prince, turned Turk, and was admitted into the Palace.

Nov. 21.—After visiting our sick, I was permitted to go with our drogerman about the town to purchase medicine; we found but a few articles. A man of 116 years of age came to have me cure him of deafness.

Nov. 24.—The Bashaw refused to furnish necessary clothing for the sick, or any thing for them to eat, but sour filthy bread.—Captain Bainbridge contracted with the Danish consul to supply the sick with beef and vegetables for soup every day.

Nov. 27.—Our men complained of their hard usage, in being compelled to lie on the cold damp ground, to eat bad bread, to work hard, and to be bastinadoed by their drivers.

Nov. 30.—One of our men in a fit of despair attempted to kill himself; but was prevented by the Turks, when in the act of cutting his throat. The wound did not prove mortal. I was permitted by the minister to call on the Spanish physician for medicine for Dr. Ridgley, who was then sick.

December 5.—The Bashaw sent for me to prescribe for himself and two officers of his body guard, and ordered me to get such medicine as was necessary of the minister, who had a medicine chest.

Dec. 6.—Visited the sick at the palace, and found them all better. I was received and treated very politely. The minister sent for me to cure him of a blindness in the left eye. I prescribed for him with very little success.

Dec. 7.—Visited the ambassador of Constantinople, who was affected with the intermitting fever. Found my patients at the palace almost well.

Dec. 8.—Received several natural curiosities of Tripoli from Mr. Nissen.

Dec. 9.—Visited the Turkish ambassador and found him better. He asked many questions about America, and treated me with coffee.

Dec. 10.—Visited the Turkish officer, where I found a captain of one of the Grand Seignior's ships of war, who came to Tripoli to carry presents to the Grand Seignior. The Tripolitan captain who took the brig from Philadelphia, captain Morris, was also there. He was very inquisitive about our country and our navy.

Dec. 12.—Was called on by the general of Marine to visit his principal secretary. Before I was permitted to give any medicine the Turks, six in number, with *Hamet,* our drogerman, summoned the sick man, and offered a prayer to

Mahomet. The sick man then told me that if I would cure him he would be very thankful, and would speak to the Bashaw in our favour.

Dec. 15.—The Bashaw had a schooner launched, which was built by the Spanish carpenters. She was tolerably handsome, and calculated to carry six guns. When she was launched, three guns were fired from the batteries, and the consuls hoisted all their colours. At sun set, a firing from the batteries announced the commencement of the Mahometan *Ramadam,* continuing a lunar month, in which they neither eat, drink, nor smoke, while the sun is above the horizon, but feast at night. In walking through the town, to visit my patients, I found the mosque and principal houses illuminated, and the people rejoicing. Passing the coffee house with our drogerman, *Lysle,* a renegado Scotchman, who was now the Tripolitan admiral, called me in to drink coffee with him and was very polite.

Dec. 16.—Visited the Marine secretary, and found him in a state of great debility. Could not prevail on him to take any medicine, or the least kind of nourishment. He said he would rather die than offend Mahomet by breaking the *Ramadam;* but would take whatever I should advise at night.

Dec. 20.—The market was so poor that we could get nothing for dinner, but a shoulder of poor dromedary.

January 1.—Was called to visit the Bashaw's child, about eleven months old. The Bashaw seemed much affected on my pronouncing the child dangerous; and wished me to pay every attention to it, saying, that any thing he could afford should be at my service.

Jan. 2.—Found the Bashaw's child better, at which he expressed great satisfaction, and offered me a horse and servant to go to his gardens, about two miles from town. I preferred walking, and took our drogerman with me. As I passed out at the gate of the city, I saw a man's head sticking on a pole. On enquiry, I found that it was the head of one of the *Bedouins,* who, about a year before, killed the son in law of the Bashaw, who commanded the army, in collecting the taxes in the back part of his dominions. About a quarter of a mile from the gate, the road passed through a burying ground full of graves. After this I came into a well cultivated country which was laid out in squares from one to six or eight acres, each surrounded with date trees, interspersed with orange, fig, olive, lemon and other trees. On coming to admiral Lysle's garden we found him there, and he invited me in. It was very beautiful. He loaded us with its fruits, and offered me access to it whenever I chose, and said I was welcome to any thing growing in it. I concluded to postpone going to the Bashaw's garden until another day.

Jan. 3.—Went to the Bashaw's garden, where I met the minister and the prince the Bashaw's eldest son. They politely conducted me through the garden, which was ornamented with a great variety of fruit trees, loaded with fruit, particularly with oranges, lemons and limes. John Hilliard died in the evening.

Jan. 4.—William Anderson died.

Jan. 12.—The Bashaw's eldest daughter was married to Selim the Bashaw's chief *Casleda* or Treasurer. Wilson, who was one of our quarter masters, and lately turned traitor and Turk, received 500 bastinadoes for quarrelling with the noted Lysle.

Jan. 14.—The minister of foreign affairs, Sidi Mahomet Docize, visited our prison. The month's fasting (*Ramadam*) ended this day at the change of the moon. The Tripolitans fired a salute from our ship which lay moored in the harbour within sight of our window.

Jan. 15.—The feast called *Byram* commenced. Every gun in Tripoli was fired in honour of the day. Every Turk put on his best suit, and there was a general rejoicing.

Jan. 16.—Capt. Bainbridge and lieutenant Porter were invited and accordingly visited the Bashaw, with all the consuls.

Jan. 17.—The *Byram* ended this evening. The consuls, the ships in the harbour, and the castle displaying their colours during the three days. The rejoicing was great, but neither elegance nor taste were discoverable.

Jan. 18.—By permission visited the triumphal arch which was built at the time the Romans conquered this country. It is dedicated to Augustus Cesar; is very large, built of fine marble, and is full of engravings and inscriptions in tolerable perfection. It stands near the marinery.

Jan. 19.—The Bashaw's agent sent us a present of tea, coffee and sugar, and a lamb, probably to induce us to buy a quantity of old clothes taken from us, for which they asked 600 dollars.

Diet at this time, two eggs and a piece of bread, with rain water for breakfast and supper; poor beef or camel's flesh, bread, and sometimes boiled cabbage, with rain water for dinner.

February 3.—Was conducted to the castle to visit the Bashaw, whom I found after passing several centinels, about fifty fierce yelping dogs, and three heavy doors loaded with irons and bolts, which were opened for us by armed mamelukes. Prescribed for the Bashaw's disorder.

Feb. 6.—The Bashaw sent for me to come to his room in the castle. He shook hands with me, received me with much politeness, and requested me to pay every attention to his family as a physician.

Feb. 10.—The Bashaw gave the officers permission to walk out into the town and country, but not to visit the consuls nor the batteries. Our droger-man, Hamet, was ordered to walk with us and direct us where to go. We went out six at a time.

Feb. 16.—Prescribed for the Bashaw's eldest daughter. Her husband offered me many civilities. At 5 o'clock, P.M. were informed that two English merchantmen were standing in for the harbour. They proved, however, to be two vessels under the command of capt. Decatur. About 11, at night, we were alarmed by a most hideous yelling and screaming from one end of the town to the other, and a firing of cannon from the castle. On getting up and opening the window which faced the harbour, we saw the frigate Philadelphia in flames.

Feb. 17.—The Turks appeared much disheartened at the loss of their frigate. A strong guard was put at our door, and we were forbid going out. I was forbid visiting our sick. It was reported that an American schooner and three boats set fire to the ship. Two Turks escaped who told this news. They said that eight Turks had charge of the ship, and they supposed the other six were carried off by the Americans. Our drogerman informed us that we were to be removed from our present habitation into the castle.

Feb. 18.—A guard of about twenty Turks was at our door. I asked permission to visit our sick, and was refused. A gloomy aspect continued on the faces of the inhabitants for the loss of the frigate.

Feb. 19.—Again asked permission to visit our sick, and was refused.

Feb. 20.—Permitted to visit the sick.—Found the town full of country militia and our guard doubled.

Feb. 21.—Our prison was kept full of Turks to guard us. The Bashaw, having got a little over his fright, consented to let us remain where we were.

Feb. 24.—We were forbid sending letters to our friends, without first shewing them to the Bashaw or his ministers. The last letters we received, were broken open by the latter, before they were delivered to us.

March 1.—We were conducted to the castle.

March 2.—Found our habitation very dark and smoky, having no light but what came through a grated sky-light.

March 3.—Not allowed to visit the sick, and our drogerman was forbid carrying letters to us.

March 4.—Captain Bainbridge received a letter from the ministers, reprimanding him on account of three men who floated ashore a few days after the burning of the frigate. The Turks pretended that they were murdered after they were made prisoners by the Americans.

March 6.—In close confinement. Hamet, our drogerman, was taken from us. The Bashaw suspected him of being too friendly to us.

March 7.—The Tripolitans got the guns from the remains of our frigate, and mounted them on their batteries. In trying them, several of the gun carriages broke down, and one of the guns burst and killed one Turk and wounded four.

March 14.—The Turks seemed much alarmed, and placed a strong guard at our door, for what reason we knew not.

March 16.—The Bashaw sent word that I should have any thing I wanted, free of expense.

March 17.—Ordered not to send our clothes out to wash.

March 24.—I was taken out of prison to visit a mameluke's wife and child. The minister of foreign affairs paid us a visit, and said many clever things.

March 26.—A truce was held between commodore Preble and the Bashaw.

From *March* the 28th to the 13th of *April,* I was violently afflicted with the dysentery, during which time the Bashaw expressed much anxiety, and offered me every assistance.

April 15.—We felt the Syroc wind, which was very oppressive.

April 24.—John Morrison died, in consequence of a hurt he received a few days before while at work under the directions of his new masters. The Bashaw permitted me, with two of my fellow officers, to go to his garden, conducted by a guard of two Turks, armed with pistols and sabres. This precaution, they pretended was taken to prevent the wandering Arabs and Moors from robbing us; but it was probably done to prevent our escaping to the squadron, then cruising of the harbour, in sight.

May 7.—Our boys caught a large scorpion in the small yard of our prison.

May 11.—Our squadron appeared off the town. The Turks were at their quarters. They had twelve gun boats armed, manned, moored out in the harbour.

May 16.—Ten of our officers took a walk to the gardens under escort of a guard. They returned with a variety of flowers and ripe apricots.

May 20.—A party of us, under escort of four Turks, walked to the desert, about four miles from our prison. We ascended a large bank of sand, where we had an extensive view of the country. The deserts have a singular and grand appearance. The[y] extend to Mount Atlas, which we could see at the distance of two day's journey. The sand is in heaps, like snow drifts in our country. There was not a house nor any other object to be seen; not a thing growing to interrupt the sight; but it appeared like an ocean of sand. On our return we visited several gardens, where we got oranges, lemons, apricots, and a variety of flowers. We were treated with sap of the date tree, which tasted much like mead.

May 29.—A party of us, under escort as before, took a walk into the desert. On our return we dined in the Bashaw's garden, under the shade of orange trees. The dinner was prepared in the Turkish style, and we ate with wooden spoons—it was simple and good. We visited several gardens, and were treated with as much respect as could be expected or desired from a foe, who held us as prisoners of war. On returning to town we saw two of our brigs at anchor off the harbour, seeming to defy all the force of Tripoli.

June 4.—We are plentifully supplied with squashes and cucumbers.

The Bashaw's eldest wife, called the queen, was delivered of her ninth child on the 18th of June. She was twenty-three years of age. H[er] first child was born when she was in her eleventh year. It was said to be common to marry at ten.

June 27.—Mr. Hodge our boatswain, Mr. Douglas the sail-maker, and Mr. Fontaine the first master's mate were taken from the prison and set to work by order of the Bashaw.

July 15.—The Bashaw, his wives and guards removed to their country seat at his garden. The season was very warm and our confinement continued. We purchased figs, watermelons, muskmelons, and cucumbers.

July 28.—I was called to visit the Bashaw's eldest son, the Bey of Tripoli (termed the *Prince of Wales of Tripoli,* by the English Consul) at his palace, about three miles from town. I found him in a lofty and airy apartment, lying on a mattras, and surrounded by his attendants. I prescribed for him and was highly entertained in the Turkish style. Saw two old women, said to have been a former Bashaw's wives.

July [2]9.—The Bey was well enough to return to Tripoli. He called at the door of our prison, which was unlocked and the bolts and bars unloosed. I was conducted to him when he expressed great satisfaction at having recovered his health, thanked me for my attendance, and promised to alleviate our misfortunes, as far as was in his power. I was then sent back to prison. The Bashaw and Bey spent a day alternately in town, on account of the expected attack by the Americans.

July 31.—I was carried with my trunk and bed, to the castle, where a room was provided for me, and the Bashaw informed me I must attend the Americans and his family as a physician.

August 3.—The American squadron, under commodore Preble, consisting of one frigate (the Constitution), two brigs, three schooners, and seven gun-b[o]ats, at about 2 o'clock, P.M. commenced an attack on the batteries and gun-boats of Tripoli. I stood on the top of the castle, where I had a fair view of the engagement. Three of the enemy's gun-boats were captured by the Americans. Two Turks swam on shore, and were carried before the Bashaw, who gave them a suit of clothes and a few dollars. They said that many were killed on both sides.

Aug. 5.—The American squadron anchored off Tripoli, I was ordered to dress the wound of a mameluke, who had his hand shattered by the bursting of a blunderbuss. I amputated all his fingers but one, with a dull knife, and dressed them in a bungling manner, in hopes of losing my credit as a surgeon in this part of the country, for I expected to have my hands full of wounded Turks in consequence of the exploits of my brave countryman.

Aug. 9.—At about 12 o'clock the alarm gun of Tripoli was fired. The Tripolitans all took their stations, and went through the Mahometan prayer, by kneeling and kissing the ground several times, with their faces towards the east, all with as much regularity as the exercise in a well disciplined army. Their military manoevuring [*sic*] was a scene of the utmost confusion. I got permission to go on the top of the castle, where I had a most extensive view of the sea and land, and saw the American squadron approaching the town. At about 1 o'clock the attack commenced, and the battle soon became vigourous, with a tremendous cannonading on both sides. I now beheld the melancholy catastrophe of the explosion of one of our gun boats. I saw the mangled bodies of my countrymen precipitated into the air. For a few moments a general silence took place, when the firing recommenced with unabated vigour. I saw the shells explode, and set fire to the town in many places; but the houses being principally built of stone, mud and mortar, the fire did but little damage: the shells and shot, however, battered the town very much, and almost destroyed some of the houses. The firing ceased at 4, P.M. when the ship John Adams joined the squadron. The Bashaw has a bomb proof room in his castle, where he staid during the action. On hearing of the explosion of our gun boat, he ventured out to take a peep, with the precaution of having a *Marabewt* or priest, to seal a small piece of paper on the top of his head, with a Turkish or Mahometan scrawl, with assurances that it would entirely secure him from all danger, but he soon returned to his cell. The Turks all wear a paper of this kind, sewed up in a little velvet bag, with assurances from the *Marabewt* that it would protect them in the greatest danger. The *Marabewt* gets a sum of money for these blessings. If a Turk gets wounded or killed, it is supposed the blessed paper was too old, or not placed in a proper manner. In the time of action the *Marabewt* gets upon some secure place and cries to Mahomet in the most dismals [*sic*] yells to let them conquer their enemies; and beckon to the vessels to run on shore or be destroyed. Such of our crew as were able, were put to work, and drove about like horses or mules.

Aug. 10.—Lewis Heximer, who lately turned Turk, went by order of the Bashaw, and told capt. Bainbridge, the particulars of the two late actions. The Bashaw informed me that the late commander of the schooner Vixen, lieut. Smith, was commodore of the gun boats in the late action, and was killed by a musket shot through his head. Our men complained of being drove and beat about at an unmerciful rate, in consequence of which they petitioned the Bashaw, in the following terms:

"*To his Excellency the Grand Bashaw of Tripoli:* The petition of the whole of the American prisoners, most humbly sheweth:—

"That your humble petitioners, when doing with all their power, as they are commanded, are most cruelly beaten by our wardens, stoned, insulted, and spit upon by the soldiers and others; required to carry burthens impossible for us to sustain; and chased and bruised, until we are, or soon shall be, unable to labour at all.

"From the many acts of justice, kindness, and generosity we have experienced from your Excellency, we cannot suppose that such conduct is authorized by your commands; or that we should be punished for what is out of our power to perform; or for the actions of others, which we have no agency in, and which we cannot prevent.

"Returning your Excellency our sincere and humble thanks for your bounty and privileges heretofore shewn, and relying on your goodness and protection, we therefore most humbly pray, that your Excellency would interpose your royal authority, and grant us a speedy relief. And your petitioners, as in duty bound, will remain your Excellency's most humble, faithful and obedient servants."

On the petition being explained to the Bashaw by Heximer, (or *Hamet Amerikan,* his new name) the Bashaw forbid the Turks striking the prisoners.

Aug. 11.—The Bashaw sent for me, and, agreeably to his orders, I took a seat by his side. He began conversation about my country, and our squadron, which was then in sight, and consisted of eighteen. He said that for two dollars he could repair all the damages that the bombardment did to his town; that but one man was hurt by the shells; that what he had been offered for the American prisoners was but fifty dollars per man; that he would make them earn that sum in two months. He asked me what I thought my country would give for me. I told him I did not know. He said he would not take twenty thousand dollars for me; to which I replied, that I might then expect to remain in slavery for life. He patted me on the shoulder and said, I must then content myself to stay with him. I asked to go and see our men, but he refused, saying, the Moors and Arabs would kill me if the[y] could catch me.

Aug. 12.—Our squadron hoisted a flag of truce, sent in a brig and schooner and fired a gun. The Bashaw did not, and swore he would not, answer it; and said he would not treat with commodore Preble. A truce however was afterwards held. Consul O'Brien wished to come on shore, but was refused.

Aug. 15.—Another truce was held, when the Bashaw demanded one million of dollars for our ransom. One hundred and twenty thousand dollars were offered and refused.

Aug. 17.—The Bashaw informed me that fifteen Americans were found drifted ashore at the westward of the town, and that one of them was an officer with an epaulet on the right shoulder. We supposed they were men destroyed by the explosion of the gun boat, at the late engagement. I asked permission to go with two or three of our men and bury them, and the Bashaw told me I might go the next day. Our squadron lay at anchor off the harbour. The inhabitants had chiefly moved out of the town, through fear of another bombardment; and the Bashaw ate, drank and slept in his bomb proof room. Several tribes of the back country inhabitants had lately come and offered their services to the Bashaw, were not more than one thousand men. Many of them had muskets without locks, but had a sort of match to put fire to them. They were almost naked, half starved, and without discipline. When they are going to battle, or appear before the Bashaw, they run to and fro, shaking their rusty muskets over their heads, all crying *Halaout Buoy?* (I am my father's son.) Every tribe has a priest, or what they call *Marabewt,* whose badge is a small green flag, which is carried in his hand or stuck up at his tent. They pretend great skill in prophecy, in which the people put the utmost faith. They prophecy success in battle, and for a small sum of money, insure any one against wounds or death in fighting a Christian. They often go on eminences, and beckon and sing to the American vessels to run on shore. They prophecied that another American vessel was to go on the rocks, and the Bashaw fully believed it.

Aug. 18.—Was not permitted to bury our dead. Our squadron stood out to sea. At evening the Bashaw went to his country seat and the Bey came in to keep the throne till his father's return. They never both leave the castle. When the Bashaw leaves it, the gates are shut till his return, for fear of incursion upon the throne. In the evening, the moon shining very bright, the prince or Bey ordered out the band of music, which was very ordinary, and made Christians, Turks, Arabs and Guinea Negroes dance before him, according to the mode of their respective countries, at which he seemed highly diverted.

Aug. 19.—Between 9 and 10 o'clock in the evening, Mr. Church, a respectable English gentleman was shot through the head in the street, on his return from visiting his neighbours.

Aug. 24.—In the morning, between 2 o'clock and day light, two of our small vessels hove about thirty shells, as was supposed for the round fort, but they all fell short of the mark. Such attempts served rather to encourage than to intimidate the Tripolitans; and the Bashaw was in high spirits on the occasion.

Aug. 26.—At about 4 o'clock P.M. the fellow who murdered Mr. Church, was executed near the spot where the crime was committed. It had therefore been a custom in this country, when a person had committed murder, to fly to a tomb of a *Marabewt* (or priest) where they were protected from justice, and a fee to a *Marabewt* would procure them absolution. This fellow fled to a palace of this kind immediately after killing Mr. Church. The English consul Mr. Langford, on being informed of the murder, addressed the Bashaw, and demanded justice. The Bashaw then found out by a boy, who accompanied the murderer when he committed the crime, the particulars of the affair; and immediately sent a file of men and ordered them to prevent any person carrying food or drink to the murderer. They watched him until night when the Bashaw sent his *Marabewt,* who coaxed him away, brought him to the castle and confined him in irons. The next day the Bashaw called his divan, when it was decided that the prisoner was guilty of wilful murder, and ought to suffer death. It appeared by the evidence and confession of the prisoner, that Mr. Church had lent a sum of money to a Spanish carpenter in this place:—that Mr. Church had pressed him for payment; and that the carpenter's wife hired the Turk to kill Mr. Church for forty dollars. The villain took his watch from his pocket after he had shot him. The boy who accompanied him and carried a lantern was bastinadoed with five hundred blows. The carpenter's wife was ordered to leave Tripoli.

Aug. 27.—Our squadron stood towards the harbour.

Aug. 28.—About 4 o'clock in the morning, I was awoke by a heavy and incessant fire of cannon, and the whistling and rattling of shot all around me. On getting up, I found that our gun-boats were close in, and were firing upon the town and batteries. Every gun in Tripoli that could be brought to bear, was returning the fire. The Tripolitan gun boats were close under the castle for protection. The firing continued until a few minutes after sun-rise, when one of the largest gun boats ventured out, with an intention of boarding the nearest American boat. As soon as she got within pistol shot, the Americans discharged their piece, loaded with grape, and killed four and wounded two of the enemy, they then put about and retreated. At the same time, commodore Preble bore down and gave the batteries to the westward of the town two broadsides. The squadron then stood out and anchored off the harbour. The damage done to the town was considerable. A large vessel was sunk in the harbour and others damaged. Many men were killed and wounded.

Aug. 29.—The Bashaw sent me to his palace in the country, to see his eldest son the Bey, whom I bled in the foot. He requested me to spend the day and dine with him, which I did. He endeavoured to have the dinner in the Christian style. It was set on a table, and consisted of a large dish of boiled rice and stewed fowls, out of which we both ate, he with a wooden spoon, and I with a silver one, without knife or fork. The prince's servant stood by him, and pulled the fowl in small pieces with his fingers, for the prince to eat. I made use of my fingers and teeth to get mine in pieces. Our dessert was dates and watermelons. Our drink was lagby, or the juice of the date tree, which we drank out of a large gold cup. He shewed me the garden, and took great pains to entertain me.

Aug. 30.—A truce was held, I took a ride upon a mule about eight miles to the westward of the town, in company with my guide, Hamet, a Turkish officer, and several footmen. I there saw a boat, which drifted on shore, with a dead man, and several muskets and swords in it. The man appeared to have been shot through the body with a cannon ball, which had also pierced the bottom of the boat. The Turkish officer collected about twenty Arabs, who hauled the boat upon the beach, dragged the dead man out of it, stripped him entirely naked, and left him on the beach. I tried in vain to hire the Arabs to bury the body; they said it was contrary to their religion to bury a Christian. I asked permission to get him buried by our countrymen, some of my fellow prisoners, but was refused. I found that our men, who were destroyed by the explosion of the gun-boat, on the 9th last lay in a state of putrefaction on the beach. They were scattered on the shore for miles, and were torn in pieces by dogs. The Bashaw had frequently promised me that these men should be buried; but refused to let me take some of our men to go and bury them.

September 2.—At about 4, P.M. our squadron commenced another attack on the town in which eight of our gun boats drove sixteen Tripolitan gun boats under the battery on the east side of the harbour; while the commodore bore down and gave the batteries at the west end of the town, several broadsides. Many of his shot came into the town and castle. Two bomb-ketches were employed in heaving shells into the town, which did considerable damage to several houses, and entirely destroyed the house of the Spanish carpenter, the Bashaw's naval contractor. I observed the utmost confusion and random-firing among the Tripolitans. It appeared they were almost out of powder. Two of their guns bursted, one of which was an eighteen pounder of the late Philadelphia frigate. The men, women and children ran out of the town in the utmost terror and distraction.

Sept. 3.—Had been to see the prince in the country, and was returning about [?] o'clock in the evening, with the Bashaw and suit, when we saw a most extraordinary light or flash, and heard heavy report. We all wheeled about, and made for the place we had left; but the Bashaw soon altered his mind, and proceeded to town, while I went to the country palace and staid all night. The explosion was a fire ship, sent into the harbour by commodore Preble, which did but little damage.

—The Turks found ten dead men near the place where the vessel blew up, on the evening of the 3d instant. The Bashaw and his people had a thanksgiving to Mahomet on the occasion. Their ceremony was prayer in doleful tone, and singing, accompanied with the sound of an instrument made by drawing a skin over a hoop.

Sept. 6.—More men were found, three of which appeared to be officers. By permission, I took our boatswain and a gang of men, and buried these bodies a little east of the wall of the town. All that I saw, who appeared to have been killed by the explosion, amounted to fourteen. The Bashaw's son-in-law told me that six more had been found drifted on the western shore; but I could not ascertain the truth of it.

Sept. 7.—John M'Donah died of a consumption, with which he had long been ill.

Sept. 9.—The Bashaw took me with him, and his suit to his country seat where we spent the most of the day. About 5 o'clock P.M. we went to see the great *Marabewt,* or Mahometan priest, in whom the Bashaw had great faith, and thought he could foretel [*sic*] events. It was said by the Turks, that he foretold the stranding and capture of the Philadelphia; and that he got offended with the Bashaw and caused and foretold her being burnt. But I had heard nothing of these mysteries until a little previous to this. He now said that the commodore's ship, the Constitution, would never return to America; that she would either be blown up, or run on shore: and that the Bashaw would have success in his warfare with America. It appeared that this great prophet was a sojourner; and that he only came to Tripoli when the Bashaw was in want of a prophet. He was encamped on the sandy desert, at a tomb of an ancient *Marabewt.* The tomb had a house over it with several rooms, and was encircled with several green trees. It was about two miles back of the gardens. We found this great *Marabewt* standing on a large mat, which was spread on the sand under the shade of a large mulberry tree. About thirty of his attendants stood back of him, paraded in form of a crescent [*sic*]. I was ordered to pull off my hat; and all approached him from the west; the Bashaw, with some of his most truly attendants [*sic*] in front. When we came near to him we all dismounted. The Bashaw run to him, kneeled before him, and kissed his hand. The mamelukes followed his example. The *Marabewt* then set down, and was followed by the Bashaw and his suit, forming a circle on the mat. During this time, I stood by my mule, about five rods from the scene, with my hat in my hand. I was soon called and ordered by the Bashaw to take off my shoes and feel the *Marabewt's* pulse. I left my shoes at the edge of the mat, or holy ground, and stepped on. I laid my hat on the edge of the mat in preference to laying it on the sand; but it was immediately taken off. I was then ordered to approach his holiness and kiss his hand. I felt his pulse; but before I had time to prescribe for him, he put his hand against me, and gave me to understand that I must go off the holy ground. Immediately stepped off; put on my shoes, took my hat, and went to my mule. The Bashaw called me back, and asked what I would do for the *Marabewt.* I recommended bleeding; but the *Marabewt,* shook his head and gave me to understand that he wanted nothing of the *kelp* (*the Dog.*) I was then told to withdraw, which I did, and took a walk round the tomb, which I found to be very ancient. The Bashaw spent about half an hour with the *Marabewt,* when he kissed his hand; and we all returned to the country. The Bashaw apologised for the impoliteness of the *Marabewt,* and said that they had a foolish antipathy to all but Mahometans.

October 22.—None of our cruisers were to be seen from the top of the castle. The Tripolitan gun boats were disarmed, and the Bashaw's gunners were employed in drawing the charges from the cannon on the battery. Many of the guns now stood in the sand, as they did when commodore Preble first attacked the town. On being fired two or three times, they recoiled into the sand so deep that they could not be worked, and were abandoned. The Bashaw told me that if he had three frigates, he would blockade America. He said he could do it as easily as a frigate and schooner could blockade Tripoli!

Oct. 26.—A great scarcity of grain. Our crew had no bread for three days. The Bashaw gave orders to all the market people, not to sell grain to any body but his household. There was no bread to be had for money. A dispute took place between the Bashaw and the renegado Lysle, about the purchasing of some barley. Lysle was considerably intoxicated, and insisted on his right to purchase grain in the market. The Bashaw was highly affronted, and flew at him with all his might, struck him, and ordered his mamelukes to disarm him and put him in prison, which they strove to obey, and carried him off. The Bashaw, however, soon ordered him released, and then ordered his servant, who was supposed to be the cause of the quarrel, bastinadoed with five hundred blows, which was immediately put into execution.

November 9.—The Bashaw had an epileptic fit, and his people thought he was possessed with the devil. They performed many ceremonies to cast him out, which they said succeeded. The Turks said they saw many ghosts the night before; and that a *Marabewt* drove the devil out of the Bashaw.

December 6.—Our men suffer for the want of provisions. The Bashaw does not allow them either victuals or cash. They get but a small allowance of bread, and that on the credit of their own country. They are beat unmercifully and compelled to work hard every day.

Dec. 7.—I was informed, that, through the influence of many Turks, the Bashaw had given orders to Sarcy, our master, to treat the American prisoners with the utmost cruelty, in order to induce the United States the sooner to make peace. He was impatient for his money.

Dec. 10.—Our men all agreed not to work unless they were fed, and accordingly when the wardens went to the prison and ordered them out, they all refused. The wardens whipped them until they were tired, and then went to inform the Bashaw, who immediately ordered them bread and oil, and they went to work.

Dec. 21.—At evening, the Bey, the eldest son of the Bashaw, was married to his first cousin, eldest daughter of the Bashaw who was driven out of Tripoli by the present Bashaw. The bride was said to be very handsome, and but twelve years old.

Our boatswain, carpenter, sail-maker, and first master's mate, who had the liberty of the town for a few months, were put in close confinement with our other officers, on suspicion of attempting to raise the crew to take the town.

Dec. 25.—The Bashaw's son-in-law, Selim, who had charge of the stores, was detected in selling a quantity of cordage to a Tunisian merchant. The Bashaw ordered him five hundred bastinadoes; but Selim fled to a *Marabewt* for protection, and escaped punishment.

January 24.—Renegado Wilson, who pretended to be a great engineer, was ordered by the Bashaw to fire hot shot at a mark, but succeeded indifferently. The Bashaw, however, was highly pleased, gave Wilson eight dollars, and promised to reward him in proportion to his exertions in his future warfare. Wilson engaged to teach the Turks how to throw bombs, hot shot, and hand grenades; and to alter and improve the fortifications, &c.

Jan. 25.—The Bashaw sent me to visit the wife of Alla Mameluke. She was once a wife or concubine to the Bashaw, who gave her as a wife to his favourite. She was sister to a wife of the Emperor of Morocco, about eighteen, and very handsome. She was in child-bed travail, attended by a number of Jewish women. She was delivered of a son, her first child, to the great joy of all the Turks in the castle, male and female. It was proclaimed by a loud yelling, with clapping of hands to and from the mouth, by the women of the castle.

Jan. 28.—The Bashaw was informed by Wilson, the renegado, that our crew were all armed, and about to rise upon the town. Search was made, and the report found to be false. But the Bashaw was much intimidated and an additional guard was placed over us.

February 1.—George Griffiths, one of our crew, having informed the Bashaw that he could build an air furnace, and cast guns, shot &c. furnished with a mason and nine of our crew, and set to work, with a promise he should have a hundred dollars for the first shot he should cast. After expending about five hundred dollars in the experiment, Griffiths this day attempted a blast in his furnace; but with all the wood and coal that the Bashaw could furnish, he could not melt the iron, and the furnace cracked in several places. It afterwards appeared that Griffiths had no intention to cast any shot.

Feb. 5.—While a number of our men were at work at the north corner of the castle, a large body of the wall fell, and killed Jacob Dowdesher. The only consolation we received from the Turks, was, that he was *amka deric* and *sansafedah*—that is, D——m *his mother, he has got no faith. Romo Kelp—He is a Christian dog.*

March 1.—An American frigate appeared off the harbour. The Turks were all at their quarters, and were manning their gun boats.

The Bashaw was preparing an armament to go against some of his refractory tribes on the borders of Egypt.

March 4.—Hassan Bey, the Bashaw's chief mameluke, was appointed to command the expedition towards Egypt, on the borders of the dominions of Tripoli. Hassan and his officers were attended by the Bashaw and several stand of colours to a *Marabewt* about three miles from town, to receive absolution and assurances of victory in the intended expedition. A great part of our crew, and many Turks and Jews were employed in packing up ammunition, &c., for the camp.

March 5.—Two frigates and a brig, supposed to be American, appeared off the harbour. The people of Tripoli were preparing and moving their effects into the country, expecting a siege by the Americans.

March 12.—Swallows appeared. Apple, peach and plumb trees were in blossom, and peas in market.

March 17.—Walking by the house called the American house, I perceived that it was full of Turks, and a strong guard was at the door. On inquiry, I found that they were the sons and nearest relations of the Bashaw's officers, who had gone in the expedition to the frontiers. The Bashaw kept these people as hostages for the fidelity of his officers, whom it appears, he was afraid to trust, least they might join in the rebellion and come against Tripoli. It was said that his highness had received a letter, stating that the Americans were making great preparations to attack Tripoli. A tent was pitched on the battery of the castle, and orders given to keep watch all night, and every night afterwards. Orders were also given to make every preparation to repel the Americans.

March 18.—The Bashaw sent his son-in-law into the country for troops to protect Tripoli.

March 19.—It was reported and generally believed that the Americans had been to Alexandria in Egypt, where they had got the Ex-Bashaw and four thousand Egyptians, and carried them to Syracuse, where they were to be landed to act in concert with the Americans against Tripoli. I perceived many private councils and long faces amongst the Turks.

March 21.—A frigate and brig appeared off the harbour. The Bashaw told me he suspected commodore Barron was dead, as he had not heard from him for a time. Not long before, he told me, that he had heard of the death of his brother the Ex-Bashaw. He seemed highly pleased at such news. Several of the sons and dearest friends of his chiefs in the country, were brought into the castle, as hostages for their fidelity to the present Bashaw. Symptoms of dissatisfaction appeared amongst the people.

March 22.—Two negroes were hung at the gate of the city for robbery.

The Bashaw's son-in-law who had been sent into the country to collect troops to protect Tripoli, returned without success. The people refused to fight for the Bashaw, because he had made unusual demands for money, and even had stripped their wives of their jewels. For several days, it had been reported that ten thousand troops were to muster on the beach near the town; and his highness was to make a speech to encourage them to fight for him against the Americans and his brother. I prepared myself to see these troops; but to my disappointment not one of them appeared.

April 7.—One of our cruisers appeared. A large gunboat was launched, which was built by re[n]egado West, who was one of our crew, and turned Turk.

April 12.—The Bashaw received an unfavourable letter from his agent at Malta, concerning the armament of the Americans. The Spanish consul presented the Bashaw three hundred stand of arms and a number of pistols, and, it is said, advised him to keep up the war, and force the Americans to pay his demand. It was concluded that the Bashaw's women and children should stay at the castle during the summer. They said that if they must be taken, they would rather fall into the hands of the Americans than the Arabs.

April 13.–16.—The Bashaw declared, that if the Americans drove him to extremities, or attacked his town, he would put every American prisoner to death.

April 19.—The Bashaw interrogated me concerning the force of my country; he asked me how many marines the United States kept in pay. My answer, for good reasons, was, ten thousand! How many troops? he asked.—Eighty thousand, said I, are in readiness to march to defend the country, at any moment; and one million of militia are also ready to fight for the liberty and rights of their countrymen! At this, his highness assumed a very serious look, and I returned to my room.

April 27.—A very oppressive Syrock wind. Several companies of Arabs had arrived within a few days: about three hundred horse and seven hundred foot.

May 3.—The Bashaw and suit went very early this morning to the great *Marabewt,* of whom some particulars have been before mentioned. He was to continue with the Bashaw during the contention with the Americans. He now assured the Bashaw that the American frigates would be destroyed; and that the gunpowder of the whole squadron would be so damaged, that the Americans would not be able to fire a gun. He agreed to attend the Bashaw, to keep the balls and shells from hurting him. He receives large sums of money from the Bashaw.

May 14.—I received a note from capt. Bainbridge, stating the inconvenience which the officers laboured under by being in close confinement and by breathing unwholsome air. I spoke to the Bashaw of the subject, and humbly solicited that our officers might be removed to the American house. The Bashaw replied, that the war between him and my country at first was about money; but now it was whether him or his brother should be the Bashaw; and that the Americans had bound themselves to his brother in such a manner that it was not in their power to make peace with him. But that his brother and the Americans were determined to take Tripoli and take off his head. He swore by the prophet of Mecca, that if the Americans brought his brother against him, he would burn to death all the American prisoners except me; that my life should be spared, because I saved the life of his child when very sick. He went off in a great passion, and mounted his horse. His mamelukes and guard, to the number of about forty, attended him, and they took a ride to his country palace. They returned about sun set, and the minister of exteriour relations and the Bashaw were in private conference.

May 19.—A spy employed by the Bashaw, arrived from Malta and Syracuse. He brought news that the American squadron sailed for Alexandria in Egypt about twenty days before; that it consisted of 4 frigates, 3 brigs, 3 schrs.[,] 24 gun boats, 6 bomb ketches, and several transports; that they were to take on board the former, or Ex-Bashaw, and to proceed along the coast of Tripoli, and take the principal towns; and then to attack and take the town of Tripoli, and put it in possession of the Ex-Bashaw. The Bashaw and his people seemed much agitated at this news.

May 21.—The Bashaw with his attendants rode into the country. According to custom he took with him on a mule, two boxes, said to contain twenty thousand *sequins,* (forty thousand dollars.) But I did not believe they contained that sum. They were light. I had lifted them both; and they were carried to and from the mule by one slave. Another mule was loaded with the packages of the Bashaw's clothing. The Bashaw always went thus provided, through fear that he might be served as he served his brother the Ex-Bashaw, who was denied to return to the castle when the present Bashaw usurped the throne. During the absence of the Bashaw, his eldest son, the Bey, had his amusement. He ordered two carpets spread on the south corner of the castle. On one of the carpets, the Bey and his attendants seated themselves, with a band of musick, consisting of two men with tamborines, and one with a sort of drum. Murat, his uncle, and myself were seated on the other carpet. Three large negroes were brought and ordered to perform before the Bey. The musick then struck up and the three negroes commenced the negro dance, with many ridiculous airs, whirling round, shaking their heads and roaring like mad bulls. This continued about half an hour, when they appeared to be raving mad. They ran about, as if to tear in pieces every body they met. One of them made a leap at me, but was prevented from reaching me, by the Bey, Murat and another Turk, who jumped between us. Two other Turks caught hold of the negro and held him, when I, by the advice of the Bey, went to the top of the north end of the castle, where I could see the sport in safety. During the frolick, I saw those negroes chase several Christians; and I was told that they often tear all their clothes off, and hurt them much by biting, &c.

May 22.—I was informed, that, in a letter which the Bashaw received the evening before, it was stated that Hassan Bey and his army were taken in Derne, by the Americans and Sadi Hamet, the Ex-Bashaw. I was desired not to mention it, because it was a great secret; and the Bashaw did not wish to let his people know it. I was also informed that the Bashaw called a council of his chiefs, and proposed to put all the American prisoners to death, but it was agreed to postpone this measure for that time.

May 23.—Twenty five of our men were sent with a cart for timber into the country. The wind from the desart was very heavy and hot. The men almost perished in the sand, which flew and drifted like a snow storm in our country. They stopped through fatigue, and asked their driver, who was a Turk, for liberty to drink at a well which was near them. The Turk replied, that they were *Romo kelps,* Christian dogs, and said they should have no water. He gave them all a severe beating with a large club, which he always carried with him to drive them with, and made them go on with the cart, which the poor fellows had to drag, loaded wi[t]h timber, through the burning sand. They returned towards night almost perished.

May 24.—At night the Bashaw dispatched a boat with powder, musket balls and money for his troops, who were collecting to oppose the approach of his brother Hamet, the Ex-Bashaw. The eldest son of Hamet, was confined in the castle by order of the present Bashaw. The Bashaw was so much agitated at the news of the approach of his brother, that he this day declared, that if it was in his power now to make peace and give up the American prisoners, he would gladly do it, without the consideration of money. His funds were so low, that his steward run in debt for the supply of the kitchen. He gave his mamelukes and domesticks, and myself, but one meal per day.—The rich Turks in town took turns in supplying his few troops. He heartily repented for not accepting the terms of peace last offered by our country.

May 26.—Three frigates in sight. At about 11, A.M. the smallest came near in, and hoisted the banners of peace. The Bashaw asked his head men of the town, who were with him in his gallery, whether it was best to hoist his white flag. All except one, the charge de affairs for Algiers, declared in favour of it, and of making peace if possible. They expressed great contempt toward the Algerine consul for his advice, and said that whoever would advise the Bashaw not to hoist the white flag at such a critical moment must be his foe and not his friend. The Algerine soon disappeared and left the castle. The Spanish consul soon after came to the castle; and the Bashaw sent him in one of his handsome boats, with *Shous Hammad* to the frigate. They returned at evening with the joyful news of a prospect of peace. There was a visible change, from gloominess to joy, in the countenance of all the Turks.

May 27.—Both Turks and Christians were all anxiously looking out for the frigates. It was said that col. Lear had promised to come on shore this morning and that the Spanish consul was preparing a dinner for the gentlemen who were expected to come with him. We were all agitated alternately by hope and despair. The terraces and every eminence in town, were covered with people of all classes and ages, who were looking for the wished for peace-maker. But not a frigate nor a sail hove in sight during the day.

May 28.—All looking out again for our squadron. A brig hove in sight in the morning, which we all at first thought was the flag ship. On discovering it was a brig, a gloominess again appeared on every countenance. The Turks began to think that the frigate had gone to fetch the whole fleet, which they heard consisted of sixty sail of different sizes. They thought that the flag of truce was only a plan of the Americans, to find out the force of Tripoli, &c. But at sun set three frigates and a brig appeared, which revived our hopes. The Bashaw shewed the greatest anxiety for peace. He was sensible of the danger he was in from the lowness of his funds and the disaffection of his people.

May 29.—Three frigates and a brig bore down upon the town and displayed the ensigns and signals of peace, which were immediately answered from the castle. The Spanish consul, *Fafah* the Jew and several Turks went on board, and did not return until late at night, when it was reported that negociations for peace were going on rapidly.

May 31.—The Spanish consul and *Shous Hammad* went on board the commodore, and returned at night. The Bashaw sent me to inform captain Bainbridge, that peace was agreed on, which I did to the great joy of the officers.

June 1.—The truce continued. Bainbridge went on board the commodore and returned at night. Our men were still drove to hard labour, and our officers kept confined.

June 2.—I received a letter from captain Bainbridge, stating that the terms of peace were agreed on, and that we should soon go on board the squadron. I immediately read this letter to our crew, who were so overjoyed that many of them shed tears. They were still drove to hard work, and many of them flogged.

June 3.—The articles of peace were signed, and salutes fired from the frigates and batteries.

June 6.—I bid the Bashaw a final adieu, at which he seemed much affected.

Further Particulars

The wood used in Tripoli, is brought in on jack-asses; six of them carry about half a cord.

There are many remains of antiquity in Tripoli. There are nine pillars to the portico of the house, in which the American officers lived. They are of marble, and have the appearance of great antiquity. There are many columns of Roman and Grecian architecture, wrought into the corners of some of the houses, without form or regularity. The streets of Tripoli are narrow and dirty, and the houses present a dead wall. Many of the houses are partly composed of broken marble, full of engravings and inscriptions, mostly defaced.

Marriages are proclaimed in Tripoli, by one or two old women, who run through the streets, making a most hideous yelling, and frequently clapping their hands to their mouths, similar to the American Indians in their *pow wows*.

The following principal articles of faith, constitute the religion of the Turks: that there is but one God, and that Mahomet is the Messenger of God. Their commandments are but five in number, viz.

1st. To pray five times a day.

2d. To fast in Lent or *Ramadam*.

3d. To give alms, and perform works of charity.

4th. To go on a pilgrimage to Mecca.

5th. To keep the body clean.

Four other points are deemed of importance, though not of absolute necessity, to salvation, viz: To keep Friday as Sabbath; to be circumcised; to drink no wine; and to abstain from swine's flesh, or things strangled. Many of the inhabitants of Tripoli strictly adhere to this religion.

END OF THE JOURNAL.

WILLIAM RAY

Horrors of Slavery

William Ray served aboard the ill-fated *Philadelphia* when it was captured in 1803 and suffered nineteen months as a prisoner in Tripoli. Unlike his shipmate, Jonathan Cowdery, Ray slept and ate with the crew and suffered the rough handling of his captors. Growing ill shortly after he arrived, Ray was spared the backbreaking work of repairing the stone fortifications that had been destroyed by commodore Preble's massive cannonades. Instead, he oversaw the captives' meals and was in charge of rationing food among the prisoners. Ray had the opportunity to read Jonathan Cowdery's narrative, and in many ways his own account is presented as a corrective to the doctor's distorted version of events.

Though he lost the journals he kept while he was aboard the *Philadelphia,* Ray constructed his narrative, *Horrors of Slavery, or the American Tars in Tripoli,* from journals he wrote while in captivity. The lengthy narrative appeared in three editions between 1808 and 1811. Several years later, Ray published a second volume entitled *Poems, on Various Subjects, Religious Moral, Sentimental and Humorous. To Which is Added, A brief sketch of the Author's Life, and of his captivity and sufferings among the Barbarians of Tripoli, with a description of the Country, and the Manners and Customs of the Inhabitants.* Like Ion Perdicaris after him, Ray also published a novel, *Sophia, or the girl of the pine woods; to which is added Lafitte, or the Barratarian chief; an American tale.* He died in 1827.

Horrors of Slavery, or the American Tars in Tripoli. Troy, NY: Oliver Lyon, 1808.

Chapter VIII

I SHALL NOW TAKE SOME NOTICE of extracts from Doctor Cowdery's journal, as published in the Balance, of Hudson, and republished in the Albany Register. As far as he adheres to strict veracity, I shall coincide with his observations; but when he deviates from correctness, or exaggerates on facts, take the liberty of differing with the learned Doctor's diary. He says—"After the signal of the Philadelphia was struck, and the officers and crew waiting the pleasure of their new masters, the Tripolitan chiefs collected their favourites, and, with drawn sabres, fell to cutting and slashing their own men who were stripping the Americans and plundering the ship.—They cut off the hands of some, and it is believed, several were killed." It is true there was a sort of mutiny and clashing of arms amongst them; but for my part I never saw any hands amputated, nor do I believe there were any lives lost; for myself and a hundred others were in the ship much longer than the Doctor, and none of us ever saw or heard of this carnage amongst themselves. After they had borrowed about ten dollars of the Doctor, and wrested his surtout from under his arm, he says—"Whilst they were picking its pockets, and quarrelling with each other for the booty, I sprung for the next boat which was waiting for me. In my way I met a little fellow who seized me and attempted to get off my coat, but I hurled him to the bottom of the boat," &c. This was certainly the most heroic action that has ever been read of any of the Philadelphia's officers. Surrounded by those horrific brigands, with "drawn sabres" and "cocked pistols," for a man, at such a critical and fearful crisis, to have the courage to collar an enemy, on his own ground, must be considered as a specimen of heroism not very common to be found among empirics of our navy. And when the Doctor mentions "hurling the *little fellow*," the reader, not acquainted with the person of the said Doctor, would really suppose him to be a mammoth of a man—quite the reverse. He further says—"they then began upon Mr. Knight, sailing-master, Mr. Osborn, lieut. of marines, and all the officers in the boat, and plundered their pockets, and took their handkerchiefs from their necks. They then landed us at the foot of the Bashaw's palace, where we were received by a guard, who conducted us into the palace, before the Bashaw. He viewed us with the utmost satisfaction, and had us conducted into an apartment where we found the captain and several officers, who arrived in another boat just before us. Here was a table set in the European style. The servants appeared to be Maltese and Neapolitan slaves. Here we supped; after which it was announced that another boat had arrived with our officers and men, who were before the Bashaw. Captain Bainbridge requested me to go and look for Doctor Harwood, whom it was feared was killed. I found him with the carpenter, before the Bashaw, stripped of every thing but their shirts and trowsers. They afterwards informed me that they were stripped in the boat when I lost my surtout, and when they got within a few rods of the shore, they were thrown into the sea, and left either to drown or swim ashore. The Bashaw gave them dry clothes, and we were all conducted before the Bashaw and formed into a half circle. He was seated on his little throne, which was decorated in the Turkish order, and made a handsome appearance. He is a good looking man, aged about thirty-five. He counted us, viewed us with a smile and seemed highly pleased with us. We were then conducted, by the minister of axterior [*sic*] relations and a guard, to the house formerly occupied by the American Consul, a very good house, with a large court, and room enough for our convenience.—We were seated here about 9 o'clock in the evening. Captain Bainbridge got permission from the Bashaw to send for the Danish Consul, who paid us a visit, and offered every assistance in his power. We slept upon mats and blankets spread upon the floor, which was composed of tiles." Although the Doctor here makes no discrimination between men and officers, it must not be understood that he includes the former when he says *we,* excepting servants— no, no, it was only the officers who were treated to a supper, and lodged in this comfortable mansion, and had mats to sleep on. You will, therefore, please to remember, that when the Doctor says *we,* it is the very same as if he had said *we officers only;* for he does not think proper to descend to the task of relating how the crew were provided for, or whether they were but half alive or all dead. I must, therefore, inform the interested and humane reader, that as soon as we were huddled into the boats, all, or the most of us, were stripped of all our clothing excepting a shirt, trowsers and hat; some, however, who were in the first boat, under the eye of our officers, fared a little better, and kept the most of their clothes. When we came near the shore, we were all precipitated into the foaming waves; for the wind blew very fresh, and left to the free exercise of our talents at swimming or wading ashore. At the beach stood a row of armed men on each side of us, who passed us along to the castle gate. It opened, and we ascended a winding, narrow, dismal passage, which led into a paved avenue, lined with terrific janizaries, armed with glittering sabres, muskets, pistols and tommahawks. Several of them spit on us as we passed. We were hurried forward through various turnings and flights of stairs, until we found ourselves in the dreadful presence of his exalted majesty, the puissant Bashaw of Tripoli. His throne, on which he was seated, was raised about four feet from the surface, inlaid with mosaic, covered with a cushion of the richest velvet, fringed with cloth of gold, bespangled with brilliants. The floor of the hall was of variegated marble, spread with carpets of the most beautiful kind. The walls were of porcelain, fantastically enamelled, but too finical to be called elegant. The Bashaw made a very splendid and tawdry appearance. His vesture was a long robe of cerulean silk, embroidered with gold and glittering with tinsel. His broad belt was ornamented with diamonds, and held two gold-mounted pistols, and a sabre with a golden hilt, chain and scabbard. On his head he wore a large white turban, decorated with ribbons. His dark beard swept his breast. He is about five feet ten inches in height, rather corpulent, and of a manly, majestic deportment. When he had satiated his pride and curiosity by gazing on us with complacent triumph, we were ordered to follow a guard. They conducted us into a dreary, filthy apartment of the castle, where there was scarcely room for us to turn round. Here we remained an hour or two dripping and shivering with the chills of the damp cells, and the vapors of the night. The Neapolitan slaves were busily employed in bringing us dry clothing to exchange for our wet. We rejoiced to see men who wore the habiliments of Christians, and sincerely thanked them for their apparent kindness. We thought them disinterested, generous and hospitable; for we expected to receive our clothes again when dry; but the insidious scoundrels never afterwards would make us any restoration. The clothes which we gave them were new, and those which they brought us in exchange were old and ragged. We were then taken to a piazza, nearly in front of the Bashaw's audience hall, where we lodged for the night. It was floored with tiles and arched above, but open, on one side, to the chilling blasts of intemperate night, and as many of us had wet clothes on, and nothing to cover us with; add to this the gloomy prospects before us, and the painful apprehensions of chains, stripes and dungeons, and you may well suppose we had not a very refreshing night's repose. In the morning, about eight o'clock, an old sorceress came to see us. She had the complexion of a squaw, bent with age, ugly by nature, and rendered frightful by art. She looked round upon us, and raised a shrill cry of *bu-bu-bu-bu,* struck her staff three times upon the pavement, and then went through and examined us. There was a black man amongst us, and him she selected and placed aside from the rest.

191191

We supposed she had chosen him for herself, but he remained in the castle, as one of the cooks for the Mamelukes. This frightful hag is held, by the Bashaw and all the Tripolitans, in the highest veneration, not only as an enchantress, but as a prophetess also. It is said by them that she predicted the capture of the Philadelphia, and believed by them that the ship struck the shoals in consequence of her incantations.

The potent Bashaw presently made his appearance, and we were ordered to rise and pull off our hats. He walked past us, into his balcony, and we were permitted to ramble for a while, through the various divisions of this chaotic pile. Some of our men had saved a little cash from the ruffian hands of our hostile pillagers; but there was nothing eatable to be purchased in the castle. We had eaten nothing for twenty-six hours, and began to feel our appetite. The Neapolitans, by paying a certain share of the profits, were permitted to retail *aqua-deut,* a spiritous liquor distilled from the fruit of the date-tree, and similar to our whisky. This they kept to sell in their cells, in the castle, around the doors of which, our shivering men thronged, and such as had money shared it with such as had not. But these villainous, mercenary knaves, taking advantage of our ignorance in the price of liquor, and of the money which they gave us in change, allowed no more than about one fourth of the real value of a dollar.

We were now collected together again, in front of a large window, which looked into a back yard. The Bashaw, his son, the renegade Scotchman, commodore Lysh, and several of the Bashaw's officers, appeared at the window, and the Commodore began to interrogate us respecting our Captain, &c. He asked us whether we thought our captain a coward, or a traitor? We answered, neither. He replied, "who with a frigate of forty-four guns, and three hundred men, would strike his colours to one solitary gun-boat, must surely be one or the other." We told him that our ship being fast on the shoals, we had no chance to defend ourselves, having thrown our guns overboard, and that although we were in no immediate danger, except from one gun-boat, we judged, and feared, that as soon as night favoured their designs, they would surround and cut us to pieces, giving no quarters. He said there was no necessity for throwing our guns overboard; that we might have known she would be got off, as soon as the wind shifted, and assured us she was already afloat—that if we had not struck our flag, they would not have ventured to board us, and highly ridiculed our captain's cowardice, if, in fact, it was owing to want of courage; he persisted in the idea, that the ship was given up by design; for he said, the captain not bringing a pilot with him, and leaving the brig, when he acknowledged himself unacquainted with the harbour, and then running so nigh in so precipitately, were circumstances weighty enough to overbalance all doubts of his treachery, or, at least, indubitable evidences of his want of judgment, and proofs of his pusillanimity. The Bashaw was very inquisitive to know the number of shipping and strength of America. We gave him surprising accounts of both. The commodore asked us, if there were any mechanicks amongst us, and said, that such as were willing to work at their trades, should be paid for their labour; if not, they would be compelled to do other work. He was informed there were ship carpenters and blacksmiths amongst us. They were selected from the rest, counted, and mingled with us again. We were then collected in a body, and marched through dark and winding alleys, to the principal gate of the castle, and different from the one at which we entered. Passing out of this, we were conducted to an old magazine, as they called it, filled with sacks of grain, meal, lumber, and useless combustibles, which we were ordered to remove to another old building, not far distant. This was the first of our labour. Our drivers began to display their ferocity, by beating several of our men, who were rather dilatory in obeying their new boatswains. When we had finished removing the rubbish, we were given to understand, that this was to be the place of our confinement. It had once been occupied as a prison, by the Swedish captains, who had shared a fate similar to ours. The prison was about fifty feet in length, twenty in breadth, and twenty-five in height, with a sky-light, and two front, grated windows. It had a most dreary appearance, was dark and fuliginous. Not a morsel of food had we yet tasted, and hunger, like the vulture of Prometheus, began to corode our vitals.

Towards evening, some coarse, white bread, was brought, and we were all ordered out of the prison, and as we were counted in again, each one received a small white loaf, of about twelve ounces. This was all we had for the day. About sun set, our keepers came, and ordered us all out, to be counted in. We were under the disagreeable apprehensions of being separated, and sold into distant parts of the country, and at every call of all hands, painful sensations would disturb our breasts. We were counted in, one by one, and as we passed the grim jailor, were under the humiliating injunction of pulling off our hats. Those who refused this devoir were sure of a severe bastinading. We had nothing to keep us from the cold, damp earth, but a thin, tattered sail-cloth; the floor of the prison was very uneven, planted with hard pebbles, and as we had nothing but a shirt to soften our beds, and nothing but the ground for a pillow, and very much crouded in the bargain, the clouds of night shed no salutary repose. Let us now return to our officers.

Doctor C. says—"This morning, Nov. 1st. the Danish Consul, Mr. Nissen, paid us another visit. Captain Bainbridge engaged him to furnish us with provisions, and such other necessaries as we might want. Our dwelling was furnished in a plain style, and we were supplied with fresh provisions that were tolerably good. We were allowed to go to the front door, and walk on the terrace, or top of the house, which commanded a handsome prospect of the sea, the harbour, the palace, and the adjoining country. Here we could see our ship on the rocks, full of Turks, and surrounded by their boats; and a constant stream of boats going to, and bringing off the plunder of the ship. We could see those robbers running about town with our uniform coats and clothing on. The minister of exterior relations promised to be friendly, and collect as much of our clothing and effects as he could, and return them to us."

The Doctor does not think it worth mentioning, that almost the whole crew were suffering intolerably, by hunger and nakedness; and it is very evident, that he thought more of uniform coats, than of his naked countrymen, who had no coats to put on. He says, also, that the ship was lying on the rocks, which was positive mendacity, for she floated clear, early that very morning! And I have observed, in all the public letters, that this circumstance has been carefully concealed.

"This day, Captain Bainbridge wrote a letter to the Secretary of the Navy, with the lamentable tale of our misfortunes, containing a brief statement of the circumstances of our capture; requesting, that arrangements might be made to meet the exigencies of himself, the other officers, and officers' servants, and adding, that the remainder of the crew would be provided for by the Regency."

How did he know this? What assurance had he from the Bashaw, that he would provide for us, any more than for himself and his favourites? It is true, he might suppose that the Bashaw would put us to labour, if we were not provided for by our government, and that, for his own benefit, he would allow us sufficient food to sustain existence; but, was this any reason, that no farther notice should be taken of us? That government should make no appropriations for the mitigation of our sufferings? How did he know, but that benevolent characters in America, might institute charitable contributions for the palliation of our miseries? How did he ever know, but that Congress might interpose for our relief? Or, how did he know but that the department of the navy might see fit to allow us some part of our rations or wages? But his declaration, that we would be provided for by the Regency, precluded, at once, the necessity of any executive, legislative, public, or private aid whatsoever. No doubt, had Captain Bainbridge made a just statement of our situation to the department of the navy, representing, that we were wholly dependent on the clemency of a faithless fratricide for the support of life, and soliciting, in our behalf, as well as for his train of servants, that some provision might be made for us, a liberal and patriotic spirit would have granted us laudable and adequate alleviation, until a ransom, or enfranchisement could be effected. For certainly those who were compelled to labour, were under greater necessity for temporary aid, and governmental munificence, than those who were cloistered in idleness. At numerous times, when we were on the very brink of starvation, and petitioned Captain Bainbridge for some part of our pay or rations, he invariably gave us to understand, that it was entirely out of his power to do any thing for us. No wonder, when he had impressed, not only the government, but all the people of the United States, with the belief that we stood in no need of assistance. The fact is an obvious one—He had committed a most flagrant blunder, and to parry off the shafts of obloquy, would hold up the idea of moderation in his demands, and frugality in his expenditures of the public money. Or, if not, his conduct evinces a total disregard and dereliction of his crew. How could an officer feast and fatten on the public benefaction, and, at the same time, be unmindful of his men, who had an equal claim on the government for similar favours? How could he be the means of debarring that claim, by asserting, that we would be provided for without it? Had not the Captain as much reason to expect that the Bashaw would make provision for him and his officers, and his officers' servants, as for us? Or, were the men whom he had brought into this distress by his blunders, totally unworthy of his regard? We were completely ignorant of this duplicity, until we returned to America, and verily thought, that Captain Bainbridge had done every thing in his power to meliorate our condition. What must we, then, think of a commander, who would give up his men to the enemy, contrary to their wishes, and then abandon them to starve, or rely on the mercy of sanguinary barbarians?

Nov. 2.—Before sunrise, the horrid clanking of huge bolts, announced the early vigilance of our keepers, who ordered us all out. They told the carpenters to stand by themselves—the blacksmiths by themselves, also—the coopers the same, and each company were appointed to their several employments, under the direction and command of Turkish masters; but they did not effect much, for a considerable time. The remainder of our men were distributed into different gangs, as we called them; some to the castle, to carry stone, dirt, lime, and mortar, where they were making repairs. Some were sent as cooks in the castle, and ten men were taken from amongst us, to be denominated cooks. Their employment was to bring water from a well, about a quarter of a mile distant, for the whole of us to drink—to bring, and serve out, the bread and oil to us, and sometimes, to boil what the Turks call *coos-coos,* which is barley ground very coarse, and neither sifted nor bolted; with which they occasionally fed us. Some were sent on board the frigate, and remained all night. About twelve or one o'clock the cooks were called, to go for bread, and presently returned with a quantity of black barley loaves, coarse, and full of straws and chaff, weighing about twelve ounces each. Of these they gave us two apiece, and, bad as they were, our men seized them with avidity. This was our allowance for twenty-four hours.

Nov. 3.—"The Bashaw sent for the carpenter to go on board the ship; he went, and found six feet water in the hold. The carpenter's crew and fifty men, were ordered, and carried on board, to work. At night, a gale of wind, and a heavy sea, hove the ship off the rocks, and the carpenter returned."

No doubt, as the Doctor says, there was six feet water in the hold; but he ought to have mentioned, that the ship was scuttled by us; otherwise it conveys the idea, that the ship filled in consequence of the shock at first, or injury on the shoals.

If our men, and all the Turks, have not uttered wilful falsehoods, or been very egregiously mistaken, the ship was hove off the rocks, the very next morning after she was captured. This morning, after a large company was sent to the ship, and the most of our crew disposed of in different avocations, and at various employments, a considerable number of us were told, after having been counted, to return into the prison, and be ready, at a moment's warning, for any emergency. Some of them, however, strayed away, went into the town, and returned intoxicated. Our keepers perceived it, and proceeded to exhibit exemplary punishment, and sate, at once, their thirst of revenge. The instrument with which they prepare a man for torture, is called a bastone; It is generally about four or five feet long, and as thick in the middle as a man's leg, tapering to the ends. At equal distances from the centre, it is perforated in two places, and a rope incurvated, the ends passed through the holes, and knotted. This forms a loop. The person is then thrown on his back, his feet put through the loop, and a man at each end of the stick, both at once, twist it round, screw his feet and ancles tight together, and raise the soles of his feet nearly horizontal. A Turk sits on his back, and two men, with each a bamboo, or branch of the date tree, as large as a walking-staff, and about three feet in length, hard, and very heavy, strip or roll up their sleeves, and, with all their strength and fury, apply the bruising cudgel to the bottoms of the feet. In this manner they punished several of our men, writhing with extreme anguish, and cursing their tormentors. They were then hampered with a heavy chain at each foot, but the next day they were taken off.

Our men began to complain much of hunger, having for this day but the two loaves of filthy, black, and sour bread. Some of them, however, who had the good fortune to save a little money, were permitted to go to the market, to purchase vegetables. Their market makes a wretched appearance. On each side of the main street in the town, commencing at the principal gate, a long string of low mud-wall huts, on each side the way, is all the market they have; at the doors of which, seated cross-legged on the ground, and a blanket wrapped round them, the Turks retail pumpkins, carrots, turnips, scallions, oranges, lemons, limes, figs, &c. &c. with a thousand trinkets, and haberdashers' wares.

At night most of our men returned from the frigate, and brought with them beef, pork, and bread, which was generously shared with those who had none, and though raw, devoured with voracity. The floor of our prison was not large enough to contain, or admit us all, stretched at full length, and many of us were obliged to sit, or stand, all night. This occasioned a strife, or crowding, at the prison door, to be the first, or, at least, not the last counted in, for the first were considered as being lawfully entitled to the spot of ground for the night, and no one attempted to eject or oust them. It was surprising to witness the invincible spirit of our tars, and a person would be at a loss, whether to ascribe it to a philosophic fortitude, or natural apathy. In the most desponding aspect of times, they would caper, sing, jest, and look as cheerful, many of them, as if they had been at a feast or wedding.

Nov. 4.—A large number of our men were again sent, and employed in bringing ashore the product of the frigate. The officers were prohibited walking on the terrace of their prison. Some of us were every day reserved for sudden avocations; to go and carry burthens, in different parts of the town, and for any other enterprize. At every emergency, or call for men, a wardman, or keeper, would enter the prison, take such as fancy, or accident pointed out, and if there was the least hesitation in obeying his commands, a severe beating was the result of such contumacy. Four of us were chosen to be the pack-horses of some unknown expedition. We were led by a grisly emissary of the Bashaw, through many crooked and dirty alleys, until we came to a house, at which he ordered us to halt. He went in, but soon returned, and gave us signals to follow him. He led us through a gloomy passage to a large court-yard. Our breasts palpitated on the way, but our fears were dissipated when we found ourselves surrounded by a dozen beautiful females, who came from the piazzas above. As the women in the streets are constantly wrapped and muffled up in blankets, which conceal their shapes and faces, except one eye, this, to us, was a novel sight; for the ladies were exposed to view, as much as the half-naked belles of our own towns. They were fantastically wrapped in loose robes of striped silk; their arms, necks, and bosoms bare. Their eyelids stained round the edges with black. Their hair braided, turned up, and fastened with a broad tinsel fillet. They had three or four rings in each ear as large in circumference as a dollar. Several of them were very delicate and handsome.—They brought us dates, olives, oranges and milk. They expressed or manifested great surprize at our appearance, and, like other ladies, were full of giggling and loquacity. Our driver then bade us follow him again into another yard, where he shewed us a large copper kettle, and ordered us to take it up and follow his footsteps. We carried it about half a mile to another house, where there was a number of women, one of which would have killed us if she had not been prevented by our master. He made us understand that her malignity arose from her husband having been killed by the Americans, in the boat at which we fired when we were on the shoals.—Here we left the kettle and returned to the prison. The streets are not paved, never swept, and are full of sharp pebbles, and having no shoes, I suffered intolerably both by the cold and in carrying burthens, until they became indurated by use.

November 5.—"Our new masters came and closed up the passage which led to the top of the house, and a guard was set at the front door to prevent our going into the street. The minister sent his chief secretary with a parole of honour, written in French, which we all signed." The Turks informed us that the reason of their closing up the passage was a suspicion that we men were concerting with the officers some plan of escape, and that the suspicion was raised from a report of this kind fabricated by the infamous Wilson, in hopes to ingratiate himself with the Bashaw. Our prison door was more effectually secured at the same time. This day several of our seamen, who were born under British colours, flattered themselves with the fallacious hope of obtaining emancipation by throwing themselves under the protection of the British government, and claiming from the English Consul the privileges or exemptions of British subjects. For this purpose they went to him and he registered a number of their names, promised to write to his government, and, if possible, effectuate their release. They returned highly elated with the prospect of freedom. But a large majority of our patriotic tars, who had adopted America as their country, laughed at their credulity and hissed at their project, positively declaring that they would not be released by a government which they detested, on account of its tolerating the impressment of seamen, and swearing that they would sooner remain under the Bashaw than George the third.

November 6.—Our treatment and provisions much the same. "The English Consul, Mr. M'Donough, paid our officers a visit, and offered them every assistance in his power." As I was walking the streets, on a return from carrying a bundle of faggots into the town, I met with a Mahometan who spoke English tolerably fluent. He informed that he had been in America, in the time of our revolution, a servant to General Fayette; and when his master returned to France, he continued in America for two years, then went to his native country, and was a soldier in the French revolution, went with Bonaparte's army to Egypt, and when the French evacuated that country, his life was despaired of, and he was left in a wretched hospital, and would have perished had it not been for the fraternal kindness of a benevolent Mussulman, who took him to his house and treated him with the affectionate attention of the nearest consanguinity, and who was the means of saving his life. While in a debilitated state both of body and mind, he was pursuaded [*sic*] by his benefactor, whose importunities it seemed ungrateful to resist, to embrace the religion of Mahomet. He was now on his way to Tunis with a travelling company, appeared to be well respected by his comrades, was decently dressed, and seemed to have plenty of money; but he asked me a thousand questions concerning America, and seriously regretted his ever having left it, and of his transmutation of religion; but he still had hopes of making his escape. He gave me a Spanish dollar which he insisted on my accepting, shook hands and bade me adieu.

November 7.—Several of our men were much indisposed from sleeping on the damp ground, and being almost destitute of clothes. A small apartment or cell adjoining our prison was appropriated for the use and retirement of the sick, and Dorman, who was loblolly-boy on board of the frigate, was appointed to attend them. Another room, contiguous to that, was the receptacle of our provisions, and the men who were called cooks were permitted to sleep in it by themselves. Another cell, at a different part of the prison-yard, was set apart for the carpenters, coopers, and blacksmiths to sleep in; so that our prison was not quite so much crouded as at first.

November 8.—"The Bashaw sent for Capt. Bainbridge and told him that John Wilson had informed him, that Captain Bainbridge, before hauling down the colours, threw overboard nineteen boxes of dollars, and a large bag of gold. Captain Bainbridge assured him it was false, and gave his word and honour that no money was thrown over to his knowledge, but that the money in question was left at Malta. In the evening the Bashaw, not being satisfied, sent for the captain's servant, and ordered him flogged if he did not tell the truth concerning the money. The boy denied having any knowledge of it. After repeating the threat several times, and the boy insisting on his not knowing any thing about the money, he was acquitted. Wilson had turned traitor, and given the enemy all the assistance in his power. He now acts as overseer of our men." This perfidious wretch was a quarter-master on board the frigate. He was born in Germany, and spoke the lingua-franca very fluently. He as yet mingled amongst us, and acted as a spy, carrying to the Bashaw every frivolous and a thousand false tales. He had not as yet assumed the habiliments of the Turks, so that he was the more dangerous. The Bashaw rode out this day, and as he returned, was to pass, with his retinue, through our prison-yard, which is approximate to the castle. Wilson came and told us that it was the Bashaw's orders that we should parade, in single file, in front of our prison, with our hats off, and when he should make his appearance we must give him three cheers. He presently made his entrance into the yard, and being marshalled according to orders, some of our silly asses swung their hats and brayed like the animal they personated; but the most of us refused, with a laudable spirit of indignation, this mean and sycophantic testimonial of a tyrant's applause. His return from his cavalcade was announced by the firing of cannon from the castle, and crackling of muskets on the beach.—He was preceded by a foot-guard at some distance. Next to the foot-guard was the high constable of the town police, mounted on an elegant Arabian grey, in his hand he held perpendicularly before him a three-pronged sceptre, richly ornamented. His majesty was mounted on a milk-white mare, sumptuously caparisoned and glittering with golden trappings. He was dressed much the same as when we first saw him, excepting a white robe, which had a head like a hood, and on the top a large tassel. At his right hand rode a huge negro, who was made one of the Bashaw's principal officers, and admitted to this distinguished honour for having assassinated the Bashaw's brother, who was a powerful and dangerous rival. Three or four of his younger children went before him, seated on mules, with Neapolitan slaves running by their sides, holding with one hand the bridle of the mule, and with the other an umbrella over the head of the child. At his left hand rode the vizier, or prime minister, his chief officers of state, and was followed and attended by his Mamelukes, or life-guards, without order or arrangement, courting his approbation by numerous feats of equestrian agility. Two large boxes flung across a mule, led by a trusty Neapolitan slave, contained his principal treasures.

November 9.—"Our captain established a credit with the Danish Consul, who supplied us with necessary provisions, and with cloth for matrasses. A guard was placed at our door to prevent our going into the street, or purchasing any books or clothing."

November 10.—The Turks appeared very savage and spit at us, and on us, as we passed the streets. The keepers or drivers beat us without any pretext, and acted more like infernal than human beings. We did not then know the cause of this altercation for the worse, but perhaps the following will account for it. "Several Turks came in and informed Capt. Bainbridge that the Bashaw had been told that Capt. Rodgers, who commanded the United States frigate John Adams, treated the Tripolitan prisoners very bad, and that they feared we should suffer for it." Several of our men were sent for and interrogated very closely concerning the money Wilson had reported was thrown into the sea; but they all unanimously corroborated the assertions of Capt. Bainbridge, that there was no money sunk.

November 11.—As I was coming in at the principal gate of the town, having been out on the sands for water, I saw a hand and foot hanging at the outside of the gate fresh bleeding, and observing a cluster of people not far distant,

I stepped to see the cause of their being collected. The object of their curiosity was a wretch with his left hand and right foot recently amputated, faint and almost expiring. The stumps had been dipped in boiling pitch. This is their mode of punishment for capital offences, and the miserable object is dragged out of town and left to breathe his last in the most exquisite agonies, unless some friend sees fit to compassionate his sufferings, and then he some times recovers; for you will see a great number of men in Tripoli hobbling about the streets thus mutilated.

November 13.—"The minister of exterior relations sent his droggerman to Capt. Bainbridge, and informed him, that if he would send an immediate order to Commodore Preble to deliver up the Tripolitan prisoners, captured by Captain Rodgers, last summer, amounting to eighty in number, we might remain where we were, but if he did not comply we should fare worse. Captain Bainbridge replied that he could not command Commodore Preble, and therefore could not comply with his request. At nine in the evening at Tripolitan officer came armed with two pistols and a sabre, and said—"to-night, nothing; to-morrow, the castle." We accordingly prepared for the castle. This day we were employed in bringing pig-iron and shot from the boats at the wharf to the magazine in the navy-yard. I was very sick, and complained to the principal keeper that I was unable to work; but the only consolation I received was that of being called a *kelp,* (dog) and told to do as I was ordered. At night our men returned from the frigate with some more beef and pork, which, eaten raw, hunger gave a delicious flavour.

November 14.—"Breakfasted early to be ready for our new habitation. At 9, A.M. a guard came and ordered us to the castle. We formed agreeable to rank, and marched to the castle. We were huddled into a gloomy cell amongst our men, where there was hardly room for us to stand. Here we spent the day without food, and were scoffed at by our foes until night, when, to our happy surprize, we were conducted back to our old place of abode." Poor Doctor! in this whining tale there are several misrepresentations. That the officers were in the prison amongst us, contaminating fellows, is true; but the Doctor and his fellow-officers, though nobody doubts their feeling very big, must be gigantic monsters indeed, if they had hardly room enough to stand in a cell at least twenty-five feet high, and which contained every night nearly three hundred men, who were chiefly absent the whole day. Neither was our prison in the castle, as he intimates; and if he remained all day without food, after having eaten a hearty breakfast, it was owing to his own fastidiousness, for our men boiled some meat which was brought from the frigate, and invited all the officers to partake of it, and several of them made a hearty repast. If this famous son of Esculapius had been three days at a time without food, as we often were, perhaps he might have had an appetite for black bread and salt beef.

While Captain Bainbridge was amongst us, Wilson came with orders to get men for some kind of drudgery, when the captain accused him of informing the Bashaw of our sinking the box of money; he prevaricated, and attempted to extenuate, though he could not pointedly deny the crime. The captain told him that he would have him hanged for a traitor if ever he returned to America, and in a violent passion threw his chain at him. A few days afterwards, Wilson, probably fearing the reality of his threats, put on the turban, and confirmed his apostasy.

November 17.—The Danish Consul sent some fresh provision for our sick, by the request of Captain Bainbridge.—Our bread was very coarse and musty. This day I saw one of the Mahometan saints or Anchorites, who are held in the highest veneration by the Tripolitans. He was seated on a tomb within a small smoky cell, where he kept a lamp incessantly burning, which he said was the spirit of the dead. He offered me a piece of bread in the name of the prophet, pitied my situation, and really appeared to possess philanthropy.

November 18.—A number of us was sent to carry powder from the quay to the castle, which is about three quarters of a mile. The powder was taken from the frigate and was still wet. I was compelled to carry a cask of it, which was very heavy; and my feet being tender, gave me insufferable pain.—What would the querimoneous Doctor think, if he had been doomed to such hardships?

November 20.—Thomas Prince was metamorphosed from a Christian to a Turk. He was a lad of about seventeen years of age, and had a mother, as he informed us, living in some part of Rhode-Island. Our men now began to construct what they termed cots. They were formed by fastening four pieces of timber at the corners, in the shape of a bedstead, and then weaving a net of ropes like a bed-cord. These were suspended from spikes driven in the wall, and composed a lodging much more comfortable and healthful than the moist earth; but materials for these cots being very scarce, but few of us could be provided with a luxury so rare and inestimable.

November 21.—Doctor Cowdery informs us that a man, one hundred and sixteen years of age, came to him to be cured of deafness. We do not know which to doubt most—the Doctor's veracity or the Turk's credulity.

November 22.—We wrote a petition to the Bashaw in behalf of the sick, praying for some kind of blankets or clothing to keep them from the earth, appealing both to his humanity and his interest. "The Bashaw refused to furnish necessary clothing for the sick; or any thing for them to eat but sour, filthy bread. Captain Bainbridge contracted with the Danish Consul to supply the sick with beef and vegetables for soup every day."

November 25.—Sixteen of us were put to boring cannon; the labour was intense, and having neither bread nor any thing else to eat, until four o'clock in the afternoon, hunger and weariness were almost insupportable. Some of our men, by some clandestine means, were found intoxicated; for which they were inhumanly beaten, and confined in shackels. Whenever instances of this kind occurred, *all* were sure to suffer for the misconduct of a *few*.

November 26.—To the disgrace of human nature be it said, that although we all had an equal share of bread allowed us, some had the meanness, the self-ishness, the brutality to steal from their companions in misery the only liga-ment of soul and body. We frequently divided our pittance, and kept one loaf over night to eat in the morning, and often when morning came we found our-selves pillaged of our stores, and nothing to silence the importunate calls of hunger. About twelve o'clock I received a small white loaf from the allowance of our officers, and never in my life did I taste a more luscious dainty. It came from Mr. Morris, who was or had been by trade a baker, and the next day I sent him the following stanzas; friendship the strain, and gratitude of muse.

THE LOAF

The best of all friends is the friend in distress,
 And more the rich morsel I prize,
Imparted when hunger and poverty press,
 Than thousands, did fortune suffice.

With gratitude, friend, to the parent above,
 And thanks to yourself not a few;
I took the sweet loaf as a token of love,
 And ate in remembrance of you.

To life-wasting hunger, to heart-piercing cold,
 To scourges of tyrants a prey;
Midst demons of slavery too fierce to be told,
 And comrades more brutish than they.

The least of my wants not a soul has reliev'd,
 Nor friendship invited a beam;
From you the first crust of regard I receiv'd—
 From you the first crumb of esteem.

Then take the fond lay as the yeast of return,
 For, while I thus indigent live,

Though my breast, like an oven, with gratitude burn,
'Tis all I am able to give.

ADDITIONAL WRITINGS BY RAY

Poems, on Various Subjects, Religious Moral, Sentimental and Humorous. To Which is Added, A brief sketch of the Author's Life, and of his captivity and sufferings among the Barbarians of Tripoli, with a description of the Country, and the Manners and Customs of the Inhabitants. New York: 1826?

Sophia, or the girl of the pine woods; to which is added Lafitte, or the Barratarian chief; an American tale. Dansville, NY: A. Stevens, 1838.

The Narrative of Robert Adams

Robert Adams set sail from New York on June 17, 1810, aboard the 280-ton *Charles*. After safely reaching Gibraltar, and taking on a cargo of wine and blue nankeens, Captain John Horton plotted a course for the Isle of May, where he hoped to top off his lading with a supply of salt. On October 11, at three o'clock in the morning, the crew heard breakers, and an hour later the ship struck in a fog so thick that the coast was completely obscured. Eventually all ten men swam to shore. Captain Horton reckoned they had foundered about four hundred miles north of Senegal, a point later identified as El Gazie. At daybreak, thirty or forty Moors set upon the weary crew, robbing them of all they owned and carrying them into the desert as slaves. For the next three years and seven months, Adams was the property in turn of several slave traders. One of these captors promised to carry him back to Mogador, where he could be redeemed only if he agreed to help capture new "negro" slaves. During this hunt, however, Adams and his masters were themselves caught and driven deep into the African interior to the town of Timbuktu.

Even though its publication history is short, editions of Adams's Barbary captivity narrative, the first by an African-American, appeared in London, Boston, Paris, Stockholm, and Amsterdam. Because Adams was illiterate, the account is told in the third person by Samuel Cook, a member of the British African Company. The African Company sought to explore the African interior, and because marvelous tales of wealth shrouded Timbuktu in mystery, the company was particularly interested in Adams's journey. Though Cook and his colleagues grew to believe Adams, who performed well under repeated questioning, others found his story riddled with incongruities. The

Fig. 14. Robert Adams discovered with his master's younger wife. (Illustration ca. 1840.) (Courtesy University of Minnesota Libraries)

Fig. 15. Robert Adams attacks his master. (Illustration ca. 1840.) (Courtesy University of Minnesota Libraries)

North American Review published a scathing attack on the narrative's veracity and the editor's naïveté. Later that year, the *Review* printed a second theretofore unknown narrative by Adams, who had apparently told his story to another inquirer in Cadiz, months before he had even reached London; this account differed considerably from the official version. The inconsistencies between the two narratives make it difficult to accept Adams's insistence that he had lived in Timbuktu, though Brian Gardner's arguments in *The Quest for Timbuctoo*[1] go a long way to clear up many of these problems. We may never clearly know whether Adams was actually the first Westerner to visit Timbuktu, though his status as a captive in Morocco is incontrovertible. That the narrative of an African-American captive was shaped and told by a white narrator, however, suggests a parallel to the American slave narrative, which also experienced an amazing rise in popularity at this time.

1. New York: Harcourt Brace, 1968.

The Narrative of Robert Adams, A Sailor, who was wrecked on the Western Coast of Africa, in the Year 1810, was detained three years in slavery by the Arabs of the Great Desert, and resided several months in the city of Tombuctoo. Ed. Samuel Cook. London: William Bulmer and Co., 1816.

Introductory Details

[The following is excerpted from Samuel Cook's original London introduction to Adams's narrative; it includes an attached letter by Joseph Dupuis, British vice-consul at Mogador, who was responsible for ransoming Adams and his shipmates out of captivity.]

IN THE MONTH OF OCTOBER, 1815, the Editor of the following pages was informed by a friend, that a Gentleman of his acquaintance, recently arrived from Cadiz, had accidentally recognised an American seaman, in the streets of London, whom he had seen, only a few months before, in the service of an English merchant in Cadiz, where his extraordinary history had excited considerable interest; *the man having been a long time in slavery in the interior of Africa, and having resided several months at Tombuctoo.*

Such a report was too curious not to have attracted the peculiar attention of the Editor at all times; but the interest of the story was much heightened at that particular moment, by the circumstance of the recent embarkation of Major Peddie and his companions, to explore those very parts of Africa which this person was said to have visited: and the Editor entreated his friend to assist him by all the means in his power, to find the seaman in question, in order to ascertain whether he really had been where it was reported, and in the hope that, either by his information or his personal services, the man might be rendered useful to the views of Government in the exploratory expedition then on its way to Africa.

Through the intervention of the Gentleman who had originally recognized the seaman, he was again found, and immediately brought to the office of the African Committee. The poor man, whose name was *Robert Adams,* was in very ill plight both from hunger and nakedness. Scarcely recovered from a fit of sickness, he had, in that condition, begged his way from Holyhead to London, for the purpose of obtaining through the American Consul, a passage to his native country; and he had already passed several nights in the open streets amongst many other distressed seamen, with whom the metropolis was at that period unfortunately crowded.

No time was lost in questioning him respecting the length of his residence in Africa, the circumstances which led him thither, the places he had visited, and the means by which he had escaped. His answers disclosed so extraordinary a series of adventures and sufferings, as at first to excite a suspicion that his story was an invention; and the gentlemen by whom he was accompanied to the office, and who were present at his first examination, were decidedly of that opinion, when they considered how widely his account of Tombuctoo differed from the notions generally entertained of the magnificence of that city, and of the civilization of its inhabitants. The Editor, however, received from this short examination, and from the plain and unpretending answers which the man returned every question, a strong impression in favour of his veracity. He accordingly took notes of the leading facts of his statement, particularly of the places he had visited, the distances according to his computations, and the direction in which his several journeys lay; and having relieved his immediate necessities, and furnished him with a trifle for his future subsistence, he desired the man to attend him again in the course of a few days.

It was nearly a week before Adams again made his appearance: but upon his return, being immediately interrogated upon all the leading points of his story, the Editor had the gratification to find, upon comparing his answers with the account which he had given on his first examination, that they were in substance the same, and repeated almost in the same terms. Thus strengthened in his previous opinion that the man's veracity was to be depended upon, the Editor resolved to take down in writing (the man himself being unable either to write or read) a full account of his travels and adventures, from the period of his departure from America in the ship "Charles" in which he was wrecked on the coast of Africa, until that of his return to Cadiz, from whence he had just arrived.

With this intention, the Editor took measures to render Adams's situation more comfortable, by equipping him with decent clothes, of which he stood peculiarly in need. He was also supplied with a trifle in money, as an earnest of the future recompense which was promised to him, provided he would attend regularly every day until the whole of his story should be taken down. It was not, however, without considerable difficulty that the man could be persuaded to remain during the period thus required. He was anxious to return to his friends after so long and perilous an absence, and had been recommended by the Consul of the United States to join a transport of American seamen which was then on the point of sailing. His desire to be gone was increased by some rumours then in circulation, of a probable renewal of hostilities between Great Britain and the United States. But his objections were at length overcome on receiving an engagement, that even if war should break out, and he, by any accident, be impressed, his discharge, either by purchase or substitute, should be immediately effected. Upon this understanding, he consented to remain as long as his presence should be required.

The Editor has been induced to enter into this detail for the satisfaction of those who might be disposed to believe that Adams had obtruded his story upon his hearers, for the purpose either of exciting their compassion, or of profiting by their credulity. To obviate such a suspicion, it is sufficient to shew with what difficulty he was induced to remain in the country to tell his story; and to state, that he was never known to solicit relief from any of the numerous gentlemen by whom he was seen and examined.

Previous, however, to Adams's agreement to stay, a Committee of the African Company having met, the Editor laid before them the notes he had taken of the heads of his story, expressing at the same time his firm belief that the man had really been at Tombuctoo; and he had the satisfaction to find that the Members of the Committee concurred in his opinion of the credibility of the man's statements; in which belief they were afterwards confirmed by their personal examination of him. They strongly encouraged the Editor to proceed in the course which he had begun; and recommended him to omit no practicable means of securing the residence of Adams in this country, until all the information he could possibly give, had been obtained from him,—whether for the purpose of increasing our general knowledge of the interior of Africa, or of obtaining information on particular points which might be useful to the expedition actually on foot.

After this arrangement was completed, Adams attended the Editor for a few hours daily during the following fortnight or three weeks, for the purpose of answering his inquiries. During these examinations upwards of fifty gentlemen saw and interrogated him at different times; among whom there was not one who was not struck with the artlessness and good sense of Adams's replies, or who did not feel persuaded that he was relating simply the facts which he had seen, to the best of his recollection and belief.

The Narrative now presented to the public is the fruit of these interrogatories.

[The following letter was included within Samuel Cook's introduction. Dupuis also provided copious endnotes to Adams's narrative, which were nearly twice as long as Adams's entire account.]

Letter from Joseph Dupuis, British Vice-Consul at Mogadore

London, 31st January, 1816

In compliance with your request, I have great pleasure in communicating to you all the particulars with which I am acquainted respecting the American seaman who is supposed to have been at *Timbuctoo;* of whom I have a distinct recollection.

In the latter end of the year 1810, I was informed at Mogadore, that the ship Charles, of New York, to which that seaman belonged, was wrecked on the Western Coast of Africa, near the latitude of Cape Blanco: and about three months after her loss, I was fortunate enough to ransom three of her crew; who informed me that their Captain was dead, that the rest of the crew were in slavery, and that two of them in particular, had been carried away by the Arabs in an easterly direction across the Desert, and would probably never be heard of again. Some time after this, I heard that the mate and one seaman were at *Wed-Noon;* and I accordingly tried to effect their liberation; but after a considerable time spent in this endeavour, I could neither succeed in that object, nor in obtaining any information respecting the rest of the crew. At length, nearly two years after the wreck of the *Kabla,* a remote Douar in the Desert, in a south-east direction from Mogadore; and subsequently I heard of the arrival of the same individual at Wed-Noon; from whence, after a tedious negociation, I ultimately obtained his release about a year afterwards.

The appearance, features and dress of this man upon his arrival at Mogadore, so perfectly resembled those of an Arab, or rather of a Shilluh, his head being shaved, and his beard scanty and black, that I had difficulty at first in believing him to be a Christian. When I spoke to him in English, he answered me in a mixture of Arabic and broken English, and sometimes in Arabic only. At this early period I could not help remarking that his pronunciation of Arabic resembled that of a Negro, but concluded that it was occasioned by his intercourse with Negro slaves.

Like most other Christians after a long captivity and severe treatment among the Arabs, he appeared upon his first arrival exceedingly stupid and insensible; and he scarcely spoke to any one: but he soon began to show great thankfulness for his ransom, and willingly assisted in arranging and cultivating a small garden, and in other employment, which I gave him with a view of diverting his thoughts. About ten or twelve days afterwards his faculties seemed pretty well restored, and his reserve had in a great measure worn off; and about his period, having been informed by a person with whom he conversed, that he had visited the Negro country, I began to inquire of him the extent of his travels in the Desert; suppressing every appearance of peculiar curiosity, or of expecting any thing extraordinary from his answers. He then related to me, with the greatest simplicity, the manner in which he had been wrecked, and afterwards carried away to the eastward, and to *Timbuctoo;* the misfortunes and sufferings of the party which he accompanied, his return across the Desert, and his ultimate arrival at Wed-Noon. What he dwelt upon with most force and earnestness during this recital, were the particulars of the brutal treatment which he experienced from the Arabs at El Kabla and Wed-Noon. He did not appear to attach any importance to the fact of his having been at Timbuctoo: and the only strong feeling which he expressed respecting it, was that of dread, with which some of the Negroes had inspired him, who, he said, were sorcerers, and possessed the power of destroying their enemies by witchcraft.

The probability of the events, the manners of his relating them, and the correspondence of his description of places with what information I possessed respecting them, led me to attach a considerable degree of credit to his Narrative. After repeated examinations, in which I found him uniformly clear and consistent in his accounts, I sent for several respectable traders who had been at Timbuctoo; and these persons, after examining him respecting the situation of that city and of other places, and respecting the objects which he had seen there, assured me that they had no doubt of his having been where he described. So strongly was my belief in the truth and accuracy of his recital now confirmed, that I wrote a detail of the circumstances to Mr. Simpson, Consul-General of the United States at Tangier: I made a chart, on which I traced his course; and observed that it extended eastward nearly to the supposed situation of Timbuctoo: I also took down in writing an account of his travels, which I regret that I left amongst my papers at Mogadore; and although in doing this I had occasion to make him repeat his story several times, I never found that he differed in any important particular from the tale he told at first.

The Narrative which you have transmitted to me appears, after a minute examination, and to the best of my recollection, to be the same, in substance, as that which I received from him at Mogadore. The chain of events is uniformly the same; but I think he entered more into detail on many points, in the relation which he gave to me. I do not enlarge upon this subject here, having pointed out in the Notes which I have made on the Narrative, the few passages in which I found it [to] differ materially from what I recollect of his statements at Mogadore. I have also mentioned such circumstances as corroborated any part of his statements; and I have added, according to your desire, such illustrations or incidental information, as occurred to me in perusing the Narrative.

Being quite satisfied from your description of the person of the American seaman, and from the internal evidence of the Narrative, that "*Robert Adams*" is the identical individual who was with me at Mogadore, I must not, however, omit to inform you, that the name by which he went in Africa was *Benjamin Rose;* by which name also he was known to those of the crew of the Charles who were ransomed.

I cannot say that I am much surprised at this circumstance, because I recollect that he once hinted during his residence at Mogadore that "Benjamin Rose" was not his real name: and from the great apprehensions which he always discovered, lest he should fall in with, or be impressed by a British Man of War, as well as from the anxiety which he shewed on being sent to Tangier, so near to Gibraltar, I could not help suspecting that he might have some reasons of his own, connected with the British Naval service, for going under a feigned name. This conjecture was in some degree confirmed by an acknowledgment which he made, that he had once been on board a British Man of War, either on service, or detained as a prisoner.

There is another circumstance which he mentioned to me at Mogadore, which may possibly have led to this change of name. He told me that he had quitted America to avoid a prosecution with which he was threatened for the consequences of an amour, which he was unwilling to make good by marriage. But on the whole, I am disposed to think that the former was the real cause; since he never expressed any reluctance to go to America, but always seemed to dread the idea of visiting Europe. I never doubted at Mogadore that he was an American, as he stated; and on one occasion, he discovered an involuntary exultation at the sight of the American flag, which seemed quite convincing. He told me that he was born up the river of New York, where his father lived when he quitted America; and I learnt, either from himself or from some other of the Charles's crew, that his mother was a Mulatto, which circumstance his features and complexion seemed to confirm.

On the whole, as I consider it not improbable that *Adams* may be his real name, and being at all events quite satisfied, that he is the person whom I knew at Mogadore, I have, (to avoid confusion) adopted the name which he bears in the Narrative, when I speak of him in my Notes.

I shall be very happy if this explanation, and the details into which I have entered in the Notes, prove of any interest: if you think them of sufficient importance, I can have no possible ground for objecting to their being made public.

JOSEPH DUPUIS

214

Robert Adams

The Narrative of Robert Adams, a Sailor . . .

CHAPTER I

Robert Adams, aged 25, born at *Hudson,* about one hundred miles up the North River, from New York, where his father was a sail maker, was brought up to the seafaring line, and made several voyages to Lisbon, Cadiz, Seville, and Liverpool.

On the 17th of June 1810, he sailed from New York in the ship Charles, John Horton master, of 280 tons, Charles Stillwell owner; laden with flour, rice, and salted provisions, bound to Gibraltar.

The crew consisted of the following persons:
Stephen Dolbie, mate,
Thomas Williams,
Martin Clarke,
Unis Newsham,
Nicholas (a Swede),
John Stephens,
John Matthews,
James Davison,
Robert Adams,
shipped at New York.

The vessel arrived in twenty-six days at Gibraltar, where the cargo was discharged. Here she was joined by Unis Nelson, another sailor: she lay at Gibraltar about a month, and after taking in sand ballast, 68 pipes of wine, some blue nankeens, and old iron, proceeded on her voyage, the Captain stating that he was bound to the Isle of May, for salt, but afterwards it appeared that he was going on a trading voyage down the coast. When they had been at sea about three weeks, Adams heard two of the crew, Newsham and Matthews, who were old sailors, and had been on the coast before, speaking to the mate, stating their opinion that the Captain did not know where he was steering: the ship's course was then south south-west: they said he ought to have steered to the northward of west.[2] They had to beat against contrary winds for eight or nine days afterwards; and on the 11th of October, about 3 o'clock in the morning, they heard breakers; when Matthews, the man at the helm, told the mate who was keeping watch, that he was sure they were near the shore; to which the mate replied, that "he had better mind the helm, or his wages would be stopped." An hour afterwards the vessel struck, but there was so much fog that the shore could not

2. [This and all subsequent footnotes in this chapter are by Cook. Ed.] These courses, whether from the fault of Adams's memory, or of the judgment of the "old sailors," hardly seem to warrant the consequences here ascribed to them.

be seen. The boat was immediately hoisted out, and the mate and three seamen got into it, but it instantly swamped. The four persons who were in it, swam, or were cast ashore by the surf: soon after a sea washed off four or five more of the crew, including Adams; but as all of the ship's company could swim, except Nicholas, and the mate, they reached the shore without much difficulty; the latter two were nearly exhausted, but no lives were lost. When morning came, it appeared that the ship had struck on a reef of rocks that extended about three quarters of a mile into the sea, and were more than twelve feet above the surface at low water. The place, according to the Captain's reckoning, was about four hundred miles to the northward of Senegal.

Soon after break of day they were surrounded by thirty or forty Moors, who were engaged in fishing on that coast, by whom Captain Horton and the ship's company were made prisoners. The vessel bilged: the cargo was almost entirely lost; and what remained of the wreck was burnt by the Moors, for the copper bolts and sheathing; but as they had no tools wherewith to take off the copper, they saved little more than the bolts. The place, which was called *El Gazie,* was a low sandy beach, having no trees in sight, nor any verdure. There was no appearance of mountain or hill; nor (excepting only the rock on which the ship was wrecked) any thing but sand as far as the eye could reach.

The Moors were straight haired, but quite black; their dress consisted of little more than a rug or a skin round their waist, their upper parts and from their knees downwards, being wholly naked. The men had neither shoes nor hats, but wore their hair very long: the women had a little dirty rag round their heads by way of turban. They were living in tents made of stuff like a coarse blanket, of goat's hair, and sheep's wool interwoven; but some of them were without tents, until they were enabled to make them of the sails of the ship; out of which they also made themselves clothes. The men were circumcised. They appeared to be provided with no cooking utensil whatever. Their mode of dressing fish was by drying it in the sun, cutting it into thin pieces, and letting it broil on the hot sand; but they were better off after the wreck, as they secured several pots, saucepans, &c. So extremely indigent were these people, that when unable to catch fish, they were in danger of starving; and in the course of fourteen days, or thereabouts, that they remained at El Gazie, they were three or four days without fish, owing to the want of proper tackle. Among the articles in a chest that floated ashore, was fishing tackle, which the crew of the Charles offered to shew the Moors how to use, and to assist them in fishing; but they refused to be instructed, or to receive any assistance. At length, having accumulated enough to load a camel, they raised their tents and departed, taking with them their prisoners.

Besides the Moors there was a young man in appearance a Frenchman, but dressed like a Moor. As captain Horton spoke French, he conversed with this man, who told him that about a year before he had made his escape from Santa Cruz, in the Canary Islands, in a small vessel, with some other Frenchmen; and that having approached the shore to procure goats, they had found it impossible to get the vessel off again, on account of the surf, and were taken prisoners; his companions had been sent up the country. As he associated, and ate and slept with the Moors, Adams was of opinion that he had turned Mohammedan, although he assured Captain Horton that he had not done so.

On the landing of the Captain and crew, the Moors stripped all of them naked, and hid the clothes under ground, as well as the articles which they had collected from the ship, or which had floated ashore. Being thus exposed to a scorching sun, their skins became dreadfully blistered, and at night they were obliged to dig holes in the sand to sleep in, for the sake of coolness.

This was not the only evil they had to encounter, for as the Moors swarmed with lice, Adams and his companions soon became covered with them.

About a week after landing, the Captain became extremely ill, and having expressed himself violently on the occasion of his being stripped, and frequently afterwards using loud and coarse language, and menacing gestures, he was at length seized by the Moors and put to death. The instrument they used on the occasion was a sword, which they found in the cabin: the Captain used no resistance; he was in fact so reduced by sickness, and was in such a state of despondency, that he frequently declared he wished for death. It was the manner of the Captain that gave offence, as the Moors could not understand what he said, any more than he could understand them. One thing in particular, about which Adams understood the Moors to quarrel with him was, that as he was extremely dirty, and (like all the party) covered with vermin, they wished him to go down to the sea to wash, and made signs for him to do so. But partly from an obstinacy of disposition, and partly from the lassitude brought on by sickness and despair, he refused to do as desired; and whenever pressed to do so, used the most threatening looks, actions, and words.

When the vessel struck, the Captain gave orders that the heads of the wine casks should be knocked in, in the hope of thereby making her float; and when he found that did not succeed, he ordered that the guns, flour, anchors, &c. should be thrown overboard, and the water started. In the confusion and alarm, the muskets and powder were also thrown overboard; otherwise the party might have had the means of defending themselves against the Moors who appeared on their first landing, the number of whom did not exceed forty or fifty people; but though the Captain was a man of courage, he appeared to be utterly deprived of reflection after the vessel had struck. He was also an excellent navigator, but relied too much upon the mate.

After they had remained about ten or twelve days, until the ship and materials had quite disappeared, the Moors made preparation to depart, and divided the prisoners among them, carefully hiding in the sand every thing they had saved from the wreck. Adams, the mate, and Newsham were left in the possession of about twenty Moors, (men, women, and children,) who quitted the sea coast, having four camels, three of which they loaded with water, and the other with fish and baggage. They travelled very irregularly, sometimes going only ten or twelve miles a day, but often considerably more, making upon an average about fifteen miles a day; occasionally going two or three days without stopping, except at night, at others resting a day or two; on which occasions they pitched the tents to recruit the camels.

Except one woman, who had an infant, which she carried on her back, the whole of the party went on foot. The route was to the eastward, but inclining rather to the south than to the north of east, across a desert sandy plain, with occasional low hills and stones. At the end of about thirty days, during which they did not see any human being, they arrived at a place, the name of which Adams did not hear, where they found about thirty or forty tents, and a pool of water, surrounded by a few shrubs, which, was the only water they had met with since quitting the coast.

In the first week after their arrival, Adams and his companions being greatly fatigued, were not required to do any work, but at the end of that time they were put to tend some goats and sheep, which were the first they had seen. About this time John Stevens arrived, under charge of a Moor, and was sent to work in company with Adams. Stevens was a Portuguese, about eighteen years of age. At this place they remained about a month.

The mate offered the Moors one hundred dollars to take the party to Senegal, which was called by the Moors Agadeer Bomba,[3] which they refused; but, as Adams understood, they were willing to take them to a place called Suerra. Not being acquainted with this place, they objected to go thither; but when they began to learn the language, they found that what was called *Suerra,* meant *Mogadore.* The mate and Newsham remained only a few days at the place at which they were stopping, when they went away with some of the Moors in a northerly direction. It was very much the desire of Adams and Stevens to continue in company with the mate and the others, but they were not permitted.

Some days after, it was proposed by the Moors to Adams and Stevens to accompany them in an expedition to Soudenny to procure slaves. It was with great difficulty they could understand this proposal, but the Moors made

3. "Agadeer Doma."

218

Robert Adams

themselves intelligible by pointing to some Negro boys who were employed in taking care of sheep and goats; and as they frequently mentioned the word "Suerra," Adams at last made out, that if he and Stevens would join in the expedition, they should be taken to that place. Being in the power of the Moors, they had no option, and having therefore signified their consent, the party, consisting of about eighteen Moors and the two whites, set off for Soudenny, taking with them nine camels, laden with water and barley flour, procured at the place at which they had stopped. After proceeding two days, they were joined by twelve other Moors, and three more camels, and then the whole party set off to cross the Desert,[4] proceeding south southeast; travelling at first at the rate of from fifteen to twenty miles a day. It was the expectation of the Moors, that by travelling at that rate for ten days, they should come to a place where water was to be procured; but the weather having been exceedingly hot, and the season dry, when they arrived at the spot (which they did in ten days) where the water was expected, which seemed to be a well about eight or nine feet deep, it was found quite dry. By this time their water running very short, they resorted to the expedient of mixing the remainder of their stock with the camel's urine, and then set out again on their journey to Soudenny, pursuing a course rather more southerly, in the neighbourhood of which they arrived in about four days more. About two days journey from this place they appeared to have left the Desert, the country began to be hilly, and they met with some small trees.

Soudenny is a small negro village, having grass and shrubs growing about it, and a small brook of water. The houses are built of clay, the roofs being composed of sticks laid flat, with clay on the top. For a week or thereabouts, after arriving in the neighbourhood of this place, the party concealed themselves amongst the hills and bushes, lying in wait for the inhabitants; when they seized upon a woman with a child in her arms, and two children (boys), whom they found walking in the evening near the town.

During the next four or five days the party remained concealed, when one evening, as they were all lying on the ground, a large party of Negroes, (consisting of forty or fifty men,) made their appearance, armed with daggers and bows and arrows, who surrounded and took them all prisoners, without the least resistance being attempted, and carried them into the town; tying the hands of some, and driving the whole party before them. During the night, above one hundred Negroes kept watch over them. The next day they were

---

4. Adams calls "the Desert" only those parts of the great Sahara, which consist of loose sand, without any traces of vegetation.

taken before the Governor, or chief person, named Mahamoud, a remarkably ugly Negro, who ordered that they should all be imprisoned. The place of confinement was a mere mud wall, about six feet high, from whence they might readily have escaped (though strongly guarded), if the Moors had been enterprising; but they were a cowardly set. Here they were kept three or four days, for the purpose, as it afterwards appeared, of being sent forward to Tombuctoo, which Adams concluded to be the residence of the king of the country.

The better order of natives at Soudenny wear blue nankeen, in the manner of a frock; but are entirely without shoes, hats, or turbans, except the Chief, who at times wears a blue turban. The distinguishing ornament of the Chief is some gold worked on the shoulder of his frock, in the manner of an epaulette; some of the officers about him were ornamented in a similar manner, but with smaller epaulettes. Their arms were bows and arrows; the former about four feet long, with strings made of the skin of some animal; the arrows were about a foot and a half long, not feathered. The Negroes frequently practised shooting at small marks of clay, which they scarcely ever missed at fifteen or twenty yards distance.

The houses have only a ground floor; and are without furniture or utensils, except wooden bowls, and mats made of grass. They never make fires in their houses. The lower order of people wear blankets, which they buy from the Moors. After remaining about four days at Soudenny, the prisoners were sent to Tombuctoo, under an escort of about sixty armed men, having about eighteen camels and dromedaries.

During the first ten days, they proceeded eastward at the rate of about fifteen to twenty miles a day, the prisoners and most of the Negroes walking, the officers riding, two upon each camel or dromedary. As the prisoners were all impressed with the belief that they were going to execution, several of the Moors attempted to escape; and in consequence, after a short consultation, fourteen were put to death, by being beheaded at a small village at which they then arrived; and as a terror to the rest, the head of one of them was hung round the neck of a camel for three days, until it became so putrid that they were obliged to remove it. At this village the natives wore gold rings in their ears, sometimes two rings in each ear. They had a hole through the cartilage of the nose, wide enough to admit a thick quill, in which Adams saw some of the natives wear a large ring of an oval shape, that hung down to the mouth.

They waited only one day at this place, and then proceeded towards Tombuctoo, shaping their course to the northward of East: and quickening their pace to the rate of twenty miles a day, they completed their journey in fifteen days.

Robert Adams

CHAPTER II

Upon their arrival at Tombuctoo, the whole party was immediately taken before the King, who ordered the Moors into prison, but treated Adams and the Portuguese boy as curiosities; taking them to his house, where they remained during their residence at Tombuctoo.

For some time after their arrival, the Queen and her female attendants used to sit and look at Adams and his companion for hours together. She treated them with great kindness, and at the first interview offered them some bread baked under ashes.

The King and Queen, the former of whom was named *Woollo,* the latter *Fatima,* were very old grey-headed people. The Queen was extremely fat. Her dress was of blue nankeen, edged with gold lace round the bosom and on the shoulder, and having a belt or stripe of the same material half way down the dress, which came only a few inches below the knees. The dress of the other females of Tombuctoo, though less ornamented than that of the Queen, was in the same short fashion; so that as they wore no close under garments, they might, when sitting on the ground, as far as decency was concerned, as well have had no covering at all. The Queen's head-dress consisted of a blue nankeen turban; but this was worn only upon occasions of ceremony, or when she walked out. Besides the turban, she had her hair stuck full of bone ornaments of a square shape about the size of dice, extremely white; she had large gold hoop ear-rings, and many necklaces, some of them of gold, the others made of beads of various colours. She wore no shoes; and, in consequence, her feet appeared to be as hard and dry "as the hoofs of an ass."[5]

Besides the blue nankeen dress just described, the Queen sometimes wore an under dress of white muslin; at other times a red one. This colour was produced by the juice of a red root which grows in the neighbourhood, about a foot and a half long. Adams never saw any silks worn by the Queen or any other inhabitant of Tombuctoo; for, although they have some silks brought by the Moors, they appeared to be used entirely for purposes of external trade.

The dress of the King was a blue nankeen frock decorated with gold, having gold epaulettes, and a broad wristband of the same metal. He sometimes wore a turban; but often went bare-headed. When he walked through the town he was generally a little in advance of his party. His subjects saluted him by inclinations of the head and body; or by touching his head with their hands, and then kissing their hands. When he received his subjects in his palace, it was his custom to sit on the ground, and their mode of saluting him on such occasions was by kissing his head.

5. Adams's expression.

The King's house, or palace, which is built of clay and grass, (not white-washed) consists of eight or ten small rooms on the ground floor; and is sur-rounded by a wall of the same materials, against part of which the house is built. The space within the wall is about half an acre. Whenever a trader ar-rives, he is required to bring his merchandize into this space for the inspection of the King, for the purpose, Adams thinks, (but is not certain,) of duties being charged upon it. The King's attendants, who are with him all the day, generally consist of about thirty persons, several of whom are armed with daggers and bows and arrows. Adams does not know if he had any family.

In a store-room of the King's house Adams observed about twenty muskets, apparently of French manufacture, one of them double-barrelled; but he never saw them made use of.

For a considerable time after the arrival of Adams and his companion, the people used to come in crowds to stare at them; and he afterwards understood that many persons came several day's journey on purpose. The Moors re-mained closely confined in prison; but Adams and the Portuguese boy had permission to visit them. At the end of about six months, there arrived a com-pany of trading Moors with tobacco, who after some weeks ransomed the whole party. Adams does not know the precise quantity of tobacco which was paid for them, but it consisted of the lading of five camels, with the exception of about fifty pounds weight reserved by the Moors. These Moors seemed to be well known at Tombuctoo, which place, he understood, they were accus-tomed to visit every year during the rainy season.

TOMBUCTOO IS SITUATED on a level plain, having a river about two hundred yards from the town, on the south-east side, named *La Mar Zarah*.[6] The town appeared to Adams to cover as much ground as Lisbon. He is unable to give any idea of the number of its inhabitants; but as the houses are not built in streets, or with any regularity, its population, compared with that of European towns, is by no means in proportion to its size. It has no walls, nor any thing re-sembling fortification. The houses are square, built of sticks, clay, and grass, with flat roofs of the same materials. The rooms are all on the ground floor, and are without any article of furniture, except earthen jars, wooden bowls, and mats made of grass, upon which the people sleep. He did not observe any houses, or any other buildings, constructed of stone.

The river *La Mar Zarah* is about three quarters of a mile wide at Tombuc-too, and appears to have, in this place, but little current, flowing to the south-

6. Or *La Mar Zahr*. It was not easy to fix the probable orthography of African names, from Adams's in-distinct pronunciation.

west. About two miles from the town to the southward it runs between two high mountains, apparently as high as the mountains which Adams saw in Barbary: here it is about half a mile wide. The water of La Mar Zarah is rather brackish, but is commonly drunk by the natives; there not being, as Adams believes, any wells at Tombuctoo. The vessels used by the natives are small canoes for fishing, the largest of which is about ten feet long, capable of carrying three men: they are built of fig-trees hollowed out, and caulked with grass, and are worked with paddles about six feet long. The river is well stored with fish, chiefly of a sort which Adams took for the red mullet: there is also a large red fish, in shape somewhat like a salmon, and having teeth; he thinks it is the same fish which is known in New York by the name of "sheep's-head." The common mode of cooking the fish is by boiling; but they never take out the entrails.

The principal fruits at Tombuctoo are cocoa-nuts, dates, figs, pine-apples, and a sweet fruit about as large as an apple, with a stone about the size of a plum stone. This latter was greatly esteemed; and being scarce, was preserved with care for the Royal Family. The leaves of this fruit resembled those of a peach.

The vegetables are carrots, turnips, sweet potatoes, negro beans, and cabbages; but the latter are eaten very small, and never grow to a solid head.

The grain is principally rice and guinea-corn. The cultivation of the soil at Tombuctoo requires very little labour, and is chiefly performed with a kind of hoe which the natives procure from the Moors, and which appears to be their only implement of husbandry. Adams never observed any cattle used in agriculture.

The guinea-corn grows five or six feet high, with a bushy head as large as a pint bottle, the grain being about the size of a mustard seed, of which each head contains about a double handful. This they beat upon a stone until they extract all the seed, and then they put it between two flat stones and grind it. These operations are performed by one person. The meal, when ground, is sifted through a small sieve made of grass. The coarse stuff is boiled for some time, after which the flour is mixed with it, and when well boiled together it makes a thick mess like burgoo. This is put into a wooden dish, and a hole being made in the middle of the mess, some goats' milk is poured into it. The natives then sit on the ground, men, women and children, indiscriminately round the mess thus prepared, and eat it with their fingers. Even the King and Queen do the same, having neither spoons, knives, nor forks. In the preparation of this food for the King and Queen, they sometimes use butter, which is produced from goats' milk; and though soft and mixed with hair, it appeared to be considered a great dainty. Some of the bowls out of which the natives eat are made of cocoa-nut shells; but most of them are of the trunk of the fig-tree hollowed out with chisels.

The animals are elephants, cows, goats, (no horses), asses, camels, drome-daries, dogs, rabbits, antelopes, and an animal called *heirie,* of the shape of a camel, but much smaller. These latter are only used by the Negroes for riding, as they are stubborn, and unfit to carry other burdens: they are excessively fleet, and will travel for days together at the rate of fifty miles a day. The Moors were very desirous of purchasing these animals, but the Negroes refused to sell them.

The elephants are taken by shooting with arrows pointed with a metal like steel, about a foot long, and exceedingly sharp. These arrows are steeped in a liquid of a black colour; and when the animal is wounded they let him go, but keep him in sight for three or four days, at the end of which he expires from the effects of the wound. Adams never saw more than one killed, which was at the distance of about two miles from the town. He was one evening speaking to a Negro, when they heard a whistling noise at a distance: as soon as it was heard, the Negro said it was an elephant, and next morning at day-light he set off with his bow and arrows in pursuit of him. Adams, the Portuguese boy, and many of the town's people accompanied him, until they came within about three quarters of a mile of the elephant, but were afraid to go any nearer on account of his prodigious size. The Negro being mounted on a heirie, went close to him, riding at speed past his head: as he passed him he discharged an arrow, which struck the elephant near the shoulder, which instantly started, and went in pursuit of the man, striking his trunk against the ground with violence, and making a most tremendous roaring, which "might have been heard three miles off." Owing to the fleetness of the heirie, which ran the faster from fear, the elephant was soon left at a distance; and three days afterwards was found lying on the ground in a dying state, about a mile from the spot where it was shot. According to the best of Adams's recollection, it was at least twenty feet high; and though of such an immense size, the natives said it was a young one. The legs were as thick as Adams's body. The first operation of the Negroes was to take out the *four* tusks, the two largest of which were about five feet long. They then cut off the legs, and pieces of lean from the hinder parts of the body, and carried them home; where they skinned the flesh, and then exposed it to dry in the sun for two days. It was afterwards boiled, but proved to Adams's taste very coarse food, the grain of the meat being as thick as a straw, and of a very strong flavour. The only thing eaten with it was salt, which is procured from a place called Tudenny wells, which will be spoken of hereafter. Upon the occasion of the elephant being killed, the Negroes were greatly delighted: and Adams frequently laughed with them, at the recollection of their appearance as they stood round the dead carcase, all laughing and shewing their white teeth at once, which formed a ridiculous contrast with their black faces.

The other wild animals which Adams saw were foxes, porcupines, baboons, wolves, and a large species of rat which frequents the river. He does not appear to have seen either hippopotami or alligators.

Besides these, there is in the vicinity of Tombuctoo a most extraordinary animal named *courcoo,* somewhat resembling a very large dog, but having an opening or hollow on its back like a pocket, in which it carries its prey. It has short pointed ears and a short tail. Its skin is of an uniform reddish-brown on its back, like a fox, but its belly is of a light-grey colour. It will ascend trees with great agility and gather cocoa-nuts, which Adams supposes to be a part of its food. But it also devours goats and even young children, and the Negroes were greatly afraid of it. Its cry is like that of an owl.

The wolves are destructive to asses as well as goats. The foxes frequently carry off young goats and guinea-fowls, particularly the former. Although he never saw either lions, tigers, or wild cats; yet the roaring of animals of these descriptions was heard every night in the neighbouring mountains.

The domestic birds are guinea-fowls. The wild birds are ostriches, eagles, crows, owls, green parrots, a large brown bird that lives upon fish, and several smaller birds. He does not recollect to have seen any swallows.

The ostriches are about double the size of a turkey, quite wild, and go in flocks. When any are observed in the day time, the place where they resort is marked, and they are caught at night by men mounted on heiries, who strike them with sticks. When they are first caught their feathers are very beautiful. The flesh of the ostrich is cooked without being previously dried in the sun, and is good eating, as well as the eggs, which are boiled: in fact, almost every thing which the Negroes of Tombuctoo eat is boiled.

The principal animal food eaten by the Negroes is goats' flesh. Adams did not see more than one cow killed during his stay; and then, he thinks, it was on account of the animal's being in a declining state. The cows are very small, and but few in number: some of them are milk-white; but the colour of the greater part is red.

There are two sorts of ants at Tombuctoo; the largest black, the smallest red; which appear at times in prodigious numbers. He has also seen bees there; but he has no recollection of having seen any honey.

Having occasionally at night, seen a light like fire on the mountains to the southward of the town, Adams had the curiosity to visit them, and found a considerable quantity of sulphur, which the natives collected. The only use to which he has seen them apply this mineral, was to mix it with a substance in black lumps which looked like opium, for the purpose of making a liquid into which they dipped the heads of their arrows. It was with an arrow so prepared that the elephant, before spoken of, was killed.

The natives of Tombuctoo are a stout, healthy race, and are seldom sick, although they expose themselves by lying out in the sun at mid-day, when the heat is almost insupportable to a white man. It is the universal practice of both sexes to grease themselves all over with butter produced from goat's milk, which makes the skin smooth, and gives it a shining appearance. This is usually renewed every day; when neglected, the skin becomes rough, greyish, and extremely ugly. They usually sleep under cover at night; but sometimes, in the hottest weather, they will lie exposed to the night air with little or no covering, notwithstanding that the fog which rises from the river descends like dew, and in fact, at that season, supplies the want of rain.

All the males of Tombuctoo have an incision on their faces from the top of the forehead down to the nose, from which proceed other lateral incisions over the eyebrows, into all of which is inserted a blue dye, produced from a kind of ore which is found in the neighbouring mountains. The women have also incisions on their faces, but in a different fashion; the lines being from two to five in number, cut on each cheek bone, from the temple straight downwards: they are also stained with blue. These incisions being made on the faces of both sexes when they are about twelve months old, the dyeing material which is inserted in them becomes scarcely visible as they grow up.

Except the King and Queen and their companions, who had a change of dress about once a week, the people were in general very dirty, sometimes not washing themselves for twelve or fourteen days together. Besides the Queen, who, as has been already stated, wore a profusion of ivory and bone ornaments in her hair, some of a square shape and others about as thick as a shilling, but rather smaller, (strings of which she also wore about her wrists and ankles) many of the women were decorated in a similar manner; and they seemed to consider hardly any favour too great to be conferred on the person who would make them a present of these precious ornaments. Gold ear-rings were much worn. Some of the women had also rings on their fingers; but these appeared to Adams to be of brass; and as many of the latter had letters upon them (but whether in the Roman or Arabic characters Adams cannot tell) he concluded both from this circumstance, and from their workmanship, that they were not made by the Negroes, but obtained from the Moorish traders.

The ceremony of marriage amongst the upper ranks at Tombuctoo, is for the bride to go in the day time to the King's house, and to remain there until after sunset, when the man who is to be her husband goes to fetch her away. This is usually followed by a feast the same night, and a dance. Adams did not observe what ceremonies were used in the marriages of the lower classes.

As it is common to have several concubines besides a wife, the women are continually quarrelling and fighting. But there is a marked difference in the degree of respect with which they are each treated by the husband; the wife always having a decided pre-eminence. The Negroes, however, appeared to Adams to be jealous and severe with all their women, frequently beating them for apparently very little cause.

The women appear to suffer very little from child-birth, and they will be seen walking about as usual the day after such an event. It is their practice to grease a child all over soon after its birth, and to expose it for about an hour to the sun: the infants are at first of a reddish colour, but become black in three or four days.

Illicit intercourse appeared to be but little regarded amongst the lower orders; and chastity amongst the women in general seemed to be preserved only so far as their situations or circumstances rendered it necessary for their personal safety or convenience. In the higher ranks, if a woman prove with child the man is punished with slavery, unless he will take the woman for his wife and maintain her. Adams knew an instance of a young man, who, having refused to marry a woman by whom he had a child, was on that account condemned to slavery. He afterwards repented; but was not then permitted to retract his refusal, and was sent away to be sold.

The practice of procuring abortion is very common. Adams was informed that in cases of pregnancy from illicit intercourse, where the woman would not submit to this alternative, it was no unusual thing for the father secretly to poison her.

The Negroes of Tombuctoo are very vehement in their quarrels. When they strike with their fists they use the under part of the hand, as if knocking with a hammer; but their principal mode of offence is by biting. On the whole, however, they are a good natured people; and always treated Adams with the greatest kindness.

It does not appear that they have any public religion, as they have no house of worship, no priest, and as far as Adams could discover, never meet together to pray. He has seen some of the Negroes who were circumcised; but he concluded, that they had been in the possession of the Moors, or had been resident at Tudenny.

The only ceremony that appeared like the act of prayer was on the occasion of the death of any of the inhabitants, when their relatives assembled and sat round the corpse. The burial is unattended with any ceremony. The deceased are buried in the clothes in which they die, at a small distance to the south-west of the town.

Adams does not believe that any of the Negroes could write, as he never saw any of them attempt it; their accounts appeared to be kept by notching sticks. Almost all the Moors, on the contrary, are able to write.

Their only physicians are old women, who cure diseases and wounds by the application of simples. Adams had a wen on the back of his right hand, the size of a large egg; which one of the women cured in about a month by rubbing it and applying a plaster of herbs. They cure the tooth-ache by the application of a liquid prepared from roots; which frequently causes not only the defective tooth to fall out, but one or two others.

He never saw any of the Negroes blind but such as were very old; of these, judging from their appearance, he thinks he has seen some upwards of one hundred years of age. Children are obliged to support their parents in their old age; but when old people are childless, there is a house for their reception, in which they live, four or five in a room, at the cost of the King.

The only tools which the Negroes appeared to possess (besides the hoes and chisels previously mentioned) were knives and small hatchets with which they cut their timber, and a few other rough instruments of iron which they procured from the Moors. Adams does not remember ever to have seen a saw.

Their musical instruments are, 1st, a sort of fife made of reeds; 2d, a kind of tambourine covered with goat skin, within which are ostrich quills laid across in such a manner that when the skin is struck with the hand the quills jar against it; 3d, an instrument which they call *bandera,* made of several cocoa-nut shells tied together with thongs of goat-skin, and covered with the same material; a hole at the top of the instrument is covered with strings of leather or tendons, drawn tightly across it, on which the performer plays with the fingers in the manner of a guitar.

Their principal and favourite amusement is dancing, which takes place about once a week in the town, when a hundred dancers or more assemble, men, women and children, but the greater number men. Whilst they are engaged in the dance they sing extremely loud to the music of the tambourine, fife, and bandera; so that the noise they make may be heard all over the town. They dance in a circle, and (when this amusement continues till the night) generally round a fire. Their usual time of beginning is about two hours before sun-set, and the dance not unfrequently lasts all night. The men have the most of the exercise in these sports whilst daylight lasts, the women continuing nearly in one spot and the men dancing to and from them. During this time the dance is conducted with some decency; but when night approaches, and the women take a more active part in the amusement, their thin and short dresses, and the agility of their actions, are little calculated to admit of the preservation of any decorum.

It has been already stated, that Adams can form no idea of the population of Tombuctoo; but he thinks that once he saw as many as two thousand persons assembled at one place. This was on the occasion of a party of five hundred men going out to make war in Bambarra. The day after their departure they were followed by a great number of camels, dromedaries, and heiries, laden with provisions. Such of these people as afterwards returned, came back in parties of forty or fifty; many of them did not return at all whilst Adams remained at Tombuctoo; but he never heard that any of them had been killed.

About once a month a party of a hundred or more armed men marched out in a similar manner to procure slaves. These armed parties were all on foot except the officers; they were usually absent from one week to a month, and at times brought in considerable numbers. The slaves were generally a different race of people from those of Tombuctoo, and differently clothed, their dress being for the most part of coarse white linen or cotton. He once saw amongst them a woman who had her teeth filed round, he supposes by way of ornament; and as they were very long they resembled crow-quills. The greatest number of slaves that he recollects to have seen brought in at one time, were about twenty, and these he was informed were from the place called Bambarra, lying to the southward and westward of Tombuctoo; which he understood to be the country whither the aforesaid parties generally went out in quest of them.

The slaves thus brought in were chiefly women and children, who, after being detained a day or two at the King's house, were sent away to other parts for sale. The returns for them consisted of blue nankeens, blankets, barley, tobacco, and sometimes gunpowder. This latter article appeared to be more valuable than gold, of which double the weight was given in barter for gunpowder. Their manner of preserving it was in skins. It was however never used at Tombuctoo, except as an article of trade.

Although the King was despotic, and could compel his subjects to take up arms when he required it, yet it did not appear that they were slaves whom he might sell, or employ as such generally; the only actual slaves being such as were brought from other countries, or condemned criminals. Of the latter class only twelve persons were condemned to slavery during the six months of Adams's residence at Tombuctoo. The offences of which they had been guilty were poisoning, theft, and refusing to join a party sent out to procure slaves from foreign countries.

Adams never saw any individual put to death at Tombuctoo, the punishment for heavy offences being, as has just been stated, slavery; for slighter misdemeanours the offenders are punished with beating with a stick; but in no case is this punishment very severe, seldom exceeding two dozen blows, with a stick of the thickness of a small walking cane.

Adams did not observe any shops at Tombuctoo. The goods brought for sale, which consisted chiefly of tobacco, tar, gunpowder, blue nankeens, blankets, earthen jars, and some silks, are obtained from the Moors, and remain in the King's house, until they are disposed of. The only other objects of trade appeared to be slaves.

The principal articles given in exchange in trade by the people of Tombuctoo, are gold-dust, ivory, gum, cowries, ostrich feathers, and goat skins; which latter they stain red and yellow. Adams has seen a full-grown slave bought for forty or fifty cowries. He never saw the Negroes find any gold, but he understood that it was procured out of the mountains, and on the banks of the rivers, to the southward of Tombuctoo.

The Negroes consume the tobacco both in snuff and for smoking; for the latter purpose they use pipes, the tubes of which are made of the leg bones of ostriches.

The chief use to which they apply the tar brought by the Moors, is to protect the camels and other animals from the attacks of large green flies, which are very numerous, and greatly distress them. Adams has sometimes seen tar-water mixed with the food of the natives as medicine, which made it so nauseous to his taste that he could not eat it. The Negroes, however, did not appear to have the same dislike to it; from which he infers, that the use of tar-water in their food, was frequent, though he only saw it four or five times. None of the persons whom he saw using it were in bad health at the time.

During the whole of Adams's residence at Tombuctoo, he never saw any other Moors than those whom he accompanied thither, and the ten by whom they were ransomed; and he understood from the Moors themselves, that they were not allowed to go in large bodies to Tombuctoo. He did not see any mosque or large place of worship there; and he does not think that they had any.

Neither Adams nor the Portuguese boy were ever subjected to any restraint whilst they remained at Tombuctoo. They were allowed as much food, and as often as they pleased; and were never required to work. In short, they never experienced any act of incivility or unkindness from any of the Negroes, except when they were taken prisoners in company with the Moors engaged in stealing them. Adams could not hear that any white man but themselves had ever been seen in the place; and he believes, as well from what he was told by the Moors, as from the uncommon curiosity which he excited (though himself a very dark man, with short curly black hair), that they never had seen one before.

There was no fall of rain during his residence at Tombuctoo, except a few drops just before his departure; and he understood from the Negroes that they had usually little or none, except during the three months of winter, which is the only season when the desert can be crossed, on account of the heat. In some years, Adams was informed, when the season had been unusually dry, there was great distress at Tombuctoo for want of provisions: but no such want was felt whilst he was there.

He never proceeded to the southward of Tombuctoo, further than about two miles from the town, to the mountains before spoken of; and he never saw the river Joliba: but he had heard it mentioned; and was told at Tudenny, that it lay between that place and Bambarra.

Being asked the names of any other places which he had heard mentioned, he recollected that the people of Tombuctoo spoke of *Mutnougo,* and of a very considerable place to the eastward called *Tuarick,* to which they traded. He had also often heard them mention *Mandingo,* and *Bondou;* but he cannot recollect what was said respecting these places.[7]

The following is a list of some of the words which Adams recollects in the language of Tombuctoo.

Man,	*Jungo.*
Woman,	*Jumpsa.*
Camel,	*So.*
Dog,	*Killab.*
Cow,	*Fallee.*
Goat,	*Luganam.*
Sheep,	*Naidsh.*
Elephant,	*Elfeel.*
House,	*Dah.*
Water,	*Boca.*
Mountain,	*Kaddear.*
Tree,	*Carna.*
Date Tree,	*Carna Tomar.*
Fig Tree,	*Carna Carmoos.*
Gold,	*Or.*
A Moor,	*Seckar.*

CHAPTER III

The ten Moors who had arrived with the five camels laden with tobacco, had been three weeks at Tombuctoo before Adams learnt that the ransom of himself, the boy, and the Moors his former companions, had been agreed upon. At the end of the first week he was given to understand, that himself and the boy would be released, but that the Moors would be condemned to die; it appeared, however, afterwards, that in consideration of all the tobacco being

7. Adams mentioned *Jinnie* to me, amongst the towns which he had heard named by the Negroes of Tombuctoo.

given for the Moors, except about fifty pounds weight, which was expended for a man slave, the King had agreed to release all the prisoners.

Two days after their release, the whole party, consisting of the

10 Moorish traders

14 Moorish prisoners

2 white men, and

1 slave

quitted Tombuctoo, having only the five camels which belonged to the traders; those which were seized when Adams and his party were made prisoners not having been restored. As they had no means left of purchasing any other article, the only food they took with them was a little Guinea-corn flour.

On quitting the town they proceeded in an easterly course, inclining to the north, going along the border of the river, of which they sometimes lost sight for two days together. They did not meet with any high trees; but on the banks of the river, which were covered with high grass, were a few low trees, and some shrubs of no great variety. Occasionally they came to a Negro hut. Except the two mountains before spoken of, to the southward, between which the river runs, there are none in the immediate neighbourhood of Tombuctoo; but at a little distance there are some small ones.

They had travelled eastward about ten days, at the rate of about fifteen to eighteen miles a day, when they saw the river for the last time: it then appeared rather narrower than at Tombuctoo. They then loaded the camels with water, and striking off in a northerly direction, travelled twelve or thirteen days, at about the same pace. In the course of this journey they saw a great number of antelopes, rabbits, foxes, and wolves, and a bird somewhat larger than a fowl, which the Moors called *Jize*;[8] it appeared to Adams to be the same kind of bird known in America by the name of cuckoo.

The soil was generally covered with shrubs, and a low kind of grass like moss. Trees were seldom seen, and those not large. From the time of quitting the river, the only persons whom they saw were Negro travellers carrying salt to Tombuctoo; of whom they met parties of about ten or twelve almost every day with dromedaries, camels, and asses.

At the end of the thirteen days they arrived at a place called Tudenny,[9] a large village inhabited by Moors and Negroes, in which there are four wells of very excellent water. At this place there are large ponds or beds of salt, which both the Moors and Negroes come in great numbers to purchase, and date and fig-trees of a large size: in the neighbourhood the ground is cultivated in the

8. *Djez*, is the Arabic name for the common domestic fowl.
9. *Taudeny*.

Robert Adams

same manner as at Tombuctoo. From the number of Moors, many if not all of whom were residents, it appeared that the restriction respecting them, existing at Tombuctoo, did not extend to Tudenny.

The salt beds which Adams saw were about five or six feet deep, and from twenty to thirty yards in circumference. The salt comes up in hard lumps mixed with earth, and part of it is red.

The Moors here are perfectly black; the only personal distinction between them and the Negroes being, that the Moors had long black hair, and had no scars on their faces. The Negroes are in general marked in the same manner as those of Tombuctoo. Here the party staid fourteen days, to give the ransomed Moors, whose long confinement had made them weak, time to recruit their strength; and having sold one of the camels for two sacks of dates and a small ass, and loaded the four remaining camels with water, the dates, and the flour, (in the proportion of eight goat skins of water, or six skins of water and two bags of dates or flour, to each camel) they set out to cross the Desert, taking a north-west direction.

They commenced their journey from Tudenny about four o'clock in the morning, and having travelled the first day about twenty miles, they unloaded the camels, and lay down by the side of them to sleep.

The next day they entered the Desert; over which they continued to travel in the same direction, nine and twenty days, without meeting a single human being. The whole way was a sandy plain, like a sea, without either tree, shrub or grass. After travelling in this manner about fourteen days at the rate of sixteen or eighteen miles a day, the people began to grow very weak; their stock of water began to run short; and their provisions were nearly exhausted. The ass died of fatigue; and its carcase was immediately cut up and laden on the camel, where it dried in the sun, and served for food; and had it not been for this supply, some of the party must have died of hunger. Being asked if asses' flesh was good eating, Adams replied; "It was as good to my taste then, as a goose would be now."

In six days afterwards, during which their pace was slackened to not more than twelve miles a day, they arrived at a place where it was expected water would be found; but to their great disappointment, owing to the dryness of the season, the hollow place, of about thirty yards in circumference, was found quite dry.

All their stock of water at this time consisted of four goat skins, and those not full, holding from one to two gallons each; and it was known to the Moors that they had then ten days further to travel before they could obtain a supply.

In this distressing dilemma, it was resolved to mix the remaining water with camels' urine. The allowance of this mixture to each camel was only about a quart for the whole ten days: each man was allowed not more than about half a pint a day.

The Moors who had been in confinement at Tombuctoo becoming every day weaker, three of them in the four following days lay down, unable to proceed. They were then placed upon the camels: but continual exposure to the excessive heat of the sun, and the uneasy motion of the camels, soon rendered them unable to support themselves, and towards the end of the second day they made another attempt to pursue their journey on foot, but could not. The next morning at day break they were found dead on the sand, in the place where they had lain down at night, and were left behind without being buried. The next day another of them lay down; and, like his late unfortunate companions, was left to perish: but on the following day one of the Moors determined to remain behind, in the hope that he who had dropped the day before might still come up, and be able to follow the party: some provisions were left with him. At this time it was expected, what proved to be the fact, that they were within a day's march of their town: but neither of the men ever afterward made his appearance; and Adams has no doubt that they perished.

Vled Duleim[10] (the place at which they now arrived) was a village of tents inhabited entirely by Moors, who from their dress, manners, and general appearance, seemed to be of the same tribe as those of the encampment to which Adams was conveyed from El Gazie. They had numerous flocks of sheep and goats, and two watering places, near one of which their tents were pitched; but the other lay nearly five miles off.

The first fortnight after the arrival of the party, was devoted to their recovery from the fatigues of the journey; but as soon as their strength was re-established, Adams and his companion were employed in taking care of goats and sheep. Having now begun to acquire a knowledge of the Moorish tongue, they frequently urged their masters to take them to Suerra; which the latter promised they would do, provided they continued attentive to their duty.

Things, however, remained in this state for ten or eleven months, during which time they were continually occupied in tending the flocks of the Moors. They suffered severely from exposure to the scorching sun, in a state of almost utter nakedness; and the miseries of their situation were aggravated by despair of ever being released from slavery.

The only food allowed to them was barley-flour, and camels' and goats' milk; but of the latter they had abundance. Sometimes they were treated with a few dates, which were a great rarity; there being neither date-trees nor trees of any other kind in the whole country round. But as the flock of goats and sheep

10. *Woled D'leim.*

consisted of a great number (from one hundred and fifty to two hundred), and as they were at a distance from the town, Adams and his companion some-times ventured to kill a kid for their own eating; and to prevent discovery of the fire used in cooking it, they dug a cave, in which the fire was made, covering the ashes with grass and sand.

At length Adams, after much reflection on the miserable state in which he had been so long kept, and was likely to pass the remainder of his life, deter-mined to remonstrate upon the subject. His master, whose name was *Hamet Laubed,* frankly replied to him, that as he had not been successful in procuring slaves, it was now his intention to keep him, and not, as he had before led him to expect, to take him to Suerra or Mogadore. Upon hearing this, Adams re-solved not to attend any longer to the duty of watching the goats and sheep; and in consequence, the next day, several of the young goats were found to have been killed by the foxes.

This led to an inquiry, whether Adams or the boy was in fault; when it ap-pearing that the missing goats were a part of Adams's flock, his master pro-ceeded to beat him with a thick stick; which he resisted, and took away the stick; upon which a dozen Moors, principally women, attacked him, and gave him a severe beating.

As, notwithstanding what had occurred, Adams persisted in his determina-tion not to resume his task of tending the goats and sheep, his master was ad-vised to put him to death; but this he was not inclined to do, observing to his advisers, that he should thereby sustain a loss, and that if Adams would not work, it would be better to sell him. In the mean time he remained idle in the tent for about three days; when he was asked by his master's wife, if he would go to the distant well to fetch a couple of skins of water, that being of a better quality; to which he signified his consent, and went off the next morning on a camel with two skins to fetch the water.

On his arrival at the other well, instead of procuring water, he determined to make his escape; and understanding that the course to a place called Wadi-noon, lay in a direction to the northward of west,[11] he passed the well, and pushing on in a northerly course, travelled the whole of that day; when the camel, which had been used to rest at night, and had not been well broke in, would not proceed any further; and in spite of all the efforts Adams could make, it lay down with fatigue, having gone upwards of twenty miles without stopping. Finding there was no remedy, Adams took off the rope with which his clothes were fastened round his body, and as the camel lay with his fore-

11. This account of the relative bearings of Woled D'leim and Wed[-]Noon is rather at variance with the details of Adams's recollected course between those two places; but it accords very nearly with what is as-sumed in the map, on other grounds, to have been his real route.

knee bent, he tied the rope round it in a way to prevent its rising, and then lay down by the side of it. This rope, which Adams had brought from Tombuctoo, was made of grass, collected on the banks of the river. The saddles of camels are made of the same material, interwoven between a frame of sticks placed together in the form of a St. Andrew's cross, so as to fit the back of the animal.

The next morning at day light he mounted again, and pushed on till about nine o'clock, when he perceived a smoke a-head, which he approached. There was a small hillock between him and this place, ascending which, he discovered about forty or fifty tents pitched, and on looking back he saw two camels coming towards him, with a rider on each. Not knowing whether these were pursuers, or strangers going to the place in view, but being greatly alarmed, he made the best of his way forwards. On drawing near to the town, a number of women came out, and he observed about a hundred Moors standing in a row in the act of prayer, having their faces towards the east, and at times kneeling down, and leaning their heads to the ground. On the women discovering Adams, they expressed great surprise at seeing a white man. He inquired of them the name of the place, and they told him it was Hilla Gibla. Soon afterwards the two camels, before spoken of, arriving, the rider of one of them proved to be the owner of the camel on which Adams had escaped, and the other his master. At this time Adams was sitting under a tent speaking to the Governor, whose name was *Mahomet,* telling him his story; they were soon joined by his two pursuers, accompanied by a crowd of people.

Upon his master claiming him, Adams protested that he would not go back; that his master had frequently promised to take him to Suerra, but had broken his promises; and that he had made up his mind either to obtain his liberty or die. Upon hearing both sides, the Governor determined in favour of Adams; and gave his master to understand, that if he was willing to exchange him for a bushel of dates and a camel, he should have them; but if not, he should have nothing. As Adams's master did not approve of these conditions, a violent altercation arose; but at length finding the Governor determined, and that better terms were not to be had, he accepted the first offer, and Adams became the slave of Mahomet.

The natives of *Hilla Gibla*[12] appeared to be better clothed, and a less savage race, than those of Vled Duleim, between whom there appeared to be great enmity; the Governor therefore readily interfered in favour of Adams, and at one time threatened to take away the camel and to put Mahomet Laubed himself to death. Another consideration by which the Governor was probably influ-

---

12. *El Kabla.*

enced, was, a knowledge of the value of a Christian slave, as an object of ransom, of which Mahomet Laubed seemed to be wholly ignorant.

On entering the service of his new master, Adams was sent to tend camels, and had been so employed about a fortnight, when this duty was exchanged for that of taking care of goats. Mahomet had two wives who dwelt in separate tents, one of them an old woman, the other young: the goats which Adams was set to take care of, were of the property of the elder one.

Some days after he had been so employed, the younger wife, whose name was *Isha*,[13] proposed to him, that he should also take charge of her goats, for which she would pay him; and as there was no more trouble in tending two flocks than one, he readily consented. Having had charge of the two flocks for several days, without receiving the promised additional reward, he at length remonstrated; and after some negotiation on the subject of his claim, the matter was compromised, by the young woman's desiring him, when he returned from tending the goats at night, to go to rest in her tent. It was the custom of Mahomet to sleep two nights with the elder woman, and one with the other, and this was one of the nights devoted to the former. Adams accordingly kept the appointment; and about nine o'clock Isha came and gave him supper, and he remained in her tent all night. This was an arrangement which was afterwards continued on those nights which she did not pass with her husband.

Things continued in this state about six months, and as his work was light, and he experienced nothing but kind treatment, his time passed pleasantly enough. One night his master's son coming into the tent, discovered Adams with his mother-in-law, and informed his father, when a great disturbance took place: but upon the husband charging his wife with her misconduct, she protested that Adams had laid down in her tent without her knowledge or consent; and as she cried bitterly, the old man appeared to be convinced that she was not to blame.

The old lady, however, declared her belief that the young one was guilty, and expressed her conviction that she should be able to detect her at some future time.

For some days after, Adams kept away from the lady; but at the end of that time, the former affair appearing to be forgotten, he resumed his visits. One night the old woman lifted up the corner of the tent and discovered Adams with Isha; and having reported it to her husband, he came with a thick stick, threatening to put him to death: Adams being alarmed, made his escape; and the affair having made a great deal of noise, an acquaintance proposed to Adams to conceal him in his tent, and to endeavour to buy him of the Gover-

13. *Àisha*.

nor. Some laughed at the adventure; others, and they by far the greater part, treated the matter as an offence of the most atrocious nature, Adams being "A Christian, who never prayed."

As his acquaintance promised, in the event of becoming his purchaser, to take him to Wadinoon, Adams adopted his advice and concealed himself in his tent. For several days the old Governor rejected every overture; but at last he agreed to part with Adams for fifty dollars worth of goods, consisting of blankets and dates; and thus he became the property of *Boerick,* a trader, whose usual residence was at Hilla Gibbila [Gibla].

The girl (Isha) ran away to her mother.

The next day, Boerick set out with a party of six men and four camels for a place called *Villa de Bousbach,*[14] which they reached after travelling nine days at the rate of about eighteen miles a day; their course was north-east. On the route they saw neither houses nor trees, but the ground was covered with grass and shrubs. At this place they found about forty or fifty tents inhabited by Moors, and remained five or six days; when there arrived a Moor from a place called Hieta Mouessa Ali, named *Abdallah Houssa,* a friend of Boerick, who informed him that it was usual for the British Consul at Mogadore to send to Wadinoon (where this man resided), to purchase the Christians who were prisoners in that country; and, that as he was about to proceed thither, he was willing to take charge of Adams, to sell him for account of Boerick; at the same time he informed Adams that there were other Christians at Wadinoon. This being agreed to by Boerick, his friend set out in a few days after, for Hieta Mouessa Ali, taking Adams with him. Instead, however, of going to that place, which lay due north,[15] they proceeded north-north-west, and as they had a camel each, and travelled very fast, the path being good, they went at the rate of twenty-five miles a day, and in six days reached a place called *Villa Adrialla,*[16] where there were about twenty tents. This place appeared to be inhabited entirely by traders, who had at least five hundred camels, a great number of goats and sheep, and a few horses. The cattle were tended by Negro slaves. Here they remained about three weeks, until Abdallah had finished his business; and then set out for Hieta Mouessa Ali, where they arrived in three days. Adams believes that the reason of their travelling so fast during the last stage was, that Abdallah was afraid of being robbed, of which he seemed to have no apprehension after he had arrived at Villa Adrialla, and therefore they travelled from that place to Hieta Mouessa Ali at the rate of only about sixteen or eighteen miles a day; their course being due north-west.

14. *Woled Aboussebàh.*
15. This bearing is not reconcileable with Adams's subsequent course.
16. This should probably be *Woled Adrialla;* but I have no knowledge of the place.

Hieta Mouessa Ali[17] was the largest place Adams had seen in which there were no houses, there being not less than a hundred tents. Here was a small brook issuing from a mountain, being the only one he had seen except that at Soudenny; but the vegetation was not more abundant than at other places. They remained here about a month; during which Adams was as usual employed in tending camels. As the time hung very heavy on his hands, and he saw no preparation for their departure for Wadinoon, and his anxiety to reach that place had been very much excited by the intelligence that there were other Christians there, he took every opportunity of making inquiry respecting the course and distance; and being at length of opinion that he might find his way thither, he one evening determined to desert; and accordingly he set out on foot alone, with a small supply of dried goats' flesh, relying upon getting a further supply at the villages, which he understood were on the road. He had travelled the whole of that night, and until about noon the next day without stopping; when he was overtaken by a party of three or four men on camels, who had been sent in pursuit of him. It seems they expected that Adams had been persuaded to leave Hieta Mouessa Ali, by some persons who wished to take him to Wadinoon for sale; and they were therefore greatly pleased to find him on foot, and alone. Instead of ill treating him as he apprehended they would do, they merely conducted him back to Hieta Mouessa Ali; from whence, in three or four days afterwards, Abdallah and a small party departed, taking him with them. They travelled five days in a north-west direction at about sixteen miles a day, and at the end of the fifth day, reached Wadinoon; having seen no habitations on their route except a few scattered tents with a day's journey of the town.

CHAPTER IV

Wadinoon[18] was the first place at which Adams had seen houses after he quitted Tudeny. It is a small town, consisting of about forty houses, and some tents. The former are built chiefly of clay, intermixed with stone in some parts; and several of them have a story above the ground floor. The soil in the neighbourhood of the town was better cultivated than any he had yet seen in Africa, and appeared to produce plenty of corn and tobacco. There were also date and fig-trees in the vicinity, as well as a few grapes, apples, pears, and pomegranates. Prickly pears flourished in great abundance.

The Christians whom Adams had heard of, whilst residing at Hieta Mouessa Ali, and whom he found at Wadinoon, proved to be, to his great sat-

17. *Aiata Mouessa Ali.*
18. *Wed-Noon.*

isfaction, his old companions *Stephen Dolbie,* the mate, and *James Davison* and *Thomas Williams,* two of the seamen of the Charles. They informed him that they had been in that town upwards of twelve months, and that they were the property of the sons of the Governor.

Soon after Adams's arrival at Wadinoon, Abdallah offered him for sale to the Governor, or Shieck, called *Amedallah Salem,* who consented to take him upon trial; but after remaining about a week at the Governor's house, Adams was returned to his old master, as the parties could not agree about the price. He was at length, however, sold to *Belcassam Abdallah,*[19] for seventy dollars in trade, payable in blankets, gunpowder and dates.

The only other white resident at Wadinoon was a Frenchman, who informed Adams that he had been wrecked about twelve years before, on the neighbouring coast, and that the whole of the crew except himself, had been redeemed. He further stated, that a vessel called (as Adams understood him) the *Agezuma*[20] from Liverpool, commanded by Captain Harrison, had been wrecked about four years before, and that the Captain and nearly the whole of the crew had been murdered. This man had turned Mohammedan, and was named *Absalom;* he had a wife and child and three slaves, and gained a good living by the manufacture of gunpowder. Adams has often seen him employed in making it, by pounding brimstone in a wooden mortar, and grinding charcoal by hand between two stones, in the manner of grinding grain. The final process of mixing he performed in a room by himself, not being willing to let any person see how it was done. He lived in the same house as the person who had been his master, who, upon his renouncing his religion, gave him his liberty.

Among the Negro slaves at Wadinoon was a woman, who said she came from a place called *Kanno,* a long way across the Desert, and that she had seen in her own country, white men, as white as "bather," meaning the wall, and in a large boat with two high sticks in it, with cloth upon them, and that they rowed this boat in a manner different from the custom of the Negroes, who use paddles: in stating this, she made the motion of rowing with oars, so as to leave no doubt that she had seen a vessel in the European fashion, manned by white people.

The work in which Adams was employed at Wadinoon, was building walls, cutting down shrubs to make fences, and working in the corn lands or in the plantations of tobacco, of which great quantities are grown in the neighbourhood. It was in the month of August that he arrived there, as he was told by the Frenchman before spoken of; the grain had been gathered; but the tobacco was

19. *Bel-Cossim-Abdallah.*
20. *Montezuma.*

then getting in, at which he was required to assist. His labour at this place was extremely severe. On the Moorish sabbath, which was also their market-day, the Christian slaves were not required to labour, unless on extraordinary occasions, when there was any particular work to do which could not be delayed. In these intervals of repose, they had opportunities of meeting and conversing together; and Adams had the melancholy consolation of finding that the lot of his companions had been even more severe than his own. It appeared that on their arrival, the Frenchman before mentioned, from some unexplained motive, had advised them to refuse to work; and the consequence was, that they had been cruelly beaten and punished, and had been made to work hard and live hard, their only scanty food being barley flour, and Indian-corn flour. However, on extraordinary occasions, and as a great indulgence, they sometimes obtained a few dates.

In this wretched manner Adams and his fellow captives lived until the June following; when a circumstance occurred which had nearly cost the former his life. His master's son, *Hameda Bel Cossim,* having, one sabbath day, ordered Adams to take the horse and go to plough, the latter refused to obey him, urging that it was not the custom of any slaves to work on the sabbath day, and that he was intitled to the same indulgence as the rest. Upon which Hameda went into the house and fetched a cutlass, and then demanded of Adams, whether he would go to plough or not. Upon his reply that he would not, Hameda struck him on the forehead with the cutlass, and gave him a severe wound over the right eye, and immediately Adams knocked him down with his fist. This was no sooner done than Adams was set upon by a number of Moors, who beat him with sticks in so violent a manner that the blood came out of his mouth, two of his double teeth were knocked out, and he was almost killed; and he thinks they would have entirely killed him had it not been for the interference of *Boadick,* the Shieck's son, who reproached them for their cruelty, declaring that they had no right to compel Adams to work on a market-day. The next morning Hameda's mother, named *Moghtari,* came to him, and asked him how he dare to lift his hand against a Moor? to which Adams, being driven to desperation by the ill treatment he had received, replied that he would even take his life if it were in his power. Moghtari then said, that unless he would kiss Hameda's hands and feet, he should be put in irons; which he peremptorily refused to do. Soon after Hameda's father came to Adams and told him, unless he did kiss his son's feet and hands, he must be put in irons. Adams then stated to him, that he could not submit to do so; that it was "countrary [*sic*] to his religion"[21] to kiss the hands and feet of any person; that in his own country he

---

21. Adams's expression.

had never been required to do it; and that whatever might be the consequence, he would not do it. Finding he would not submit, the old man ordered that he should be put in irons, and accordingly they fastened his feet together with iron chains, and did the same by his hands. After he had remained in this state about ten days, Moghtari came to him again, urging him to do as required, and declaring that if he did not, he should never see the Christian country again: Adams, however, persevered in turning a deaf ear to her entreaties and threats. Some time afterwards, finding that close confinement was destructive of his health, Hameda came to him, and took the irons from his hands. The following three weeks he remained with the irons on his legs, during which time, repeated and pressing entreaties, and the most dreadful threats, were used to induce him to submit; but all to no purpose. He was also frequently advised by the mate and the other Christians (who used to be sent to him for the purpose of persuading him), to submit, as he must otherwise inevitably lose his life. At length, finding that neither threats nor entreaties would avail, and Adams having remained in irons from June till the beginning of August, and his sufferings having reduced him almost to a skeleton, his master was advised to sell him, as if longer confined, he would certainly die, and thus prove a total loss. Influenced by this consideration, his master at last determined to release him from his confinement; but though very weak, the moment he was liberated he was set to gathering in the corn.

About a week afterwards, *Dolbie,* the mate, fell sick. Adams had called to see him, when Dolbie's master (named *Brahim,* a son of the Shieck) ordered him to get up and go to work; and upon Dolbie declaring that he was unable, Brahim beat him with a stick to compel him to go; but as he still did not obey, Brahim threatened that he would kill him; and upon Dolbie's replying that he had better do so at once than kill him by inches, Brahim stabbed him in the side with a dagger, and he died in a few minutes. As soon he was dead, he was taken by some slaves a short distance from the town, where a hole was dug, into which he was thrown without ceremony. As the grave was not deep, and as it frequently happened that corpses after burial were dug out of the ground by the foxes, Adams and his two surviving companions went the next day and covered the grave with stones.

As the Moors were constantly urging them to become Mohammedans, and they were unceasingly treated with the greatest brutality, the fortitude of *Williams* and *Davison* being exhausted, they at last unhappily consented to renounce their religion, and were circumcised; and thus obtained their liberty; after which they were presented with a horse, a musket, and a blanket each, and permitted to marry; no *Christian* being allowed at any of the places inhabited by Moors, to take a wife, or to cohabit with a Moorish woman.

As Adams was the only remaining Christian at Wadinoon, he became in a more especial manner an object of the derision and persecution of the Moors, who were constantly upbraiding and reviling him, and telling him that his soul would be lost unless he became a Mohammedan, insomuch that his life was becoming intolerable; when, only three days after Williams and Davison had renounced their religion, a letter was received from Mr. *Joseph Dupuis,* British Consul at Mogadore, addressed to the Christian prisoners at Wadinoon, under cover to the Governor; in which the Consul, after exhorting them most earnestly not to give up their religion, whatever might befal them, assured them that within a month, he should be able to procure their liberty. Davison heard the letter read apparently without emotion, but Williams became so agitated, that he let it drop out of his hands, and burst into a flood of tears.

From this time Adams experienced no particular ill treatment; but he was required to work as usual. About a month more elapsed, when the man who brought the letter, who was a servant of the British Consul, disguised as a trader, made known to Adams that he had succeeded in procuring his release; and the next day they set out together for Mogadore.

On quitting Wadinoon, (where Adams is confident he stayed more than twelve months; the second year's crop of tobacco having been completely got in before his departure) they proceeded in a northerly direction, travelling on mules at the rate of thirty miles a day, and in fifteen days[22] arrived at Mogadore. The first night they stopped at a village called *Akkadia,* situated at the foot of a high mountain. Here, for the first time, Adams saw olive trees, and palm trees from the nuts of which oil is extracted. The place consisted of about twenty houses; some of them two stories high. Having slept there, they set out the next morning at four o'clock, and the following day about sun-set reached another village, the name of which he does not remember. Here were only a few houses, but a great many tents, and in the neighbourhood large fields of wheat, Indian-corn, and barley. Adams thinks this place was all the property of one man.

The place at which they next stopped, having travelled that day in a northeast direction, was the residence of a great warrior named *Cidi Heshem,* who had with him upward of six hundred black men and Moors, most of them armed with muskets, which they kept in excellent order. Adams was informed that he admitted into his service any runaway Negroes or Moors; to whom he gave liberty on condition of their entering into his service. He appeared to be very rich: having numerous camels, goats, sheep, and horned cattle, and abundance of piece goods of various kinds, as also shoes and other manufac-

22. The detail of Adams's course from Wed-Noon to Mogadore, makes only *thirteen* days.

tures which were exposed for sale in shops kept by Jews. The place was called after its owner, *Bled de Cidi Heshem,* in the district of Suz, and to the best of Adams's recollection, contained from twenty to thirty houses. Here he saw a great quantity of silver money, principally dollars. Cidi Heshem was at war with Emperor of Morocco.

After staying one night and part of the next day, Adams and his companion proceeded on their journey; and the following night slept at a place where there were only two huts. The next day they arrived at a place of a similar description, and then set out, expecting to arrive at a large town, situate on a high hill by the sea side named in English *Santa Cruz,* (where he was told, formerly a British Consul resided), but called by the Moors *Agadeer.* They did not, however, get so far; but reached a place called *Cidi Mahomeda Moussa,*[23] situate in a wide sandy plain, where the harvest being just got in, the inhabitants were holding a market, at which there appeared to be assembled not less than four thousand persons from all quarters, who had goods of all descriptions for sale. This market, he was told, is held once a year, and lasts for five days. Here Adams's companion was met by several persons of his acquaintance, who seemed greatly delighted at his success in effecting his (Adams's) liberation: some of them spoke English.

After remaining there one day, they set out again on their journey, and by one o'clock reached *Agadeer.* As soon as they arrived, the Governor sent for Adams, and said to him in the Moorish language, "now, my lad, you may consider yourself safe." He afterwards made particular inquiry as to the treatment Adams had met with; and on being told with what inhumanity he had been used at Wadinoon, the Governor said he well knew their manner of treating Christians; but that they were savages, and not subjects of the Emperor: he added, that having the good fortune now to be in the dominions of the Emperor, Adams might rest satisfied that he was perfectly safe, and would meet with nothing but good treatment; an assurance that afforded him the greatest satisfaction, although ever since his departure from Wadinoon he had felt a confident belief that his complete deliverance was at hand. The next day they resumed their journey, and from this time travelled northerly for five days without meeting with any other habitation than occasional huts. About twelve o'clock on the fifth day, ascending a hill, they discovered the town of Mogadore beneath them, and square rigged vessels lying in the harbour; the sight of which, says Adams, "I can no otherwise describe than by saying, I felt as if a new life had been given to me." In about half an hour afterwards they en-

---

23. There is a sanctuary near Santa Cruz, called *Cidi Mohammed Monsoul,* but Adams appears to have confounded it, (probably from the similarity of the names) with *Cidi Hamet a Moussa.*

tered the town, and immediately went to the house of the Governor, who sent Adams to Mr. Dupuis, the British Consul; by whom he was received into his house, and treated with the utmost kindness. "Never," says Adams, "shall I forget the kindness of this good gentleman, who seemed to study how to make me comfortable and happy."

On the arrival of Adams at *Mogadore,* it appeared to be the wish of the Governor to send him to the Emperor; but to this Mr. Dupuis objected, and Adams remained with him the following eight months; in the course of which time, Mr. Dupuis frequently interrogated him upon the subject of the several places at which he had been in Africa, and sent for travellers for the purpose of comparing their statements with those given by him; after which he expressed a strong desire that Adams should come to England for the purpose of giving an account of his travels, as he said many gentlemen would be glad to receive it. But as England and America were then at war, Adams was apprehensive lest he might be made a prisoner, and therefore declined the pressing offers and solicitations of the Consul that he should take his passage in an English vessel, bound to London. Finding Adams thus averse from going to England, and the only vessels which were lying at Mogadore being bound thither, Mr. Dupuis wrote to the Emperor of Morocco, and also to Mr. Simpson the British[24] Consul at Tangier with the view of procuring permission for Adams to go to Tangier, from whence he hoped he might get a passage by some Spanish vessel to Cadiz. This being at length agreed to, Adams took leave of Mr. Dupuis in the month of April, 1814, who sent him under the protection of two Moorish soldiers, to *Fez,* the residence of the Emperor.

They travelled on mules; but as they stopped two days at *L'Arrache,*[25] and travelled but slowly, it was eighteen days before they arrived at Fez. On their arrival the Emperor was absent at *Mequinez,* and they accordingly proceeded thither the next day, and went to the house of Doctor Manuel, a Portuguese physician, who informed the Emperor of Adams's arrival. Adams was then ordered into the presence of the Emperor, who first asked him of what country he was; he replied, "an Englishman." He then inquired into the treatment he had met with, and whether he liked the Moors as well as the Europeans, to which Adams answered, "No." The Emperor then ordered that Adams should be taken to the Governor; who, the next day, sent him in the charge of two soldiers to Tangier, where, travelling on mules, they arrived in three days.

Immediately upon his arrival at *Tangier,* Adams was presented to the Gov-

24. Mr. Simpson was *American* Consul.

25. Adams has evidently forgotten the situation of *El Araische.* He could not have touched there on his journey from Mogadore to Fez; though he might very probably pass through it on his way from Mequinez to Tangier. The place he alludes to must be either *Rhabatt* or *Sallee.*

ernor, and then conveyed to the Consul, Mr. Simpson; who two days afterwards procured him a passage on board a Spanish schooner bound to Cadiz,
where he arrived the next day, being the 17th of May, 1814, making *three years
and seven months,* since he was wrecked in the Charles; during which period,
except from the effect of the severe beating he received at Wadinoon, and the
weakness produced by his long confinement at that place in irons, he never was
sick a single day.

After remaining about fourteen months at Cadiz as a servant or groom, in
the service of Mr. Hall, an English merchant there; peace having in the mean
time been restored; Adams was informed by the American Consul that he had
now an opportunity of returning to his native country with a cartel, or transport of American seamen, which was on the point of sailing from Gibraltar. He
accordingly proceeded thither; but arrived two days after the vessel had sailed.
Soon afterwards he engaged himself on board a Welsh brig lying at Gibraltar,
in which he sailed to Bilboa, from whence the brig took a cargo of wool to Bris-
tol; and, after discharging it there, was proceeding in ballast to Liverpool. But
having been driven into Holyhead by contrary winds, Adams there fell sick,
and was put on shore. From this place he begged his way up to London, where
he arrived about the middle of October, completely destitute; and had slept
two or three nights in the open streets, before he was accidentally met by a gentleman, who had seen him in Mr. Hall's service at Cadiz, and was acquainted
with his history; by whom he was directed to the office of African Committee.

END OF THE NARRATIVE.

ADDITITIONAL WRITINGS BY ADAMS

"Interiour of Africa." *North American Review* 5, no. 13 (May 1817): 11–26.

❧ ELIZA BRADLEY

An Authentic Narrative

Eliza Bradley's narrative has long been read as a rare account of a female ship-wrecked off the Moroccan coast. Keith Huntress, however, has documented the considerable evidence that the Bradley narrative is a work of anonymous fiction that also plagiarizes large sections from James Riley's best-selling account. That the narrative has long been read as true and believable, and that it also sold well, suggests that it didn't greatly violate the captivity genre while positing the character of a female in a traditionally male role. Indeed, what stands out in Bradley's account is how closely in general it adheres to previous shipwreck narratives. The narrator admits she receives preferential treatment from her captors, including the convenience of a camel to ride, a tent for shelter, and a bible to read, but she is never subjected to sexual advances nor forced to perform domestic labor as we might expect. Her access to the bible, however, figures her as the repository of piety who frequently frames the events of the narrative within the larger story of Christian suffering and who offers encouragement and emotional succor to her husband and his flagging crew, who crawl through the sand behind her.

That Eliza Bradley claims to be from Liverpool rather than from a New England town is likely more a function of the publisher's ruse than a specific comment on nationality. The first U.S. publisher claimed his edition was a copy of the original British edition, the veracity of which was testified to by those who "knew" the Bradleys. No record of the publication of any such authoritative edition exists, but at least thirteen U.S. editions were published, and no one in this country would have been expected to vouch for Eliza Bradley and the authenticity of her story.

Fig. 16. Eliza Bradley riding a camel to her encampment. (Courtesy Special Collections and Rare Books Department, University of Minnesota Libraries)

Fig. 17. Eliza Bradley taking succor from the Bible. (Courtesy Special Collections and Rare Books Department, University of Minnesota Libraries)

An Authentic Narrative of the Shipwreck and Sufferings of Mrs. Eliza Bradley, the Wife of Capt. James Bradley of Liverpool, Commander of the Ship *Sally*, which was wrecked on the coast of Barbary, in June 1818. Boston: James Walden, 1820.

Chapter One

I WAS BORN in Liverpool, Eng., of creditable parents, in the year 1783—in the year 1802, at the age of 19, I was married to Capt. JAMES BRADLEY, my present husband. Who, having been bred to the seas, was possessed of no other means of support, and knew of no other way to obtain a livelihood; hence, my endeavors, after our marriage, to induce him to pursue some other occupation, attended with less dangers, proved, unfortunately, ineffectual. In May, 1818, my husband was appointed to the command of the ship Sally, bound from Liverpool to Teneriffe: and I having expressed a wish to accompany him on a former voyage to Madeira, he insisted on my accompanying him [on] this.—The ship was freighted with all possible dispatch, and on the morning of the 18th of May, we embarked, thirty-two in number, comprising the ship's crew and passengers, of which I was the only female.—Nothing worthy of record transpired on our voyage, until nearly five weeks from the day of our departure, when we experienced a tremendous storm, which continued to rage with unabated fury for six days; and to add to our distress, it was discovered that the ship, from the violent working of the sea, had sprung leaks in several places; both pumps were kept continually going, and were found almost insufficient to free the ship of water. The whole crew began now to turn their eyes upon my husband, who advised the immediate lightening of the ship, as the only measure that could be adopted to preserve our lives—the hatches were torn up, and the ship discharged of the most weighty part of her cargo: but the storm continued to rage, and the leaks increasing, it was soon concluded by the officers utterly impossible to save either the ship or their effects; the preservation of their lives becoming every moment more difficult to them, they now began to apply every thought and deed to that consideration. Since the commencement of the furious storm, they had not been enabled to keep any reckoning, and had been driven many leagues out of their course.

Such was our perilous situation from the 19th to the 24th June; in the evening of which the storm began to abate—the morning ensuing, although the sea had become much more calm, there was so thick a fog, that the ship's crew found it impossible to discern an object three miles a-head of them, and to add to our consternation, by the colour of the water, it was discovered that we were on soundings, while the breakers were distinctly heard at the leeward.—The storm had rendered the ship unmanageable, and she was considered so complete a wreck, that the officers thought it their wisest plan to put her before the wind, until they could discover the land, (which they imagined not far off) and then attempt gaining the shore with the boats—but, the day closed without any discovery of land being made, although the roar of the surf indicated that it could not be far distant. The ship's crew, nearly worn down with fatigue, as many of them as could be spared off deck, now sought a little necessary repose below; but, about midnight, they were suddenly aroused from their slumbers from the violent striking of the ship against a chain of rocks, and with so much violence as to open her stern! Even the little hope that the ship's crew had 'till then preserved seemed to fail them at once—on the instant the ship resounded with their lamentable exclamations, imploring the mercy of their Creator! [I]ndeed to form an adequate idea of our distress, one must have been a witness of it. The reader cannot suppose but that I too, in a moment like this, must have shared the terrors of the crew; but my fortitude, by the blessings of Heaven, was much more, probably, than what would have been exhibited by many females in my situation—the extremity of the misfortune, with the certainty of its being inevitable, served to supply me with a sort of seeming firmness. My poor husband, in his endeavors to reconcile me to my fate, seemed to forget his own situation; indeed, his visible steadiness and resolution happily imposed so far upon the whole crew, that it inspired them even in the instant of destruction, with such confidence in him, that rendered them attentive and obedient to his directions.

Never could a night be passed in more wretchedness! [T]he storm again gathered, and while the rain fell in torrents, the waves rising every instant, covered our bark, and rolled their mountains over our heads—in such a situation, stretched along on the outside of the hulk, fastening ourselves to every thing we could lay hold of, drenched through with rain, spent with constant efforts, we were obliged to exert against the fury of the waves which endeavored to wash us off from our hold, we at length perceived the morning's dawn, only to afford us a clearer view of the dangers we had passed, and those we had yet to encounter.

This prospect of our situation appeared still more tremendous; we perceived indeed, that we were not far from land, but we saw it was not possible for us to reach it. The raging of the sea would have daunted the stoutest and most expert swimmer; for the waves rolled with such fury, that whoever attempted to gain the shore, must have run the risk of being washed back into the main ocean or dashed to pieces against the ship or shore. At this sight and reflection, the whole crew was seized with the extremity of despair; their groans and exclamations redoubled, and were repeated with such strength and fervency, that they were to be heard amidst the raging of the winds, the roaring of the thunder, and the dashing of the waves, which, all joined together, augmented the horror of the sound.

The day was once more near closing, we reflected with terror on the last night, and trembled beforehand at that which was to come—there was indeed a small boat attached to the ship, but in no condition to weather, even the short passage that appeared to be between us and the land. We passed the night with feelings more horrible, if possible, than on the former; the exhausted state we had been reduced to, by our past labor, left us hardly power to sustain the present.

The succeeding morning our spirits were a little revived by beholding the sun arise, a sight all absolutely despaired of, when we saw it setting, and when death, by putting an end to our calamities, would certainly be a blessing; but the care of life, is the strongest passion in the human breast; it continues with us to the last moment of existence; the miseries one feels may weaken, perhaps, but rarely extinguish it. Our first emotion, on finding ourselves still clinging fast to the vessel, was to offer up our thanksgivings to Heaven, for having still preserved us alive even in such a deplorable situation, to raise up our suppliant hands in petition to Providence, to complete its miracle, by affording us some unforeseen means of escaping to the shore—there never was sure a more fervent prayer. Heaven at length seemed to look down with compassion on our miseries and danger—the wind began to abate, and the various agitation of the sea to subside to that degree, that the officers conceived it possible for us to reach the shore in the ship's boat.

The boat was but small, it could not contain above a third part of our number: we could not attempt to embark all at once without sinking it: every one was sensible of the difficulty, but no one would consent to wait for a second passage; the fear of some accident happening to prevent a return, and the terror of lying another night exposed on the hulk, made every one obstinate for being taken in the first—it was, however, unanimously agreed by all, that my husband and myself should be among the number who should go first into the boat. The sea having now almost become a calm, the boat containing as many as it was thought prudent to take on board, left the wreck, and in less than half an hour, we reached the shore, and were all safely landed; and were soon after joined by the remainder of the ship's crew, who were as fortunate as ourselves in reaching the shore, and with as little difficulty.

Being now placed on dry land, we soon perceived that we had new difficulties to encounter; high craggy rocks nearly perpendicular, and of more than two hundred feet in height, lined the shore as far as the sight could extend. The first care of the crew was to seek among the articles floated ashore from the wreck, for planks and pieces of wood, to erect a covering for the night; and they succeeded beyond their hopes—the night was extremely boisterous, and nothing beneath us but sharp rocks on which to extend our wearied limbs, we obtained but little repose. Early the ensuing morning it was to our sorrow discovered, that but little of the wreck was remaining, and those of the crew who were best able to walk, went to reconnoitre the shore, and to see whether the sea had brought any fragments of the wreck; they were so fortunate as to find a barrel of flour and a keg of salt pork—soon after they had secured these, the tide arose and put an end to their labour.

Captain Bradley now called together the ship's crew, and having divided the provision among them, enquired of them if they consented to his continuing in the command; to which they unanimously agreed; he then informed them, that from the best calculations he could make, that he had reason to believe that we were on the Barbary coast; and as we had no weapons of defence, much was to be apprehended from the ferocity of the natives, if we should be so unfortunate as to be discovered by them. The coast appeared to be formed of perpendicular rocks to a great height, and no way could be discovered by which we might mount to the top of the precipices, so steep was the ascent. Having agreed to keep together, we proceeded along the sea side, in hopes to find some place of more easy ascent, by which we might gain the surface of the land above us, where we were in hopes of discovering a spring of water, with which to allay our thirst—after travelling many miles, we at length found the sought-for passage, up a precipice, which resembled a flight of stairs, and seemed more the production of art than of nature. We soon gained the summit of the cliffs; but instead of springs of water, or groves to shelter us from the rays of the scorching sun, what was our surprise, to see nothing before us, but a barren sandy plain, extending as far as the eye could reach.

The day was now drawing to a close, and despairing of meeting with relief, I threw myself upon the sand, and after wishing for death a thousand times, I resolved to await it on the spot where I lay. Why should I go further to seek it, amidst new miseries? I was, indeed, so determined to die, that I awaited the moment with impatience as the termination of my misery. Amid these melancholy reflections, sleep at length overpowered me. My poor husband did everything in his power to alleviate my sufferings, he represented to me the probability of our meeting with friendly aid, by the means of which we might be conducted to some commercial port, at which we might probably obtain a passage for Europe. We passed the night at this place, half buried in the sand. At the dawn of day we again put forward, travelling in a south-east direction. The cravings of hunger and thirst, became now more pressing than ever, and we found nothing to appease them—before the close of the day, we were, however, cheered by the account of one of the sailors who had been dispatched a-head on the look out, who informed us that he had travelled the rocky borders of the shore, until he had discovered an extensive flat almost covered with mussels. We hastened to the spot, where we passed the night, and the next morning found ourselves so much strengthened, that we resolved to remain there the whole day, and following night.

At the dawn of day, we took our departure, and before the setting of the sun, it was conjectured that we had travelled nearly thirty miles; but without any prospect of relief—indeed, every hour now seemed to throw a deeper gloom over our fate. Having in vain sought for a resting place, we were this night obliged to repose on the sands. This was, indeed, a crisis of calamity— the misery we underwent was soo [*sic*] shocking to relate. Having existed for three days without water, our thirst was too great to be any longer endured. Early the ensuing morning we resumed our journey, and as the sandy desert was found to produce nothing but a little wild sorril, it was thought advisable again to direct our course along the sea shore, in hopes of finding some small shell-fish that might afford us some refreshment, although but poorly calculated to allay our thirsts.

Believing from our present feelings, that we could not possibly survive a day longer without drink, and no signs of finding any appearing, the last ray of hope was on the eve of fading away, when, about mid-day, the second mate, (who had been sent forward to make discoveries) returned to us with the joyful tidings, that he had found a pool of brackish water! [A] revelation from heaven could not have cheered us more! Conducted by the mate, we hastened to the pool, which contained about half a barrel of stagnated water; but impure as it was, it served as a very seasonable relief to us, for without something to allay my thirst, I am sure I should not have survived the night. Having at length succeeded in reaching the sea shore, we were miserably disappointed by the state of the tides, which prevented our obtaining any kind of shell-fish.

The next day brought no alleviation of our miseries—necessity impelled us to proceed, though hope scarcely darted a ray through the gloom of our prospects. My dear husband, seeming to forget his own miseries, did every thing in his power to alleviate mine—from the time of our shipwreck, he was never heard once to murmur: but by precept and example, endeavored to keep up the spirits of those who had as little cause to murmur as himself—for my own part, the miseries that I had endured since that melancholy event, had afforded me but little leisure to reflect upon the situation of any one but my-self. At the fall of the tide, we were so fortunate as to find a few mussels, and then following the windings of the coast, we pursued our journey for three or four days, over sharp craggy rocks, where perhaps no human being ever trod before, uncertain which way to proceed, incommoded by the heat, and ex-hausted by the fatigues of our march. In this, our most deplorable situation, however, and at the very instant that we were all nearly famished with hunger, Heaven was pleased to send us some relief when we least expected it—some of the crew who led the way, had the good fortune to discover a dead seal on the beach—a knife being in possession of one of them, they cut up their prey, dressed part of the flesh on the spot, and carried the rest with them.

As we were now in possession of provision, and could not expect to find wa-ter by traversing the sea shore, it was thought most advisable once more to bend our course backward, in search of it among the barren sands: for from our feelings we judged that we could not possibly survive a day longer without drink; our tongues were nearly as dry as parched leather. Fear of meeting with the natives (from whom they expected no mercy) appeared to be the prevailing principle of the actions of most of the crew, which must have been very power-ful in them, when it was superior to the prevailing calls of hunger and thirst. As we traversed the sandy desert, we searched in vain for some sorts of nourish-ment: there were neither roots nor vegetables fit for eating to be found. Our thirst increased every moment, but the hope of being able to assuage it, sus-tained us every step, and enabled us to travel on till the afternoon. We cast our eyes around, but could see nothing to rest our wearied sight upon, but a boundless and barren waste, extending on all sides. Such a horrid prospect threw us into the most shocking state of despair, and our exhausted spirits died within us; we no longer thought of continuing our hopeless and uncertain route, in which we could not possibly foresee any end to our wants and mis-eries, except what we might have received upon the spot, where we then laid ourselves down, from death alone—not until this moment did my fortitude forsake me—the weight of my misfortunes had now become too heavy for my strength, or rather weakness, to support—I felt as if the earth I pressed, had been heaped upon me! I exhorted my husband to leave me here, and to avail himself of the powers that he had yet remaining, to hasten forward to some in-habited part of the country, from whence he might have an opportunity of once more returning to our native land. My dear husband could only answer with tears and moans, while I continued to persuade him to our separation, urging the absolute necessity of it, in vain. "No, my dear wife, (said he) I will never consent to abandon you while life remains—with the Almighty nothing is impossible—if we put our trust in Him, He may prove compassionate towards us, & give us strength to pursue our journey, and support us in our tri-als—if it is His will that we should perish in a foreign land, far distant from kindred and friends, the will of God must be done, and we ought not to mur-mur.—He certainly orders every thing in the best possible manner, and He who takes care of the ravens, will not forsake His own children in the hour of affliction." My husband now kneeled down by my side, and offered up a peti-tion for our speedy relief; in which he was joined by the whole crew. After our pious devotions were over, it was agreed by the company that a part of their number should remain with me, and the remainder (who were the least fa-tigued) should go in search of water.

The sun was now near setting, and I fell into a state of torpid insensibility, without motion, and almost deprived of all reflection, like a person between sleeping and waking; I felt no pain, but a certain listlessness and uncomfort-able sensation affected my whole body.

About two hours after the party had departed in search of water, they re-turned nearly out of breath, and apparently much affrighted, and informed us that they had been pursued by a party of the natives (some of whom were mounted on camels) and that they were then but a short distance from us! [T]hey had scarcely finished their story, when a dreadful yell announced the arrival of their pursuers! Their appearance, indeed, was frightful, being nearly naked, and armed with muskets, spears and scimeters.

Our company having no weapons with which to defend themselves, they approached and prostrated themselves at the feet of the Arabs (for such they proved to be) as a token of submission. This they did not, however, seem to re-gard, but seizing us with all the ferocity of cannibals, they in an instant stripped us almost naked. For my own part such had been my sufferings, that I no longer felt any fear of death—such was my thirst at this moment, that I think I should have been willing to have exchanged my life for a draught of fresh water.

As soon as the Arabs finished stripping us, a warm contest arose among themselves, each claiming us individually as his property. This contest lasted for more than an hour, nor could I compare the combatants to any thing but hungry wolves contending for their prey!—sometimes we were laid hold of by a dozen of them at once, attempting to drag us off in different directions—they aimed deadly blows at each other with their scimeters, within two feet of my head, and inflicted wounds which laid the flesh of their bodies open to the bone! Becoming weary of the bloody contest, an old Arab (who probably was chief) at length commanded them to desist, and promising them, as I have since learned, that we should be possessed by those only who had the best claim to us—this point being at length amicably settled among them, and each Arab having taken possession of what had been apportioned to him as his rightful property, my husband by signs [exhibiting his mouth as parched and dry as the sand under foot] gave them to understand that our thirst was too great to be any longer endured, and that if we were not provided with something immediately to allay it, they must expect soon to be in possession of nothing but our dead carcasses!

As the Arabs appeared now to esteem us [poor miserable objects] of too much value to suffer us to perish for any thing within their power to afford us, they drove up their camels and took from the back of one of them, a goat skin, sewed up like a wallet, and containing about four gallons of brackish slimy water, which they poured into a callabash and gave us to drink. Bad as this water was, and nauseous to the smell, I think we could have drank half a gallon each; but having finished the contents of the skin, they refused us any more; but pointing to the east, gave us to understand that although water was with them a precious article, they in a few days should arrive at a place where they should obtain a plentiful supply, and we might drink our fill.

The Arabs now began to make preparation to depart—the one by whom I was claimed, and who I shall hereafter distinguish by the title of MASTER, was in my view more savage and frightful in his appearance, than any of the rest. He was about six feet in height, of a tawny complexion and had no other clothing than a piece of woollen cloth wrapped around his body, and which extended from below his breast to his knees: his hair was stout and bushy, and stuck up in every direction like bristles upon the back of a hog; his eyes were small but were red and fiery, resembling those of a serpent when irritated; and to add to his horrid appearance, his beard [which was of jet black and curly] was of more than a foot in length!—such, I assure the reader, is a true description of the monster, in human shape, by whom I was doomed to be held in servitude, and for what length of time, Heaven then only knew!

The draught of water with which I had been supplied, having revived me beyond all expectation, my master compelling his camel to kneel, placed me on his back. My situation was not so uncomfortable as might be imagined, as they have saddles constructed to suit the backs of these animals, and on which a person may ride with tolerable ease—the saddle is placed on the camel's back before the hump and secured by a rope under his belly. Thus prepared, we set out, none of the captives being allowed to ride but myself. The unmerciful Arabs had deprived me of my gown, bonnet, shoes and stockings, and left me no other articles of clothing but my petticoat and shimmy, which exposed my head, and almost naked body, to the blazing heat of the sun's darting rays. The fate of my poor husband, and his companions, was, however, still worse: the Arabs had divested them of every article of clothing but the trowsers; and while their naked bodies were scorched by the sun, the burning sand raised blisters on their feet, which rendered their travelling intolerably painful. If any, through inability, slackened their pace, or fell in the rear of the main body, he was forced upon a trot by the application of a sharp stick which his master carried in his hand for that purpose.

About noon, we having signified to the Arabs our inability to proceed any further, without some refreshment, they came to a halt, and gave us about half a pint of slimy water each: and for food some roasted insects, which I then knew not the name of, but afterward found they were locusts, which abounded very much in some parts of the desert. In my then half starved state, I am certain that I never in my life partook of the most palatable dish, with half so good an appetite. Having refreshed, we were again hurried forward, and were not permitted to stop again until about sunset when the Arabs came to a halt for the night, and pitched their tents—my master ordered me to dismount, and after he had turned his camel loose to feed upon the juiceless shrubs that were thinly scattered about the tent, he presented me with about half a pint of water, and a handful more of the insects! after which, I was permitted to lie down in the tent, to repose for the night; this was an indulgence that was not allowed the other captives, and would not probably have been allowed me, had it not been for my very weak state, which caused my master to fear, that without proper attention he might lose his property; for it appears, by what I have since learned, that they considered us of about as much value as their camels, and to preserve our lives, were willing to use us with about as much care and attention. My poor husband and his companions were compelled to take up their lodging on the dry sand, with nothing but the canopy of heaven to cover them. I this night, as I did every succeeding night before I closed my eyes, returned thanks to Almighty God for preserving me and enabling me to bear up under my heavy afflictions during the day past; to Him I looked, and on Him alone depended for a deliverance from bitter captivity— nor did I each morning fail to return Him thanks for his goodness in preserving me through the night.

At day light we were called on to proceed. The Arabs struck their tents, and I was placed as before on my master's camel; while the other captives were compelled to hobble along on foot as well as they could. A few moments before we commenced our journey, I was permitted to exchange a few words with my husband—he informed me with tears in his eyes, that his bodily strength began to fail him, and that if he did not meet with better treatment, he was fearful that he should not survive many days: in the mean time expressing a hope that God would preserve my life, and again restore me to my friends. I comforted him all I could, assuring him that if we put our trust in God, He cer-

Eliza Bradley

tainly would remember mercy in the midst of judgment, and would so far re-
strain the wrath of our enemies, as to prevent their murdering us. And the
more to encourage him, I then repeated the two following texts of scripture: "I
shall not die, but live; And declare the works of the Lord." Psalms cviii. 17.—
"Why art thou cast down, O my soul? And why art thou disquieted with me?
Hope thou in God: for I shall yet praise him, who is the health of my countenance, and my God." Psalms xiii. 11.

By sunrise we were again on our march, and travelled until night, over a
sandy desert, without sight of any living creature but ourselves—sands and
skies were all that presented to view, except now and then small spots of sun-
burnt moss—indeed, before us, as far as the eye could reach, presented a
dreary prospect of sun-burnt plains, without grass, stick or shrub. Some of my
poor unfortunate fellow captives being unable to proceed any further, the
Arabs came to a halt a little before sunset; and pitched their tents, and having
unloaded their camels, they dispatched two of their companions with a camel
to the west. We were now presented with a like quantity of water and food, as
on the day proceeding, and permitted to lie down under a corner of a tent to
rest our wearied limbs. Here I had another opportunity to converse with my
husband, and to witness more minutely the wretched condition of my other
companions in distress; some of whom appearing to be on the eve of exchang-
ing a world of trouble and sorrow, for a better. The sustenance allowed them
was hardly sufficient to keep the breath of life in them—having been deprived
of nearly all of their clothing and their bodies exposed to the sun, they were
rendered so weak, emaciated and sore that they could scarcely stand—they all
thought that they could not live another day! I exhorted them not to fail to call
on the Supreme Being in a proper manner for help, as He alone had power to
deliver them from the hands of their unmerciful masters; and if ever so fortunate as to meet with a deliverance, and to be once more restored to their fami-
lies and friends, never to let it be said of them as of Israel—"They forgat his
works, and the wonders he shewed them: they remembered not his hand, nor
the day that he delivered them from the enemy."

A little after sunset, the two Arabs, who had been dispatched with the
camels to the west, returned, driving the beast before them. As soon as they
reached the tent, we discovered that they had brought a skin of fresh water
[which they had probably been in quest of] and a quantity of a small ground
nut, which in appearance resembled European ground-nuts, and were equally
agreeable to the taste. Of the water they allowed us nearly a pint each, which
was a seasonable relief, for without it, I am certain that some of my companions would not have survived the night. It was pleasing to me to witness the apparent gratitude, which every one of the crew now manifested toward Him

who had wrought their deliverance from immediate starvation—after we had partaken of our scanty meal, it was proposed by me that we should all kneel, and individually return thanks to God for this wonderful proof of his infinite goodness—a proposition that was cheerfully agreed to by all, the Arabs in the mean time standing over us, apparently much diverted with a view of the attitude in which we placed our bodies during our pious devotions.

The ensuing morning we started very early, travelling west, and about noon arrived at the well, from which the water brought us had been obtained the day previous—the well had the appearance of having been dug many years, and contained five or six feet of water, of a quality too inferior to be drank by our meanest brutes, if any better could be obtained.—Preparations were now made to water the camels, they having never drank a drop to our knowledge, since the day we fell into the hands of the Arabs.—Troughs sufficiently large to contain half a barrel, were filled twice, and the whole drank by a single camel—nature seems to have formed these animals, for the express purpose of crossing the sandy deserts, and when watered, to drink a sufficient quantity, to last them from four to six weeks; was this not the case, they certainly must perish in travelling from well to well, which are situated many miles from each other. For my own part, so great was the quantity of water given to the camels, that I was under very serious apprehension that none would be left for us; for so great now was our thirst, that had we been permitted, we would have gladly thrust in our heads, and drank out of the same trough with the camels; but this we were not allowed to do, nor would they allow us to approach the well, until the camels had been supplied with as much water as they could drink: this being done, the troughs were next filled for us, when we were permitted (in imitation of the camels) to kneel down, thrust in our heads, and drink until we were satisfied. I am confident that I drank three pints, and without producing the serious effects that one would apprehend after suffering so much from thirst. I now by signs begged of my master for something to eat; but he gave me only a very small quantity of the roots heretofore described, at the same time by signs, giving me to understand that in two or three days, we should reach the place of their destination, where his family dwelt, and who would supply me with as much food as I should want.

The Arabs next proceeded to fill their goat-skins with water, which having done, they slung them on each side of their camels; the camel belonging to my master was next ordered to kneel, and I again placed on his back—thus prepared, we again resumed our journey, travelling east. The face of the desert in every direction had still the same barren appearance, and at noon day the rays of the sun had a most powerful effect upon our almost naked bodies—having been deprived of my bonnet, and having nothing to defend my head from the sun's scorching rays, the pain that I endured was extremely excruciating: yet, I praised God that I was not doomed to walk on foot, and at night to lie in the scorching sands, as my fellow-sufferers were compelled to do. During the day we continued our dreary route without the discovery of any thing that could serve to relieve the cravings of nature—we continued, however, to travel until eight o'clock in the evening, when the Arabs came to a halt, and pitched their tents for the night. To attempt to describe the situation of my poor husband, as well as the rest of his unfortunate fellow captives, at this time, would be a thing impossible for any one to do but those who witnessed it. The sun had scorched and blistered their bodies from head to foot: I will not pretend to describe their feelings; the compassionate reader will paint our distress in his imagination in stronger colors than can be described by words. We had nothing now left to eat; our masters, however, had the humanity to give us as much water as we could drink, and after returning thanks to heaven, as usual, for our preservation through the day, we retired to seek repose for the night.

The next morning we were ordered early to arise and prepare for our journey; but three of my unfortunate fellow captives (one of whom was a lad of but 12 years of age) signified to their masters, by signs, inability to proceed one step further, unless they were provided with some sustenance, of which they had been deprived for the last thirty-six hours. The unmerciful Arabs thereupon became greatly enraged, and beat those who had complained of their weakness most unmercifully: but the blows inflicted upon the poor wretches only increased their inability to travel. The Arabs finding that blows had no effect, and unwilling to part with any of us, they next consulted together what was best to be done to preserve our lives, it being evident to them that none of us could survive another day without some kind of nourishment, of which they were themselves now destitute; they at length agreed to kill one of their camels; and the one on which I rode, being the oldest of the drove, they obtained the consent of my master to butcher that; the business being thus settled, they began to make preparation for the slaughter. They compelled the poor animal to kneel down in the usual manner, as when about to be relieved from or to receive a load, and then with a rope hauling his head back nearly to his rump, they with one of their scimeters, cut his throat; the blood they caught with in a bucket as it flowed from the wound, and were extremely careful not to lose a drop—such was our hunger at this time, that we would have gladly have [*sic*] drank it as it streamed warm from the beast. Indeed such was the state of our stomachs, that I am confident that we should not have loathed animal food, even in a state of putrefaction.

The camel was now dressed by the Arabs in much the same manner as the Europeans dress a butchered ox; but there was not a particle of any thing belonging to the carcase, but was esteemed of too much value to be wasted: even the hide and entrails were carefully preserved. The Arabs, assisted by the captives, next busied themselves in gathering small twigs and dry grass, with which to cook a part of the animal. The blood was first poured into a copper kettle, and set on the fire to boil, the Arabs stirring it with sticks until it became a thick cake; this being done, the entrails (with very little cleaning) were next deposited in the kettle and set on the fire to bake or stew, after which the whole was distributed among the captives to eat; this was a relief that none of us anticipated when we arose in the morning; nor did I fail on this occasion, to pour out my soul in rapturous effusions of thankfulness to the Supreme Being, nor did I find it very difficult to persuade my fellow captives to follow my example; this our wonderful deliverance, while on the very brink of starvation, was to me another proof of the mercy and goodness of God, and that with us in the present instance he had eminently fulfilled the word contained in Psalms cvi. 46: "He made them also to be pitied of all those who carried them captives."

While we were devouring the food allotted us, the Arabs were employed in cutting up and roasting the carcase, which done they, like ravenous wolves, devoured more than one half of it, and the remainder deposited in their bags slung upon their camels. Preparations were now made for our departure. I begged of my master to indulge me with the privilege of conversing a few moments with my husband, before we resumed our journey, as he had informed me, in a few words the evening previous, that he had something important to communicate: after a good deal of persuasion the indulgence was granted me, and my husband having begged the same indulgence and obtained the same liberty of his master, we were permitted to seat ourselves in one corner of the tent to converse. My husband now informed me that by what he could learn from the Arabs (as they were of different clans,) we were soon to be separated and conveyed to different parts of the country, and retained as captives, until they could have an opportunity to dispose of us to some of their brethren bound to the capital of Morocco, where an English consul resided—and of whom they expected a good price, as they knew it was his duty to redeem all the European captives that should fall into their hands. That he had done all in his power to persuade his master to purchase me, to prevent our separation, but without any success; his master informing him that my master could not be persuaded to part with me, as he well knew that the English Consul would pay double price for the redemption of a female captive; that he then by signs gave him to understand that the female captive was his wife, and that the Consul would be willing to give him four times the sum for the redemption of both together, (that they might be each other's company to their own country) than he would be obliged to redeem them separately at different periods; but his master could not be persuaded either to purchase me or to part with him. Here my poor husband concluded by observing, that as I was used with less severity by the natives than any of the other captives, he hoped that I should be so fortunate as once more to gain my liberty, by the intercession of some friend who might hear of my captivity; but as for himself, he had become so extremely feeble, in consequence of the treatment which he met with from the natives, that he despaired of living to regain his liberty. I begged of him not to despair while life remained—that if he put his trust in God, he would be his friend, and not forsake him, but in his own good time restore us all to our liberty and our friends; that it might prove good for us that we were thus afflicted, and as God certainly knew best what was for our good, we ought to pray that God's will be done; that the Almighty had enabled us thus far to surmount difficulties, and to perform tedious journies [*sic*] each day of many miles, when we conceived it almost impossible for us in the morning to travel half the distance. My husband now told me that he had been informed by one of the sailors that his master had taken a bible from him, which he found in his knapsack, and which the Arab had then in his possession: which being of no use to him as he could not read it he thought he might be persuaded by my master to part with it, if seasonable application was made.—This was indeed pleasing news to me, as in case of a separation from my poor husband, I could find in this sacred volume the consolation which no human power on earth could afford me.

The hoarse voices of our masters were now heard, commanding us to separate and prepare to continue our journey. Since the camel I rode had been slain, not a thought until this moment entered my mind whether I should any longer be thus indulged, or be compelled like the other captives to travel on foot; if the latter was their intention I was certain that my situation would be infinitely worse than that of my husband; for as the Arabs had robbed me of my shoes and stockings, were they to compel me thus to travel, they would very soon find the necessity of either leaving me behind to perish with hunger, or of dispatching me at once with their scimiters; but my anxious doubts were very soon removed by the appearance of my master, leading a camel, which being compelled to kneel, I was ordered to mount.

We set forward in an easterly direction, and in consequence of the food with which we had been supplied, travelled with much better spirits than we had done for many days before—a little before sunset, we came to a well of tolerable good water, where were a large company of Arabs, watering their camels; the strangers were all armed with muskets, and were double our number. Our masters were all mounted, but instantly leaped off their camels, and unsheathing their guns, prepared for action should the strangers prove enemies. They approached us hastily with a horrible shout—I expected now to see a battle; but when they had arrived within half a gun-shot of us, they stopped short and demanded who we were? of what country we (the slaves) were? and where our masters had found us? To which questions my master briefly replied, assuring them that the place where we had been shipwrecked was but a very short distance, not more than two days travel; and that they had left the beach strewed with many articles of inestimable value, which they were unable to bring away with them—this was stratagem made use of by my master, to prevent the strangers molesting us; for as they live by stealing, they conceive that property belongs to no one, unless he has power to defend it. The strangers, elated with the prospect of obtaining their share of the booty, hastily mounted their camels and departed for the place, where our masters assured them they would find the wreck, and the valuable property they had described to them.—They were to the very great satisfaction of our masters, soon out of sight, and left us in peaceable possession of the well. Here we had once more an opportunity to quench our thirst, but not, however, until the camels and their masters had drank their fill.

As the sun had now set, a dispute commenced between the Arabs whether we should pitch our tents here for the night, or proceed a few miles further. It was argued by those who were against stopping here, that the Arabs who had gone in quest of the wreck, might alter their minds, and return in the course of the night and possess themselves of their prisoners. As an Arab had rather part with his life than his property, it did not require much argument to satisfy those who were at first of a different opinion, that to proceed to a place of more safety, would be the wisest step. Having filled their skins with water, and permitted us to take a second draught, they quitted the well near an hour after sunset, and after ascending and descending prodigious drifts of dry sand until our strength had become nearly exhausted, our masters at length found a snug retreat, surrounded on all sides by high sand drifts. As it was nearly midnight, they thought it not worth while to pitch their tents, but compelled us to lie down in the deep sand, and charged us not to exchange a word with each other, or make the least noise. Here, in our most exhausted state, were we compelled to lie on the bare ground, without the smallest shelter from the heavy dews of the night, and enduring, beside the cravings of hunger, excruciating pains in all our limbs. Our masters accustomed to such hardships did not even complain of fatigue.

As soon as day-light appeared they allowed us a small portion of what remained of the camel, after which we were called upon again to pursue our journey. The Arabs were exceedingly careful in their preparations to depart, not to make the least noise, and forbid our uttering a word, lest they should be discovered by an enemy more powerful than themselves. By sun rise we were on our march—they compelled my husband and his poor fellow captives to keep up with the camels, although their feet were extremely sore and swollen—for my own part (next to hunger and thirst) the most that I had endured was from the scorching rays of the sun, beating upon my bare head; but having now gone so long bare-headed, my head had become accustomed to heat, and though it remained uncovered, it did not pain me. Since my captivity, I had many times begged of my master that he would return me my bonnet, as the only means by which he could expect me to preserve my life; but he always, by signs gave me to understand that it was the property of another, who could not be prevailed upon to part with it.

The desert now before us had the same sandy appearance we had before observed—all was a dreary, solitary waste, without a tree or shrub to arrest the view within the horizon. We continued on our route, however, as well as our situation would admit, until an hour after sunset, when the Arabs pitched their tents as usual, and we were permitted to retire to rest, although our extreme hunger (having eaten nothing but a morsel of camel's flesh for the last 24 hours) deprived us of sleep. In the morning, so reduced were many of the captives by fatigue and hunger, that they were scarcely enabled to stand on their feet. It was in vain that the cruel Arabs beat them unmercifully, to force them to renew their journey—their legs were too weak to support even their emaciated bodies. The Arabs became at length satisfied that food must very soon be obtained or they would lose some of their prisoners. While they were debating on what was to be done, the fresh track of camels was discovered by some of the company, a short distance to the west of where we were encamped. The Arabs seemed overjoyed at the discovery, and eight or ten of them mounted on the best camels set out in pursuit of the travellers, to beg a supply of provisions, if friends, and to take it by force, if enemies.

As we were likely to remain here some time [at least till the return of those who had been dispatched in quest of provision] I solicited, and was so fortunate as to be allowed the privilege of another interview with my poor unfortunate husband. I found him laboring under a still greater depression of spirits, than when I last had the privilege of conversing with him—he said that every hour now seemed to throw a deeper gloom over his fate, and that nature could not possibly hold out but a short time longer! and indeed, that such was the state of wretchedness to which he was reduced, that [as regarding himself] death was stripped of all its terrors; I once more reminded him of the power of the Almighty to relieve us, and of the necessity of relying on his mercy, that through his divine goodness, we ought to be thankful that our lives had been so long miraculously preserved—that although our afflictions had been very great, and might still be even greater, yet the Lord was able to support us, and might in proper season be pleased to effect our deliverance; as he had declared to us in Psalms 6, 15. "And call upon me in the day of trouble, I will deliver thee, and thou shalt glorify me."

My husband now informed me, that his suspicions that we were to be separated and conveyed to different parts of the desert without a prospect of seeing each other again, had been confirmed by the chief of the clan, with whom he had had much conversation respecting our future destiny—the chief giving him to understand that it was the intention of our masters to retain us as slaves until an opportunity should present to dispose of us to some of their countrymen bound to the Moorish dominions, where a high price would be paid for us by the Sultan's friend [British Consul] that he had tried to prevail on him to purchase me, and to convey us both to Morocco (or Marockish as the Arabs term it) where he assured him we had friends who would pay a handsome price for us! but without any success—his master assuring him that my master could not be prevailed upon to part with me, for all the property he was worth, and that he would not engage to carry him (my husband) to Marockish for the price of his life; as he should have to pass through many tribes with whom they were at war—"thus my dear wife, [concluded my husband] you see that the prospect of our speedy redemption is very small; and I am confident that if our captivity continues a month longer, and we are not treated with more lenity, not one of us will be found alive, for every one of my unfortunate fellow captives are if possible, in a more deplorable situation than myself."

Such indeed as had been represented by my husband, was the situation of those victims of misfortune! overwhelmed with fatigue, unable to obtain repose, tormented with hunger, and consigned, without any human assistance, into the hands of merciless barbarians. These ferocious monsters whenever they uttered a murmur, appeared so enraged against them, that when they spoke to them, the fire flashed from their eyes, and the white, so perceptible in the Moors and Arabs, could not be distinguished—and even in their most debilitated state, they were guarded with such vigilance, that an Arab with a spear or a musket in his hand, attended them on every occasion; the barbarians being apprehensive that they might escape, or that their prey might be taken from them by force.

The Arabs sent in pursuit of the travellers returned about noon, and brought with them the bones and entrails of a kid, a small portion of which they gave to us. It was sweet to our taste, though but a morsel, and we pounded, chewed and swallowed all the bones. They now finished their last sack of water, having taken a plentiful drink themselves, they gave us the relicks, which was inferior to bilge water.—The Arabs having concluded to proceed no further this day, they had the humanity to suffer the weakest of the captives to lodge at night under a corner of their tent. The ensuing morning they compelled us to start as soon as it was light, and travelled very fast until noon, when they came to a halt to let their cammels [*sic*] breathe, and feed on a few shrubs that were thinly scattered among the sand drifts. We were here so fortunate as to find a few snails which the captives were privileged to roast and eat, which in some measure allayed the cravings of hunger—having thus refreshed, we were ordered by our masters once more to put forward, and taking a northeasterly course, travelled rapidly through prodigious sand drifts until late in the evening—my master by words and signs encouraging me, that if my strength did not fail, he should reach the village the day ensuing: where I should be plentifully supplied with victuals and drink. The Arabs having found a convenient spot, pitched their tent, and again gave us permission to occupy a corner of it; but being allowed nothing this night wherewith to allay our hunger, our fatigues and sufferings may be more easily conceived than expressed; yet as we were sheltered from the dews of the night, we slept very soundly until we were roused up to continue our journey.

The next day about noon we had the good fortune to discover a well of pure water—this was a happy circumstance, for having been deprived of that precious article for the last twenty-four hours, our misery from thirst had become so intolerable, that some of the captives had been induced to attempt to make use of that as a substitute, which decency forbids me to mention. For this unexpected relief, our souls were overwhelmed with joy: nor did we fail to raise our eyes and hearts to heaven, in adoration and silent thankfulness, while tears of gratitude trickled down our haggard cheecks [*sic*]. While our masters were watering their camels, and filling their sacks, some of the captives had permission to go a short distance in search of snails, and were so fortunate as to collect, in less than half an hour, about three quarts, which, after being roasted, were shared among the captives.

During our halt at this place, I had yet another circumstance to record, which I then esteemed, and still esteem of more importance to me, if possible, than even the discovery of the well of water. My master having ordered me to dismount, that he might water his camel, I seated myself on a hard sand drift, a few rods from the well—here I remained until I saw him returning, leading his camel—as he approached, I perceived that he had something in his hand, and on his near approach, what were my emotions, to find that it was the sacred volume, that my husband informed me was in possession of one of the Arabs, who had taken it from the pack of a fellow captive—the Arab it appeared, having conceived it of little value [being opposed to the Christian faith] and unwilling to be burthened with it any longer, threw it upon the sand with an intention of there leaving it. My husband being made acquainted with his determination, after much persuasion, prevailed upon my master to pick it up, and convey it to me; this he would by no means have done [being a strict Mahometan] had not my husband satisfied him by repeated assurances, that with this precious volume in my possession, I should be enabled to endure the hardships to which we were then subject, with more fortitude than I had done. My feelings on receiving so rich a present from the hands of one, whose very nature was at enmity with our Christian religion, may perhaps be conceived, but I cannot attempt to describe them—to form a correct idea of my emotions at that time, let him, and him alone, who has full faith in the religion of Christ, and at whose hands he has found mercy, and is not ashamed to confess him before the world, transport himself in imagination to the country where I then was; a distant heathen clime, a land of darkness, where the enemy of souls reigns triumphant, and where by an idolatrous race the doctrines of a blessed Redeemer are treated with derision and contempt: and none but such wretches for his companions—thus situated, after having been more than two months deprived of the blessed book, which is so peculiarly calculated to afford him comfort and consolation in the trying hour of affliction and woe, let him imagine himself presented with the sacred volume, and by one who has been taught to despise its precious contents!

Although my master, in presenting me with the book, which to me was of inestimable value, consulted only his own interests, yet I could not but feel grateful to him for a treasure of more value, than any thing with which he could then have presented me. As soon as it was in my possession, I turned to Jer. 21, 16, and read the following passage, which afforded me great consolation: "Thus saith the Lord refrain thy voice from weeping and thine eyes from tears for thy work shall be rewarded, and they shall come again from the land of the enemy."

But a very few moments were allowed me at this time to examine the contents of my new acquired treasure, as the Arabs having completed their watering, in less than an hour, were prepared to pursue their journey; nor did I then suspect that our next encampment would be that at which I should not only be separated from my dear husband, as well as from every one of my other fellow captives, but the place where I should be doomed to pass many months in captivity!—my master had, indeed, intimated to me the day previous, that we should on this day arrive at our place of destination, but, as he had proved himself a liar in a similar promise, which he had made many days before, I placed but little reliance on his word in the present instance—but such, however, proved to be the fact.

We travelled in an easterly direction over a sandy, although extremely uneven country for about six hours, at the rate I should judge of about four miles an hour; about sunset the Arabs commanding the captives to halt, as they did themselves, they set up a most tremendous halloo, in which they were immediately answered by some one who appeared to be but a short distance from us. They now pushed instantly on, and in a few moments, were met by six or eight on foot, each of whom were Arabs, a part women, being armed with a spear, ten or twelve feet in length—these I soon found were my master's friends, and a part of them his own family. They welcomed the return of their friends by rubbing their limbs with dry sand, and then throwing handfulls of it in the air, after which they saluted the captives by spitting on us, pelting us with stones, and throwing sand in our faces, accompanied with the word "fonta" [bad]— the females were not less backward to insult me then the men, and I think that I should have met with very serious injury, had I not been protected by my master, at whose command they desisted, and appeared disposed to treat me with less severity. One of them having snatched my bible from under my arm, was compelled by my master to return it. We were now conducted to their village, if I may be permitted so to term it, which was composed of only a few tents, of a similar construction to those which the Arabs carry with them in their excursions. The village was situated in a valley which had no more the appearance of fertility than the barren desert which we had passed, except a few shrubs and thorn bushes on which the camels were feeding. When we arrived, the Arabs who remained at the tents were engaged in their evening devotions—some were kneeling down, and bowing their faces to the ground, and others standing and rubbing the naked parts of their bodies with dry sand, in the mean time constantly repeating the words "Allah Hookibar."

Having finished their devotions, and the captives being secured in an old tent allotted them, the female camels were driven up by the women and milked. A bowl containing about six quarts of the milk, mixed with two or three quarts of barley flour, was presented to the captives to eat. This was the first time that I had ever tasted of camel's milk, and in my hungry state, was, I think, the most delicious food I ever tasted. My poor fellow captives, reduced by hunger to skeletons, seated themselves around the bowl, and having nothing but their hands to eat with, they devoured its precious contents in less than three minutes. After this, about three quarts of roasted snails, and about the same quantity of brackish water were presented us, which were as quickly devoured—indeed, to such a state of starvation were we reduced, that I believe half a roasted camel would not have been sufficient for us. While we were partaking of this repast, our masters [whose appetites were probably nearly as sharp as ours] were busily employed in cooking a kid, the entrails of which we were in hopes we should obtain, but in this we were disappointed.

I had now another opportunity (and the last in Arabia) to converse with my husband, who was yet decided in his opinion that our separation was soon to take place, and that without the kind interposition of Heaven in his behalf, that separation he was fearful would prove a final one. By hearing the Arabic so much spoken, he had understood and heard enough to satisfy him that the village in which we then were was the place of my master's abode only, of our company—that I should be retained here in captivity, and the remainder of them conveyed, probably, to more remote parts of the desert. He labored under the same impression, that if his sufferings continued without alleviation, death must soon terminate them. Here he begged of me, that if I should be more fortunate, and Heaven should thereafter be pleased to effect my deliverance, that I should do all in my power to ascertain what had been his fate, and if still alive and in captivity, that I would interest the British Consul at Mogadore in his favor to effect his deliverance.

It may excite the surprize of the reader, that while my husband and his wretched companions were in such a state of despondency, I should support my sufferings with so great a share of fortitude. It may be easily accounted for, as there was a very material difference in our treatment—for while the other captives had been compelled to travel the whole journey without shoes or stockings, on foot, through burning sands, and if they slackened their pace, were beat unmercifully by their masters, I was conveyed on the back of a camel the whole distance, without being compelled to walk five rods; and when I had occasion to mount or dismount, the camel was compelled to kneel for me; and though I endured much fatigue at first from their mode of riding, yet when I became more used to the Arabian saddle, I suffered but very little inconvenience on that account: indeed, I set as easy as in an arm chair. I was also most generally indulged each night with the privilege of occupying a corner of their tent, while my unfortunate fellow captives were compelled, with one or two exceptions, to sleep in the sands, with no other covering but the canopy of heaven. Hence, while these poor unfortunate people were by ill treatment as well as hunger, reduced to mere skeletons—their whole bodies burned quite black by the powerful rays of the sun, and filled with innumerable sores: their feet blistered by the hot sands, or severely gashed by sharp stones: and their heads, for the want of an opportunity to cleanse them, overrun with vermin, I, blessed be God, suffered but little but from hunger and thirst.

It was a pleasing thing to me to see these unfortunate captives almost without an exception, although but a few months before conducting as if strangers to the gospel of Jesus, on their bended knees imploring the mercy and protection of an offended God. O that they may continue to be ever grateful to Him for past favors, and learn to trust in Him for the time to come—surely then above most others they have reason to say "it is good for us that we have been afflicted." By their request I read many passages in my bible, which seemed most appropriate to the situation, and which appeared to afford them great consolation—among which were the following:—"Wait on the Lord, be of good courage, and he shall strengthen thine heart, wait, I say, on the Lord." Psalms 20. "I shall not die, but live, and declare the works of the Lord: the Lord hath chastised me sore, yet he hath not given me over to death." Psalms 118, 17, 18. "Cast thy burthen upon the Lord, and he shall sustain thee." Psalms 55, 22. "I know, O Lord, that thy judgments are right, and thou in faithfulness hath afflicted me." Psalms 119, 75.

As it was now quite dark, we retired to rest upon a few old mats, that the Arabs had thrown into our tent for us to repose on: but the apprehension of being separated the ensuing morning, deprived us of sleep: indeed the night was spent in a state of anxiety not easy to conceive of. While we remained in this situation until day light, our masters were engaged the whole night in debate, there appearing by what little we could understand, still some difficulty in deciding to whom each one of us belonged; the dispute, however, at length subsiding and the time of milking the camels having arrived, our masters presented us with a pint of milk each, warm from the beast, which refreshed us very much. Our tents were now visited by the wives and children of the Arabs, who having satisfied their curiosity by gazing at us for half an hour, to express their disgust, the children were encouraged by their mothers to spit and throw sand in our faces—as soon, however, as this was discovered by our masters, they were ordered off.

The Arabs now commenced their morning devotions, by bowing themselves to the ground, rubbing their faces, arms, legs, &c. with dry sand, as in the evening before, after which another kid was butchered and cooked, of which they gave us the entrails. Having finished their repast, they began to saddle and load their camels, and in a few moments after, my unfortunate fellow captives were commanded to come forth to pursue their journey—I too [as if ignorant of the intentions of my master] obeyed the summons; but, no sooner had I stepped without the tent, than the barbarian forced me back with the britch of his musket!

The fears that I had entertained of being separated from my poor unfortunate husband, and his wretched fellow captives, were now realized—it would be impossible for me to describe my feelings at this moment, and the reader can have but a faint conception of them! I begged that I might exchange a few words with my husband, previous to his departure; but even this privilege was denied me; in a fit of despair, I threw myself upon a mat, where I remained in a state of insensibility until the captives were far out of sight. As soon as I had recovered sufficiently to support myself on my knees, I sent up a prayer to

Heaven, imploring her protection in my then, still more wretched, situation. I then laid myself down to rest, but could not sleep. My mind, which had been hitherto remarkably strong, and supported me through all my trials, distresses and sufferings, and in a great measure had enabled me to encourage and keep up the spirits of my frequently despairing fellow captives, could hardly sustain me: My sudden change of situation seemed to have relaxed the very springs of my soul, and all my faculties fell into the wildest confusion.

Soon after the departure of the other captives, I was again visited by a motley group of the natives, who came merely to satisfy their curiosity, when the children were again encouraged by their parents to insult me, by spitting and throwing sand in my face; this was more than I could bear; tears of anguish, which I had not the power to controul, now gushed from my eyes; and my almost bursting heart vented itself in bitter groans of despair! It soon appeared, however, that the abuse offered me by these unfeeling wretches, was not countenanced by my master; for on his arrival, viewing the sad condition that I was in, with my eyes and mouth filled with sand, he became greatly enraged and beat the vile authors of it unmercifully—and, indeed, the severe chastisement which they then received, had a lasting and very happy effect; for from this time, until the period of my redemption, I was not once again insulted in this way.

My master having retired, soon returned with a bowl of camel's milk, and another of the flour similar to that with which I had been before presented; and of which I made a very delicious meal, and returned thanks to God for the wholesome repast. In two hours after I was again visited by my master, accompanied by a very aged, and the most respectable looking Arab that I had seen; who, having seated himself on a mat, accosted me with "who de do Christiano." I was indeed, very much surprised to hear a language that I could understand, and was much pleased with the prospect of having found one, who, as an interpreter, might be of essential service to me. The old man could speak but very broken English, but with the assistance of my partial knowledge of the Arabic [which I had obtained during my captivity] we could converse with each other tolerably well. He informed me that he belonged to a village much larger than the one in which my master had now encamped, and many miles nearer Morockish—that he had obtained his partial knowledge of the English language, by having once in his possession three or four English captives, who with a number of their countrymen, had been shipwrecked on the coast. That they were with him about two years, when, with the exception of one that died, they were redeemed by the Sultan's friend at Moroccash.

The old man was very inquisitive and anxious to learn of what the ship's cargo was composed, and whether there was much cash on board; how many miles we had been travelling since we quit the wreck, and on what part of the coast we were wrecked—how many persons there were on board, and if the whole of our number were captured. To these questions I gave correct answers, which were interpreted to my master. I embraced this opportunity to ascertain, if possible, what would probably be the fate of my husband and his unfortunate companions; and whether there was any prospect of their gaining their liberty again; and what were my master's intentions with regard to myself. Agreeable to my request these enquiries were made, and my master's replies interpreted by the old man; which apprized me, that the prospect of my companions being soon redeemed was very great, as their masters resided much nearer the Sultan's dominions, where information of their captivity might be easily conveyed; and as soon as the Sultan received the information, he would immediately communicate it to his friend, the British Consul, at Sewarah [*sic*] who would dispatch a person with cash to redeem them. That as regarded myself, it was the intention of my master to retain me in his own family until he could find an opportunity to dispose of me at a good price, to some one of his countrymen bound to Swearah. I suggested to the old man the improbability of my living long if not more tenderly treated, and more bountifully supplied with wholesome food; without being interpreted to my master, I was assured, that if I behaved myself well, I should have my liberty to walk about the village where I pleased, and should always have my share of food.

As I had always been under serious apprehension of being deprived of my bible (which was now my only remaining companion) or that I should be compelled to engage with them in their idolatrous worship of the Supreme Being, I hinted to my interpreter, that although we believed in one and the same Grand Spirit, yet, there was a difference in our mode of worshipping Him: and that while they peaceably pursued theirs, I hoped that I should not be disturbed while engaged in mine: and what was a still greater consideration with me, I hoped that none might be permitted to take from me my bible, but that I might be allowed to devote a few hours each day in perusing it. To this my master assented, on condition that I would never worship or peruse the book in his presence, or any of his family; for as they believed Christians, fonta (bad) he could not answer for the conduct of his family if they found me thus engaged.

My master having informed me that the tent in which I was then confined, was allotted me as my place of residence until he should have an opportunity to dispose of me, now granted me liberty to walk about the village where I pleased, hinting at the same time that an attempt on my part to escape from him, would be punished with instant death! all this was interpreted to me by the old Arab, who having promised me that if he should meet with an opportunity to send [me] to Swearah, he would inform the Sultan of my situation, with my master withdrew, and left me to return thanks to Him, by whose kind interposition I was so fortunate as to meet with one, in that barren and inhospitable desert, who was not only enabled to acquaint me of what would probably be the ultimate fate of my poor husband, but what were the views of my master with regard to myself.

Being now left entirely alone, I embraced the opportunity to peruse more attentively the sacred volume, which alone was calculated to yield consolation to a miserable captive like myself; a volume calculated also to convey the most affecting views, and awaken the sublimest sensibilities on a thousand topics; a volume full of entertainment as well as instruction, composed by a great diversity of authors, and all of them divinely taught. Methinks I see them one after another (in this moment as in that of my tribulation) presenting for my improvement, their respective writings with an aspect of dignity and sweetness, combining, the dignity of truth, and the sweetness of benevolence; both derived from Him, who inspired them to be the teachers of mankind. Methinks I hear them severally addressing me in the name of God, with an authority that can only be equalled with their mildness on subjects the grandest and most important. What book is there but the bible, that contains so much to inform, impress, and delight reflecting minds, laid together in a manner extensively adapted to their various turns of understanding, taste and temper; which people of different and distant countries, through a long succession of ages, have held in so much reverence, and read with so much advantage; where it is so difficult to determine, which are more distinguished, ease and simplicity, or sublimity and force, but where all are so beautifully united; where there is so little to discourage the weakest spirit, if docile, and so much to gratify the strongest, if candid—where the frailties, disorders and distresses of human nature, are so feelingly laid open and the remedies which Heaven provided are so tenderly applied.

And ought I to omit to declare, that although misfortune had placed me in the hands of a barbarous people, although separated from every christian friend and experiencing all the hardships and privations peculiar to those who are so unfortunate as to fall into the hands of a merciless race, yet, from this sacred volume, I derived more comfort, more sweet consolation, secluded as I was from the civilized world, than the most fashionable amusements of the most populous cities in Europe, could have afforded me! Ah! ye fair ones of Britain, who doat [*sic*] on the parade of public assemblies, and sail along in the full blown pride of fashionable attire, of which the least appendage or circumstance must not be discomposed; thoughtless of human woe; insensible to the sad condition of those like myself pining in many a solitary residence of want—ye gaudy flutterers, "with hard hearts under a soft raimente," how much more brilliant as well as beautiful would ye appear in the eyes of saints and angels, were you to employ your leisure hours thus devoted to the attaining a knowledge of that sacred scripture by which alone ye can expect to attain eternal life. I blush for many of my country-women possessed of understanding, who have never yet learned its noblest and happiest use; in whose ears the circulated whisper of a well dressed crowd, admiring their appearance, is a more grateful sound than the praise of the ever-living Jehovah! How much more praise-worthy would it be, were it your object only to appear beautiful in the eye of God; to be beloved by the Monarch of the Universe! to be admitted, if I may be permitted to use the phrase, as so many fair and shining pillars into her temple below: while he contemplates each with a pleasing aspect, and purposes to remove them in due time to his sanctuary on high, where they shall remain his everlasting delight, as well as the never-ceasing admiration of surrounding cherubims [*sic*]. Great Creator! what can equal such exaltation and felicity! and can any of you, my fair readers, be so destitute of every nobler sentiment as not to aspire after privileges like these! Unmoved by such ideas, can you turn away with impatience, and run to scenes of dress and show with the same little inglorious passions as before; preferring to the approbation of the Eternal the slightest regards from the silliest mortals? Go thou senseless creatures, and boast of being admired by the butterflies of a day; see what they will do for thee, when He, whose favor thou neglectest, and for such things shall cause thy "beauty to consume like a moth," and thy heart to sink within thee like a stone. Imagination shudders at the thoughts of that day, when thou shalt enter trembling, forsaken and forlorn, these dismal regions which the voice of adulation cannot reach, and nothing shall be heard but sounds of reproach and blasphemy and woe; where stript of every ornament that now decks the body, and stript of that body itself, thy mind must appear without shelter or covering, all deformed and ghastly, mangled with the wounds of despairing guilt, and distorted by the violence of envenomed passions, while demons shall mock at thy misery. May the Almighty Redeemer be pleased to save us all from a doom so dreadful! and my fair readers would you concur to prevent it? Begin with restraining the love of ornament; or rather turn that dangerous affection into a higher channel, and let it flow; it will then become safe, useful, noble. Here you will have a scope for the largest fancy. To the adorning of your minds we wish you to set no bounds. In dressing the soul for the company of saints, of angels, of God himself you cannot employ too much time or thought. In a word, all the best things in the creation, together with the Creator himself, concur in loving and honoring a beauteous mind.

But, to return—

The liberty granted me by my master, to peruse the sacred scriptures, I faithfully improved at this time. I perused the whole book of Job and derived much consolation therefrom, after which, to prevent its destruction by the natives, I buried my inestimable treasure in the sand; unaccompanied by any one, I was now permitted to walk about the village, as it was termed, which was composing of no more than 10 or 12 wretched tents, containing from six to ten persons each. As a more minute description of the inhabitants—their employment, dress, habits, customs, &c. may be gratifying to some of my readers, I will here record them as correctly as my recollection will enable me, from observations made during my captivity.

The Arabs are of a tawny complexion, and when full grown, are generally from five to six feet in height with black sparkling eyes, high cheek bones and thin lips—their hair is black, long and very coarse; and being occasionally clipped by the men, they leave it sticking out in every direction from their head, which gives them a very savage appearance—their beards they permit to grow to the length of seven or eight inches. The only clothing they wear is a piece of coarse cloth of their own man[u]facture, which they tie round their waists, and which extends to their knees. The women are in general not so tall as the men, but in other respects resemble them very much. They appear, in their natures, as if created expressly for the country which they inhabit, as no human beings can endure thirst, hunger and fatigues better than they. When they rise in the morning, their first employment is to milk their camels, after which the whole village, old and young (the women excepted) assemble to attend prayers and their other religious devotions, which they perform in the following manner; they first strip themselves nearly naked, and then with dry sand rub every part of their bodies, after which, bending their bodies nearly to the ground, they cry aloud "Allah Hookiber"—"Allah Sheda Mahommed!"—at night, before retiring to rest, they again assemble, to worship in the same manner.

The cloth with which the Arabs cover their tents they manufacture out of camel's hair, which work is performed by the women in the following manner; having first spun the hair into thread, by means of a hand spindle, and it having gone through the operation of doubling and twisting, they drive into the ground two rows of pegs, placing them about three feet apart; the warp is attached to the pegs and the filling is then carried by a shuttle over the thread of the warp, and under another; the women, in the mean time beating up the threads with a flat piece of stick. Every tent is occupied by a separate family, who have no further furniture but a mat, which serves them for a bed—a small brass kettle in which they sometimes boil their provisions, a calabash to hold their milk, and a wooden trough, in which they water their camels.

If the Arabs are provided with water, they never fail to wash before they eat, but in the choice of their food, they are less particular, esteeming a mess of roasted snails preferable to any other dish. Their principal food, when encamped, is camel's milk, and occasionally feast themselves on a kid, but never on a camel, unless in case of real necessity, or when they have become too old to travel. Frequently, however, in travelling the desert, the Arabs have been driven by hunger to such extremities, as to devour animals and insects of any kind in a state of putrefaction.

The Arabs have a plurality of wives to whom they are very severe and cruel, exercising as much authority over them as over their slaves, and compelling them to perform the meanest drudgery—their husbands consider them as their inferiors, as beings without souls, and will not permit them to join their devotions. While engaged in weaving they carry their infant children on their backs, which are secured by a fold of a piece of cloth, which they wear for the purpose over their shoulders; by being kept constantly at work, they become very filthy in their persons, and are covered with vermin.

The children of the Arabs are taught to read and write, and every family has a teacher for that purpose, but for paper they substitute a piece of smooth board about two feet square, and on these they are taught to make their Arabic characters with sharpened reeds—they are early instructed to read the Koran, agreeable to their Mahometan faith, and are taught to write verses therefrom. O, what a pity is it that they are not taught the superior excellence of the Christian religion, and to worship the blessed Jesus, instead of the impure and idolatrous worship of objects prescribed by Mahomet.—Weep, O my soul, over the forlorn state of the benighted heathen! Oh! that all who peruse this narrative would join in their fervent requests to God, with whom all things are possible, that these deluded people may soon be brought to worship the true and only Jesus, and to drink freely of the waters of salvation!

Although my master had promised me that I should receive a plentiful supply of food, I soon found that he was by no means in a situation to fulfill his promise; for with the exception of the small quantity of milk that the camels yielded, I found that they had nothing themselves to subsist on, for the most part of the time but ground nuts, and a few snails, which they found in the sand. Each family possesses two or three kids, but they will sooner starve than kill them unless it is on a particular occasion.—There were two wells of tolerable good water in the neighborhood, which was the only convenience that the miserable village could boast of.

While some of the wives and children of the Arabs viewed me with scornful eyes, frequently uttering the word "fonta" (bad); others appeared more amicably disposed, and treated me with compassion. They all, however, appeared to be anxious that I should be taught to labor like themselves, and for the first week attempted to instruct me how to weave after their manner—but as I was sure that if they taught me to be useful to them in this way, I should be allowed but little time to rest or to peruse my bible, I did not prove so tractable as they expected to find me, and they finally gave up all hopes of rendering me serviceable to them in this way. I was, however, compelled every night and morning to drive off the camels, to milk, and to devote two or three hours each day in collecting snails and ground nuts.

After performing the duty allotted to me, I usually retired to my tent, and spent the remainder of the day in serious meditation and in perusing the sacred scriptures. During my captivity I read my bible, the Old and the New Testament, twice through from the beginning to the end. O it is impossible for me to bestow too much praise on this sacred book—the consolation that I derived therefrom in the hour of tribulation was very great indeed: it was that and that alone that now enables me to say, "blessed be the hour that I became a convert in the land of the heathen!" O, how precious, how exceedingly valuable is the word of God! how exceedingly precious is the religion of Jesus—how unlike that of Mahomet, how different from any which the carnal heart can invent!— O, it was this that sustained me in the hour of affliction, in the day of my captivity.

Five months having nearly passed since my separation from my poor husband and his unfortunate companions, and at the moment of despairing of being ever redeemed from cruel bondage, I was one morning very early aroused from my slumbers by the hoarse voice of my master, commanding me to come forth; the summons I instantly obeyed; but my surprise may be better imagined than expressed, when on reaching the door of my tent, I was presented by my master with a letter directed to me, and which I immediately recognized to be the hand writing of my husband! With my master was a stranger mounted on a mule, and although of a tawny complexion, had not otherwise the savage appearance of an Arab. As soon as I came within view of him, with a smile on his countenance, he accosted me with "how de do Christiano;" that he was the messenger of pleasing news, I did not doubt. I broke open the letter, and with emotions that I cannot describe, read as follows:

MOGADORE, Dec. 10, 1818.

MY DEAR ELIZA—

This will inform you that I am no longer a slave; by the blessings of God, I once more enjoy my liberty—I was brought to this place with three of my crew by the Arabs, a few days since, and humanely redeemed out of their hands by our excellent Consul (Mr. Willshire) who resides here. I have informed him of your situation, and he has kindly offered me his assistance in effecting your redemption and restoring you to liberty—the bearer of this letter (should he be so fortunate as to find you) is a man in whom you may place the utmost reliance, and who will conduct you in safety to this place, should your master be pleased to comply with the proposals of Mr. Willshire, to whom he has directed a letter written in Arabic, offering seven hundred dollars for your redemption, provided he conveys you in safety to this place.

I am affectionately yours, &c.

JAMES BRADLEY

Having finished this letter, so great was my joy, that I could not refrain from shedding tears, and it was some time before I could become sufficiently composed as to beg of my master permission to retire to my tent, where, on my bended knees, I might return thanks to an all-wise and beneficent Creator, through whose goodness there was a prospect of my being once more restored to my husband and friends.

The terms offered my master being such as he was pleased to accept of, the necessary preparations were immediately made for our departure, and the morning ensuing, my master and myself being mounted on a camel each, accompanied by the Moor [for such he proved to be] mounted on his mule, set out for Mogadore, a distance of more than seven hundred miles. We were nearly twenty days in performing the journey, the greater part of the way being a sandy desert, yielding little for man or beast.

Were I to record the occurrences of each day, while on our journey, it would swell a volume to too great an extent. I would rather confine myself to a few particulars which I esteem of the most importance to the reader, and which is calculated to give him a correct idea of my situation, until the day of my redemption—and that of the country through which we passed. My master loaded the camels with as much provision as they could well carry, which, with the little they were enabled to collect on the way, served us until we reached a more fertile country. My master seemed disposed to treat me with more humanity than ever, and of whatever provision was obtained, if there was scarcely sufficient for a moderate meal for one, I was sure to receive one half; nor was time refused me each morning before we set out on our journey, to return thanks to Heaven for the protection afforded me through the night, and to read a chapter in my bible.

After travelling ten days, we came to the country inhabited by the Moors, and passed several walled villages, enclosing some well stocked gardens. The further we proceeded on our journey, the more the fertility of the country seemed to increase. We passed large fields of Indian corn and barley, and gardens filled with most kinds of vegetables, and the surrounding country presented beautiful groves of date, fig, pomegranate and orange trees. The Arabs and Moors not being on the most friendly terms, and the latter being as great enemies to christianity as the former, we might have starved amidst plenty, had we not fortunately a Moor for a companion, without whose aid we could not have gained admittance to any of their villages.

In fifteen days from that on which we left the village of my master, we entered the dominions of the Emperor of Morocco, and in two days after arrived at Santa Cruz, the most considerable frontier town of the Emperor's dominions. We were met at the entrance of the town by a large body of Moors of all ranks and ages and while some of the most respectable appeared disposed to protect me, from another class I received every insult that they could devise means to bestow upon me. My master, on attempting to defend me from the outrages of these merciless wretches, received but little better treatment himself, as the Moors harbor the most contemptible opinion of the Arabs of the interior. My master however, gained permission of the Governor to tarry in the town until the ensuing morning, and promised us his protection. I was then conveyed to the small dirty hut, situated at the extreme part of the town, and therein barricaded as securely as if I had been one of their largest and most formidable enemies in existence. I ought not, however, to fail to mention, that I was here for the first time since I became a captive, plentifully supplied with good and wholesome provision in abundance. The town abounded with fish of a most excellent quality, which they understood the cooking of equal to Europeans, and of which they allowed me more than could possibly eat; with an equal proportion of sweet barley bread. Although I felt grateful for such liberality, yet I could not but view its authors as nothing more than instruments in the hands of the Supreme Being employed to alleviate the sufferings of one of his most unfortunate creatures, who day and night had unceasingly solicited his protection. O, I have infinite reason to confess my obligation to that Almighty Power; who so wonderfully preserved and supported me in the day of bondage. May my future life evince my gratitude, and every thought be brought into subjection to the Father of Spirits—surely a "soul redeemed demands a life of praise."

Early the ensuing morning we quit Santa Cruz and proceeded on our journey, travelling through a beautifully cultivated country. The sea on our left covered with boats of various sizes, was in full view.—About 3 o'clock the day following, having reached the summit of a mountain which we had been since morning ascending, the Moor suddenly cried out, pointing to the east, "see, see Mogadore!"—the town was indeed fair in view, and did not appear to be more than fifteen or sixteen miles distant from us.

The harbor was soon in view, and the flags of ships of different nations floating at their mizzen tops was viewed by me with unbounded pleasure.—It is impossible to state my feelings at this moment, on the reflection that in a few hours I should in all probability be enabled to meet my husband, and enjoying that liberty of which I had been so many months deprived. I could not fail to look up to heaven with adoration, while my heart swelled with indescribable sensations of gratitude and love, to the all-wise, all-powerful, and ever merciful God of the universe, who had conducted me through so many dreadful scenes of danger and suffering; had controlled the passions and disposed the hearts of the barbarous Arabs in my favor, and was finally about to restore me to the arms of my husband.

As we approached the city, we were met by considerable bodies of the Moors, whom curiosity had brought from the city, to view a Christian female—many appeared disposed to offer me insult, but were prevented by those who apparently possessed a greater share of pity for one who was really a spectacle of distress. At half past seven o'clock, we entered the city, and was conducted by a company of soldiers immediately to the house of the British Consul. Mr. Willshire met me at the door, and had this truly benevolent and humane man been my own brother, he could not have given me more welcome reception—he actually shed tears of joy at the prospect of having it soon in his power to restore me to the arms of my husband, who he informed me had been impatiently awaiting my arrival, and had been daily at his house to ascertain if any information had been received of me, since the departure of the Moor dispatched in quest of me.

The news of my arrival soon reached the ears of my husband, who with the remainder of the captives who had been redeemed, and had not left the country, hastened to the Consul's house to see me. Happy meeting! It was some time before my husband or myself could exchange a syllable with each other—the joy which we both felt in being enabled to meet again, and under circumstances so different from those under which we parted, deprived us for some time of the power of speech; indeed, if there was ever a moment in which it became an unfortunate people like ourselves to offer up prayers of thankfulness to an adorable Creator, for his mercy and goodness in so long protecting us during our many months captivity, and for finally effecting our redemption out of the hands of the unmerciful Arabs, this was the moment. It is certainly the Almighty who is the bestower and giver of all our good things—all our mercies come to us by a divine providence and ordering; not by casualty or accident—neither are they of our own procuring and purchasing—it is God who returns the captivity of Zion. "When the Lord turned again the captivity of Zion, we were like them that dream: then was our mouth filled with laughter, and our tongue with singing.—Then said they among the heathen, the Lord has done great things for them. The Lord hath done great things for us: where of we are glad: Turn again our captivity, O Lord." Psalms cxxvi. The very heathen acknowledge the good things bestowed upon and done for the church, to be from God; and God's own people acknowledge Him for the mercies granted, and humbly supplicated mercies from Him for the future. It is God who gathers the outcasts of Israel: It is He who takes away the captives of the mighty, the prey of the terrible; who contends with them that contend with us, and saves our children. It is God who dispenseth and gathers again. Sometimes God in a more immediate and extraordinary way and manner, confers his blessings and mercies; sometimes in a more ordinary and mediate way; but His providence is to be acknowledged in all; not one single mercy comes to us, without a commission from that God by whom our very hairs are all numbered.

Scarcely any of Mr. Willshire's domestics who witnessed the happy meeting of myself and husband, could refrain from tears. The poor sailors who had been so fortunate as to obtain their liberty, seemed really overjoyed at the prospect of my being once more restored to the bosom of my family.—Each seemed anxious to relate to me a narrative of his sufferings and treatment which he received from the Arabs from the moment of our separations, until that of their redemption. While some appeared to have been treated with a small degree of lenity, others bore the marks of the most savage cruelty, and certainly could not have survived much longer under such sufferings had they not been providentially redeemed out of the hands of the unmerciful barbarians. By the account given me by my husband, of his deprivations and sufferings from the time of our separation, it appeared that he had fared no better than the rest—two days after my separation from them the Arabs reached another village, which was the place of residence of three or four more of the company, and where another separation of the captives took place. My husband, however, being not of this party he was still compelled to travel on under the most disagreeable circumstances; he became so weak and emaciated, and his faculties so rapidly declined that he could scarcely hear or see, and a vertical sun was so continually darting his beams so intensely upon him, that for the last two days of his journey he could scarcely move one foot before the other. But, having at length succeeded in reaching the village of his master, by the intercession of one of his sons in my husband's behalf, he was treated with more humanity, until an opportunity fortunately presented in which he was enabled to forward a line to Mogadore, by a man, informing Mr. Willshire of his situation, as well as that of his fellow captives. On the receipt of my husband's letter, that gentleman, who is so renowned for his humanity, did not spare a moment to effect his redemption, and adopted such means as were attended with success; and by his means seven more of the unfortunate captives obtained their liberty, and returned with us to England in the same ship, which, thanks to the Supreme Disposer of all events they were enabled to do, after having been held in captivity for nearly six months, in which they had suffered hardships and trials seldom known to human nature.

The hospitable Mr. Willshire insisted on our remaining at his house, until such time as he could procure passages for us to Europe. There indeed was not a European or white man of any nation, in the harbor, who did not come to see us, and who generously supplied us with such articles of clothing, &c. as we stood most in need of. Having refreshed ourselves by these good people's bounty, and meeting with so many christian friends at this place, we began to feel new life, and almost to think ourselves restored to our former strength and vigor; though in reality we were still in a most deplorable condition.

In justice to the Europeans that we found at Mogadore, I must say that we received from them marks of the most tender interest, and the most generous compassion! I think I can never sufficiently express the sense that I shall ever entertain for the kindness and humanity of Mr. Willshire, whose whole employment it appeared to be for the several days, to contrive the best means to restore us to health and strength. By him I was advised to bathe every morning, and to confine myself to goat's milk, except a few new laid eggs, together with moderate exercise. After a week he allowed me to take some light chicken broth with a morsel of the wing. By means of this diet my health and strength were in a great measure restored.

The Almighty, by whose will I had probably very justly suffered, was at length pleased to deliver me into the hands of a benevolent man, whose kindness I experienced in every instance. What would have been our condition if we had met with a person of less sensibility; who thinking he had sufficiently answered the duties of his office, in redeeming us out of the hands of the Arabs, had left us to shift for ourselves with regard to all other necessaries! I can never reflect without the most grateful sensibility on the goodness and charity of him whom I am proud to claim as my countryman, and who certainly is an honor to the country which gave him birth. At our departure, when my husband attempted to make acknowledgements for his bounties, "I must beg leave (said the Consul) to interrupt you on this subject; you have deserved every thing I did for you, because you needed it, and I have done nothing more in your instance than I should have a right to expect myself in the same circumstances. But my consideration for your distress, (continued he) ought to extend beyond the immediate exigencies of your situation."

Having continued at Mogadore until we had perfectly recovered our health and strength, a passage was procured for us to Liverpool; but we did not quit the Barbary coast, however, until I had the pleasure of communing with God. There was a small English church at Mogadore, of which our excellent friend Mr. Willshire was the principal founder; for among the other qualifications of this good man, I am happy to say that I found him a true believer in the religion of Jesus. How sweetly calculated were the gospel ordinances here performed to enliven the hearts of believers, surrounded as they are by a race of idolators, on whom no light of revelation beams; where there are no other sanctuaries—no communion tables—no bread and wine to remind them, that a Savior shed his blood on Calvary for them! O thou blessed Redeemer, for poor lost sinners, thou who didst commission thy disciples of old to preach the gospel to every creature; wilt thou send forth laborers [to] make the wilderness a fruitful field, and cause the wilderness to blossom like the Rose.

Having taken an affectionate leave of our friends at Mogadore, on the 1st of February, 1819, we were in readiness to embark for our native country. Beside my husband and myself, there were six others of my husband's original crew, who had agreed to work their passage. In forty days from that on which we bid adieu to the coast of Barbary, we were all safely landed on the shores of Old England, and the day succeeding I was restored to the arms of my friends in Liverpool, who joined with me in returning thanks to the Almighty for my wonderful deliverance.

Here Mrs. Bradley concludes her affecting narrative.—Subsequent accounts from Mogadore state that five more of the crew had found their way back to that place by the interposition of Mr. Willshire.

ॐ I on H. Perdicaris

In Raissuli's Hands

The abduction of an American millionaire from his home in Tangier just a month before the Republican convention in 1904 pricked Teddy Roosevelt into action. Within a few days of the kidnapping, he sent both the South Atlantic and European squadrons—a total of seven powerful warships—to Morocco to back up his demand that the American, Ion Perdicaris, and his British stepson, Cromwell Varley, be freed immediately. Despite the unfolding of these dramatic events overseas and the threat of a possible Moroccan invasion, the Republican national convention promised to be the dullest in history. Something sensational was needed, and Secretary of State John Hay provided the necessary bombshell in the form of a telegram to Morocco that, in part, read: "We want either Perdicaris alive or Raisuli dead." The convention suddenly came alive and the magic slogan quickly became linked to candidate Roosevelt. If the conventioneers had learned any one of three things, the jubilant mood would have changed dramatically: (1) that Perdicaris was not a U.S. citizen; (2) that the second sentence in Hay's bellicose cable warned the consul general to "not land marines or seize customs without the Department's specific instructions"; and (3) that Perdicaris had already been released *before* Hay wired the message. However, it wouldn't be until after the election that any of this would come to light.

Ion Hanford Perdicaris was born in 1840, the son of a Greek immigrant who amassed a fortune in the illuminating gas industry. At the time of the American Civil War, Perdicaris fled South Carolina, and in 1862 registered himself in Athens as a Greek subject to avoid enlistment in the Confederate army and the confiscation of his property. In the late 1860s, Perdicaris moved to England, fell in love with a married woman, and stole off to Germany with

Fig. 18. Ion Perdicaris, captive in Morocco (1904) who had unbeknownst to U.S. officials renounced his citizenship. (Courtesy University of Minnesota Libraries)

Fig. 19. Perdicaris's captor, Muali Ahmed er Raisuli, called a "Sherif, warrior and philosopher, saint, tyrant and psychologist." (Courtesy University of Minnesota Libraries)

his new bride. After much traveling in Europe and the United States, the couple and her four children eventually settled in Tangier, where Perdicaris bought Villa Aidonia, a former royal residence. It was from here, on May 18, 1904, that Perdicaris and Cromwell Varley were seized by a group of Riffians under the command of Muali Ahmed er Raisuli, a direct descendant of the prophet Muhammad.

Raisuli had been one of many local rebels challenging the new sultan, Abd-el-Aziz IV, who had drifted from traditional policies and had increasingly begun to accept aid from the West. To hold a rich American hostage,

Raisuli reckoned, would effectively hold the sultan himself hostage to American demands. Abd-el-Aziz's inability to regain Perdicaris would illustrate the sultan's impotence, humiliate the ruler on the international stage, and open the door for Raisuli's own challenge. Thus Raisuli wanted virtually nothing from the United States and treated Perdicaris, whom he had met before, with the greatest courtesy.

"In Raissuli's Hands: The Story of My Captivity and Deliverance May 18 to June 26, 1904." *Leslie's Magazine* 58 (September 1904): 510–22.

Tsarradan, Morocco, June 8, 1904.

THREE WEEKS AGO TO-DAY we were at home, surrounded by those who are dear to us, and free to come and go at our pleasure. Now we are captives in this Kabyle village, high amongst the Beni Arroze hills, whilst armed guards, posted everywhere about, follow us wherever we move. Yet our condition is so much better than seemed probable at the outset that we feel there is much for which to be thankful.

Indeed, as I write these lines, my heart overflows with gratitude to the friends, not only in Tangier but in other countries, and especially in the United States, who have spared no effort to secure our release or to mitigate the most trying features of our detention. The British Minister, Sir Arthur Nicolson, and the Hon. S. R. Gummere, the representative of the United States, occupy naturally, as well as officially, the first place.

I shall especially never forget the solicitude shown by the latter on the night of our capture, when Mr. Gummere, in spite of the distance and the lateness of the hour, rode out at once to Aidonia, my summer residence on the Djebal Kebir, where a little group of relations and devoted friends hastily gathered to protect and encourage the ladies of the family. Subsequently Mr. Gummere and Sir Arthur Nicolson went the very same night to Hadj Mohammed Torres, the Sultan's representative at Tangier, to insist upon prompt measures being taken for our rescue. That I should feel grateful to the friends who have intervened so actively and constantly on our behalf, and to the authorities at Washington who instructed the admirals in command of the cruisers and battleships now lying in Tangier Bay to insist upon my release is natural enough. How could any American fail to be deeply touched and most profoundly grateful at such a proof of his country's solicitude for the welfare of its citizens and for the honor of the flag!

But to revert to that Wednesday evening and to the immediate circumstances of our capture. The members of our family had gathered after dinner in the drawing-room, when we were startled by loud screams from the servants' quarters. I rushed out of the room, followed by my step-son, Cromwell Varley, both of us under the impression that the French "chef," who was an ex-zouave, had again attacked the German housekeeper, since between the two there was a long-standing and bitter feud. On our way through the hall we met the butler, also a German, flying madly past us. "Ah!" I thought. "The zouave has been too much for the Fatherland all along the line!" On reaching the servants' hall I found a number of armed Moors, whom I took for the moment to be our own guards, who had also come, as I imagined, to the rescue of the housekeeper.

On inquiring what had happened, these armed natives smiled blandly. What was my amazement then when I saw these Moors, whom I now discovered to be strangers, seize the butler, who at this moment rushed back pursued by other armed natives, and club him violently with the stocks of their rifles!

I interfered to protect him, when I was immediately seized, clubbed and my arms bound behind my back, almost before I could realize what had occurred.

With Varley, who is very vigorous and who had grappled with them, they were much rougher—though their blows were not delivered, apparently, with any downright, malignant intention. One of his assailants drew his knife across Varley's hand to force him to release his hold upon the throat of one of the band, whilst another dealt a more serious blow at the unfortunate housekeeper, who at this moment endeavored to escape from the adjoining room, felling her to the floor. In the meantime Varley and I were hustled out at the back of the house by the conclusive argument of gunstocks thrust into our backs and ribs.

I managed, however, to get to the guardhouse, in front of which hangs a light, where I found most of my native guards and servants covered by the rifles of the enemy. Here I noticed for the first time a fine, dark-bearded and turbanned Moor,[1] with whom my government soldiers, though disarmed, were remonstrating against this attack upon us, asserting that I was a friend to their people and should have been spared such an outrage.

Lifting his hand, the leader of the band exclaimed in a loud voice: "I am the Raissuli. I swear by all we hold sacred that if there is no attempt at escape or rescue no harm shall come to these people, but they must mount and ride with us! In a few days they will be safely back amongst you!"

I was familiar with the name—it was indeed one with which to conjure. Not a native government official but would quail at the mention of it. I knew, also, something of the speaker's antecedents, of which more presently.

---

1. The other mountaineers, for such they were, wore their cloth gun-covers bound about their heads. [Perdicaris's note]

"I accept your assurance, Raissuli," I replied in Arabic, "but we cannot go with you thus, in evening dress and slippers, we must have hats, overcoats and boots."

He ordered us at once to be unbound. "Send one of your men for what you require," he said, "but let there be no delay."

I despatched one of the natives, but he could not find what we wanted. Then a Spanish waiter was unbound and soon hurried back with some of the articles, but before I had laced up even one of my boots, Raissuli, becoming impatient, insisted upon our mounting.

Three of our horses had been brought up from the stables unsaddled with the exception of one on which they had put an old saddle used occasionally by the grooms. Upon this saddle I was lifted, while Varley was hoisted upon a pack mule. All this in the midst of an indescribable confusion, as the horses, all of them restive and excited, engaged in a free fight, during which one of my servants was knocked down and trampled upon. I nearly met with the same misadventure myself, but, once in the saddle, one of Raissuli's men leading the animal by the bridle, we were hurried through the grounds in the opposite direction from Tangier. We were dragged in the dark down steep and rocky slopes, where I would not take my horses in the daylight, towards the plain of the Bubana, sometimes used as the town racecourse. But how different it all seemed now! No crowded stands, no applauding public; only the black night, the wild mountaineers striking our horses with their guns and dragging us over rocks and across streams, with, it is true, an occasional but impromptu water-jump. A water-jump, let me remark, with someone else hanging on to your bridle and riflestocks to drive your steed along, is not quite the sport that even the most ardent gentleman jockey would select.

Presently we circled round three tombs or saint's shrines to avoid passing a military post and soon found ourselves heading for the interior. All night we were hurried along and when day broke we were halted on a hillside for a short rest. As I saw Raissuli dismount from a fine black steed in Moorish trappings, when I then noticed was one of my own horses, I approached and asked whether it would be possible to send a note to my wife, explaining to him that I was an invalid, and that if kept too long without the remedies upon which I depended I might break up altogether.

To my surprise he produced a pocket book, took out some note paper and envelopes and offered them with a pencil. When I had written, he asked me whether I would guarantee that the bearer of this note should not be arrested and, on my giving the required assurance, he called up one of his men. The latter seemed but little pleased at being sent back, but finally accepted the mission, kissed Raissuli humbly, yet devotedly on the shoulder, and, mounting one of my own mules, rode back towards Tangier.

I now had an opportunity to observe Raissuli himself more closely; I was struck by the natural dignity of his bearing and by his singular gentleness, so different from that of his rough, wild followers, of whom there were about twenty.

We were, however, soon again in the saddle and, towards the afternoon, began to climb the foothills behind which rise the more mountainous districts inhabited by the Beni M'Saour, the Beni Idder and the Beni Arroze. These powerful Kabyles are united in a league against the Government and against the intrusion, not only of Europeans, but even of natives not belonging to, or connected by marriage with themselves.

I soon began to suffer from the discomfort of the situation. The night had been cold but the sun now blazed down upon us and, as when the day dawned we had been compelled to replace our solar tepees by turbans and to hide our European garments beneath Moorish *jilabas* and *sulhams* we were half suffocated by the heat, whilst our only food was clammy, native bread, a few dirty dried figs, and muddy water from a broken *berada* or native jug. The wretched saddle I was riding also kept slipping back, the girths being old and rotten. Meanwhile the path or rather our erratic course, along which we were led in order to avoid everything in the shape of a village or hut, grew steeper and wilder, whilst I became more faint and weary with every hour in the saddle. At last, about four p.m., just as my horse was scrambling up the side of a steep ravine through which ran a mountain torrent, the animal missed his footing, and swerved violently; the saddle slipped, the rotten stirrup leather broke, and I fell, heavily, down the steep and rocky side of the hill, hurting my thigh badly. From that time until ten or eleven p.m. when we reached our destination,—a mountain village, perched upon a spur or extended flank of Mount Nazul—I was in great pain. I could not lift my leg, which was soon swollen from the calf to the waist, so that getting into the saddle or out of it, was simply excruciating. When we reached the village we were shown into a hut containing two rooms, the outer one with a large hole in the thatch—and the inner, or sleeping quarter, with a raised clay floor; the room itself being about nine by eight feet with a cave ceiling, resting on oaken rafters, so low that we could not stand upright. The one little, unglazed window, with shutters frail as cardboard, opened out directly onto a pool of stagnant water and the whole place swarmed with flies, mosquitoes and vermin. We were given, each, a woolen *haik* or blanket, with one, also, for one of my native servants who had asked to be allowed to accompany us.

Thus, aching in every bone, I lay, devoured not merely by every kind of biting insect, but my mind a prey to the keenest anxiety. In the first place I feared the effect of the awful anxiety upon my wife's health, since she has suffered frequently of late from trying heart attacks. Then I, myself, am a confirmed invalid of long standing, and lastly I have always had a peculiar horror of being carried off and held for ransom, for my father, a naturalized citizen of the United States, was, by birth a Greek from Macedonia where so many such deeds of horror have been perpetrated. I contemplated nothing, therefore, less than being starved or otherwise reduced to accede to any terms my barbarous captors might impose. Between us and such a fate only one possible saving clause intervened, and that was the character and antecedents of Raissuli himself.

In order that both the weight of my fears and the grounds of any hope I might entertain may be appreciated, I must relate some incidents which have already been reported by the press but which readers at a distance may not recall.

Summer before last, the fire of sullen discontent against the Moorish Government, which had long smouldered, burst into flame in the immediate neighborhood of Tangier.

The Basha, or military governor of the town, Mohamed Bargash, rode out one day into the Fahas or neighboring agricultural district, accompanied by his followers, to collect men for the *harka* or military levy in accordance with orders from Fez.

Now the Fahas people assert that thrice already the levy had been collected either in men, or in money paid as exemption fees, and amounting to some thirteen thousand dollars in all, a large sum for so poor a district. Amongst the Basha's attendant officers was one Abd-el-Malek, very well known to the writer, who had been, it was asserted, particularly active in enforcing these illicit claims since, legally, the *harka* could only be summoned once in the twelve months.

When Basha Bargash and his following reached a village called Zeenats he was suddenly surrounded by an angry crowd of armed natives who seized upon Abd-el-Malek, hustled the Basha himself, and drove him and the rest of his attendants off. The little group of alarmed officials rode hurriedly back to Tangier and the unfortunate Abd-el-Malek was left in the hands of his enemies—who, after torturing him for forty-eight hours, finally, deliberately burnt out his eyes with the branding irons that are used to mark the cattle.

The poor wretch, even then, was not released but held until all the men of the villages belonging to this league, who were imprisoned at the time at Tangier or elsewhere, had been released and the Basha himself had engaged never to press for further collections or unjust taxation.

The negotiations for Abd-el-Malek's final release and for the exchange of prisoners were carried out by the young Wazani Chereef, Mulai Ahmed.

This outrage has never been punished.

Last summer again we heard of Zeenats, when the Sultan's troops surrounded that village in an attempt to seize Raissuli, the latter having been thrown off his guard by friendly assurances from the then newly appointed Basha of Tangier, Hadj Mohamed Abd-el-Saduk, who was a foster brother and also a former friend of Raissuli. The latter, though he had only thirteen followers with him, held the village until the men of the Kabyles gathered from the hills and drove off the assailants.

It was during this fray that Mr. Walter B. Harris, the correspondent of the London *Times* was captured, nor was he released until the Moorish Government, under pressure from the British Legation, acceded to Raissuli's demands for the release of his followers who had been taken prisoners at various times. The negotiations connected with Mr. Harris' release were also conducted by the same young Wazani Chereef, Mulai Ahmed.

I was in Switzerland at the time and felt greatly concerned as to the future security of life at Tangier, when I found that no attempt was, or apparently could be made by the Sultan's government to punish Raissuli.

On my return to Tangier in October I found, however, that government troops had been sent down from Fez, but either the force was not sufficiently strong or the soldiers would not fight. The pretense of punitive operations was, however, maintained, and only a few weeks before my own capture I had heard the shouts of triumph with which a party of these soldiers, including some of the local garrison of Tangier, drove past my gateway a group of wretched prisoners with their arms bound behind them. These men, I found on inquiry, had not been captured in open fight, but had been persuaded by the Basha, on false assurances of safe conduct, to come into his camp carrying presents instead of arms, in order to negotiate a general submission of the hostile Kabyle.

This incident I subsequently found had been the immediate cause of my own capture. But to return to our experiences.

For two days after my arrival at Tsarradan I had been confined to my bed, or, rather, had lain upon the floor in the hut owing to the effects of my fall, but we had in the meantime been allowed by Raissuli to communicate freely with our friends in Tangier. Raissuli had, moreover, shown much apparent concern at my condition and frequently came to see me and talked freely with me. Thus I learned that he had no wish to harm me or to exact any personal ransom for my release, but I also found with dismay that the terms he demanded from the government were singularly exorbitant. First, he demanded from the Moorish government not merely the removal of the Basha of Tangier, together with the release, not only of the men from the village of M'zorra, so treacherously seized, but also of all his friends, partisans or relations, actually in the hands of the government authorities, but also an indemnity of no less than seventy thousand dollars to be paid by the Abd-el-Saduks to cover the losses inflicted upon the Raissuli faction. For the members of his faction, moreover, he demanded a complete pardon and safe conduct for the future.

Whilst I was thus, on the one hand, relieved to find that I, personally, was not to be held to ransom or treated as an enemy, yet I was in despair as to the outcome of the whole affair, for if such complete satisfaction and absolute immunity for his raids should be accorded, who or what would be henceforth safe in Tangier?

I discussed this with Raissuli himself.

"I am the accredited leader," he replied, "of three of the most powerful hill Kabyles in the neighborhood of Tangier, the Beni M'Saour, the Beni Idder and the Beni Arroze, which have been driven into revolt against the Sultan's authority by the illegal exactions of the Abd-el-Saduks, by their acts of treachery and by the repeated violation of their plighted word.

"So far as you yourself, your security and that of your property are concerned, you have nothing to fear. No member of these Kabyles will interfere with you. On the contrary, they will protect you from harm to the best of their ability. If you will accord us your friendship we shall do all in our power to merit your esteem, and if you will allow me to visit you I will be glad to discuss with you the questions affecting the interests both of Tangier and of our own districts, for we know that you are well disposed toward our people."

Little by little, as we became better acquainted, he talked to me freely of his past life and of all that he had suffered at the hands of his enemies. His father, a member of the wealthy clan of Raissuli, a Chereefian family and a sub-division of the Beni Arroze, had died whilst Mulai Ahmed—or my Lord Ahmed, to give Raissuli the appellation by which he was addressed—was still a child. On one pretext or another the widow and her orphaned children had been stripped of the farms and plantations owned by the family. "This and the neighboring villages which you see," said Raissuli, "are all inhabited by members of one family, all descendants of one man, a direct descendant of the Prophet Mohammed, who settled here in this mountain district just four hundred and twenty-seven years ago. My grandfather, however, moved down to Zeenats in the plain near Tangier, where he owned a large *azeeb,* or farm. He built a house there, and subsequently, as other relatives gathered, the place became the village you know, which contains some three hundred houses. By my energy in defending our interests I became, whilst still a young man, the acknowledged head, first of the Raissuli, then of the entire Beni Arroze Kabyle, and finally, by treaty with our neighbors, the chieftain also of the two nearest Kabyles—a confederation with which I hope to associate other and more distant Kabyles. We do not dispute the Sultan's authority nor refuse to pay the tax prescribed by the Koranic law; that is, the tenth of our crops, but beyond this we resist oppression by force.

"Now some eight years ago Abd-er-Rahman Abd-el-Saduk, then the Basha of Tangier, finding that he could not subdue our resistance by the troops at his disposition, made overtures of peace and, sending me a safe conduct, invited me to come and discuss a friendly solution of our difficulties. My friends warned me not to go, or if I would, begged me to allow them to accompany me, arms in hand. I replied that Abd-er-Rahman and I had been friends in our youth and that I would trust his plighted word. I went to this official residence alone and unarmed—and, while we sat at table (literally—about the tray—) I was suddenly seized, bound, hurried to prison and heavily ironed, an iron band was riveted about my neck, handcuffs with intervening bars so that I could not bring my two hands together were fastened on my wrists, and similar fetters were also riveted about my ankles. Then, by a special refinement of cruelty, I was sent to Mogador and there confined, not with imprisoned officials or offenders of the better sort, but with the lowest criminals who reeked of filth and who swarmed with insects—these latter cut into my flesh as did also my irons. Thus I remained four long years, chained to the walls so that I could not lie down, until at last the neck band and handcuffs were removed. After that I passed still another whole year in that horrible prison. Do you now wonder," he asked, "at the oath I swore to be revenged upon so treacherous an enemy? From that day no scissors have touched my hair!" Here he showed me a long plat concealed by the fall of his turban over the back of his neck. "This," he added, "will disappear only when my wrongs are avenged—mine and those of my people! You know," he continued, "of the column of Government troops lately sent against us. They dared not venture here among the hills. They remained in the valley, yonder, capturing defenseless peasants at the plough, and violating their daughters of whom eighteen, amongst them children of six years old, have been thus dishonored. Then came the treacherous capture of the M'zorra deputation who went at[2] Hadj Abd-er-Selam Abd-el-Saduk's summons, bearing, not arms, but presents in their hands. Then I de-

---

2. Also an Abd-el-Saduk, nephew of Abd-er-Rahman and at this time also Basha of Tangier. [Perdicaris's note]

termined to seize upon some European and to hold him till these men should be released and until the Abd-el-Saduks make restitution for all the wrongs we have suffered at their hands!"

Thus it seems I have been brought here, where, they assure me, no European, or any foreigner, has ever set foot, not to be plundered, but merely as a means of coercing the Government to render, even though it be unwillingly, some measure of tardy justice.

It was five days after our capture that the young Wazani Chereefs, who had negotiated for Abd-el-Malek's release appeared upon the scene to again negotiate over the last result of the Zeenat outrages. Their approach was announced by signal guns fired by the watchful Kabyles. Indeed it was Raissuli, himself, who knew we had summoned these friends to our assistance, who called us out upon the village green to witness their approach. What a blessed moment it was for us, as, presently, we saw the long escort, on foot and on horse, appear, winding along the distant hill-side.

After a long conference, alone, with Raissuli, the younger brother, Mulai Ahmed, returned to inform the authorities at Tangier as to Raissuli's conditions, whilst the elder, Mulai Ali, pitched his camp near us, placing a handsome tent at our disposition. Here we dined together, joined often by Raissuli who had treated us, daily, more and more like honored guests rather than like prisoners, and who, as he realized that we bore him no perceptible ill will for having thus deprived us of our liberty, displayed an almost affectionate consideration. His singular gentleness and courtesy, the freedom with which he discussed both our immediate interests as well as subjects of more general concern, the unfailing good temper with which he "rose" to Varley's chaff, together with the readiness of his happy repartees, quite endeared him to us.

Could we, however, have realized the anguish of our friends at home, owing to the treatment of my wife and Mrs. Varley—whom we had pictured to ourselves as remaining unconsciously in the drawing-room until our brief struggle was over, but who had actually been hurled by the brutal band violently down a flight of stone steps to prevent their agonized intervention—could we have realized the despair of our friends at the menace of our death in case Raissuli's terms should not be complied with—a threat of which we were entirely ignorant—we should not have so sympathized with the story of Raissuli's own wrongs nor so easily have forgiven his aggressions.

Still even now (for this account, begun at the village of Tsarradan, has been completed here at Tangier), I feel that we should not judge Raissuli by our own standards of right and wrong. As he himself said, speaking as a Moslem, "We return wrong for wrong—not good for evil, and the injury my enemy does me I will repay a hundred fold."

Accepting such a standard, Raissuli still stands head and shoulders above most of his compatriots. Especially is he superior to those who occupy official positions, many of whom are credited with crimes of even deeper hue than the ones that soil the tarnished record of the Abd-el-Saduks, four of whom have held the post of Basha in Tangier, during my own residence there. And although I feel some distrust as one who has listened only to *ex parte* statements, yet I must confess that I not only honestly sympathize with Raissuli, but that I consider him rather in the light of a patriot who is using every means within his reach, even means which we cannot but condemn, to defend the independence of these Berber Kabyles who, since the days of the Roman Empire, have resisted every attempt to subdue their wild love of freedom.

But to return to our own situation. Mulai Ali, whom we had known from his childhood, had remained with us at the village. He is a most accomplished type of a young Moorish prince, speaking perfectly English, his mother tongue, and French as well as Arabic. He is an aide-de-camp to the Bey of Tunis, and possesses an acquaintance with the farthest limits of Morocco, Algiers and Tunis equaled by few travelers. As one of the sons of the late Grand Chereef of Wazani, Mulai Ali outranks most of the nobles of his native land, and it was very interesting to notice his apparently unconscious acceptance of the homage paid him by members of the Raissuli clan, who are all Chereefs or descendants of the Prophet, and between whom and the Wazani there is indeed a distant relationship. The primacy of the former is due to the fact that the Wazani are the official heads of the Mulai Taib, one of the most numerous and influential of the great religious fraternities of North Africa. Mulai Ali on this occasion had been charged with the task of conducting the negotiations for our release by Sir Arthur Nicolson, with the assent of M. St. Rene de Taillandier, the French Minister, for the Wazani Chereefs are protegees of France, and also the recipients of a subvention from the French government, which was awarded to the late Grand Chereef of Wazan and to his immediate descendants in consideration of services rendered during the Bou Amema and other risings in Algeria.

And now, even as I write these lines, the news reached us simultaneously from various sources that the government couriers had returned from Fez with the Sultan's unconditional assent to all of Raissuli's stipulations, and that the imperial order removing the younger Abd-el-Saduk and appointing his successor to the governorship of Tangier had already been read in the mosque at Tangier in conformity with the usual formula of official proclamation.

Many weary days of continued disappointment and delays intervened, however, before the difficulties connected with the payment of the indemnity and the exchange of prisoners could be effected.

It had been settled that we should accompany Raissuli to a *donar* called Bou Rabish, which one might almost describe as the castle of another robber chieftain, on the confines of the Beni M'Saour Kabyle, where the younger of the Wazani Chereefs should bring the indemnity and the liberated prisoners, who had been collected by steamer or convoys from the prisons of Tetyan and the coast towns. But El Zelal, the owner of this *donar*, perched upon the hill, became frightened on account of his relations with the Raissuli band, and until he was reassured by a formal request from the Sultan's representative, he would not consent to allow the transfer to take place at his castle.

The last night we passed at Tsarradan I was troubled by a revelation, communicated by one of Mulai Ali's retainers, to the effect that the hut I occupied had been the scene of a ghastly tragedy.

Whilst His Excellency Senor de Ojeda, now the Spanish Ambassador at Washington, presided at the legation at Tangier, a young Spanish girl and her brother had been carried off by the Moors from the neighborhood of Arzila. In spite of the efforts of the Spanish authorities these captives had never been recovered. According to some accounts they had been murdered, whilst others asserted they had been carried off to some of the inaccessible Kabyles of the Riff Mountains.

According to my informant, these unfortunate captives had been seized by the owner of this very hut which I now occupied—a man with whom I was now necessarily in daily contact. When the pressure from Tangier threatened danger to their captor, who dared not release these poor children for fear of the tales they might have told the authorities, he took these two unfortunate Christians from the very room in which I slept and cut their throats in the garden, just beneath my window where my horses were now tethered. There, in the garden, a few yards from where I slept, they had been buried.

I never know, in this country inhabited, as the natives themselves declare, by liars and by the sons of liars, what to believe or what to doubt. But certainly that night, in spite of the ordeal of the morrow's fatiguing journey, I barely slept an hour or two at the most.

The reader can perhaps conceive how I dreaded lest some new delay might yet intervene to keep me in this horrible place, amongst this band, many of whom, if not all, are murderers and cut-throats, such as this man was described to be.

However, the morning came at last. At four o'clock every one was on foot, and by five we were all in the saddle, thanks especially to the help of Mulai Ali's people, and soon the long cortege started again for Mount Nazul. Yet, even now, I could scarcely feel that we were really safe. So many contingencies had been suggested. Our friend, Mulai Ali himself, fully believed that the Beni

Arroze Kabyle might yet intervene to wrest us from the hands of Raissuli, so as to themselves reap the rich rewards he had demanded.

Raissuli himself betrayed no concern, though both of his own followers and those of the Wazani Chereef looked to their cartridges, and I noticed that when we halted each band drew up separately, on either side of the way, nor were the two leaders on better terms.

Some allusion was made to the squadrons of the American fleet in Tangier Bay and I knew that Raissuli himself had heard of their arrival with perfect equanimity, merely remarking, "Now the Sultan's authorities will be compelled to accede to my demands!" Indeed, he always spoke to me of his desire to be on good terms with the foreign Powers. My fear had been that Raissuli might, in case of an armed attempt to affect [*sic*] his own capture, compel us to accompany him to some more distant Kabyle, where we should no longer be able to communicate with our friends.

Even where we then were, more than one of the inhabitants had never before seen any but fellow Mohammedans or native Israelites. One Chereef from a neighboring town, naively remarked, on seeing us, "Why these are like human beings!"

On the day of our return, we reached the mountain heights just as the rays of the rising sun painted all the pinnacles of the hills around us in lines of amethyst and rose. It was, indeed, one of the most gorgeous effects upon which I ever gazed.

Raissuli was riding beside me on his great, gray charger, having returned to me all the horses he had seized on the night when he attacked Aidonia. He smiled as he saw how lost I seemed in admiration of the gorgeous panorama that the lifting clouds of fleeting vapor revealed, and asked me whether I altogether regretted now, my involuntary expedition.

For hour after hour we traversed these mountain glades, down one slope and ever up and farther on. The long line of horse and foot crept along the treacherous steeps or followed the crest of the dangerous hills, ever on towards the north, until, at last, we overlooked the distant plain and saw afar off where the blue sea kissed the almost invisible shore, one radiant gleam of white betraying where lay the town which had, now, indeed, become to us in very truth what the Moorish official documents declare it to be, Tangier, the blessed of God.

And still we rode on and on, until we saw, close beneath us, Bou Rabish, the semi-fortified abode of El Zellal, hanging to the side of the deep slope beneath. Here, a halt was called and runners were sent forward to make sure that no enemy was concealed behind the walls or garden hedges. When these advance guards had signalled back satisfactory assurance that "the coast was clear," we proceeded with some difficulty to urge our horses down the giddy descent. As we passed through the gateway I thought I noticed Raissuli grasp his rifle with a tighter hand as he looked suspiciously about him.

The place seemed, however, almost deserted. A brother of the owner and a few servants alone were visible. They invited us to dismount and enter a long room, where a Moorish bed, with embroidered hangings and triple mattresses and a bridal coffer in gaily painted wood, completed the usual equipment of such apartments. Upon some mattresses along the walls we were glad to rest our weary limbs. Mulai Ali, Varley and I, sat together, whilst Raissuli and the brother of our absent host sank upon the cushions in front of the bed and engaged in an inaudible, whispered conference.

I resigned myself, but I fear with most manifest impatience! I confess, however, the sight of preparations for tea, conducted by Mulai Ali's servants seemed to me singularly appropriate after a ride of six hours.

Later a more substantial lunch was served. "But where," I asked, "are Mulai Ahmed, your brother, the prisoners and the seventy thousand dollars, the essential conditions of our release?"

"They have been summoned," replied Raissuli, himself.

About two hours later, Mulai Ahmed, accompanied by Zellal and various others, appeared in the doorway. These all proceeded, as we had done, to take their places silently after mutual, solemn salutations. Tea was again served, then a second luncheon, this time served by Zellal's people, was placed before us, of which etiquette compelled us, also, to partake before business could be discussed.

However, we now saw boxes of bullion being unloaded from mules in the court without. After we had finished luncheon several sturdy negroes brought the boxes, each containing, as we afterwards found, two thousand silver Spanish dollars, into an inner room—but later these were again removed to another apartment where Zellal, Mulai Ahmed-el-Wazani and Raissuli proceeded to superintend counting the cash.

When it is remembered that we were under instructions to reach Tangier that night, to avoid the danger of an attack from the Kabyles, my anxiety to get away from *these* hills and from *that* cash, which seemed as though it never would get counted, may be appreciated.

Then after all this was slowly, solemnly and with due decorum accomplished, Raissuli took me aside under a quaint, old, arched veranda, all the arches running up the side of the hill, each arch independently, on its own account, without any regard to the architecture in general, and he assured me that he looked to me to warn him of any danger in the future, adding, "And I, on my part, will come with all my men to your rescue if you are ever attacked."

I wondered whether I was living in the days of Robin Hood and Friar Tuck or in this prosaic twentieth century. Then we parted. I mounted the handsome black steed that once had been his, then mine by purchase, then his by capture, and now mine again—and shall I confess it?—Yes! I was actually sorry to leave one of the most interesting and attractive personalities I have ever encountered, and so, grieved yet rejoicing, I rode off, leaving Raissuli standing under that strange, topsy-turvy veranda—as topsy-turvy even as my own sentiments.

It was pitch dark long before we got near Tangier, and I never saw the flag, as I had hoped to do that afternoon, waving over the *Brooklyn* and the *Olympia*. But what I did see, when we were nearing the town after midnight, as I struggled out of the mule litter which my Wazani friends had so kindly brought to me, to mount the black horse to escape from the crowd, were the signal lights on the mastheads of the frigates announcing my return, and then I whispered to myself: "Thank Heaven, it is *that* flag, and *that* people—aye, and *that* President, behind *those* frigates, thousands of miles away, who have had me dug out from amongst these Kabyles! That flag and no other!"

ADDITIONAL WRITINGS BY PERDICARIS

"The General Situation in Morocco." *North American Review* 181 (1905): 745–53.

The Hand of Fate. London: Holden & Hardingham Ltd: 1921.

Mohammed Benani: A Story of Today. London: Sampson, 1887.

"Morocco, 'The Land of the Extreme West' and The Story of My Captivity." *National Geographic Magazine,* March 1906: 117–57.

Appendix

Publishing History of the American Barbary Captivity Narrative

We have no bibliographies of Barbary captivity narratives, and while this list doesn't claim to be comprehensive, I hope it moves us toward a fuller understanding of the genre's publication history. No doubt there are many more narratives among newspaper accounts, unpublished diaries, sermons, letters, travel narratives, captain's logs, and miscellany. I have included the seemingly fictitious accounts that were printed in the United States—Vandike, Velnet, Martin, Nicholson, Bradley, and Laranda—and with the exception of the Nicholson narrative, all of these were reputedly written by non-Americans but published exclusively in the United States. Excluded from the list are narratives like James Sutherland's that were written by non-Americans and published outside of the United States, though several editions were also printed there. (Bradley appears to be an exception to this case since the U.S. editor writes that he has typeset from the original British version, but there is currently no record of such an edition.) When one casually glances at the 149 editions listed here and recalls the great number of English-language captivity narratives published outside the United States as well as those printed in foreign languages, the overwhelming size of the genre becomes clear. When one adds to this the numerous novels, plays, poems, films, and operas that depict and reimagine the North African conflict, and the rippling effect of historical contact among Africans, Europeans, and Americans, the truly great breadth of the genre begins to emerge.

The list is arranged chronologically by year of captivity.

Joshua Gee, 1680
Narrative of Joshua Gee of Boston, Mass., While he was Captive in Algeria of the Barbary pirates 1680–1687. Intro. Albert Carlos Bates.
Hartford: Wadsworth Atheneum, 1943.

Cotton Mather, 1703
The Glory of Goodness. The Goodness of God, Celebrated; in Remarkable Instances and Improvements thereof: And more particularly in the Redemption Remarkably obtained for the English Captives, Which have been Languishing under the Tragical, and the Terrible, and the most Barbarous Cruelties of Barbary.
Boston: T. Green, 1703.

Appendix

James Leander Cathcart, 1788

The Captives, Eleven Years a Prisoner in Algiers. Compiled by J. B. Newkirk.

LaPorte, IN: Herald Print, 1899.

LaPorte, IN: 1902.

Partial manuscript published as "The Diplomatic Journal and Letter Book of James Leander Cathcart, 1788–1796." *Proceedings of the American Antiquarian Society* 64 (1954): 303–436.

John Vandike, 1791

Narrative of the Captivity of John Vandike, who was taken by the Algierines in 1791, An account of his escape, bringing with him a Beautiful Young English Lady Who was taken in 1790, The ill usage she recieved from her Master. The whole in a Letter to his Brother in Amsterdam. Trans. James Howe.

Leominster, MA: Chapman Whitcomb, 1797.

Leominster, MA: Chapman Whitcomb, 1801.

Daniel Saunders, 1792

A journal of the travels and sufferings of Daniel Saunders, Jun. a mariner on board the ship Commerce, of Boston, Samuel Johnson, Commander, which was cast away near Cape Morebet, on the coast of Arabia, July 10, 1792.

Salem: Thomas C. Cushing, 1794.

Leominster, MA: Charles Prentiss, 1797.

New Haven: W. W. Morse, 1802.

Hudson: A. Stoddard, 1805.

Salem: Joshua and John D. Cushing, 1824.

Exeter: A. Brown, 1830.

Penrose, M'Shane, and others, 1793

"Letters from Captains Penrose, M'Shane, and sundry other American captives, with a description of the treatment those prisoners experience." In *A Short Account of Algiers, and of its several wars against Spain, France, England, Holland, Venice, and other Powers of Europe. From the Usurpation of Barbarossa, and the Invasion of the Emperor Charles V to the Present Time. With a concise view of the Origin of the Rupture between Algiers and the United States . . . to which is added, a copious appendix, containing Letters.*

Philadelphia: Mathew Carey, 1794.

Mary Velnet, 1797

The Captivity and Sufferings of Mrs. Mary Velnet, Who was Seven Years a Slave in Tripoli, three of which she was confined in a dungeon, loaded with irons, and four times put to the most cruel tortures ever invented by man. To which is added, The Lunatic Governor, and Adelaide, or the Triumph of Constancy, a Tale.

Boston: William Crane, 1800.

Boston: William Crane, 1804.

Boston: William Crary, 1804.

Sag Harbor, NY: Alden Spooner, 1806.

Boston: T. Abbot, 1828.

An affecting history of the captivity and sufferings of Mrs. Mary Gerard, an Italian lady. Who was seven years a slave in Tripoli, three of which she was confined in a dungeon, loaded with irons, and three times put to cruel torture [rewritten version of the above] . . .

Boston: Artumus Belcher, 1810.

John D. Foss, 1798

A Journal, of the Captivity and Sufferings of John Foss; several years a prisoner in Algiers: Together with some account of the treatment of Christian slaves when sick:—and observations on the manners and customs of the Algerines.

Newburyport: A. March, 1798 (1st ed.).

Newburyport: A. March, 1798 (2d ed.).

Maria Martin, 1800

History of the captivity and sufferings of Mrs. Maria Martin, who was six years a slave in Algiers: two of which she was confined in a dark and dismal dungeon, loaded with irons: to which is annexed a history of Algiers, a description of the country, the manners and customs of the NATIVES—their treatment to their slaves—their laws and religion—&c, &c.

Boston: W. Crary, 1806.

Boston: W. Crary, 1807.

Philadelphia: Joseph Rakestraw, 1809.

Philadelphia: Jacob Meyer, 1811.

Trenton: James Oram, 1811.

New Haven: Sidney's Press, 1812.

New York: n.p., [1812?]

New York: Evert Duyckinck, J. Oram, 1813.

Philadelphia: Thomas T. Stiles, 1813.

Saint Clairsville, OH: John Berry, 1815.

Rutland, VT: Fay & Davison, 1815.

Brookfield, MA: E. Merriam, 1818.

History of the captivity and sufferings of Mrs. Lucinda Martin, who was six years a slave in Algiers . . . written by herself. To which is prefixed a history of Algiers [rewritten version of the above].

Elijah Shaw, 1803

A short sketch of the life of Elijah Shaw, who served for twenty-two years in the Navy of the United States, taking an active part in four different wars between the United States & foreign powers; namely, first—with France, in 1798; second—with Tripoli, from 1802 to 1805; third—with England from 1812 to 1815; fourth—with Algiers, from 1815 to 1816: and assisted in subduing the pirates from 1822 to 1826.

Rochester: Strong & Dawson, 1843.

Rochester: E. Shepard, Mammoth, 1845.

Jonathan Cowdery, 1803

American Captives in Tripoli; or, Dr. Cowdery's Journal in Miniature.

Boston: Belcher and Armstrong, 1806.

Boston: Belcher and Armstrong, 1806 (2d ed.).

Boston: Lemuel Austin, 1810.

William Ray, 1803

Horrors of slavery, or, the American tars in Tripoli containing an account of the loss and capture of the United States frigate Philadelphia: treatment and sufferings of the prisoners: description of the place: manners, customs, &c. of the Tripolitans: public transactions of the United States with that regency, including Gen. Eaton's expedition: interspersed with interesting remarks, anecdotes, and poetry, on various subjects: written during upwards of nineteen months' imprisonment and vassalage among the Turks.

Troy, NY: Oliver Lyon, 1808.

The American Tars in Tripolitan Slavery containing an account. . . . [same as the above, under a different title]

New York, William Abbatt, 1911.

Thomas Nicholson, 1809

An Affecting Narrative of the Captivity and Sufferings of Thomas Nicholson [A Native of New Jersey] Who has been Six years a Prisoner among the Algerines, And from whom he fortunately made his escape a few months previous to Commodore Decatur's late Expedition. To which is added, a Concise Description of Algiers of the Customs, Manners, etc of the Natives—and some particulars of Commodore Decatur's Late Expedition, Against the Barbary Powers.

Boston: G. Walker, [181?].

Boston: N. Coverly, jr., 1816.

Boston: H. Trumbull, 1816.

Boston: N. Coverly, jr., 1818.

Robert Adams, 1810

The Narrative of Robert Adams, A Sailor, who was wrecked on the Western Coast of Africa, in the Year 1810, was detained three years in slavery by the Arabs of the Great Desert, and resided several months in the city of Tombuctoo.

London: William Bulmer and Co., 1816.

London: John Murray, 1816.

Boston: Wells and Lilly, 1817.

Paris: L. G. Michaud, 1817.

Stockholm: A. Gadelius, 1817.

Amsterdam: J. C. Sepp en Zoon, 1818.

[Anthologized in *Robinson Crusoe's Own Book; or, The Voice of Adventure, from The Civilized Man cut off from his Fellows, By Force, Accident, or Enclination, and from The Wanderer in Strange Seas and Lands*. Ed. Charles Ellms.]

    Boston: William Perry, 1842.

    Boston: Joshua V. Pierce, 1843.

    Boston: Joshua V. Pierce, 1846.

    Boston: Joshua V. Pierce, 1848.

"Interiour of Africa." *North American Review* 5, no. 13 (May 1817): 11–26 [this is the earlier Cadiz narrative, never published in book form].

James Riley, 1815

Loss of the American brig Commerce, Wrecked on the Western Coast of Africa, in the Month of August, 1815. With an Account of Tombuctoo, and of The Hitherto Undiscovered Great City of Wassanah.

    n.p., [18 ?].

    Hartford: Riley, 1817.

    New York: Riley, 1817.

    New York: James Riley, 1818.

    New York: Collins & Co, 1818.

    Chillicothe: Riley, Bailhache & Scott, 1820.

    Lexington, KY: Riley, 1823.

    Hartford: Andrus & Judd, 1828.

    Hartford: Silas Andrus, 1829.

    Hartford: Silas Andrus, 1831.

    Hartford: Andrus & Judd, 1833.

    Hartford: Judd & Loomis & Co, 1836.

    Hartford: William Andrus, 1843.

    Hartford: S. Andrus & Son, 1844.

    Hartford: S. Andrus & Son, 1846.

    Hartford: S. Andrus & Son, 1847.

    Hartford: S. Andrus & Son, 1848.

    Hartford: S. Andrus & Son, 1850.

    Hartford: S. Andrus & Son, 1851.

    New York: Leavitt and Allen, 1859.

    London: J. Murray, 1817.

    Paris: Le Normant, 1818.

    Dordrecht: Blusse en Van Braam, 1818–19.

    Hartford: Andrus & Judd, 1928.

Sufferings in Africa: Captain Riley's Narrative . . . [first half of the above].

    New York: Clarkson N. Potter, 1965.

Appendix

Sequel to Riley's narrative; being a sketch of interesting incidents in the life, voyages and travels of Capt. James Riley, from the period of his return to his native land, after his shipwreck, captivity and sufferings among the Arabs of the desert, as related in his narrative, until his death.

    Springfield: A. R. Wright, 1851.

    Columbus: G. Brewster, 1851.

    Detroit: Negro History Press, 1970–1.

Goodrich, Samuel Goodrich [Peter Parley, pseud.] *The Story of Captain Riley, and his Adventures in Africa* [children's book based on Riley's narrative].

    Philadelphia: Henry F. Adams, 1834.

    Boston: Carter, Hendee, 1834.

    New York: J. P. Peaslee, 1835.

    Philadelphia: Henry F. Adams, 1837.

    Philadelphia: Henry F. Adams, 1841.

    Philadelphia: Lippincott, Grambo, & Co., 1854.

    Philadelphia: J. B. Lippincott & Co., 1861.

    New York: World Publishing House, 1876.

Archibald Robbins, 1815

Journal, Comprising an Account of the Loss of the Brig Commerce, of Hartford, (Con.) James Riley, Master, Upon the Western Coast of Africa, August 28th, 1815; Also of the Slavery and Sufferings of the Author and the Rest of the Crew Upon the Desert of Zahara, In the Years 1815, 1816, 1817; with Accounts of the Manners, Customs, and Habits of the Wandering Arabs; also, A brief Historical and Geographical view of the Continent of Africa.

    Hartford: Andrus & Judd, [18 ?].

    Hartford: F. D. Bolles, 1817.

    Rochester: E. Peck, and Co., 1818.

    Hartford: Silas Andrus, 1818 (3d ed.).

    Hartford: Silas Andrus, 1818 (4th ed.).

    Hartford: Silas Andrus, 1818 (5th ed.).

    Hartford: Silas Andrus, 1818 (6th ed.).

    Hartford: Silas Andrus, 1818 (7th ed.).

    Hartford: Silas Andrus, 1818 (9th ed.).

    Hartford: Silas Andrus, 1819 (10th ed.).

    Hartford: Silas Andrus, 1820 (12th ed.).

    Hartford: Silas Andrus, 1821 (13th ed.).

    Hartford: Silas Andrus, 1821 (14th ed.).

    Hartford: Silas Andrus, 1822 (15th ed.).

    Hartford: Silas Andrus, 1823 (16th ed.).

    Hartford: Silas Andrus, 1824 (17th ed.).

    Hartford: Silas Andrus, 1825 (18th ed.).

Hartford: Silas Andrus, 1826 (18th ed.).

Hartford: Silas Andrus, 1828 (20th ed.).

Hartford: Silas Andrus, 1829 (20th ed.).

Hartford: Andrus & Judd, 1831.

Hartford: Andrus & Judd, 1833.

Hartford: Andrus & Judd, 1835.

Hartford: Judd, Loomis & Co. 1836.

Hartford: Andrus, Judd & Franklin, 1838.

New York: Robinson & Franklin, 1839.

Hartford: E. Strong, 1842.

Hartford: S. Andrus & son, 1847.

Hartford: S. Andrus & son, 1848.

Hartford: S. Andrus & son, 1850.

Hartford: S. Andrus & son, 1851.

Greenwich, CT: Conde Nast, 1931.

Detroit: Negro History Press, 1971.

Judah Paddock, 1815

Narrative of the shipwreck of the ship Oswego, on the coast of south barbary, and of the sufferings of the master and the crew while in bondage among the arabs; interspersed with numerous remarks upon the country and its inhabitants, and concerning the peculiar perils of that coast. In *An Authentic Narrative of the loss of the American Brig Commerce, Wrecked on the Western Coast of Africa, in the Month of August, 1815. With An Account of the Sufferings of her Surviving Officers and Crew, who were enslaved by the wandering arabs on the Great African Desert, or Zahahrah; and Observations historical, geographical, &c. Made during the travels of the author, while a slave to the arabs, and in the empire of Morocco.*

London: Longman, Hurst, Rees, Orme, Brown, 1818.

New York: Collins & Co, 1818.

New York: James Riley, 1818.

Eliza Bradley, 1818

An authentic narrative of the shipwreck and sufferings of Mrs. Eliza Bradley, the wife of Capt. James Bradley of Liverpool, commander of the ship Sally, *which was wrecked on the coast of Barbary, in June 1818 . . . Written by herself. . . .*

Boston: James Walden, 1820.

Boston: George Clark, 1821.

Boston: James Walden, 1821.

Boston: Jonathan Howe, 1823.

Boston: James Walden, 1823.

Exeter: Abel Brown, 1824.

Exeter: Abel Brown, 1826.

Concord: L. Roby, 1829.
Boston: John Page, 1832.
Ithaca: Mack, Andrus, & Woodruff, 1835.
Ithaca: Mack, Andrus, & Woodruff, 1837.
Lowell: H.P. Huntoon, 1848.
Fairfield, WA: Ye Galleon Press, 1985.

Viletta Laranda, 1829

Neapolitan Captive: Interesting Narrative of the Captivity and Sufferings of Miss Viletta Laranda, A Native of Naples, Who, with a Brother, was a passenger on board a Neapolitan vessel wrecked near Oran, on the Barbary coast, September 1829, and who soon after was unfortunately made a Captive of by a wandering clan of Bedowen Arabs, on their return from Algiers to the Deserts—and eleven months after providentially rescued from Barbarian Bondage by the commander of a detached Regiment of the victorious French Army.

New York: Charles C. Henderson, 1830 ([3d ed.?]).
Middletown, CT: Lemuel Austin, 1831 ([4th ed.?]).

Ion H. Perdicaris, 1904

"In Raissuli's Hands: The Story of My Captivity and Deliverance May 18 to June 26, 1904." *Leslie's Magazine* 58 (September 1904): 510–22.

"Morocco, 'The Land of the Extreme West' and The Story of My Captivity." *National Geographic Magazine* 17, no. 3 (March 1906): 117–57.